Nazis, Islamists, and the Making
of the Modern Middle East

Nazis, Islamists, and the Making of the Modern Middle East

BARRY RUBIN

AND

WOLFGANG G. SCHWANITZ

Yale UNIVERSITY PRESS

New Haven & London

Archival research by Wolfgang G. Schwanitz for this book was partially made possible by the Education Fund of the Middle East Forum in Philadelphia, Pennsylvania.

Yale University Press books may be purchased in quantity for educational, business, or promotional use. For information, please e-mail sales.press@yale.edu (U.S. office) or sales@yaleup.co.uk (U.K. office).

Set in Sabon type by Integrated Publishing Solutions.
Printed in the United States of America.

Library of Congress Cataloging-in-Publication Data

Rubin, Barry M.
   Nazis, Islamists, and the making of the modern Middle East / Barry Rubin, Wolfgang G. Schwanitz.
      pages cm.
   Includes bibliographical references and index.
   ISBN 978-0-300-14090-3 (hardback)
   1. Middle East—Foreign relations—Germany. 2. Germany—Foreign relations—Middle East. 3. National socialism and Islam. 4. World War, 1939–1945—Participation, Muslim. 5. Middle East—History—20th century. I. Schwanitz, Wolfgang G., 1955– II. Title.
   DS63.2.G4R823 2014
   327.43056—dc23
   2013028622

A catalogue record for this book is available from the British Library.

This paper meets the requirements of ANSI/NISO Z39.48–1992 (Permanence of Paper).

10 9 8 7 6 5 4 3 2 1

To the memory of relatives killed in the Shoah: Dolhinov, Poland: Haya Rubin Perlmutter and Azriel, Haim, and Yaakov Yermiyahu Perlmutter. Shmuel, Rahel Leah, Leah Rivka, Pinkas Leib, Ethel, and Moshe Grosbein. Rahel Dimenshtein and Yirimayahu and Moshe Dimenshtein. Turo, Czechoslovakia: Maria, Jozef, Artur, Ilsa, and Erika Dub
—*Barry Rubin*

Dedicated to my parents: Margot Schwanitz and Wolfgang Schwanitz (1929–2013)
—*Wolfgang G. Schwanitz*

Contents

Preface

The story of Nazi Germany's involvement in the Middle East has hitherto largely been viewed as a dramatic tale of might-have-been that was nevertheless marginal to Middle East history and the course of World War II. In fact, however, this episode was central to the modern history of the Middle East and continues to reverberate many decades later given its profound effects on Arab nationalism, Islamism, and the course taken by the Palestinian Arab movement.

The recent release by the U.S. government of massive quantities of both wartime and postwar documents coupled with the translation of previously unused German documents and Arabic-language accounts permits a much fuller telling of the story of the interactions among Arabs, Muslims, and Germans.

To understand this history requires bringing together several elements. First, there was the German strategy, beginning in the late nineteenth century, that saw Berlin's interests in the Middle East as being linked to an Islamic jihad against Germany's European rivals conducted with the help of Muslim organizations.

On the other side were radical forces of nationalism and Islamism in rebellion against the regional status quo. These latter groups would become not merely Nazi Germany's protégés but its partners due to common interests and a set of parallel ideas. This was, then, neither purely an alliance of convenience nor a situation in which the Nazis were the teachers and the Middle Easterners were the pupils.

Beyond the world war itself and the collapse of Nazi Germany these events were to have long-term ramifications for Middle Eastern history going far beyond 1945. The Middle East was the only part of the world where the local allies of Nazi Germany and those holding so many of the same ideas actually emerged triumphant in the postwar world.

Again, these forces were not Nazi or fascist—they would later draw many ideas from the Communist bloc—but radical nationalist and Islamist forces that held certain parallel views and at times converged and created syntheses. Their political triumphs came not so much against their external opponents but over their more moderate Arab and Muslim rivals. During the first round, despite the defeat of their European allies, these forces were able to destroy and discredit nonauthoritarian thinking and methods in the late 1940s and throughout the 1950s. Their success was so thorough that liberal democratic forces—not uncommon in the Arabic-speaking world before the 1930s—did not again emerge as contenders for power until the first decade of the twenty-first century.

Today there is a second round in that battle. Revolutionary Islamism, one of the movements that cooperated with Imperial Germany up to 1918 and Nazi Germany up to 1945, has reemerged to challenge its former partner, militant Arab nationalism, which had crushed it in the 1950s. Once again, moderate democratic views are facing a three-way battle in which they are at a considerable disadvantage. At any rate, the ideological debates and political battles reflected in and unleashed, beginning in 2011, by the "Arab Spring" which, according to many observers, seemed to have turned into an "Islamist Spring," can only be fully understood with reference to the earlier eras documented here.

We thank those who assisted us in granting Freedom of Information Act Requests to the U.S. National Archives for CIA records, especially the coordinator for information, Scott Koch, in Washington, D.C.; and likewise Caroline Lugato for arranging access to the Bundesnachrichtendienst collections in the German Federal Archives.

Our gratitude is due to the Global Research in International Affairs (GLORIA) Center and especially to Yeru Chernilovsky. We want to give warmest thanks to the archivists Lars Amelung, Ludwig Biewer, Birgit Kmezik, Oxana Kosenko, Martin Kröger, Larry McDonald, Michael Petersen, Knut Piening, Christoph Stamm, Christiane Stegemann, Gabriele Teichmann, and Dominik Zier. We have researched private collections, among them those of Joseph W. Eaton, Hannelore Grobba, Maria Pawelke, and Manfred G. Steffen. Our thanks go to colleagues Wajih Abd as-Sadiq Atiq, Xavier Bougarel, Joel Fishman, Rainer Karlsch, Jacob M. Landau, Walter Z. Laqueur, Bernd Lemke, Astrid Ley, Jamal Malik, Sean McMeekin, Bernard Lewis, Stefan Meining, Chantal Metzger, Daniel Pipes, Wladimir J. Sacharow, Hans-Ulrich Seidt, Abd ar-Rauf Sinnu, and Matthias Uhl. And last but not least, we thank our agent Andrew Stuart; our editor, Sarah Miller and her assistant, Heather Gold; and our copy editor, Gavin Lewis, and our senior editor Margaret Otzel, for all their efforts.

Archive Abbreviations

USArchBDC	U.S. National Archives, Berlin Document Center, 1994 BA, Berlin
USArchII	U.S. National Archives II, College Park, Maryland
VerArchAGH	Vereinsarchiv, Amtsregister, Hamburg
VerArchAGM	Vereinsarchiv, Amtsregister, Munich

Nazis, Islamists, and the Making
of the Modern Middle East

1 From Station Z to Jerusalem

It began as another normal summer day in June 1942 at the Sachsen-hausen concentration camp near Berlin, the place where SS trainees were taken to see how the Master Race's captive enemies should be treated.[1] Three barracks in a separate section housed Jewish prisoners, mainly Polish citizens or men deported from Berlin. On that particular day, a squad of shouting guards ordered the Jewish prisoners of Bar-rack 38 to line up for four special visitors participating in an SS tour.[2]

As a model SS facility Sachsenhausen was run with the utmost ef-ficiency and discretion. Whenever a prisoner was murdered or died, the nearby town's officials filled out a routine death certificate, as if his passage from life had been an ordinary one. Only the wafting smell of death from the cremation chimneys suggested otherwise.[3] Yet this visit was handled with even greater care. Fritz Grobba, the Nazi regime's chief Middle East expert and liaison with its Arab allies, emphasized the event's importance. Everything must be perfect.[4] So seriously did the Reich's leadership take this occasion that SS chief Heinrich Himmler personally drove to Sachsenhausen beforehand and took the planned tour himself.

The timing was carefully selected. In May, just one month earlier, the Germans had begun a new project in Sachsenhausen that they wanted to show off to their allies. It was codenamed Station Z. The choice of the letter "Z," the alphabet's last letter, was to symbolize that this place would mark the end of the road for Jews, not only in Sachsenhausen but throughout Europe.

For years, the Nazis had experimented with the best method for exterminating Jews and others. Starting with individual hangings, they moved on to shooting people in groups, more efficient but still slow. The breakthrough in mass producing death came in 1941 with the development of camouflaged gas chambers. These had just been installed at Sachsenhausen along with four new crematoria to speed up disposal of corpses. In May, Himmler ordered the killing of 250 Jews in the camp as a test run. The system worked flawlessly.[5]

And so, in June 1941, four special Arab guests visited the prototype for future death camps. Their interest had a very practical purpose. One day, they planned to create their own Station Z's in the Middle East near Tunis, Baghdad, and Jericho to eliminate all the Jews in the region.

That goal had been set in a January 1941 letter that Amin al-Husaini, the Palestine Arab political and religious leader, sent German Chancellor Adolf Hitler. Al-Husaini asked Hitler to help Arabs solve the Jewish question in their lands the way it was being done in Germany.[6] To succeed they must learn the Nazis' techniques and obtain their technology.

This was why four officials from Germany's Arab allies were at Sachsenhausen in June 1942, preparing for the day they would return home behind Hitler's army. One interpretation of the documents has been that they were all aides, one of al-Husaini and three working for Germany's other main Arab ally, Rashid Ali al-Kailani, Iraq's former ruler who had been overthrown by a British invasion the previous year and fled to Berlin. The delegation's Palestinian Arab member would have been either al-Husaini's security adviser, Safwat al-Husaini, or another nephew, Musa al-Husaini, who handled propaganda and agitation.

Another interpretation, however, is more dramatic: the four visitors might have included Germany's two main Arab allies in person—al-Husaini and al-Kailani—each with one aide. The evidence points to at least al-Kailani's personal presence.[7] Grobba had written, "There shouldn't be concerns about the participation of al-Kailani himself in this inspection."[8] Foreign Ministry Under Secretary Martin Luther asked "Why al-Kailani and his entourage had visited that camp."[9] The visitors most likely, then, included al-Kailani, an Iraqi and a Palestin-

Figure 1. On July 15, 1942, at his East Prussian headquarters near Rastenburg, Hitler meets the former Iraqi premier Rashid Ali al-Kailani, a member of the al-Qadiriyya brotherhood, which together with seven similar Islamist organizations played a key role in Berlin's Middle East policy from 1894 on. On May 15, 1942, al-Kailani promised Hitler in a secret letter "to fight the common enemy until final victory."

ian Arab whom their bosses had assigned to the SS course, along with either a second Iraqi assistant or, less probably, al-Husaini himself.

Whether or not he personally visited the death camp on that occasion, the grand mufti emerged as Nazi Germany's main Arab and Muslim ally. He and his entourage had first fled British arrest for stirring a bloody revolt in Palestine, and had then—after a stay as al-Kailani's guest in Baghdad—fled to Germany ahead of the British army. On November 28, 1941, Hitler gave al-Husaini a long audience as a mark of special favor, during which they agreed to cooperate in committing genocide against the Jews.

The path leading to that moment started in 1871, when Prussia led neighboring states into the creation of a united Germany. Arab intellectuals later saw this as a model for doing the same thing. Before World War I, Germany's monarch, the kaiser portrayed himself as patron of Muslims and Arabs. During the war, Germany fomented a jihad to encourage Muslims to fight on its side.

After the war, the thinking of Hitler and al-Husaini had developed along parallel lines. Both the grand mufti and Hitler developed the idea that only exterminating the Jews would let them achieve their goals.[10] The two men each sought allies with a similar worldview.[11] When Hitler became Germany's chancellor in 1933, the grand mufti visited the German consulate in Jerusalem to offer cooperation. That same year, Hitler's autobiography, *Mein Kampf,* was serialized in Arab newspapers and became a best-selling book.

Nazi Germany and its ideology became popular among Arabs for many reasons. They, too, saw themselves as a weak, defeated, and humiliated people, much like the Germans after World War I. Germany was also an enemy of Britain (which ruled Egypt, Sudan, Jordan, Palestine, and Iraq); France (which ruled North Africa, Lebanon, and Syria); and the USSR (which had large Muslim-populated areas).

In addition, many Arabs hoped to copy Nazi Germany's seemingly magic formula for quickly becoming strong and victorious by having a powerful government mobilizing the masses by passionate patriotism, militant ideology, and hatred of scapegoats. That fascist Italy offered the same model reinforced the idea.

The grand mufti later wrote that many Arabs proclaimed, "Thank goodness, al-Hajj Muhammad Hitler has come."[12] The regimes that would later rule Iraq for forty years, Syria for fifty years, and Egypt for sixty years were all established by groups and leaders who had been Nazi sympathizers.

The alliance between these two forces was logical. Al-Husaini's 1936–39 Palestinian Arab rebellion received weapons from Berlin and money from Rome. In 1937, he urged Muslims to kill all the Jews living in Muslim lands, calling them "scum and germs."[13] But al-Husaini's ambitions went further. He wanted German backing not only to wipe out the Jews in the Middle East but also to make him ruler over all Arabs. In exchange for Berlin's backing, he pledged to bring the Muslims and Arabs into an alliance with Germany; spread Nazi ideology; promote German trade; and "wage terror," in his own words, against the British and French.

The Nazis were eager for this partnership. They established special relationships with the Muslim Brotherhood, the Ba'th Party, the Young Egypt movement, and radical factions in Syria, Iraq, and Palestine. Berlin also hoped to build links with the kings of Egypt and Saudi Arabia.

In 1939, for example, Hitler met Saudi King Abd al-Aziz Ibn Saud's envoy, Khalid al-Qarqani, telling him: "We view the Arabs with the warmest sympathy for three reasons. First, we do not pursue any territorial aspirations in Arab lands. Second, we have the same enemies. And third, we both fight against the Jews. I will not rest until the very last of them has left Germany."

Al-Qarqani agreed, saying that the prophet Muhammad had acted similarly in driving all the Jews out of Arabia. A Muslim could make no more flattering comparison. Hitler asked al-Qarqani to tell his king that Germany wanted an alliance and would arm both Saudi Arabia and al-Husaini's men.[14]

But first, Hitler had to decide precisely how "the very last" of the Jews were to leave Germany. As late as 1941, Hitler thought this could happen, in the words of Hermann Göring in July, by "emigration or evacuation."[15] Yet since other countries refused to take many or any Jewish refugees, Palestine was the only possible refuge, as designated by the League of Nations in 1922. If that last safe haven was closed, mass murder would be Hitler's only alternative.

The importance of the Arab-Muslim alliance for Berlin, along with the grand mufti's urging, ensured that outcome. And al-Husaini would be present at the critical moment Hitler chose it. In November 1941, al-Husaini arrived in Berlin to a reception showing the Germans saw him as future leader of all Arabs and Muslims, perhaps even reviver of the Islamic caliphate. He was housed in the luxurious Castle Bellevue, once home to Germany's crown prince and today the official residence of Germany's president.

Al-Husaini was paid for his personal and political needs an amount equivalent to about twelve million dollars a year in today's values.[16] The funds were raised by selling gold seized from Jews sent to concentration camps.[17] Following this pattern, al-Husaini requested and received as his office an expropriated Jewish apartment. His staff was housed in a half-dozen other houses provided by the Germans. In addition, al-Husaini was given a suite in Berlin's splendid Hotel Adlon and, for vacations, luxurious accommodations at the Hotel Zittau and Oybin Castle in Saxony.[18]

On the German side, Grobba was his guide and handler; Ernst von Weizsäcker, a state secretary and SS general, his liaison with the Foreign Ministry. Von Weizsäcker preferred courting Turkey rather than

Figure 2. Hitler in conversation with Grand Mufti al-Hajj Amin al-Husaini, November 28, 1941. At their meeting they concluded the pact of Jewish genocide in Europe and the Middle East, and immediately afterward, Hitler gave the order to prepare for the Holocaust. The next day invitations went out to thirteen Nazis for the Wannsee Conference to begin organizing the logistics of this mass murder.

the Arabs since it had a large army—thirty-six brigades easily expandable to fifty—while all Arab countries combined had just seven, and those mostly under British officers.[19]

But Hitler had a higher opinion of the grand mufti's value. All his other Arab or Muslim partners had followers in just one country; al-Husaini had transnational influence. The grand mufti sought to prove himself worthy of these high expectations. At the Bellevue, he met not only Arab politicians but also exiled Muslim leaders from the USSR, India, Afghanistan, and the Balkans.

Foreign Minister Joachim von Ribbentrop was impressed, telling al-Husaini, "We have watched your fight for a long time. We have always admired you, fascinated by your dangerous adventures. . . ." Von Ribbentrop assured al-Husaini of the Reich's support.[20] The Germans accepted al-Husaini's claim that the Arab masses would rally to their side if Berlin guaranteed independence from British and French rule as well as stopping all Jewish immigration into Palestine. In March 1941, Berlin secretly promised to support Arab independence.[21] In October, Berlin and Rome publicly announced that policy.[22]

Among themselves, German officials called al-Husaini the most important Muslim cleric and leader of the Arabs in Lebanon, Syria, Palestine, Transjordan (today Jordan), Iraq, and elsewhere.[23] Hitler called him the "principal actor of the Middle East, a realist, not a dreamer."[24] A contemporary U.S. intelligence assessment agreed, claiming al-Husaini was seen throughout the Middle East as "the greatest leader of the Arab peoples now alive."[25]

In recognition of this estimate, Hitler gave al-Husaini a ninety-minute meeting on November 28, 1941. Hitler's preparatory briefing, written by Grobba, stressed that al-Husaini was in tune with Germany's ideological and strategic interests.[26] The red carpet was rolled out with the Nazi regime's considerable talent for dramatic pomp. The grand mufti stepped from his limousine to see a two-hundred-man honor guard and a band playing military music. Hitler greeted him warmly, "I am most familiar with your life."

His Arab guest returned the compliments, pleased to find Hitler not only a powerful speaker but also a patient listener. Al-Husaini thanked the German dictator for long supporting the Palestinian Arab cause. The Arabs, he asserted, were Germany's natural friends, believed it would win the war, and were ready to help. Al-Husaini explained his plan to Hitler. He would recruit an Arab Legion to fight for the Axis; Arab fighters would sabotage Allied facilities while Arab and Muslim leaders would foment revolts to tie up Allied troops and add territory and resources for the Axis.

Hitler accepted, saying the alliance would help his life-and-death struggle with the two citadels of Jewish power: Great Britain and Soviet Russia. At that moment, the Third Reich was at the height of its victories. German forces were advancing deep inside the Soviet Union and nearer its border with Iran. General Erwin Rommel was moving into Egypt and many Egyptians thought Cairo might soon fall. When the day of German victory came, Hitler continued, Germany would announce the Arabs' liberation. The grand mufti would become leader of most Arabs. All Jews in the Middle East would be killed.[27] When al-Husaini asked for a written agreement, Hitler replied that he had just given him his personal promise and that should be sufficient.[28]

For al-Husaini, the meeting could not have gone better. Not only was the might of triumphant Germany, Europe's master, sponsoring the Arab cause, but the world's most powerful man was backing him personally. Hitler was also pleased. Afterward, he called al-Husaini "the principal actor in the Middle East," a sly fox, a realist, and—with his blond hair and blue eyes—an Aryan, too. And so Hitler forgave al-Husaini what the German leader called his sharp and mouse-like countenance.[29]

Germany's certification of the grand mufti as its candidate to be Arab and Muslim leader was confirmed in a uniquely Nazi manner. The day after the meeting, the grand mufti went to see a physician, Dr. Pierre Schrumpf, whose thorough physical checkup lasted six hours. The doctor concluded that al-Husaini was no mere Arab but a Circassian, thus a Caucasian, and hence an Aryan. His pseudoscientific diagnosis rested on distinctively unphysical reasoning. An Arab could never have kept up the battle against the British and Jews, the doctor explained, but would have sold out to them. Al-Husaini's steadfastness proved he was an Aryan. And since he was an Aryan he would be a faithful ally for Nazi Germany.[30]

But there was another consequence of the al-Husaini–Hitler meeting to cement their alliance. A few hours after seeing the grand mufti Hitler ordered invitations sent for a conference to be held at a villa on Lake Wannsee. The meeting's purpose was to plan the comprehensive extermination of all Europe's Jews.

Considerations of Muslim and Arab alliances, of course, were by no means the sole factor in a decision that grew from Hitler's own anti-Semitic obsession. But until that moment the German dictator had left open the chance that expulsion might be an alternative to extermination.

When Hitler first told Heydrich to find a "final solution," the dictator had included expelling the Jews as an option. Already, the regime estimated. it had let about 500,000 Jews leave Germany legally during seven years of Nazi rule. Yet if the remaining Jews could only go to Palestine, and since ending that immigration was al-Husaini's top priority, emigration or expulsion would sabotage the German-Arab alliance.[31] Given the combination of the strategic situation and Hitler's personal views, choosing to kill the Jews and gain the Arab and Muslim assets necessary for his war effort was an easy decision.[32]

Consequently, Hitler ordered the Wannsee Conference to devise a detailed plan for genocide.[33] Since this decision was linked to the alliance with al-Husaini he would be the first non-German informed about the plan, even before it was formally presented at the conference. Adolf Eichmann himself was assigned to this task.

Eichmann briefed al-Husaini in the SS headquarters map room, using the presentation prepared for the conference. The grand mufti, Eichmann's aide recalled, was very impressed, so taken with this blueprint for genocide that al-Husaini asked Eichmann to send an expert— probably Dieter Wisliceny—to Jerusalem to be his own personal adviser for setting up death camps and gas chambers once Germany won the war and he was in power.[34]

As a first step, it was agreed that once Rommel captured Egypt, an SS unit commanded by Walther Rauff, Heydrich's thirty-five-year-old aide who had developed mobile gassing vans, would arrive in Cairo to eliminate the Jews there before following the Wehrmacht into Palestine for an encore.[35] In June 1942, Rauff did begin this project, killing twenty-five hundred Jews in German-occupied Tunisia. If the Germans had taken Egypt and then Palestine, this would have been the rehearsal for larger operations. With German armies approaching the Middle East near the Libya-Egypt and Soviet-Iran borders, the idea that within a year German-advised Arabs might have murdered all of the Jews in the region seemed realistic.

And that was why an Arab delegation was invited for a preview at the Sachsenhausen camp. They were briefed by the camp's SS commander, Colonel Hans Loritz, who, with eight years' experience, was the Reich's top expert in running concentration camps. After fielding questions he led the tour of the barracks, eating halls, washrooms, kitchens, and dispensary. Leaving nothing to chance, the Germans had prepared a dramatic event. A group of sixty Soviet officers, singing enthusiastically, marched out of the camp dressed in new German army uniforms. These were, Loritz explained, prisoners of war who had volunteered to fight the Communist regime.[36] The guests got the message. Everyone wanted to be on the winning side, and if Germany could turn Soviet officers against Stalin, Arabs could recruit Muslims to fight Churchill.

One German official, however, was horrified by that visit. The Foreign Ministry's undersecretary, Martin Luther, demanded that Arabs not be allowed into any concentration camp lest they tell others about what they saw. If Germany's enemies discovered mass murder was happening they would use this as a propaganda weapon against the Third Reich.

Luther, a party veteran, also worried that leaks would sabotage his job of convincing German satellite or allied states to turn over their Jews for transport to the death camps. If word got out, those regimes might balk at cooperating due either to Allied pressure or to fear of future punishment.[37] Infuriated, Luther complained to Grobba that von

Ribbentrop had promised him the visit wouldn't happen.[38] Luther's request to suspend this particular tour was denied[39] The SS promised him there would be no more tours in future but held them anyway, including a likely later visit by al-Husaini to Auschwitz.[40] As for Luther, in 1943 he went too far in conspiring to replace von Ribbentrop's job and was sent to Sachsenhausen himself.

The importance of Nazi Germany's connections with Arab and Muslim allies was quite clear to Hitler and most of his lieutenants. They saw this alliance as vital to their war effort and the key to conquering the Middle East. Hitler thought al-Husaini would emerge as leader of a vast Arab empire that would be his junior partner. Yet what was the background of this German fixation with Arab revolts and Islamic jihad, and precisely how did this alliance develop on both sides?

2 A Christian Imperial Strategy of Islamic Revolution

Nazi Middle East strategy would be rooted in debates begun a half-century earlier, in the 1880s, and on how that policy was implemented during World War I. That German strategy was to portray itself as champion of downtrodden Muslims and to promote jihads against Germany's enemies.

The original debate setting German policy on this course was between the two men who dominated modern Germany's origin, Chancellor Otto von Bismarck and Kaiser Wilhelm II. Conservative and cautious, Bismarck urged that the new country focus on economic development rather than seek to be Europe's leader or a global power. In an 1888 speech to Parliament, he explained why not following his advice would lead Germany to catastrophe.[1]

First, von Bismarck said, Germany must avoid war because of its poor geographical situation that left it open to attack on three fronts simultaneously since it was surrounded by Russia, France, and Great Britain. In comparison, Britain was an island fortress protected from invasion by its rule over the seas, while France and Russia were only vulnerable along their borders with Germany.

Second, Germany should avoid making enemies because the common interests of Britain, France, and Russia gave them good reason to ally against Germany rather than to support it.

Third, by the time Germany became a united country in 1871, Great Britain, France, and Russia already had large overseas empires. Germany couldn't catch up. Von Bismarck's lack of interest in Middle East colonies made him remark that gaining territory in the Ottoman Empire wasn't worth the bones of a single German soldier.[2]

Instead of seeking empire, von Bismarck concluded, Germany should focus on commercial opportunities. Middle East peace was in German interests while any attempt to alter the regional situation would set off a losing war in Europe.[3]

Some powerful Germans, however, contemptuously dismissed von Bismarck's arguments. They thought that not having an empire consigned Germany to be eternally a second-rate power. Reversing von Bismarck's geopolitical analysis, General Hermann Count von Schlieffen replied that only overseas expansion would let Germany leap over its encirclement within Europe.[4]

Wilhelm II, who came to the throne in 1888, agreed with von Schlieffen. Within twelve months of being crowned, Wilhelm forced von Bismarck into retirement and reversed his policy. For the kaiser, in addition to finding raw materials and markets for Germany's growing industry, empire or at least a sphere of influence in the Middle East was imperative.[5] Alongside practical considerations was a considerable romantic element. Fascinated by the Middle East, Wilhelm dreamed of being an oriental potentate or reincarnation of Alexander the Great. Two trips to the Ottoman Empire, in 1889 and 1898, convinced him that this was his destiny.

In a January 1896 message to Russia's Tsar Nicholas II, Wilhelm tactlessly complained that the British wrongly thought the Mediterranean an "English Sea" and that their hold on the Middle East was unbreakable.[6] Wilhelm confidently explained that a friend of his had met a Muslim prophet so influential in India[7] that a signal from him would spark revolution there. Losing India would reduce Britain to a third-rank power.[8]

This man's name was Sayyid al-Kailani and the kaiser's "friend" was Max von Oppenheim, who had met al-Kailani in 1893.[9] Sayyid was descended from Abd al-Qadir, a twelfth-century preacher who founded a group that spread to China, India, Pakistan, Turkey, the Balkans, and

Africa. Von Oppenheim also told the kaiser of eight similar brother-hoods, for example the as-Sanusiyya of North Africa, that Germany might use to organize a jihad against its enemies.

While Sayyid al-Kailani (from the Persian highland area Jilan, Kilan in Arabic and in Iraqi also al-Kailan) himself would never launch a pro-German revolt, one of his descendants would do so almost a half-century after von Oppenheim's prediction and at a time when von Oppenheim was still a top German agent. That man, Rashid Ali al-Kailani, would lead a pro-German coup that took over Iraq in May 1941. So in a sense the kaiser's prophecy would come to pass, albeit to fail.

The immediate effect of the kaiser's bragging was to hurt himself. The Russians were so alarmed by the kaiser's ambition that they shared this message with the British and later entered an anti-German alliance with London and Paris. After all, Berlin could also try to launch a jihad against them in their own Muslim-populated areas. And that concern would also prove accurate.

The British, hypersensitive to interference with their lifeline to India and protectorate over Egypt, saw the kaiser's interest in the region as a serious threat. Some news of these German plots would eventually reach the British novelist and intelligence official John Buchan. While working for the War Propaganda Bureau during World War I, he wrote a successful spy novel, *Greenmantle,* about a villainous German conspiracy to seize the Middle East as a base for conquering Europe. Through a charismatic Muslim preacher (whose codename is "Green-mantle"), a high Foreign Ministry diplomat explains to the novel's narrator, a German-backed jihad will "astonish the world . . . The war must be won or lost in Europe. Yes; but if the East blazes up, our effort will be distracted from Europe. . . . The stakes are no less than victory and defeat."[10]

To implement this strategy, Germany turned not only to individual religious leaders or brotherhoods but also to the Ottoman Empire whose monarch, as caliph, nominally led all Muslims. As such, he could declare jihad for every Muslim in the world, setting off what the kaiser called a "furor Islamiticus," an Islamic fury against British (but not German) infidels.[11] Seeing the Ottoman Turks as a kindred people, Germans dubbed them "the Germans of the Middle East."[12]

The father of this policy and the man who persuaded the kaiser to implement it was Max von Oppenheim. His historic role was as impor-

Figure 3. Kaiser Wilhelm II leaves his camp at Jerusalem to inaugurate the Lutheran Church of the Redeemer on October 31, 1898, after starting off his official policy toward Islam with a visit to the Ottoman Sultan Abdülhamid II in Istanbul. The diplomat Max von Oppenheim, posted in Cairo, had sent the monarch his report 48 on the "Pan-Islamic Movement," advising the use of "Islamism"—the Kaiser's term—to inspire Muslim revolutions in enemy colonies in the event of a European war.

tant, especially since he played it over a far longer period, than that of his better-known British counterpart, T. E. Lawrence, known as Lawrence of Arabia.[13]

Born in 1860, von Oppenheim descended from a Jewish banking family in Cologne that had converted to Catholicism in his infancy.[14] In 1868, Abraham, the brother of Max's grandfather, had become the first Jew to be made a baron by Prussia's monarchy, giving family members the right to add the aristocratic "von" to their names. Max received his law degree in 1883 but preferred to be an explorer, and his wealthy family was willing to pay for his travels. He set off, first through Syria and Iraq in 1883–84, then to Morocco in 1886, and afterward all the way to the Persian Gulf and India in 1893–94. He studied Arabic in Egypt and achieved a fair mastery of the language. On his return, von Oppenheim published his observations in two volumes. His reputation rose as the country's leading expert on the contemporary Middle East.[15] Von Oppenheim was a good observer of the region's life and politics. His rival, Lawrence of Arabia, a great writer in his own right, would call von Oppenheim's book the best on the area available before World War I.[16]

Germany's Foreign Ministry, concerned about Islam's spread into its African colonies, wanted an independent source of information on the topic. In 1896, through a family connection with a high-ranking Foreign Ministry official, von Oppenheim became an attaché to the German consulate in Cairo. During his service there, until 1909, he sent 467 reports to Berlin. Building a good network of contacts, von Oppenheim learned a great deal, though not all of it accurate. Ironically, despite being sent to Cairo to study Islam as a threat, von Oppenheim became convinced that, on the contrary, it offered Germany a tremendous opportunity. Soon his dispatches, including a long 1898 report on the Pan-Islamic movement, were being sent on to the kaiser.[17]

The Ottoman Empire was sponsoring Pan-Islamism to counter nationalism's inroads into its subject peoples' loyalty. The empire had already lost the Christians of southeastern Europe who had rebelled under the inspiration of Greek, Serbian, Bulgarian, and Romanian nationalism. It hoped to hold Arabs, Turks, Kurds, and others by persuading them that their Muslim identity should come first and the sultan was their caliph, endowed with full Islamic legitimacy. For the Germans, however, it was not these defensive but Pan-Islamism's offensive aspects that were of greatest interest. What if the peoples of French-ruled North Africa and those under British control in India or Egypt would also demand an Islamic government? What if Russia's Muslim subjects sought the same? That would be the best way to subvert Germany's rivals.

On the eve of Kaiser Wilhelm's 1898 Middle East trip, von Oppenheim advised him to back Islamism as a political movement.[18] He explained that Muslims wanted to end the reign of Christian powers (that is, Britain, France, and Russia) over Muslim-majority lands. In part, this was a response to spreading Western culture and political power; in part, a realization of Islam's command to unite and make their societies follow its precepts. Muslims, von Oppenheim wrote, had established a unified state in the seventh century and sustained it for centuries. Starting in the 1860s the Ottomans had revived this effort by using Islam to retain the loyalty of its Muslim subjects. Von Oppenheim thought this campaign had succeeded, and that Muslims were increasingly viewing the Ottoman sultan-caliph as protector of Islam and its holy places. This was good for Germany which, he claimed, was the Muslims' favorite European country since it had no colonies in the area and was friendly to the Ottoman Empire.

Von Oppenheim was more enthusiastic than accurate in many of his conclusions, misled by wishful thinking or informants' eagerness to tell him what he wanted to hear in hope of gaining Berlin's financial and political support. To answer criticisms, von Oppenheim responded that it was easy to underestimate the sultan's massive religious influence. Just because his empire was militarily weak did not mean it was not potentially mighty. If as caliph the sultan were to proclaim jihad and Muslims had been prepared properly, von Oppenheim predicted, that decree would be an unconventional weapon of massive power.

The most impressive example von Oppenheim could muster to make his case was the Sudan, where a charismatic leader, Muhammad Ahmad bin Abd Allah, the mahdi, had led a victorious jihad uprising against the British. Starting with nothing, he built a large army, defeating and wiping out regular British forces on several occasions. He captured Khartoum, established an Islamist state, and ruled it for thirteen years. Only after his death had the British, in the 1898 battle of Umm Durman, finally succeeded in defeating and destroying that state.

Von Oppenheim's report on Islamism was submitted three months before that battle, when the mahdi's state still existed. If the mahdi could achieve so much with so little and no foreign allies, the Ottoman sultan—with a half-millennium of legitimacy, a large state apparatus, and recognition throughout the Muslim world—could shake the world with Germany behind him! Von Oppenheim was not alone in advocating this strategy. Other government officials and experts like Ernst Jäckh, a specialist on the Ottoman Empire, were spreading similar ideas.[19] Thus, Germany's ruler accepted von Oppenheim's proposal. In the event of war, the kaiser decided, Berlin would aid the Ottomans while the sultan would raise a jihad against Germany's European foes in British-ruled India, French-ruled North Africa, and Russian Asia. Not

Figure 4. Max von Oppenheim, the German "Abu Jihad" ("father of jihad") and mastermind of the jihadization of Islam from 1893 on, sits in his tent, carpeted and hung with texts from the Qu'ran in the style of an Arab chieftain. He was responsible for both the 1914 German-Ottoman plan for jihad in the British, French, and Russian empires, and the 1941 German-Arab "Union Jack" plan for jihad in the British mandatory areas of the Middle East after the fall of Paris in mid-1940.

everyone in the German government was entranced with this scheme and none less so than Friedrich Rosen, a Foreign Ministry expert on the region. Rosen, who spoke better Arabic than von Oppenheim and had been Germany's envoy in Baghdad and Jerusalem, mocked von Oppenheim's idea as ignorant of the region's real conditions. He joked that the idea's real father was Karl May, the popular German writer of Wild West stories and romantic tales about the Middle East.[20] But what Rosen or others said didn't matter because von Oppenheim had the kaiser's ear.[21]

The most prestigious expert, Carl Heinrich Becker, at first had mixed feelings about von Oppenheim's thesis.[22] He believed there was a real possibility of a massive jihad revolt—in fact, he made the case far better than von Oppenheim—but doubted the Ottoman sultan was the man to unleash it. True, Becker said, one of Islam's basic requirements was for Muslims to fight for it through jihad until Islam ruled the world. It was also true, he added, that Europe's advance had made Muslims realize their military and technological inferiority to Christian civilization. In turn, this gave Muslims greater solidarity among themselves and strengthened Islam's political appeal. They yearned for a mahdi to restore Islam's primacy through revolution.

But that wasn't the whole story, Becker explained. Short of the true mahdi, a divinely inspired messiah who would come to bring the world's end, nobody, including the Ottoman sultan, could claim to be the one rightful Islamic ruler. There was no "Muslim pope," Becker pointed out, and while sultans had always found Muslim theologians to back their claims, they were really just worldly rulers with no true religious authority. Sultans merely pretended to possess that authority in order to gain support from their own subjects and European powers. Moreover, Becker explained, discontent with the Ottoman sultan could just as likely provoke a Muslim uprising against him as foment a jihad under his leadership. Further, the possibility of a big transnational jihad was weakened by splits among Muslims. Turks, Arabs, and Persians all had quarrels, as did Sunni and Shia Muslims. The solidarity of Islam was a phantom, said Becker.[23]

Becker's conclusions were more accurate than those of von Oppenheim, yet they also did not offer the prospect of a victorious Germany. Moreover, since the kaiser's mind was set, Becker would not openly contradict him. So Becker eventually turned around and endorsed the idea he had previously ridiculed.

There were seeds of truth in von Oppenheim's analysis and yet much error, too, as later history showed. The strong feeling of solidarity among Muslims was countered by deep divisions based on religious views, ethnicity, region, differences of opinion, and self-interest. Numerous Muslim leaders and groups—the Egyptian Jamal Abd an-Nasir, the Muslim Brotherhood, Iraqi dictator Saddam Husain, Iran's Ayatollah Ruhollah Khomeini and his successors, Libyan ruler Muammar al-Qaddafi, and Usama bin Ladin—trying to set off such transnational revolts always failed and were defeated.

As Becker originally noted, there were other weaknesses as well to von Oppenheim's thesis. On paper, the Ottoman caliph's power looked legitimate and overwhelming but in reality it had withered. The Ottomans were not so popular in Arabic-speaking lands and of relatively little importance elsewhere. The British and French had their own Muslim assets, including an ideological import from Europe: ethnic nationalism. Finally, von Oppenheim was short on practical measures. How would Germany prepare and organize the masses to unleash, in his words, a "Muslim fanaticism that borders on insanity," to set off the nuclear chain reaction of militancy he envisioned?[24]

All of these problems were ignored by the kaiser, and when he visited the sultan's domain, in October–November 1898, the alliance with Islamism and the launching of jihad were officially adopted as German policy.[25]

The nominal purpose for the kaiser's trip was to inaugurate the new Lutheran Church of the Redeemer on the Muristan hill in Jerusalem, and in his public speeches, the kaiser's message of peace differed sharply from his aggressive plan. Speaking in Istanbul, the German monarch explained the mutual benefits of peaceful competition between peoples of different faith and background. As he schemed to fight fellow Christians through a Muslim revolt, the kaiser told an audience in Bethlehem that he regretted how quarrels among Christians set a bad example for the rest of the world.

The U.S. representative in Jerusalem, Consul Selah Merrill, was impressed: "The Emperor and Empress were constantly busy in sightseeing, visiting churches, schools, colonies, hospitals, and orphanages that belong to the Germans. Without being partisan, the Emperor showed that he was a stalwart supporter of the great principles and doctrines of Protestantism, and at the same time he conducted himself in such a manner as to make a most favorable impression upon all classes."[26] But the kaiser was not trying to win over the empire's non-Muslim or dissident subjects. In 1898, the Ottoman Empire appeared a stronger horse than scattered Arab nationalist intellectuals, Jewish ideologues, and Armenian activists with no troops or money behind them. Thus, the Germans turned down Armenian requests for help against the Ottomans. Wilhelm associated the growing Zionist movement in Germany[27] with his enemies in the Social Democratic Party.[28] While the visiting kaiser praised the young Zionist settlements and met the movement's leader, Theodor Herzl, at the entrance of the Mikveh Israel agricultural school, he insisted that Jewish immigration must be in the context of recognizing the sultan's sovereignty over that land.[29] Consequently, Armenians would turn toward Russia and both Zionists and Arab nationalists toward Great Britain for support.[30]

The kaiser's endorsement of the Ottoman Empire's continued authority and Islam's power to inspire political action required some remarkably mixed symbolism, as seen in the trip's most striking event, in Damascus on November 8, 1898, when the kaiser visited Salah ad-Din Yusuf al-Aiyyub's tomb.

Born around 1140, Saladin, as he is generally known, became the greatest Muslim general fighting the Christian Crusaders, many of whom were Germans. At the battle of Hittin in 1187 he destroyed his foes and then wiped out their strongholds, culminating in his conquest of Jerusalem. He became the symbol of Muslim triumphs over Europe, Christianity, and the West. Now here was one of Europe's leading monarchs, many of whose countrymen had been Saladin's victims, praising that general as "a fearless knight who had taught even his enemies the proper way to chivalry."[31] The kaiser proclaimed himself friend to the world's Muslims as he planned to harness the power of Islamic fervor to create some new Saladin to unleash against his enemies. The Germans printed his words on postcards mailed to influential Muslims in many countries.

That German strategy's ultimate backfiring was perfectly symbolized by the fate of the bronze laurel wreath the kaiser left as a gift at Saladin's tomb. Twenty years later, almost to the day, the Allies entered Damascus in triumph after defeating the Ottomans and their German allies in World War I. Lawrence of Arabia picked up the wreath and sent it as a war trophy to London, where it is still on display today at the Imperial War Museum.

As has so often happened in the modern Middle East, a mistaken Western strategy ended in catastrophe. But as also has so often happened, local rulers were manipulating the Western power that thought it was doing the stage-managing. On his trip, the kaiser seems to have succeeded in winning the admiration of Muslims and of the Ottoman

Figure 5. A postcard in German and Turkish displays the kaiser's words of 1898, pledging always to be the friend of the Ottoman sultan and the three hundred million Muslims who revere him as their caliph. The postcard was produced two years after the Ottoman sultan and caliph Abdülhamid II had been condemned throughout Europe for massacres against his Armenian subjects that shocked all "minorities of infidels."

government. Yet Ottoman agents were systematically exaggerating the sultan's religious authority in order to make the kaiser think as he did.

Thus Shaikh Abdallah, a cleric on the Ottoman payroll, told the kaiser that 300 million Muslims all over the world viewed the sultan as their spiritual ruler and now saw the German monarch as their friend, too. The kaiser was so impressed with this compliment that he thereafter used the "300 million" number himself as the measure of his influence among Muslims. The exaggerations, however, were not all on one side. The kaiser's speech at Saladin's tomb became a legend among some Muslims, part of the tale of "al-Hajj Wilhelm," the Christian emperor so moved by his visit that he converted to Islam. Around evening camp fires and in marketplaces, colorful details were added to this story.

How much political capital all this gave Berlin was unclear. But now

Germany had a long-term Middle East strategy, and one that was profitable in the short term, too, since Wilhelm's trip led to an agreement for
Germany to build the Ottoman Empire's railroads.[32] By the turn of the
century, Berlin's influence there was rising and offering serious competition to Britain and France. And when it came to producing new Saladins,
Germany had been training the empire's officers and selling weapons
to the Ottomans since the 1880s. As a result, there was a strong pro-
German faction in the Ottoman military. The British, worried about
this link, referred to such officers as being "made in Germany."[33]

Germany's Middle East gambit was accompanied by production of
an extensive literature on the region including novels, travelers' reports,
translations, and scholarly writings. Students and scholars flocked to
Middle East studies. By 1900, Germany had fifty-seven professorships
in the field at twenty-one universities.[34] That same year, the kaiser received von Oppenheim royally and congratulated him for having proposed such a successful strategy, and von Oppenheim retired from the
diplomatic service in 1909 with his policy set as Germany's own.[35]

Yet Germany's success in the Middle East had, as von Bismarck foresaw, stirred up dangerous antagonism from the British, French, and
Russians. The British satirical weekly *Punch* mocked the kaiser as following a strategy of "Germany Over Allah," a play on the German
national anthem, "Deutschland über Alles" (Germany Above All).

The British press published lurid articles about the kaiser converting to
Islam, seeking naval bases to challenge British primacy in the Mediterranean, or taking over countries; in the words of one headline, "Teutons
colonize Mesopotamia!" (the name used for Iraq at the time). The idea
of a German-backed Berlin to Baghdad railroad—it had extended into
Iraq by 1914 though it did not reach Baghdad until 1940—became the
symbol for the British and French of their rival's threatening influence
in the area.

The Germans tried to soothe these fears and—except for one slip
by the kaiser in referring to a German "foothold in Mesopotamia"—
maintained that their strategy was not a colonialist one. Chancellor
Bernhard von Bülow stressed that Germany had no political interests in
the Middle East.[36] "Germany does not seek any kind of economic mo-
nopoly in Turkey nor would this be in Turkey's interest," insisted one
German article in 1898.[37] Some European diplomats accepted the idea
that German ambitions were limited to economic opportunities rather
than seeking colonies.[38] So did later scholars, who used such phrases

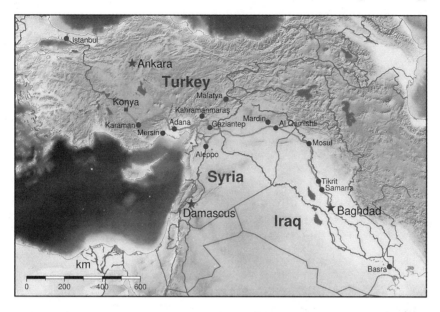

Figure 6. The map shows the eastern section of the Berlin to Baghdad railroad, built between 1903 to 1940 and running for a thousand miles through modern-day Turkey, Syria, and Iraq—a long-term German project for gaining influence in the region that aroused the suspicions of all its imperialist rivals.

as the "imperialism of free trade,"[39] or spoke of "ethical imperialism" or "peaceful imperialists"[40] whose goal was merely to build profitable railroads.[41] Indeed, contemporary internal German government documents show that this was true.[42]

The German economic push went far beyond railroad-building. In 1906, the German Orient Bank was established in Berlin, led by two Jewish bankers, Eugen and Herbert M. Gutmann, to develop business connections with the Middle East. It was a big success and became the leading regional-oriented bank in the world, with projects in Egypt, Morocco, Sudan, and the Ottoman Empire.[43] Three years later, Germany's gigantic Deutsche Bank opened a branch in Istanbul, linking directly with Ottoman financial institutions. A deal with British interests the following year brought the Deutsche Bank into financing oil production in Iran. In the period leading up to World War I, Germany was, after Britain and France, the Ottoman Empire's third largest trading partner.

This emphasis on commercial ties, then, seemed to be in the tradition

of von Bismarck, who had declared his distaste for "French-style colonial conquerors" and preferred economic relations instead.[44] Yet the
strategy also contradicted von Bismarck's warning to avoid even the
appearance of aggressive intensions or else risk fomenting war. Bringing von Bismarck's worst fears to fruition, London and Paris formed an
alliance, joined by Russia in 1907, directed against Germany.

The Germans could well argue that this was unfair. The French and
British had carved up Africa; the Russians and British had split Persia's oil wealth between them while begrudging Germany colonies or
even control of overseas resources. But, unfair or not, Germany was
seen and portrayed by others as the aggressive newcomer in the Middle
East.[45] The kaiser's visit to Morocco in March 1905, for example, was
met with British and French screams about "German imperialism."
Frustrated by France's growing power over Morocco—contradicting
Paris's promise to maintain an open door there for all European states
equally—the Germans sent their gunboat *Panther* to visit in July 1911.
This "leap of the *Panther*," as it was dubbed in the British press, again
set off alarm bells in London and Paris.[46]

An even greater shock for Germany's rivals, albeit one based on mistaken assessments, was the idea that Germany had gained complete
control of the Ottoman Empire. In July 1908 there was a revolution
by the Young Turks, mostly German-trained young officers. Many of
them revered Germany as a role model of how a single ethnic group
(in those days the term usually used was "race") could unite in a single
nation-state. The new regime's leaders adored the head of the German
army's training mission, General Colmar von der Goltz, as their father
figure and viewed his writings on war as sacred texts.

The Young Turks were not Islamists but modernizing ethnic nationalists who wanted their country to be like Germany. Still, the kaiser
wrongly saw them as Islamist in politics and took the upheaval as
proof that he was right about the emergence of Islamic political power.
He even used the term "Islamism." If the great powers continued to
interfere in the Middle East, the kaiser speculated, the Ottoman sultan
could merely raise the green flag of Islam, Muslims in all corners of
Asia and Africa would shout, "Allahu Akbar," and Christians—at least
non-German ones—would be driven out of the region.[47] If this were
true, the kaiser thought, Christians, at least non-German ones, were
finished in Ottoman lands.[48] But the idea that Christians and other

minorities might be massacred—as had happened with the Armenians and Greeks on a number of occasions in the late nineteenth century—did not discourage the German strategy of promoting Islamism and allying with the Ottomans.

One of the most powerful Young Turks was Ismail Enver Pasha, military attaché in Berlin from 1908 to 1911 and a strong Germanophile. He became war minister in 1913 and one of the ruling Young Turk triumvirate at the age of thirty-one. As a result, relations between Germany and the Ottoman Empire became tighter than ever. In December 1913, General Otto Liman von Sanders arrived with forty officers to become inspector general of the Ottoman army. He reorganized it and put German advisers into key positions.[49]

Thus, the stage was set for World War I: Germany would cast its lot with the Ottoman Muslims and hope the sultan's call for jihad would destabilize French and British colonies from Algeria through Egypt and all the way to India. The Allies would respond by backing the nationalism of Arabs, Jews, and Armenians. Most Arab officers did remain loyal to the Ottomans but overall the Allied strategy was far more successful.

Yet in history there is always a longer run. Already, even before the first act—a first world war—of the drama had begun, the scene was being prepared for the second round. Two young men affected by the kaiser's policy would play a central role in those future developments.

The first of these was a young Austrian named Adolf Hitler. Born in 1889, the same year the kaiser first visited the Ottomans, he arrived in Vienna to study painting. A high school drop-out, he failed the entry exam to the Academy of Fine Arts. Angry, bitter, and with no profession, he turned his attention to architecture, theater, and politics. Having grown up in a village, he was fascinated by Vienna's imperial buildings like the Court Museum, the Opera, and the Parliament. For hours he gazed at the skyline, feeling an "enchantment out of The Thousand and One Nights."[50] Hitler drew on Middle Eastern imagery surprisingly often, and the Middle East is the most neglected influence on the thinking of this most-studied person in modern history. He was eager to devote his life to some higher mission. But what should that be? With his unimpressive physique, unsteady eyes, pale face, and tendency toward ranting monologues, he seemed a most unlikely person ever to play a great role in public events.

Hitler lived in a house for impoverished men built by donations from two Jewish families, the Gutmanns, who had established the German Orient Bank, and the Rothschilds.[51] The struggling painter, used to a thoroughly ethnic German environment, went into culture shock in the cosmopolitan city where German, Czech, Italian, Romanian, Hungarian, Yiddish, and Russian were spoken in the streets and even the Parliament.[52] To him, Vienna appeared "a Babel of languages and races" with no coherence.[53] He saw the city that had in effect rejected him as filled with "filth, prostitution, and scum."[54] Why was he impoverished, his genius unrecognized, while all those others went around like lords, dividing wealth and honors among them?

The answer he found was that the cities had become "mixed-language danger zones" where the "de-Germanization" of life led to "Judaization, Slavization, bastardization, and Niggerization." With an eye to the nearby German Empire, he thought about an "Aryan and pan-German" alternative in "racial self-awareness," influenced by Charles Darwin's *The Origin of Species.*

The atmosphere in Vienna fed these attitudes. He attended debates on the "gypsy plague" and heard proposals to send them to forced labor camps and tattoo numbers on their arms.[55] At first, he was more favorably inclined toward Jews, seeing them as the first civilized nation that went from polytheism to monotheism, as an intelligent people who stuck together and succeeded in politics and culture. As Jewish refugees arrived in flight from Russian pogroms, Hitler met for the first time an Orthodox Jew in a black caftan and asked himself: "Is this a Jew or a German?"[56] He missed a chance to further his ambition to become an artist when he recoiled from being interviewed by a Jewish professor, Alfred Roller.[57] Hitler concluded that "neither assimilation nor conversion can turn a Jew into a non-Jew"; associated Jews with socialism, Marxism, and antinationalist thinking; and believed in a social Darwinism requiring survival of the "fittest race and elimination of the weak."[58] Hitler described himself as a "fanatical German nationalist."[59]

All of this has been much discussed, but less appreciated is one other element in his evolution: a romantic fascination with the Middle East and with Islam. A key role here was played by Karl May, the same man to whose adventure stories about the Wild West and the exotic East Friedrich Rosen had sarcastically compared von Oppenheim's ideas about fomenting jihad. In May's books, which Hitler lovingly absorbed, he discovered the world of Muslims, Turks, and Arabs "exerting the magic spell" of Mecca as he later recalled. He was devoted to such books as *A Desert Ride,* even reading at night by candlelight or with a magnifying glass, using the moon as his lantern.[60]

May was born in 1842 into a poor working-class family with fourteen children, nine of whom died before adulthood. His career as a teacher was wrecked by an accusation that he stole a colleague's watch. Twice imprisoned and having suffered a nervous breakdown, he began writing in jail in the 1870s. His imagination soared beyond the bars as he made up stories about distant people and dramatic adventures encountering his German heroes. For his Middle Eastern novels, May created the first-person German narrator, Kara Bin Nimsi and his Muslim servant al-Hajj Khalif Umar.[61] On and on they traveled, through *The Oil Prince* (1877), *Travel Adventures in Kurdistan* (1882), the three-volume *In the Land of the Mahdi* (1891–1896), *From Baghdad to Istanbul* (1892), *The Black Persian* (1892), and *In the Desert* (1892). In 1899, May actually traveled himself through the Middle East.

Hitler's fascination with May intensified when he attended a lecture by the author in March 1912. In an argument back at his hostel that evening, Hitler defended the literary quality of May's work. Ten days later, May suddenly died. Hitler seemed to have felt himself the recipient of May's final message, even the heir of his vision.

May promulgated no political doctrine. Among his fans were the humanitarian missionary doctor Albert Schweitzer, the antifascist writer Hermann Hesse, and the Jewish physicist Albert Einstein. May admired Native Americans, had no apparent anti-Semitic prejudice, and wrote sympathetically—albeit with excessive imagination—about a wide variety of non-European peoples. The only Jewish character in May's book *A Desert Ride,* though, is Sir David, an Anglicized Jew who is a British agent. Hitler would later view Britain and the Jews as his united enemy.

May himself was something of a pacifist who at his career's end revealed a mystical, utopian turn of mind. While he wrote about violence, he stressed that his heroes would only kill someone when absolutely necessary. Indeed, the only time Hitler saw May speak reflected those tendencies, the title of May's lecture being, "Upward into the Noble Man's Realm," based on his mystical idea of how everyone could raise himself from materialistic Ardistan (pidgin Arabic for the country of the earth) to noble Jinnistan (May's pseudo-Arabic for the high land of the spirit).[62]

While one can see how this thinking played into the mystical idealism of later Nazism, May's moralistic thought had to be twisted greatly to fill that function. May's importance for Hitler, then, had nothing to do with the ideology of Nazism as such but with several other aspects of his work, relating more to its tactics, style, and what might be called its idealization of the tribe. The basic plot of both May's Middle Eastern and Western novels was always the same. A group of noble, brave natives are fighting local, tribal enemies. The German explorer makes an alliance with them to destroy their enemies. This was the model Hitler would use in befriending Arabs and Muslims by helping them against the Jews.

Another effect of May on Hitler and many of his later followers was to fill their Walter Mitty–like heads with a thirst for adventure, breaking out of the stolid bourgeois conformism so powerful in German society. In this context, Hitler would make even May's lack of experience with the places and peoples about which he wrote into a plus. Years later he told senior aides that May's writing proved that "It was not necessary to know the desert in order to direct troops in the [North] African theater of war. . . . It wasn't necessary to travel in order to know the world."[63]

Finally, May's writings functioned for Hitler as von Oppenheim's books and dispatches had for the kaiser, making him feel that he knew everything necessary about the Arabs and Islam. May even met von Oppenheim in Cairo in 1899. At von Oppenheim's home, Bab al-Luq, they spoke at length about Middle East rulers, Muslim brotherhoods, and tribes. May was fascinated by "the consul," as he called the diplomat, and von Oppenheim was equally impressed, describing May as handsome, tall, and with a full blond beard.[64] For his part, May was familiar with von Oppenheim's books and seems to have drawn on them for his own novels.[65]

Just as May's hero Kara Bin Nimsi led his Arab Muslim servant al-Hajj Khalif Umar Bin Khalif, Hitler would dream of doing the same for the Muslims and Arabs in general. From Hitler's perspective, Arabs seemed proud desert warriors in whom could be glimpsed an echo of the ancient Germanic tribes, that ideal group Hitler wanted his Aryans to emulate. In 1939, Hitler would tell a Saudi envoy that his sympathy and support for the Arabs had begun with his reading of May's novels in his early youth.[66]

How did May characterize Arabs? In his works, they talk a lot but don't necessarily follow through on what they say. Some are heroes, some are cowards, but they are all very religious—Islam is the main force driving them—and they want to convert everyone to their religion. The strategic import of this portrait for Hitler was, as with von Oppenheim and the kaiser, the idea that allying oneself with Islam was the political key to success in the region.[67]

The other young man of the time who would play a leading role in the second round of Germany's efforts to raise the Islamic world in rebellion against rival powers was al-Hajj Muhammad Amin al-Husaini. To Hitler's Kara Bin Nimsi, al-Husaini would play the part of al-Hajj Khalif Umar Bin Khalif. Born in 1897 to one of the most important families in the Ottoman province of Syria, al-Husaini's uniqueness was in his bringing together all the factors that would make a powerful Arab and Muslim leader.

First he had a strong education in Islam. Al-Husaini was taught to memorize the entire al-Qur'an and made the pilgrimage to Mecca as a teenager, accompanying his mother to the holy city in 1913.[68] He was well connected for becoming a high-level Muslim cleric, being heir to one of the area's most powerful clans whose members often held such posts. The al-Husaini family claimed a noble ancestry, in both Arab and Islamic terms, from Muhammad himself. They were said to have left western Arabia for Jaffa and in 1380 to have settled in Jerusalem. From that time, the family's members often served as mayors or, like al-Husaini's father and his brother Kamil, as muftis of Jerusalem.[69]

Then, too, he was taught other skills. In a land still governed in the Ottoman Turkish tongue, he was given private lessons in Arabic and Arab history, thus preparing him for the Arab nationalist movement. He learned French from Catholic priests, enabling him to communicate with Europeans both linguistically and socially. Later he would write to Hitler in French with a fine handwriting. Another advantage in this regard was that Amin himself was European-looking, with light skin, a reddish beard, and blue eyes.

After his early education, al-Husaini was sent to study at al-Azhar in Cairo, the most influential Islamic university in the Muslim world. He also sat in on courses at Cairo University. Al-Husaini also embarked on political activism, and in 1914 he organized a meeting of twenty Arabs to form an anti-Zionist group.[70] As Hitler inherited old anti-Semitic concepts and transmuted them, so did al-Husaini. He was told in his religious education how Jews had corrupted the holy book given to them by God and had later refused to become Muslims, and how Muhammad—whose acts are always defined as righteous—had massacred Jewish tribes, killing the men, selling the women and children into slavery, and expelling all the Jews from Arabia.[71] Al-Qur'an told him not to befriend or trust them.

One of al-Husaini's teachers was the leading Arab intellectual of the day who blended Islamism, nationalism, and modernization. The Syria-born Rashid Rida argued that by adopting certain elements of the modern world and uniting, Muslims could best resist Western incursions and return to early Islam's golden age. Amin quarreled with his father, who was more of a traditionalist and didn't like the politicization of Islam that was producing this new Islamist movement.[72]

Back in Germany, after von Oppenheim's retirement from the Foreign Ministry his place as the kaiser's chief adviser on Islam and the Middle East was taken by Ernst Jäckh. This young man, born in 1875, had spent much of his career in journalism, wasn't really an academic expert, and spoke little if any Turkish, but he was a strong enthusiast for the Ottoman regime and the Young Turks in particular. Since 1902, Jäckh had been an organizer for Germany's liberal movement. He saw the Young Turks as kindred spirits, reformers dedicated to constitutionalism and modernization. There was truth in this concept, but they were also militaristic and chauvinistic nationalists, aspects he failed to understand.

Since Germany ruled few Muslims, Jäckh suggested, it had little to fear from a jihad against European Christian rule. In August 1914, as the war began, he wrote that once the Ottoman sultan-caliph ordered a jihad,

> Then Islam rises up against Great Britain, France and Russia. In Iran are ten million Muslims ready to march against Russia and England. Russia rules over 20 million Muslims who could turn against her. London has to take into account 100 million Afro-Asian Muslims, among them 60 million in India.

It will be a global war from Morocco through India and Iran to the Caucasus. The stage is set "for the mighty sword of Islam."[73]

It seemed that the kaiser's dream of a second front in the colonial hinterland that would sweep Germany to victory was about to be realized. Or was it?

3 A Jihad Made in Germany

On June 28, 1914, Archduke Franz Ferdinand of Austria and his wife were assassinated in Sarajevo. The event set off a diplomatic chain reaction two decades in the making. Austria-Hungary issued an ultimatum demanding huge concessions from Serbia, which it held responsible for the murders. Serbia refused and turned to its ally, Russia; Russia looked to its allies Britain and France for support. Austria sought Germany's backing. A month later the Austrians declared war on Serbia and all the powers joined battle.

In Berlin, the war lit the fuse for Germany's secret weapon. On July 30, the kaiser explained: "Our consuls and agents in Turkey, India and Egypt are supposed to inflame the Muslim regions to wild revolts against the British." If the plan worked, "England shall lose at least India."[1] Von Oppenheim, author of Germany's Islamic strategy, returned to the Foreign Ministry on August 2, nominally as head of the news department but actually to run covert warfare in the Middle East, implementing the program he had advocated for twenty years.[2] As von Oppenheim had put it in 1898, his mission was to unleash "Muslim fanaticism that borders on insanity."[3]

Of the experts recruited for this purpose, the most important were Carl Heinrich Becker, Hugo Grothe, and Eugen Mittwoch, all brilliant scholars but not necessarily well-informed regarding how to organize a jihad.[4]

Becker was a thirty-eight-year-old professor of Oriental Philology at Bonn University and editor of the journal *Der Islam*. Despite earlier reservations about the jihad strategy, he was eager to implement it. Since he had been rejected for military service due to poor health, this was the way he would serve the Fatherland.

Grothe, forty-five years old, knew Turkey and India well and had traveled across Iran in 1907, but was mainly an economist and made basic factual errors in discussing Islam. A strong partisan of the Turks, he referred to Armenians' "cheating and usury" and to them as the "main supporters of the terrorists in the Caucasus,"[5] and blamed previous Turkish massacres on the Armenians' "bloodsucking activities."[6]

Mittwoch, thirty-eight years old, would have the strangest career. In 1916, he succeeded von Oppenheim in running the German jihad campaign, and after the war he became the University of Berlin's professor of Semitic studies. An at least partly observant Jew, Mittwoch was praised by one of his students, Rabbi Joseph B. Soloveitchik, the Lubavitcher rebbe and one of the greatest figures of modern Jewish history.[7] His scholarship was so highly regarded that the Nazis rescinded his firing in 1933 and kept him on for two more years, and even then gave him emeritus status due to intervention by Italian dictator Benito Mussolini, who admired his research on Ethiopia. He headed the office of an American Jewish organization in Berlin until he could escape in 1939, dying three years later in London.

In August 1914, Becker, Grothe, and Mittwoch agreed that their duty was to use their knowledge for Germany's benefit.[8] They all believed that the longer, more deadlocked the war in Europe, the more vital it was to open a front in the Middle East.[9]

On one point the experts and the kaiser were quickly proven correct. In early 1914, the Turks secretly asked for an alliance with Germany, and on August 2, as the war was beginning, the two countries signed an agreement in which the Ottomans would enter the war if Russia did so and if the Germans provided support and equipment.[10] This achievement was the culmination of a decades-long German dream.[11] The head of the kaiser's war cabinet, Moriz von Lyncker, expressed both hope and ambivalence about German strategy. "Eventually all of

Islam might turn against England," he agreed, but asked how much of a contribution that would really be to the German war effort.[12]

While von Oppenheim organized his team and wrote a master plan for launching jihad,[13] the three experts assembled a program entitled "Germany and Islam." Their mission was to inform the German elite and prepare the general public for an unprecedented—in Becker's phrase—and frightening undertaking: a European Christian–manufactured jihad against other European Christians. Becker dealt with German policy toward Islam in general; Grothe, with Turkey; and Mittwoch, with the doctrine of jihad.[14]

While examining potential problems, the German experts were up-beat, claiming alliance with the Ottomans plus jihad would be unstoppable. "We have to win the war ourselves," they explained, but the Ottomans would be an important force in that victory.[15] They could stir huge Islamic revolts, Mittwoch wrote, because, "Culture and religion, state and church, nation and community of faith are for Muslims all the same."[16] He predicted that Ottoman troops accompanied by German officers could even advance into India and inspire a massive anti-British revolt there.[17]

Of course, the authors admitted, there were risks, especially that of unleashing an Islamic genie that would escape Berlin's control, launching an all-out offensive against all Christians. Or, perhaps the Allies might discredit the Ottoman sultan as a pawn of German "infidels" and raise an Islamic-flavored Arab revolt against him. Becker revived his old idea that the jihad strategy wouldn't work because the Ottoman sultan was not a real caliph.[18]

But Becker and his colleagues quickly brushed aside these objections. At this point, they believed, Germany had no choice but to try the scheme. At a minimum, a jihad would tie up Allied troops in the Middle East so they could not be sent to the European front. If, however, the jihad succeeded the prize would be enormous. A huge, modernized Muslim state dominated by the Ottoman Empire, the Islambund, with Istanbul as its capital, would become a close ally and valuable economic partner. Iran and Afghanistan would be linked to it in an Islamic Triple Alliance.[19] And Germany would be predominant throughout the Middle East.[20]

On August 5, 1914, just three days after the German-Ottoman alliance was concluded, Chief of the German General Staff General Helmuth

Figure 7. Enver Pasha, Ottoman war minister during World War I, who also unleashed the German-Ottoman jihadization of Islam with a 1914 call for Afro-Asian jihad in the colonies of Great Britain, Russia, and France. After the war he briefly joined the Soviet "leftist jihad" in the service of world revolution, but was eventually killed fighting for Central Asian Muslim opponents of the Bolsheviks.

von Moltke asked the Ottomans to invade Egypt to trigger pan-Islamic revolts. Ottoman War Minister Enver Pasha agreed and gave the order to prepare the operation. He told a visitor from Berlin: "I am conducting this war according to orders from the German General Staff. I have asked for [German] advisers in all ministries. And this shows my real intention."[21]

Enver cooperated closely with the German naval attaché, Hans Humann, a boyhood friend.[22] The Turkish-speaking Humann's background exemplified Germany's prewar role in the empire. His father, Carl Wilhelm, was an engineer who traveled widely building roads and railroads, as well as a great amateur archaeologist. His great accomplishment was the excavation of Pergamon, an almost intact ancient Greek city near Izmir. It was in that latter place where Hans was born in 1878.

Together, Hans Humann and Enver established the *tashkilat-i mahsusa,* an organization to spread revolt and jihad throughout the Russian-ruled Caucasus.[23] Enver created another such group, the Bureau for Revolutionizing Middle Eastern Lands,[24] to do the same for Arab-populated regions.[25] Meanwhile, Enver received the promised German military advisers and equipment. On October 21, 1914, he became Ottoman commander in chief,[26] and the next day he told Berlin his war plan.[27] Within a week, the Ottoman navy, under the command of German Admiral Wilhelm A. Souchon, was ordered to attack Russian Black Sea ports.[28] On November 2, Russia declared war on the Ottoman Empire, followed by Britain and France three days later.

On the covert operations front, von Oppenheim sent his 136-page plan, "The Revolutionizing of the Islamic Territories of our Enemies," to the kaiser in November.[29] It was quickly approved and funded.[30] The prime goals were to take Egypt away from Britain and raise serious revolts in India and Afghanistan. Toward this end, Germany would bribe tribes to revolt and distribute propaganda to persuade Muslim troops in enemy armies to desert and join the German side. The Suez Canal, water supplies, and oil pipelines would be sabotaged. War would be waged against the British in Iran, the Persian Gulf, Afghanistan, and India, against the French in North Africa, and against the Russians in the Caucasus and Central Asia. Since the plan identified the enemy as not only the British, French, and Russians but also non-Muslim minorities, Christians and Jews who supported the Allies, this meant Germany's endorsement of a war against civilians and spreading religious hatred. Thus, German strategy would be intimately involved in the Ottomans' mass murder of Armenians.

Would the sultan's religious prestige suffice for Muslims to follow him in fighting their Christian rulers?[31] It is easy to see these schemes as fantasies, but there was a real basis for believing Islam could be Germany's secret weapon. Aside from the millions in enemy territory, almost 500,000 Muslim soldiers served in Allied armies: in the French forces, they came from Algeria, Morocco, and Tunisia; and in the British forces, from India.[32] And belief that the sultan was the proper ruler and guardian of Islam's holiest sites, Mecca and Medina, did keep almost all of the Ottoman army, including Arab officers, and the empire's Muslim population loyal throughout the war.

Von Oppenheim quickly established propaganda bases throughout the empire, the main ones being in Medina, Jaffa, Jerusalem, Cairo, Baghdad, and the Shia Muslim centers of Karbala and Najaf. To assemble his team required the services of a variety of characters. One of them was the Young Turk activist Munis Tekin Alp who wrote pro-German propaganda and extolled Pan-Turkish ideas.[33] Although a convinced Turkish nationalist, he had been born Marcel Cohen in Salonika.[34]

Alp's writing stressed Pan-Turkish nationalism and enmity toward Russia; Arab and Arabic-speaking German agents wrote similar materials that put the emphasis on Pan-Islamist religious ideology and Britain as the enemy. Alp's 1915 pamphlet, *The Turkish and Pan-Turkish*

Ideal, spoke of uniting all Turkic peoples—including those ruled by Russia—into a great nationalist-Islamist empire that would be allied to a Germany that dominated Europe.[35] In comparison, the Russians were portrayed as enemies of all Turkic and Muslim people; the English as degenerate friends of the tsar; and the French as foes of Turkish nationalism and Islam. Germany, claimed Alp, "is the only country" that would help create and sustain the new Turkey, respecting its national independence and territorial integrity.[36]

But one German operation in the Ottoman Empire, involving an agent as flamboyant as Alp, would not only dwarf the impact of all the others but decisively change world history. Israel Lazarevich Gelfhand, better known as Alexander Parvus, was simultaneously a revolutionary thinker and a counterrevolutionary spy. Born in 1867 in a Russian shtetl, he was raised in cosmopolitan Odessa where he joined the Jewish Socialist Bund. Moving to Switzerland and Germany, Parvus became a Marxist and became friends with Vladimir Ilyich Lenin, joining his Bolshevik group Parvus was considered one of the early movement's most brilliant minds. His writings, especially his thoughts about how revolutionaries could ally with the tsar's enemies in an international war to bring down the regime, drew German intelligence's attention as early as 1905.

Continuing his remarkable permutations, Parvus moved to Istanbul where he became a millionaire arms merchant and adviser to the Young Turks.[37] German ambassador Hans von Wangenheim, another admirer, sent Parvus to Berlin in March 1915 with a proposal to use German money to back the Bolsheviks in overthrowing the tsar and taking Russia out of the war. Soon, through Parvus's networks in Denmark and Istanbul, money started flowing to Lenin. Success came in March 1917 when the Germans arranged Lenin's return to Russia in a sealed train to foment a revolution. Before the year ended, Lenin seized power and did take Russia out of the war, a large, though not ultimately fatal, blow to the Allies. Germany could then transfer hundreds of thousands of troops from the Eastern to the Western Front for its final offensive in 1918.

Ironically, the operation intended to create a Muslim jihad to destroy Germany's Russian enemy unexpectedly succeeded in that goal by helping set off a Communist revolution instead! It was ironic that Hitler and al-Husaini[38] would both claim that the hated Jews were be-

hind the Bolshevik revolution when actually the real culprit was argu-
ably the kaiser.

As Buchan's novel *Greenmantle* showed at the time, British intelligence knew a great deal regarding the German jihad plan. But the
man who most publicly spilled the beans was a soft-spoken, respected
Dutch scholar, C. Snouck Hurgronje, who read what his counterparts
in Berlin wrote and was horrified at what he called this "jihad made in
Germany." Unleashing a plague of religious hatred, he warned, would
provoke mob violence and massacres beyond anyone's control. Hurgronje correctly pointed out in an article that while the caliph was
formally endowed with the right to call a jihad and that Islam's most
sacred texts held jihad to be every Muslim's duty, this did not cor-
respond to what happened in the real world: "The jihad program assumes that the Mohammedans, just as at their first appearance in the
world, continuously form a compact unity under one man's leadership.
But this situation has in reality endured so short a time, the realm of
Islam has so quickly disintegrated into an increasingly large number of
principalities, the supreme power of the so-called caliph, after flourish-
ing for a short period, has become a mere word. . . ."[39]

This was especially embarrassing for Becker, who viewed Hurgronje
as one of his mentors. The German scholar retorted that when the Allies used Muslim troops against the Central Powers, Berlin had every
right to incite jihad in the colonial territories of its enemies to undermine that recruitment.[40]

Another leak came through German ambassador Wangenheim in Istanbul who blabbed too much to his neutral American counterpart,
Henry I. Morgenthau. Puffing away on a big black cigar in his office,
Wangenheim claimed that the Ottoman army was far less important
than the sultan's ability to proclaim a jihad. The ambassador explained,
Morgenthau later recalled, "Quietly and nonchalantly, as though it had
been the most ordinary" matter, Germany's plot "to arouse the whole
fanatical Muslim regions against the Christians."[41]

But as it had been since von Oppenheim first raised the idea many
years earlier, this was still all big talk. What could the Germans actually
do to raise and direct such a jihad?

Von Oppenheim's team worked closely with Rudolf Nadolny, a former diplomat who had been posted in the Middle East and now served
in the German General Staff's political section, and the Foreign Min-

istry's Middle East expert Otto von Wesendonk. Insisting he wanted real experts, not adventurers, von Oppenheim quickly hired a dozen German experts and two dozen, mostly Muslim, non-Germans. By the war's end, about sixty such people worked for him. Among them were the Tunisian Salikh ash-Sharif at-Tunisi; the Algerian Rabah Bukabuya; Mamun Abu al-Fadl, from western Arabia; and the Egyptians Ahmad Wali, Mustafa Mansur Rifat, and Abd al-Aziz Jawish. After the war, Jawish would be a key adviser of Hasan al-Banna in the founding of the Muslim Brotherhood.

Von Oppenheim also hired Caucasian Muslims like the Tatars Said Effendiev, Shamil Safarov, and Muhammad Kazakov. There were also Indian and Persian sections. One of the more capable collaborators was Rabah Bukabuya, a French Muslim officer from Algeria who deserted to the German side in 1915. Also in Berlin, the Lebanese Druze Pan-Islamist Shakib Arslan and the Egyptian nationalist Muhammad Farid become advisers.

Arslan would ultimately be the most famous and influential of them all. In 1893, von Oppenheim had met members of his clan.[42] Forty-five years old in 1914, Shakib Arslan was a Druze prince who had been a member of the Ottoman Parliament. Influenced by the ideas of the influential pioneer Islamist Muhammad Abduh, who had also influenced al-Husaini, Arslan viewed the Ottoman Empire as Islam's defender against European colonialism.

The other staffer of note, and the only one with a real political base in his home country, was the forty-six-year-old Egyptian Mustafa Farid, former president of the National Party, Egypt's main nationalist group. An advocate of expelling Britain from Egypt, he was exiled by Egypt's king in 1912, after which he sought Ottoman and then German help.

During World War I, von Oppenheim's office produced over one thousand publications in nine European and twelve Middle Eastern and Asian languages—four hundred of them in 1914 and 1915 alone—and distributed three million copies of books, newspapers, journals, pamphlets, and leaflets. These materials included such Pan-Islamic, anti-Allied materials as "They Cheat God and the Infidels," "England and the Caliphate," "Russian Massacres," and "Jihad and French Troops."[43] Von Oppenheim placed propaganda with sympathetic news agencies like Agence Ottomane.[44] In November 1914, the Germans opened a reading room in nearby Medina to attract those making the pilgrimage to Mecca until the area's ruler, Sharif Husain—already involved in secret talks that would lead to his joining the British the next year—closed it.[45]

The most important readers for von Oppenheim's publications were, literally, a captive audience: Muslim prisoners of war—mainly Indians from the British forces and North Africans from the French armies—held by Germany. There were about nine hundred of them at first. To indoctrinate and recruit them, these potential turncoats were moved into two special camps near Berlin, each with a mosque. They were given classes in Islam along with intensive German propagandizing by lectures and literature, including a multilingual weekly appropriately named *al-Jihad*.[46]

The means for actually carrying out the grand plan were limited. Nevertheless, the long-awaited moment arrived. On November 14, 1914, the sultan-caliph's call for all faithful Muslims to wage jihad against the British, French, and Russians was proclaimed. Non-Ottoman Muslims also had to participate, said the fatwa—published in Arabic, Persian, Urdu, and Turkish—to rescue the Ottoman Empire as the heart and soul of the *umma*, the international community of all Muslims. In a special ceremony, Sultan-Caliph Mehmed V was given an ancient Ottoman sword. Grand Mufti Ürgüplü Khairi Bey, the empire's highest Muslim cleric and the fatwa's main author, unrolled what was said to be Muhammad's original battle flag. The sultan himself addressed the troops while War Minister Enver Pasha thundered, "Three hundred million Muslims sigh under chains," and must be liberated.[47]

A large crowd, some on horseback, marched from the mosque to the German embassy. They included a woman acting the part of Aisha, one of Muhammad's wives. On the balcony stood the German ambassador and some special surprise guests: fourteen Muslim ex–prisoners of war who had decided to join the German-Ottoman side. One of them, a huge Moroccan from the French army, made a speech in Arabic praising Germany and saying that Muslim soldiers were badly treated in the French military. The kaiser himself had approved the plan to take these men from Berlin to Istanbul on the luxurious Orient Express. To keep the operation secret, they had been disguised as acrobats.[48] After cheering the kaiser, the crowd moved on to the embassy of Germany's ally, Austria-Hungary, where they repeated the ceremony.

The declaration of jihad was calculated to make Muslims' blood

Figure 8. The rulers of the Central Powers in World War I meet in Vienna, 1916. Left to right: Kaiser Wilhelm of Germany, Tsar Ferdinand of Bulgaria, Kaiser Franz Joseph of Austria-Hungary, and Sultan Mehmed V Reshad of the Ottoman Empire.

boil with indignation and eagerness to fight. Enemies, the declaration began, have attacked the Islamic world, seized and pillaged Islamic countries, and taken Muslims as prisoners. The "warships and armies" of Russia, England, France, and their allies: "Attack the Seat of the Islamic Caliphate and the Imperial Dominions and strive (God forbid) for extinguishing and annihilating the exalted light of Islam. . . . [Consequently] it is also incumbent upon all Muslims that are being ruled by these governments to proclaim jihad against them and to attack them."[49] Any Muslim who did not wage jihad, the declaration continued, was committing "a great sin and deserve[s] Divine wrath and punishment." Even if the Allies threatened him with death or the extermination of his whole family, to fight against the Ottomans violated Islamic law and made them deserving of "hell-fire." All Muslims "be they young or old, on foot or mounted, [must] hasten to partake in the jihad."

This imperial decree was followed by many other fatwas, some engineered by the Germans, others translated and distributed by them. Typical was a 1915 fatwa by Hibat ad-Din Muhammad ash-Shahrastani, translated by Helmut Ritter of the Sixth Ottoman Army in Baghdad and Carl Brockelmann of Halle University. Becker checked the text and von Oppenheim's organization distributed it widely. An Iranian, Muhammad Farisi of Karbala, added notes.[50]

The fatwa began with a question: "Germans are Christians and now helpers of Muslims. But they are also infidels like the Russians, English, Italians, and French. Why is it allowed for us as Muslims to be friends with the Germans while the killing of other infidels is an obligation, and since all the infidels are of one nation?" Ash-Shahrastani answered, "There are two kinds of infidels. The friendly ones do not seek to plunder the houses of Muslims and to rape their religion. The other kind of infidels—the French, British, and Russians—are our religious foes. They want to loot our houses and destroy our national independence and state. The Sharia [Islamic law] does not allow us to treat them nicely but orders us to be hostile and wage war against them."

As examples of Germany's pro-Muslim policies, ash-Shahrastani recalled how the kaiser had honored Saladin and called himself a friend and protector of Muslims. Germany's ruler had sent Muslim prisoners of war taken from the French and Russian armies to Istanbul, city of the caliphate, to fight for the Ottomans. Finally, Farisi noted the military training and weapons Germany gave the Ottomans. In contrast, ash-Shahrastani listed the Allies' sins, some of them fabricated: British "Foreign Minister" William Ewart Gladstone (he was prime minister but never foreign minister) supposedly had told Parliament that England could not succeed unless the Muslim holy book, al-Qur'an, was defiled. Prime Minister Lord Salisbury had allegedly stressed that only if the Kaaba, Islam's holiest site in Mecca, was eliminated could London control Muslim countries. An unidentified French ruler was quoted as advocating that Mecca and Medina be captured so that Muhammad's body could be put in the Louvre and Muslims lured to come live in France. To this list, Farisi added the Crusades (deleting the large German role in them), Russian expansionism, French and British colonialism, and the 1907 Anglo-Russian treaty dividing Persia into spheres of influence.

Ash-Shahrastani's arguments, down to the accusation that Gladstone was behind a war on Islam, would be recycled by al-Husaini before and during World War II. Echoes of this World War I propaganda can also be found in the documents of Hamas, al-Qaida, and the Muslim Brotherhood in the twenty-first century.

The fatwas promulgated were precisely as von Oppenheim prescribed to the kaiser back in 1896: jihad was the duty of all Muslims, the caliph could order them to jihad, the Ottoman ruler was the caliph, so all Muslims should obey him.

Could this chain of logic win the war for Germany and the Ottoman Empire? The problem was that German experts erroneously assumed that Islam's doctrines would be implemented by its adherents. Yet in practice things were quite different. Outside the Ottoman Empire the sultan's fatwa was largely ignored. Shia Muslims, who formed the majority in Iraq and Iran, did not accept this claim that they must obey a Sunni Muslim Ottoman ruler.

Even among Sunni Muslims, there were many who never heard of the fatwa or were indifferent, who put ethnic considerations as Arab nationalists above loyalty to the Ottomans, did as local political or religious leaders ordered, thought a non-Arab Turk could not be the proper caliph, benefited from working with the colonial rulers, or simply didn't want to risk their lives or property. This distinction between the theory of Islam and the actual daily lives of Muslims would be one that many would miss in future, both in the West and among Muslims themselves, such as in the foiled expectations of Usama bin Ladin decades later.

In Istanbul, the immediate aftermath of the fatwa's issue confirmed the idea that inflaming passions might end with killing Christians. U.S. Ambassador Morgenthau described how after the ceremony, Enver visited Morgenthau and promised, "There will be no massacres," a statement that did more to heighten than assuage the American ambassador's concern. At the very moment Enver was speaking, Morgenthau's secretary entered the office and whispered in his ear that a mob was demonstrating against foreigners and assaulting an Austrian-owned shop that had a sign saying, "English clothes for sale"—ironic since Austria was Germany's leading ally—and a French clothing store. This was just a mistake, Enver said, and left.

Later in the day, Morgenthau called Enver to find out what had happened. Enver tried to calm him by saying that the U.S. embassy had nothing to fear. Meanwhile, though, the mob—with Ottoman policemen in the lead—marched through the area where most foreigners lived.[51] One target was the famous Armenian-owned Tokatlian hotel and café on the Grande Rue de Péra. Men used poles with hooks on the end to break its mirrors and windows. Others smashed marble-topped tables. Within minutes, the place was gutted. Suddenly, one of the policemen drew his gun and shot straight into a fine English grandfather clock. Even von Oppenheim's deputy, Karl E. Schabinger, who later succeeded him as head of the News Department, was shaken by the violent passions aroused. "This is the way the Holy Jihad war is starting."[52]

Quickly, Enver, who was simultaneously planning the deportation and massacre of Armenians, realized that the violence had to be focused against his and Germany's enemies. He asked Salih ash-Sharif at-Tunisi of von Oppenheim's staff to write a supplementary analysis of the fatwa to show that only war against the Christians of France, Britain, and Russia was good, but that attacking German Christians was bad. Al-Tunisi produced a pamphlet entitled "Truth of Jihad."[53] He explained that peace between Muslims and European Christians could only be achieved if there was no longer any foreign occupation of Islamic lands. Since Germany had no colonies, it would be sufficient to expel Britain, France, and Russia from Muslim lands, and German willingness to help in this effort proved they were good infidels.[54] Von Oppenheim's organization published the booklet in several Middle Eastern languages, with the German Society for the Study of Islam bringing out a German edition.

In March 1915, von Oppenheim left Istanbul to oversee field operations. During the next few months, he toured Ottoman Syria, giving talks in Beirut and Damascus calling for jihad and a close Ottoman-German alliance.[55] More prosaically, a British intelligence report following his activities, perhaps drawn from local rumors and eager-to-please informants, also accused him of "consorting with Muslim prostitutes while intriguing with Muslim married women." Von Oppenheim later seemed to admit this was at least partly true.[56]

As a result of all these activities, von Oppenheim claimed, his organization had established seventy-five reading rooms, mostly managed by locals, all over the empire to make literature available, gather intelligence, and recruit agents. Within two days, he boasted, he could spread a piece of propaganda all over the sprawling, technologically backward country.[57] In early 1916, the German liberal politician Gustav Stresemann inspected two of von Oppenheim's reading halls in Istanbul and was impressed. Thousands of people were using them, he noted, even if only—because they were illiterate—to look at the pictures. "This is great for us since it is not obvious . . . that they are German-controlled

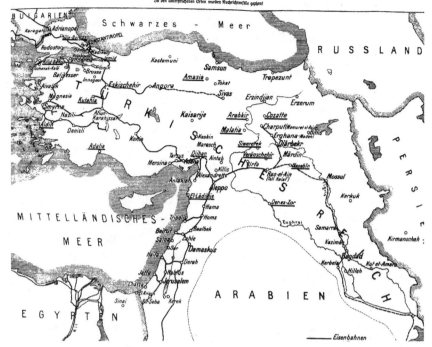

Figure 9. Map of Max von Oppenheim's news operation in the Ottoman Empire, with seventy-five centers for jihad propaganda open or planned. The agitation for war was often coordinated with local Young Turk leaders. In 1916 the German politician Gustav Stresemann visited two centers in Istanbul and commented that "it is not obvious . . . that they are German-controlled operations."

operations."[58] Morgenthau was less favorable. In trying to make public opinion hostile to the Allies, he reported, the halls use "streams of slander." Huge maps posted on the walls showed Muslim-inhabited territories snapped up by the British, French, and Russians; cartoons portrayed the Allies as greedy animals harrying poor Turkey.

The local hero in this propaganda was Enver Pasha. The other idol was the kaiser: "Hajji Wilhelm," he was called as if he were a Muslim who had made the Mecca pilgrimage. Another theme was the claim that Muslims of India and Egypt were about to revolt and throw out the British tyrants. People were taught the German motto, which took on an even more intense meaning for Muslims: "Gott strafe England!"— "God Punish England!"[59]

Outside the Ottoman Empire, von Oppenheim organized news halls wherever possible in neutral countries, like Tabriz, Iran, and Misrata in Italian-ruled Tripolitania, as well as distributing materials in the neutral Netherlands and Switzerland. In 1916, he founded a newsreel company to make propaganda films for use in the Balkans and Middle East.

Less publicly, von Oppenheim's group produced "how-to" manuals for jihad. One of the most widely circulated was by the Egyptian Jawish who worked both for the Germans and for Enver's intelligence operation in Berlin.[60] Morgenthau obtained a copy and was horrified. The booklet called for assassinations and the systematic "inciting of hatred to the foreign infidel." Jawish gave three methods for jihad: individual killings of Europeans or any non-Muslims, bands to slay infidels, and operations supporting Ottoman army campaigns.[61] Referring to the many Christians serving as officials on Ottoman railroads, von Oppenheim advised they should be threatened and "members of their families taken hostage to ensure they would not engage in sabotage."[62]

Von Oppenheim's top objective was Egypt. Forcing the Suez Canal's closure would be a tremendous blow to Britain's war effort. There were, he estimated, 11 million Egyptians, mostly Muslims, but only 37,000 British troops in the area. If an Ottoman army crossed into Egypt, he claimed, the vast majority of Egyptians would support it and overwhelm the British.[63] To achieve this result, von Oppenheim recommended, agents should be sent to spread revolt and Egyptians recruited into death squads "under Egyptian and Turkish officers to kill the English all over, beginning with the countryside."[64]

Von Oppenheim continued:

> Let us incite the Egyptians in the name of the sultan-caliph. Foment revolts there. Target especially the al-Azhar Mosque, the religious brotherhoods, and so on. Arrange as many strikes and assassinations as possible, regardless of whether they succeed or not. This helps us by confusing the British. . . . [British] reprisals are to be expected: the more cruel . . . the more they will hit the innocent civilians, the more it will deepen the people's fury and fanaticism. This gets them ready . . . to fight until the bitter end and to throw the British out.[65]

While World War I was a brutal, bloody conflict in which hundreds of thousands of soldiers died and poison gas was used, Germany's de-

cision to launch a campaign of state-sponsored terrorism against civilians was nonetheless shocking at the time. Both Morgenthau and
the Austro-Hungarian military adviser to the Ottomans, Joseph Pomiankowski, whose country was allied with Germany, thought so and
questioned whether this strategy would lead to mass murder.[66]

Except for small-scale sabotage successes however, the covert German
war in Egypt achieved little. In January 1915 the Austro-Hungarian
engineer Georg Gondos and the linguist Paul M. Simon led a band of
twenty men, including Ottoman soldiers, that tried but failed to destroy
oil installations in the southern Sinai near the Red Sea. A few mines
were placed near the Suez Canal.[67] German operations from Sudan and
Italian-ruled Libya sought to strike into Egypt.[68]

Von Oppenheim's efforts were a bit more successful in North Africa than in Egypt but didn't lead anywhere either. Italy's loose hold
on Libya let the Germans operate there with impunity. Twice, the
German Arabic-speaking agent Edgar Pröbster infiltrated into Libya
by submarine and distributed money to the rebellious Sanusiyya
brotherhood.[69]Another German agent, Otto Mannesmann, lived with
that group as an adviser until killed by bandits in 1916.[70]

Subversive efforts against Egypt and Libya were ultimately more
counterproductive than useful. Italy's alarm about von Oppenheim's
efforts in Libya was one factor driving Italy to enter the war on the
Allied side in 1915. Aware of the threat in Egypt, the British tightened
their control and replaced pro-German ruler Abbas Hilmi with his pro-
British uncle Husain Kamil. Hilmi's German patrons helped the exiled
monarch found the International Muslim Office in Lausanne, another
of von Oppenheim's many front groups.[71]

But the main difficulty was the German-advised Ottoman army's in-
ability to break through against the British on the Egyptian front. Its
offensives failed in February 1915 and the summer of 1916. In contrast,
the 1917 British offensive from Egypt succeeded, capturing Jerusalem
and then Damascus. On the Iraq front they took Baghdad. Similarly,
the British came out on top in Arabia. Von Oppenheim, knowing this
was an extremely religious area, hoped to persuade Sharif Husain of
Mecca, ruler of the west Arabian Hijaz kingdom, and his prestigious
Hashemite family to join the jihad. His first agent was the journalist
Max Roloff who volunteered to go disguised as a Muslim pilgrim. In
late 1914 he returned to report on his perilous journey. But Roloff had

Figure 10. The German-Ottoman alliance at work, October 1917. Kaiser Wilhelm II visits Gallipoli, site of Ottoman victory over Australian, British, and New Zealand forces with Ottoman General Esad Pasha, Enver Pasha, and German Vice Admiral Johannes Merten while non-Muslims like Armenians and Jews became the first victims of Islamism, an ideology that was used by the German-Ottoman jihad of the kaiser and the "Three Pashas," Enver, Talat, and Cemal.

merely made up the story.[72] Next, the German ethnologist Leo V. Frobenius was sent to Medina in 1915 to buy up Islamist preachers for the jihad cause while Othmar von Stotzingen tried to build a support base in southern Arabia.

The most able German agent in that region was Alois Musil, a Czech-born theology professor and Catholic priest. His mission was to win over the two key figures in Arabia, Sharif Husain and Ibn Saud, leader of the east Arabian kingdom in Nejd. For the first time, Enver balked at a German operation, concerned that the discovery that Musil was a priest could bring massive violence as local Muslims would suspect him of preaching Christianity. At last, though, Enver's concerns were assuaged. Musil spoke fluent Arabic and had a deep understanding of local customs and Islam. The Arabs dubbed him *mumathil al-muluk ath-thulatha,* envoy of the three kings—Germany, Austria, and the sultan. But even Musil backed by a monarchical trio could not mobilize a pro-Ottoman movement.[73]

Instead, Britain successfully raised rebellion in Arabia by winning over Sharif Husain with bribes of gold and promises of territory. As for Ibn Saud, he mistrusted the Ottomans, from whom he had long struggled to maintain independence.[74] The Germans had ignored the fact that backing the Ottomans was costly in a place where many saw the sultan as an enemy. While the British persuasively promised Sharif Husain a vast Arab kingdom carved from Ottoman territories if he joined them, Germany could only offer continued submission to Ottoman rule. For the tribesmen, loyalty to their leaders was more compelling than fighting for a distant supposed caliph who wasn't even an Arab and whom they know only through resented tax collections. Then, too, even if they had no sophisticated sense of nationalism, the Arabs of the peninsula proved easier to rouse against Turkish governors they knew than against European Christians they had never glimpsed.

Aside from Egypt and Arabia, the main German target was India. Von Oppenheim's twenty-five-member Indian section trained exiled nationalists to use explosives, preparing them for assassinations and even suicide attacks, then tried to infiltrate them back into India.[75] He toyed with such daring operations as a naval attack to free five hundred anti-British Indian nationalists held prisoner on the remote Andaman Islands. German navy officers were ready to try but the plan was put aside due to more pressing demands on the Reich's ships and men.[76] In Berlin and Switzerland, von Oppenheim's network established an eighteen-member Indian Committee whose men, as a German document put it, "were willing to die and kill any traitors."[77] But Germany vastly overestimated both the ease of stirring revolt there and the subcontinent's Muslims' interest in what the sultan said.

One operation was even conducted in the then-neutral United States. The key figure was Franz von Papen, German military attaché in Washington. He had already established an arms business, the Bridgeport Company, to make explosives and buy up weapons for the German war effort. Some were destined for anti-British revolutionaries in India.

In 1914, the Indian Committee in Berlin obtained an official German promise of arms and money to fight for the country's independence. The committee sent that message to Indian troops in the British army to subvert their loyalty: "Revolution is round the corner, independence in reach." The plan was to ship German weapons via the neutral Dutch East Indies, today Indonesia. Von Papen sent $250,000 worth of war materiel on two ships, the *Annie Larsen* and the *Maverick*. An Indian revolutionary, Manabendra Nath Roy, traveled to Java to take delivery,[78] but the British discovered and blocked the plot. A year later, a trial in San Francisco of eight of von Papen's Indian agents would reveal his involvement in a wide range of espionage and sabotage activities in America, including an effort to set up a military training base for pro German Indians in upstate New York.[79] As a result of these plots, the United States declared him persona non grata in early 1916.

Von Papen became chief of staff of the German army's Asia Corps under General Erich von Falkenhayn on the Iraqi front.[80] During his service, von Papen developed contacts with many Ottoman officers and political figures, including Mustafa Kemal who, as Kemal Atatürk, would lead the postwar Turkish republic. During this time, von Papen also befriended a young staff officer in Istanbul named Joachim von Ribbentrop. When von Ribbentrop became Nazi foreign minister, he remembered the favor. Von Papen would return to the area to play a leading role as Germany's ambassador to Turkey during World War II.[81]

The other part of Germany's India campaign was two adventurous but ultimately unfruitful overland treks by agents through Iraq, Iran, and Afghanistan to raise rebellion in those countries and establish bases for operations into India. One group, which set off in January 1915, was headed by former German military attaché to Iran Fritz Klein. Its immediate task was to destroy British facilities near the Iran-Ottoman border, but the more ambitious goal was to raise jihad among the Shia Muslims of Iraq. A German officer, Edgar Stern-Rubarth, persuaded Shia leaders in Karbala to issue a fatwa calling for jihad in February 1915 and to praise Germany as the Muslims' friend.[82] Von Oppenheim's group ensured that this declaration was relayed to India. But there was no uprising:[83] tribal leaders simply took money from both sides and did nothing.

In an even more dramatic effort a German-Ottoman group of about forty men traveled by horse and camel from Istanbul through Iran all the way to Kabul. They included Werner Otto von Hentig, who would be the Foreign Ministry's top Middle East expert during World War II, and the Indian nationalist R. Mahendra Pratap. Two men who traveled with them part of the way, Wilhelm Wasmuss and Max von Scheubner-Richter, both former German consuls in Iran, were dropped off to raise the tribes in, respectively, the southern and northern parts of that country.

Scheubner-Richter took as his assistant Paul Leverkuehn, who would later head German military intelligence in the region during World War II.[84] Later, Scheubner-Richter was one of the first to join the Nazi Party. Close to Hitler, he undoubtedly discussed his experiences and views on the region with the future dictator, for whom he served as a fundraiser. During Hitler's abortive 1923 coup in Munich, Scheubner-Richter was killed while standing beside him.

Wasmuss and Scheubner-Richter tried in November 1915 to make a deal with Persian Prime Minister Mustosi al-Mamalik to gain his support for Germany in the war. They did win over the German-educated governor of Shiraz, who helped them destroy some British telegraph lines and oil pipelines.[85] They also built good networks of contacts, one of whom was a military officer named Reza Khan who after the war would overthrow the Qajar dynasty and make himself shah.[86] That development, too, would have an important impact on German fortunes in the region during World War II.

The rest of the expedition moved on to Afghanistan. In August 1915 it showed the governor of Herat—a spy reported the details to British intelligence—the sultan's and the Shia clerics' jihad proclamations. Berlin, they said, would supply Afghanistan with new rifles and military advisers, and if it joined them in attacking India they promised a lot of Russian and Indian territory after Germany won the war.[87] Arriving in Kabul late in 1915, they made the same offer to the monarch, Amir Habib Allah.[88] He toyed with them, signing a German-Afghan Pact of Friendship after a month of talks, but took no action.[89] The pact specified that the Germans would supply 100,000 rifles and 300 artillery pieces along with all necessary supplies. But the Afghan monarch was not so naïve as to take on Russia and England simultaneously on the word of a few weather-beaten travelers. He would act, the amir said, when 100,000 German or Ottoman troops arrived to cover his rear against Russia.[90]

The Afghanistan expedition nonetheless did benefit German interests. Aware of these contacts, the British kept more soldiers in the area than they would have done otherwise. As in Iran's case, furthermore, the German contacts in Kabul had a delayed effect. In May 1919, after the war ended, a coup brought to power a new ruler, Aman Allah, who did declare a jihad against the British, and in the subsequent fighting the Afghans temporarily invaded Indian soil. But that was too late to help the Germans.

Another achievement was the establishment of an anti-British Indian nationalist base in Kabul. On December 1, 1915, Pratap, who had accompanied the expedition, announced himself president of Free Hindustan's government in exile. The British put a price on his head but for the next thirty years he continued to cooperate with the Germans and later the Japanese. After India became independent in 1947 he was allowed to return home.

In general, though, the jihad strategy, so long in development and high in hope, had fizzled. Many Arabs within the Ottoman Empire and most Muslims outside of it either no longer cared about the sultan, didn't accept his credentials, had other priorities, or just didn't believe the Young Turks, the empire's real rulers, were sincere in their religious pretensions.[91]

But the most momentous immediate event arising from the German jihad strategy was the mass murder of Ottoman Armenians. Von Oppenheim either urged or supported Ottoman repression of the Armenians and Jews, as well as the execution of Arab nationalists, groups he saw as favoring the Allies. When German officials warned about massacres of Armenians, von Oppenheim told them to shut up.[92]

On April 24, 1915, the Ottoman government began rounding up and deporting Armenians after some groups began a revolt to coordinate with the Russian advance against the Ottomans, hoping the tsar would give them control over areas where they lived in eastern Turkey. Pomiankowski, the Austro-Hungarian military attaché who sympathized with the Armenians' plight, wrote that Ottoman leaders were enraged at how the insurrection damaged their military situation. Muslim Turks were killed by Armenians. Enver and other Ottoman rulers had warned the Armenians at the war's start of severe punishment if they sided with the Russians.[93]

Von Oppenheim's aide, Scheubner-Richter, sent three vivid reports to German Ambassador von Wangenheim on the cruelties against Armenians in the Lake Van region. Scheubner-Richter reported rumors that deportations were being conducted according to German advice. Personally, he explained, he didn't believe the story and tried to help ease the pressure on the Armenians, but von Wangenheim ignored his request for intervention.[94] If the Germans had wanted to stop, or at least mitigate, Ottoman policy and behavior toward the Armenians they could easily have done so. For example, on October 8, 1915, von Oppenheim received a report that the Ottoman government's goal was the extermination of the Armenians.[95] Only one week later, however, he was telling Berlin that the deportations were justified war measures because the Armenians were betraying the Ottomans by supporting their Russian enemy.[96]

One of the few Ottoman leaders who openly criticized the massacres was the grand mufti who wrote the jihad decree, Ürgüplü Khairi Bey. He was an opponent of the Young Turks' secularism and of executing Arab clerics for disloyalty to the regime. Precisely because he was a very traditional Muslim he complained about the alliance with the infidel Germans, too, and as a result was forced from his post in mid-1915.[97]

Meanwhile, German consuls, bankers, and clerics in the empire were telling a different story from what von Oppenheim reported to Berlin.[98] During the second half of 1915, they warned of how jihad rhetoric was inflaming Muslim hatred of Christians and determination to annihilate them; how the jihad was just a cover for systematic looting, killing, and terror toward Armenians; and they provided detailed accounts of mass deportations, killings, and concentration camps.

These Germans said they often heard the slogan from Muslims that jihad should begin by killing local Christians. They also noted that Ottoman officers and officials frequently said that Germany wanted the Armenians killed. German bankers told how Armenian employees and customers were disappearing. The Ottoman government then informed them that it was seizing the Armenians' assets. The official explanation for German inaction was that Germany needed Turkey's help as an ally and so could say nothing.[99]

By early 1916 German officials in the Ottoman Empire had no doubt about what was happening. Even the kaiser heard the news. The head of his military cabinet, Moriz von Lyncker, wrote in his diary on August 8, 1916: "Most terrible how the Turks rage against Christian Armenians, their subjects. Thousands—men, women and children—are slaughtered, others are driven purposely to death by starvation. Our diplomats appear at this point powerless."[100] But in fact the German government never made the slightest attempt to discourage the mass murders.

Soon, the Armenians disappeared entirely from eastern Anatolia.[101] Enver told a visiting German that there was "No Armenian question any more."[102] He said that Armenians had killed between 125,000 and 150,000 Muslim Turks, and that the Turks had killed—the figures are hotly debated to this day—up to one and a half million Armenians.[103]

The mass murder of Ottoman Armenians was the largest organized massacre against a civilian minority since medieval and probably since ancient times. While it was carried out by the Ottomans, the Germans broadly inspired it, were well aware of it, and didn't interfere with it. There is no definitive evidence for the story that Hitler later said

Germany could get away with the Jewish Holocaust because nobody remembered the Armenian massacres, but this certainly seems to be what he thought.

Meanwhile, on the war's Western front, Corporal Hitler received the Iron Cross at the end of 1914.[104] Heavily wounded at the Somme two years later and sent to the Beelitz hospital near Berlin, he heard there about developments in the Middle East. Later, Scheubner-Richter gave him an eyewitness account of how the Ottomans gained popularity and strengthened their strategic situation by making a minority community scapegoat for the country's problems and murdering them.

The kaiser himself was not particularly anti-Semitic or even anti-Zionist, though his alliance with the Ottomans was a higher priority for him.[105] Moreover, the Jews, who would be the target of Germany's own jihad in the next war, fared better in the Ottoman Empire. Many of the Zionists who had immigrated were Russian citizens and thus subjects of the Ottomans' foe, though they had no love for the tsar's regime. Some hoped the British would support their project for a Jewish state, and a small group led by botanist Aaron Aaronson founded the Nili spy ring to help the Allies.[106]

Since the Ottomans assumed Jews would be disloyal, they arrested and deported some and planned to expel them all. Cemal Pasha, Ottoman governor of Greater Syria and Fourth Army commander, wanted to, as a contemporary Zionist report put it, eliminate "alien subjects and to resettle those areas with Turks."[107] Cemal ruled with such an iron hand that the Arab inhabitants called him "as-Saffah," the blood-shedder or killer, according to al-Husaini, one of his officers.[108]

On December 17, 1914, eight hundred Jews with Russian citizenship were deported by ship to Egypt.[109] But later deportation decrees were reversed due to intervention by several foreign envoys, especially Morgenthau, himself a German-born Jew, and Richard Lichtheim, a leader of the German Zionist movement. Berlin urged a stop to Ottoman attacks on the Zionist settlements, and the Ottomans canceled the projected mass deportation partly because Germany warned that the Allies would make propaganda out of any anti-Jewish actions.[110]

On March 31, 1917, however, Cemal again ordered the deportation of all Jews from the area, an operation Jews feared would be a cover for massacres similar to those against the Armenians.[111] Von Oppenheim's deputy, Schabinger, who had tried to stop the killings of Armenians, was at the time German consul in Jaffa. Schabinger estimated that there were sixty thousand Jews in Jerusalem alone. Ahmad Munir, Cemal's deputy in Jerusalem, told Schabinger that the deportations could not be carried out "without starvation and death." A Jewish delegation from the town of Petah Tikva asked Schabinger for help, and he, in turn, asked Munir, "How am I supposed to explain this to my fellow Germans?" He and the German consul in Jerusalem threatened to protest publicly, and pointed out that the Germans had carried out effective propaganda against Russia precisely because it mistreated Jews. Cemal's German chief of staff, Kreß von Kressenstein, agreed with the diplomats. Cemal relented and the order was again withdrawn. Ironically, Schabinger, who may have saved tens of thousands of Jews, joined the Nazi Party fourteen years later.

As an Ottoman officer stationed in Syria with the Fourth Army, al-Husaini closely watched these events as he built strong personal ties to the Germans. Al-Husaini later wrote how pleased he was with the kaiser's honoring of Saladin during the monarch's 1898 visit.[112] Al-Husaini supported the jihad, did not participate in Arab nationalist underground movements, and viewed the Jews as traitors to the empire. He later claimed that the Nili ring was uncovered by his friends, military intelligence officer Juwad Rifat Aitelkhan and an army doctor named Hasan al-Fuad Ibrahim. According to al-Husaini—though this story is almost certainly untrue—Ibrahim found a pigeon in his room, where Jews had formerly lived, carrying a coded message intended for the British. Ottoman troops captured Sara Aaronson, Aaron's sister, who was tortured and three days later committed suicide.[113]

Yet before the war ended, the Germans decided, and persuaded the Ottomans, to change their policy toward Zionism. They realized the value of courting Jewish support. The British wanted to gain Jewish political backing to keep Russia in the war after its March 1917 revolution and to ensure strong U.S. support for the Allied side; the Germans hoped to do the exact opposite.

The British government, however, moved faster and more decisively. Negotiating with Zionist leader Chaim Weizmann, Foreign Secretary Arthur Balfour believed a pro-Zionist declaration would keep Russia in the war, encourage the Americans to fight, and beat German efforts to win over the Zionist movement. On October 31, 1917, the Cabinet approved the proposed text favoring a Jewish national homeland, which was published November 2, immediately after the British captured Gaza.[114]

The Germans and Ottomans had a mixed response to the Balfour Declaration. On the one hand, they tried to use it to hold the Arabs' loyalty, spreading the word that Britain had sold their land to the Jews. Many Arabs who heard this at first, however, assumed the claim to be German propaganda.[115] Yet, at the same time, the Germans and Ottomans rushed to make their own offer to the Jews. In August 1917, Cemal Pasha met German Zionist leader Lichtheim while on a visit to Berlin. Cemal was coy at first, simply repeating the Ottoman stance that Jews could settle anywhere in the empire except in the territory they hoped to make into a state some day, but then he hinted that this policy could change in future.[116]

Meanwhile, the new German ambassador to the Ottomans arrived in Istanbul. Johann-Heinrich von Bernstorff had spent ten years as a diplomat in Washington and held a high opinion of Jewish influence on the U.S. government. He lobbied with Ottoman leaders to support the policy shift and in October, before the British issued the Balfour Declaration, persuaded him to make a deal with the Zionists. The Ottomans would offer a Jewish national home under their rule after the war. Talat thought he had nothing to lose by doing so since, he predicted, the Arabs would eventually kill all the Jews who went there.[117]

As the British gained ground in the fighting, both the Germans and the Ottomans became desperate, especially after the British captured Jerusalem in December 1917. The Ottomans were reluctant to change policy, though, saying that the Zionist dream of autonomy conflicted with the empire's sovereignty.[118] Von Bernstorff continued his efforts, however, joined in July 1918 by German and Austrian Jewish leaders.[119] They were now negotiating, however, over an area largely controlled by the British, not the Ottomans. Von Bernstorff urged the Jews to drop political demands for the time being because if the land was reconquered, they could get open immigration after the war and eventually reach their goal. While the Germans didn't want to go too far and get into conflict with the Arabs, he continued, the kaiser would like to see Germany's Jewish problem solved by emigration.[120]

The Ottomans, too, were finally ready to act. On August 12, 1918, Talat issued a statement that was the Ottoman equivalent of the Balfour Declaration:

> The Council of Ministers had just decided . . . to lift all restrictions on Jewish immigration and settlement in Palestine.

Strict orders have been given . . . to secure a benevolent treatment of the Jewish nation in Palestine based on complete equality with the other elements of the population. . . . I declare . . . my sympathies for the establishment of a Jewish religious and national center in Palestine by well-organized immigration and colonization. I am convinced of the importance and benefits of the Jewish settlement in Palestine for the Ottoman Empire.

I am willing to put this project under the high protection of the Ottoman Empire. I am willing to promote it by all means according to the sovereign rights of the Ottoman Empire which do not affect the rights of the non-Jewish population.

A commission was set up to write a detailed proposal for the Ottoman Parliament.[121] Before this could happen, though, the Ottoman Empire surrendered to the Allies on October 30. Talat fled three days later in a German submarine on a voyage that would end in Berlin. But it is still significant that the last Muslim government ruling the area accepted the idea of a Jewish national home, as did both sides in the war.

Equally, though, the war also laid the basis for Nazi Middle East policy. The German strategy and many of the same individuals would be involved in World War II. Hitler would later say that all in his leading circle were from the generation of World War I soldiers, and that many of those men had served in the Middle East.[122]

The parallels between the kaiser's and Hitler's regional policies included the following.

First, Germany's policy in both conflicts was based on stirring Muslim revolt against its enemies. Germany cast itself in the role of being the Muslims' and Arabs' true friend and patron, champion of the downtrodden, and sworn enemy to colonialism. Those who fought on Germany's side were said to be acting faithfully in the interests of Islam and Iranian, Indian, or—in French-ruled areas—Arab nationalism; anyone who supported the Allies was a traitor to Islam.

Second, racism was a key element in German policy, laying a basis for its use by the Nazis in setting their Middle East (and other) policies. The Armenians were vilified on racist grounds while the Turks were praised as fellow warriors and rulers. As one German newspaper article put it in 1898: "The sick man [of Europe, a term used for the declining Ottoman Empire] will be cured, so thoroughly that when he wakes up from his sleep of recovery he will be difficult to recognize. One would think he has got blond hair, blue eyes, and looks quite

Germanic. In our loving embrace we have injected so much German essence into him that he will be hard to distinguish from a German."[123] On the other hand, German policy looked down on Middle Eastern Christians, especially Armenians. Von Oppenheim said they deserved their reputation "as being cowards, and great at plotting and scheming."[124] This racial theme would continue under the Nazis, with some non-Europeans such as the Japanese and Arabs, granted "honorary Aryan" status, like the Turks in World War I. And of course by then the main target was the Jews.

Third, in deliberately stirring passionate hatred, Germany anticipated and accepted the idea that this would produce mass murders of minorities, Christians and Jews, as well as other civilians not on Germany's side.

Fourth, German policymakers believed that powerful forces could be set in motion by charismatic individuals possessed with semimystical legitimacy. In both wars the Germans erred in expecting Muslims to react as a bloc rather than being divided by local, dynastic, ethnic, and other loyalties. At the same time, the Germans believed themselves able to control wildly fanatical forces. Such stories as those of the Sorcerer's Apprentice or Frankenstein are based on ample historical experience that genies unleashed from bottles do not willingly return to their prisons.

Fifth, Germany accumulated during World War I a large cadre of experts and soldiers who knew the Middle East well and had extensive contacts there. About one hundred of them remained active in key positions during the Nazi era and continued their work in the region before and during World War II. Likewise, many Middle Easterners who had cooperated with Germany during the first war did so again in the sequel.

Sixth, Hitler would draw a lesson on the uses of genocide. The Armenians' fate furnished a model for what he would do to the Jews since he believed that the Ottoman regime had benefited from the mass killings. The deep German complicity in the mass murders of the Armenians set a precedent. German officials were aware of these killings and other war crimes, hid them from the public eye, often justified them, and never acted to stop or reduce their scope though they could easily have done so. German officials who advocated the murders paid no price for their actions, while those who objected were silenced or ignored.[125]

Finally, the German concept of Islam and nationalism in the Middle East would reinforce Hitler in his romantic idea of a "racial"-based community prepared to wipe out entire peoples seen as rivals. While Germany had its own long history of anti-Semitism, Hitler developed the Middle East–influenced idea of staging a systematic jihad-style struggle against the Jews.

But there were also two lessons not fully absorbed by the Germans that would cost them dearly. One was that battlefield success would play the main role in determining whether political agitation could trigger revolts in the Middle East. The factor that sank von Oppenheim's theories was military defeat, despite thirty thousand German troops fighting with the Ottoman army, two attempts to capture the Suez Canal, and hard-fought wars against the British in Iraq and against the Russians in the Caucasus. Even the fact that German advisers literally ran the Ottoman army—General Hans von Seeckt was the last Ottoman chief of staff—wasn't enough to turn the tide.

The other thing the Germans didn't learn, despite the failure of the sultan's jihad, was skepticism about Arab and Muslim politicians' promises to raise revolts and bring huge forces onto Germany's side.

Hence the World War I experience of failure had not settled the issue as far as the Germans involved were concerned. Schabinger, von Oppenheim's lieutenant, had said that the seeds of a mass uprising had been planted, positing that one day Middle Eastern peoples would turn against the British, French, and Russians.[126] The idea that "the Muslims" or "the Arabs" could be united and mobilized in order to seize control of the entire region would be a central theme in Middle East history throughout the twentieth and into the twenty-first centuries. The kaiser, Hitler, the USSR, Jamal Abd an-Nasir, Saddam Husain, Usama bin Ladin, and a variety of other Arab and Muslim leaders would try and fail to bring it to fruition.

Yet one thing was certain: Germany's first effort to foment a jihad that would bring it victory would not be the last. The Germans would try the same strategy in a second round, seeking to use the Middle East in its attempt to conquer Europe and even the entire world.

4 An Islamism Sheltered in Berlin

The years between Germany's defeat in the Great War ending in 1918 and the day the Nazis took power in Berlin a mere fifteen years later saw enormous changes in the Middle East. During that time, Hitler and al-Husaini absorbed the lessons of the past German-Muslim alliance and moved toward a new version.

When this period began, though, none of the coming events seemed even remotely possible. No longer a great power, Germany had to pay massive indemnities. The country was wracked by internal instability and rapid inflation, its territory and population drastically reduced, and Allied troops occupied its rich western region. The army was strictly limited in size and weapons while all of its colonies—six times larger than the mother country itself—were lost.[1] Postwar Germany was in no shape to play a role in world affairs even if the victors had let it do so.

Passing through Germany en route to Moscow in 1919, the Indian nationalist, now Communist, Manabendra N. Roy, who had worked closely with von Oppenheim's apparatus, saw hordes of beggars in frayed military uniforms, many with amputated limbs and disfigured faces or suffering from shell shock. They often wore a cardboard sign on strings around their necks with the accusing slogan: "I fought for the Fatherland."[2] Little good had it done them, or the war for Germany.

German Middle East assets were either looted by the winning side or destroyed in the fighting. The German Orient Bank alone lost 30 million marks, including murdered Armenian clients' accounts first confiscated by the Ottoman Empire and then taken by the French and British after the war.[3]

The psychological trauma of defeat was as bad as the losses of lives, land, and wealth. As late as spring 1918, a German offensive had almost succeeded before an Allied counteroffensive drove it back and advanced until poised to invade the exhausted Fatherland. Germany gave up in November 1918. Ironically, a clever policy that avoided invasion, occupation, and even more destruction led many Germans to believe that victory had been snatched away by traitors at home rather than lost on the battlefield.

On November 10, 1918, as Corporal Hitler lay in the Pasewalk, Pomerania, medical center almost blinded by a gas attack he had barely survived, he heard about the revolutionary upheaval and the kaiser's abdication. Hitler would recall that as the moment he decided to become a politician to seek revenge on those he held responsible for betraying Germany.[4] He would write six years later that if only the thousands of Jews who had been corrupting the nation had been gassed to death as had the best German soldiers at the front, those killed in battle would not have died in vain.[5]

Right-wing circles echoed this psychologically self-serving view.[6] In using the fact that some Jews had been among the revolutionaries and politicians who brought the war to an end in order to blame them for defeat, Hitler merely echoed popular views. The postwar German democratic state was called the "Jewish Republic of Weimar" on the basis of a Jewish-leftist-stab-in-the-back theory. In 1920, as the Nazi Party formed, the swastika symbol had already appeared on the helmets of right-wing militia units fighting Communists and Socialists. Among those so engaged were many of the thirty thousand German veterans from Middle East campaigns, including von Papen and Oskar von Niedermayer.

Meanwhile, the Middle East's new era was influenced by President Woodrow Wilson's Fourteen Points address to Congress on January 8,

1918.[7] Seeking to promote democracy and stability, Wilson wanted to banish the great powers' imperial machinations, which he blamed for the war, and enthrone local nationalism. He demanded the abolition of secret deals like the Sykes-Picot Agreement that had partitioned the Ottoman Empire between Britain and France, and backed free trade.

Thus, though not by design, U.S. policy served Germany's interests. The less power wielded by Britain or France and the more open the region was to others' economic efforts, the better for Germany. Free trade and minimum colonialism had also been the kaiser's program, since otherwise Germany could not compete with the British and French empires. Middle Eastern nationalists were also enthusiastic about Wilson's program. Nationalism was seen as the wave of the future; Islamism a remnant of the obsolete Ottoman past. But there were Muslims who did not accept this verdict and German experts who still believed that the Islamist ideology had a future.

Wilson was positioning America into the niche that Germany had tried to fill: a great power that wasn't interested in gaining territory but was friendly to local aspirations and working for mutual enrichment through trade and development. If Middle Eastern nationalists wanted to avoid colonial rule, the United States seemed the only alternative. But when local leaders invited Washington to take a mandate over Greater Syria or Armenia they were turned down.[8] The United States was entering an isolationist period. The United States did not join the League of Nations in 1919, much less play an active role in distant places of whose existence it was barely aware.

When Nazi Germany returned to the region in the 1930s, it reclaimed the role of anti-imperialist ally and role model for Arabs and Muslims that pre-1918 Germany had played. In the 1920s, though, Germany was in no shape to play that role. The British and French controlled the Middle East through their mandatory governments, and local elites had made their peace with these new rulers to preserve their wealth and power.

At the same time, though, the British and French competed in subverting each other's rule. François Picot, the French diplomat who had demanded his country's total control over Syria and Lebanon, told a group of Muslims in Jerusalem in 1919 that the British "had promised Palestine to Zionism" but staunchly Catholic France "Would not let the land of Jesus go to those who crucified him." After Picot left, however, his Muslim host declared of the French: "God annihilate them, they lie. Britain would never do such a dirty trick."[9]

It was in this murky situation of conflicting loyalties and interests—pro-Ottoman Islamism versus Arab nationalism and revolutionary Islamism; Germany fighting the Allies; Arab factionalism; and British-French rivalry—that al-Husaini made his career. He had been one of those Arabs who had at first remained loyal to the Ottoman Empire on imperial Islamist grounds, serving as an officer in its army and fighting alongside Germany. Then he changed sides to support the anti-Ottoman Arab revolutionaries and became a British agent. It was that fact, never revealed until now, that explains why the British were eager to support his political ambitions in the 1920s and into the 1930s.

In 1916, al-Husaini was a lieutenant in the Ottoman 46th Division at Izmir (Smyrna).[10] That November, he became ill, was given leave, and returned to Jerusalem for three months. Al-Husaini, like Hitler, had his vision of the future while in hospital during the war. Early in 1917 he made a momentous decision. Instead of returning to the German-backed Ottoman army he joined the British-backed Arab revolt. Ironically, al-Husaini, who played a direct role in the Ottoman Empire's destruction, would later describe that event as an "imperialist plot."[11]

Be that as it may, al-Husaini worked on behalf of that "plot" and took a salary in British gold as a recruiter for the army of the Arab revolt against the Ottomans. He signed up about fifteen hundred Arabs from what was then called southern Syria—later, Palestine—to join the forces fighting alongside Lawrence of Arabia.[12] Junior as al-Husaini was, his being one of the few active supporters of the British and their Hashemite allies from that area marked him as a person of importance for the Allied cause.

But the British were also backing those who would be al-Husaini's future enemies, the Zionists. In July 1918, the German envoy in Istanbul sent a report arguing that Berlin might use British support for Zionism to mobilize Arab support for its war effort. Foreseeing a Jewish state's eventual emergence, he explained, Arabs and Ottomans would fight harder to resist it.[13] But while the dispatch was prophetic in the longer term, it did not prove useful as an immediate strategy. Al-Husaini, who would soon emerge as leader of the Palestinian Arabs, was fighting for those who had issued the Balfour Declaration.[14]

Already fluent in French, al-Husaini taught himself English during 1918. He served six months with the British Occupied Enemy Territory Administration, working for General Gabriel Haddad, the Christian Arab adviser to Ronald Storrs, British military governor of Jerusalem. When Haddad was made commissioner of public safety in Damascus, al-Husaini went there too, with the rank of detective agent.[15]

Arriving in Damascus with the victorious British army and its Arab auxiliaries in late 1918, al-Husaini's job was to support the British and his own former commander in the Arab revolt, Faisal, son of Sharif Husain of Mecca. Al-Husaini and the British were undermining London's wartime promise to Paris that France would rule Syria. Al-Husaini wanted those who would later be called Palestinian Arabs, then known as "southern Syrians," to become part of an Arab-ruled Greater Syria. To further this goal, he wrote articles for a Jerusalem newspaper, *Southern Syria,* edited by his friend, Arif al-Arif.[16]

Much of al-Husaini's work was in the General Syrian Congress which, on March 8, 1920, proclaimed Faisal to be Syria's king, as the British wanted. Of course, the British could not openly pursue this goal since it directly violated their pledges to France under the Sykes-Picot Agreement, which is why they needed trusted agents like al-Husaini. As a secret agent, al-Husaini reported to the British on the activities of Arab political groups.

One of al-Husaini's activities was to lobby the United States on behalf of Syrian Arab nationalism. President Woodrow Wilson sent a commission to the Middle East in 1919 headed by theologian Henry King and businessman-philanthropist Charles Crane.[17] Their task was to suggest who should rule the former Ottoman lands of Greater Syria and Anatolia.[18] The commission met with the General Syrian Congress which wanted a large, independent Syrian Arab state.[19] Al-Husaini must have been involved in preparing those testifying, successfully so since the commission endorsed the congress's stance.

While working as a British agent, however, al-Husaini was increasingly critical of British policy, disappointed both with the implementation of the Balfour Declaration and with London's refusal to do more to help Faisal and the Greater Syria cause. Meanwhile, though, he gained great personal advantage from having feet in multiple camps.

For example, in June 1918 he founded in Damascus the Arab Club, which had about five hundred members by the end of 1919, and the

Literary Club. The former supported Faisal; the latter, dominated by the powerful an-Nashashibi clan—later al-Husaini's chief rivals and victims—marked the start of a Palestinian Arab nationalist movement.[20] By 1920, he also helped organize the first anti-Jewish underground military organization in southern Syria, al-Fidiya ("the Sacrifice,").[21] The busy al-Husaini also found time to back the Christian-Muslim Association.

During this period, al-Husaini saw himself as an Arab nationalist and a Syrian Islamist who regarded Britain as the best ally against French ambitions. There were certainly contradictions in this stance. After all, on January 18, 1919, Faisal had met with Zionist leader Chaim Weizmann at the Versailles peace conference and made a deal to accept Zionist aspirations in exchange for Jewish support to establish his own Syrian domain.[22]

This dream of Greater Syria, however, did not materialize. France accepted a League of Nations mandate to rule Syria in April 1920 and seized control in July, brushing aside an Arab force in a minor battle, and Faisal was expelled. In compensation, the British made him Iraq's king in 1921 and many Arab officers from the Ottoman and Arab nationalist armies followed him to Bagdad. Al-Husaini was not among them.

These developments forced al-Husaini to rethink his views, identity, and ambitions. The Ottomans and their idea of an all-inclusive empire based nominally on Islam had collapsed to be replaced by Turkish nationalism, which had nothing to offer him. So al-Husaini turned toward Arab nationalism and Syro-Palestinian Islamism. It was Syrian, not Palestinian Arab, nationalism that first attracted him. Yet soon, the idea of an independent Greater Syria also disintegrated. During that transitional period, however, al-Husaini did not have to make an immediate choice. He could combine four seemingly disparate, if not outright contradictory, doctrines.

First and foremost, he was a Pan-Arab nationalist, seeking a large Syrian state that would include what are today Syria, Lebanon, Israel, Jordan, the West Bank, the Gaza Strip, and perhaps more. Even after Faisal's defeat, al-Husaini did not have to give up this goal or the idea that the British could be persuaded to favor it. After all, though Britain was allied with France, it didn't want to share power over the Middle East with that partner.

Second, al-Husaini, who functioned as a completely secular political figure at this point, did not have to choose between Arab nationalism and Islamism in setting his political identity. The two standpoints seemed compatible.

Third, and least important, al-Husaini was a leading figure among the then largely passive group of those who would later define themselves as Palestinian Arabs. Focusing on this group was al-Husaini's best career move. After all, he was of no importance in Faisal's entourage—especially when it moved to Iraq—and would be even less so in French-ruled Syria. But in the relatively backward area of Palestine and especially in Jerusalem he had almost no competition, came from an important family, and thus could realistically hope to become leader himself.

Finally, al-Husaini was advancing himself by accepting British patronage. In later years, this type of behavior was denounced—even by al-Husaini himself—as that of an imperialist lackey and traitor. This connection, kept secret throughout his long life, explains the mystery of why the British would promote and back a young, unknown, and troublesome man to a position of such power.

If al-Husaini's employment by the British settles that particular historical mystery—why London promoted the ambitions of such a seemingly antagonistic political figure—another secret was the identity of his other patrons. With the French taking over in Damascus and Faisal's supporters kicked out, why was the vocal al-Husaini able to remain there? According to U.S. intelligence reports, the reason was simple: he went to work for French intelligence.[23] This not only gave him further protection—and a quarter-century later the French would save him from punishment as a Nazi ally and war criminal—but also a sponsor happy to see him subvert British rule in Palestine.

Thus, within a few months, al-Husaini had fought with the Ottomans to suppress Arab nationalists and beat the British, then with the Arab nationalists against the Ottomans and Germans, next for the British to help Syrian Arab nationalists against the French, and finally for the French to undermine British rule on behalf of Palestinian Arab nationalists. By 1920 and 1921, al-Husaini was involved in numerous organizations in both Damascus and Jerusalem, spending time in both cities.

At this point an event took place that would rocket al-Husain overnight into the position of the Palestine Arabs' leader for more than three decades and help determine the fate of the entire Middle East.

Palestine's Arabs themselves had nothing to do with selecting al-Husaini as their chief. Instead, that choice was made by Herbert Samuels, who was Jewish, pro-Zionist, and Britain's first high commissioner in Palestine. He appointed al-Husaini as grand mufti of Jerusalem on May 10, 1921, making him the country's highest Muslim cleric and providing the basis for al-Husaini to become the political leader, too.

Since no one knew about al-Husaini's British intelligence activities, the decision seemed inexplicable at the time. True, he was from a distinguished family and half-brother of the previous grand mufti. Al-Husaini was also still only twenty-four years old, yet he was being given a post usually awarded to a much older man. He was no religious scholar with advanced studies or even a cleric at all, though he held the equivalent of an undergraduate degree in religious studies from al-Azhar University. Moreover, he had made many anti-British statements and been involved in subversive groups.

Clearly, his previous service had convinced the British that al-Husaini would be reasonably loyal to their interests. It was one of the most remarkable errors of judgment ever made in a region rife with them. What makes this strategy even more incredible was that al-Husaini had not so long before been sentenced by a British military court to ten years' imprisonment for sedition.[24] On April 4, 1920, a little more than a year earlier, al-Husaini had made a passionate Syrian nationalist speech at the Nabi Musa religious procession in Jerusalem. The fired-up crowd responded with shouts of "Death to Zionism" and "King Faisal for Ruler," then rioted and killed a number of Jews.[25] The British put out an arrest warrant and al-Husaini fled across the Jordan River.

Was there a secret agreement between al-Husaini and the British to secure his pardon? Whatever happened, Samuel voided al-Husaini's conviction, let him return to Jerusalem, and then made him grand mufti.

Next, Samuel asked him, on August 24, 1921, to create a Supreme Muslim Council to supervise all Muslim charities, foundations, and courts in the British mandate of Palestine. This gave al-Husaini tremendous patronage power and a large, secure source of revenue. It would be virtually impossible for any other Palestinian Arab to compete with him. On January 9, 1922, the council elected al-Husaini as its president. This nominally philanthropic body would become the Palestinian Arab political leadership.

Thus, the British had elevated the man who would become their worst enemy in the Middle East. But this mistake only became fully apparent in the late 1920s. During the immediate postwar period it was the changes in Turkey that seemed most important for Europeans and especially for Germany.

The wartime Allied plan had been to divide Turkey into British, French, Italian, and Greek zones of occupation. The Sèvres peace treaty, signed August 10, 1920, was intended to fulfill that goal. Then, however, everything changed. The Turks came together under the leadership of Mustafa Kemal (Kemal Atatürk), a former Young Turk and successful officer in World War I. The British, Italians, and French had no desire to fight. Only the Greeks pursued their territorial claims but were soundly defeated.

As a result, an armistice was concluded on September 23, 1922, followed by the Treaty of Lausanne on July 24, 1923. Turkey won full independence, and Atatürk would create a secular republic that sought to emulate and join the Western world. Before that happened, however, there was a now-forgotten period when Turkish thinking echoed the wartime German-Ottoman cooperation on jihad. The Turkish-Afghan treaty of March 1, 1921, established an Islamic Confederation, an Islamic United States of the Orient, as one Turkish official called it, with the idea of adding Iran as a third partner.[26]

Turkey and Afghanistan agreed to cooperate if one of them declared a jihad, but pledged not to declare any jihad against each other.[27] The two countries also agreed to fund and direct Islamic groups promoting revolts in British-ruled South Asia and Soviet-ruled Central Asia.[28] Sultan Ahmad Khan, Afghan envoy to Ankara, claimed the Indian revolution would triumph as the Islamic world awakened.[29] Some of those involved were former Ottoman officials who had worked closely with Berlin, among them the Turkish envoy to Kabul, Abd ar-Rahman Peshawari, who had participated in the German-Ottoman expedition to Afghanistan during the war.[30]

The British were worried that the Kemalists ruling Turkey might take an Islamist route, following the prewar Young Turks' policy. There were signs in 1921 and 1922 that they might be right. Atatürk revived the Jemiet ul-Islam association to promote Islamic revolutions under Ahmad as-Sanusi, formerly one of von Oppenheim's men from an anti-Christian Islamic brotherhood group.[31]

The Turkish leader threw a banquet in as-Sanusi's honor and gave five million pounds to found Pan-Islamic centers to agitate for a new jihad.[32] Turkey sponsored as-Sanusi,[33] arguing, in Atatürk's words, that he would "consolidate the Turkish Empire as fulcrum of the Islamic world."[34] Another old von Oppenheim collaborator, the Egyptian al-Jawish, was appointed by Atatürk to head the Ulama Council of Muslim Scholars.[35]

As late as May 1922, British intelligence assessments were that Turkey was enthusiastically promoting Pan-Islamism in pursuit of a Federation of Muslim Communities under Turkey's leadership.[36] This was not, however, the direction Atatürk finally chose. In March 1924, definitively rejecting Islamism in favor of secular Turkish nationalism, Atatürk abolished the caliphate.[37] The last caliph, Abdülmecid II, who had been deposed eighteen months earlier as Ottoman ruler, was expelled from Turkey with his family.[38]

For the first time since Islam had been founded twelve hundred years earlier there was no caliph to make at least a pretense of leading a united Muslim religion and empire. Not only the Ottoman Empire but also the Ottoman dynasty, Germany's old ally, was at an end. Atatürk closed Islamic schools, forced people to wear Western clothes and hats, introduced European legal codes, gave voting rights to women, and changed written Turkish from Arabic to Roman letters.

The torch of modern Islamism, once lit with the kaiser's help, now briefly passed to a surprising new sponsor: the atheistic, Communist Soviet Union. One of the key people in this strange alliance was once again as-Sanusi, a veteran of both German and Turkish Islamist campaigns. The Kremlin promised weapons for his Pan-Islamic schemes.[39] Hearing of these contacts confirmed Atatürk in his belief that Islamic politics were dangerous for Turkey's interests, and he kicked as-Sanusi out of the country.[40]

Abolition of the caliphate came as a great shock to Muslims in many countries despite the fact that they had largely ignored it for centuries and had ignored the caliph's call for jihad in World War I.[41] Still, Islamic loyalty had been a major factor in holding together the Ottoman Empire. The loss of something hitherto taken for granted was a reminder to Muslims of how far they had declined since their glory days. Usama Bin Ladin would remind them of this shame seventy-five years later when he called for Muslim unity and a global war against the Jews and the Christian "crusaders."

In this way the question was raised, as it has been again in the twenty-first century, about who might fill the vacuum of transnational Islamic legitimacy. There were several self-declared candidates.

Just two days after the Turks deposed the caliph, Sharif of Mecca Husain Bin Ali, Faisal's father and ruler of the Hijaz in western Arabia, declared himself caliph, but nothing came of it since he had so many enemies. In 1925 his own kingdom was conquered by Ibn Saud, who annexed the Hijaz and went on to create Saudi Arabia.

Another claimant to leadership over all Muslims was a new group, the Muslim Brotherhood, whose founding in 1928 marked the start of the modern Islamist movement. As an organization rooted in the Ottoman-German jihadization of Islam, it would also develop close relations with Germany during the following decade. Thus, Islamism remained alive in the 1920s, available for use by Nazi Germany in the 1930s.

When the British general Edmund Allenby spoke at the ceremony opening the British military cemetery in Ramallah, Palestine, he had echoed the slogan that World War I had been a war to end all wars. Unfortunately, this assessment proved inaccurate.[42] True, the postwar settlement had produced a seemingly stable system in the Middle East in which moderate elites accepted a leading role. But militant Arab nationalists and Islamists were dissatisfied with British and French rule.

The League of Nations was established—albeit without U.S., Soviet, or German membership—in 1919 and soon issued mandates for British rule over Iraq, Palestine, and Transjordan. The June 1922 Palestine mandate incorporated the Balfour and the similar Ottoman Declaration's goal of creating a national home for the Jewish people. The French received a mandate in September 1923 to rule Syria and Lebanon.[43]

How would von Oppenheim's former agents, both German and local, find a place in this new order? Many of them carried on with their earlier efforts during the Weimar Republic era, like Grobba, von Hentig, and Nadolny. Formerly military coordinator of von Oppenheim's jihad plan, Nadolny became German ambassador to Ankara and, after the Nazis took power, briefly to Moscow.

Others pursued revolutionary activities, sometimes with former Ottoman comrades.[44] One such man was a former German officer, Wilhelm Hintersatz. As a pilot, he had survived the perilous skies, though frigid air paralyzed the right side of his face in 1916. At age thirty, he switched to service with von Sanders in the Ottoman army. Learning Turkish and Arabic, he became commander of all the Ottoman Empire's machine-gun units. Wounded several times in combat, Hintersatz worked closely with Enver and even converted to Islam in Istanbul. As he later explained, he did so fully aware of the conflicts of loyalty it brought him as a German. The *shaikh ül-islam,* the empire's highest cleric, Musa Kazim Effendi, honored him with a Muslim name that had been that of a ninth-century caliph, Harun ar-Rashid, who had both fought and developed good relations with Germanic kings.

Returning to work for the German government, Harun ar-Rashid Hintersatz helped his old friend Enver wage Pan-Turkish nationalist and Islamist wars in Central Asia. As head of the Turkish treasury ministry's security force, he oversaw depots full of Ottoman weapons supposed to be scrapped under the peace agreement, managing to smuggle much military equipment to his wartime comrade fighting the Soviets in the Caucasus.[45] Indeed, Hintersatz was soon himself battling the local version of the Soviets when he returned to Berlin and commanded right-wing militia forces against revolutionaries there.

Enver, who had been Germany's main ally in the Ottoman regime, had equally remarkable adventures. He and five other leaders fled to Germany within hours of the Ottoman surrender in October 1918. It was a wise move. The next year he was sentenced to death for leading the empire into war and for the mass murders of the Armenians.[46]

In the early 1920s, the leading role in fomenting revolutionary movements in the Muslim world had passed from Germany to the Soviets, who urged Muslims to overthrow their European rulers.[47] Enver therefore next went to Moscow and offered his services to the new Soviet government, becoming director of its Asian department and winning the personal support of Lenin. Remarkably, Enver would persuade Lenin to support an Islamic religious revolt based on a plan drawn up for the kaiser.

At the September 1920 Baku conference, the Soviets sought to rally the "people of the east" for their cause. Grigory Zinoviev, the Communist International's thirty-seven-year-old head, tried some fancy dialectical footwork to justify these contradictions. Pan-Islamism was not a Soviet idea, he explained, but "we are now faced with the task of kindling a real holy war against the British and French capitalists." The combatants in World War I, Zinoviev continued, had tried to present

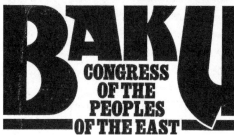

Figure 11. "Red Holy War." At the September 1920 Baku Conference, the Soviet agitators Grigory Zinoviev and Karl Radek incited Pan-Islamism and jihad against the "Anglo-French capitalists" in the name of the Communist International.

that slaughter as a holy war. Now, he rationalized, the peoples of the east must proclaim the real jihad against the Anglo-French robbers.[48]

Communist leaders realized that they were playing with fire. Karl Radek, the Communist International's secretary, admitted that the call for jihad appeals to "warlike feelings which once inspired the peoples of the East when they advanced upon Europe" as in the days of Genghis Khan and the caliphs of Islam. Yet this was different because it was in a good cause. When you draw your daggers and revolvers, Radek told the assembled Muslims, it was not for purposes of conquest or to turn Europe into a graveyard but to build a new civilization of free workers and peasants. This was no wave of barbarism or a new horde of the Huns. This was "The Red East, which together with the workers of Europe will create a new civilization under the banner of Communism."[49] The delegates applauded wildly.

Enver's Soviet-approved plan for jihad against Britain's empire in the Middle East and India was basically just his and von Oppenheim's wartime scheme. One comrade explained that as German allies the Ottomans under Enver were merely liberating lands from Russian or British imperialism to hand them over to German or Turkish imperialism, but now it was the power of the masses that would triumph.[50] Yet there was little and nothing particularly Marxist or proletarian about Enver's strategy. To build a base in Afghanistan and the formerly tsarist territories of eastern Turkestan in order to strike at India, he promised to enlist Afghanistan's ruler, King Amanullah, who had been involved in the German-Ottoman strategy, as well as some of his contacts among Indian Muslims.[51] Enver also turned to still another old German collaborator, the Indian Roy who had now become a Communist. His task was to prepare a base near the Afghan-Indian border, a job similar to what he had done for the Germans a few years earlier.[52]

Enver, however, was still loyal to Islamism and Turkic nationalism. After fighting for the Soviets against Muslim rebels in the Caucasus for a while, he then defected to the Islamic forces, training them along German lines. When he visited Berlin in 1922, he asked Hintersatz to join him. Hintersatz agreed and applied for a visa at the Iranian embassy, planning to cross over into the rebel area. But Hintersatz never heard from Enver again.[53] In Tajikistan, the Red Army caught up with Enver in August 1922. In a case of poetic justice, the unit that killed him was commanded by an Armenian.

For his part, Hintersatz carried on preparing for the battles to come. He advised Italian intelligence during that country's war in Ethiopia. Under cover as a reporter for Turkish newspapers, he himself went to Ethiopia as an Italian spy and won the confidence of Emperor Haile Selassie. Hintersatz was convinced that the great battle between the Germans and British to decide the world's fate would take place in the Middle East. When World War II came, he would command a German army unit of Azerbaijani Muslims, recruited in cooperation with al-Husaini.[54]

But these events lay well ahead. Germany in the 1920s was uninterested in foreign adventures, especially in the Middle East. The prime concern was individual and national survival. Two days before World War I ended, the Red Flag was flying over German government buildings.[55] Kaiser Wilhelm abdicated and went into exile in the Netherlands,[56] and a new liberal democratic constitution was adopted.

Germany was defeated, disarmed, blamed for the war, and forced to pay France's war costs and to give up much territory.[57] Isolated, marginalized, and excluded from international organizations until 1926, Germany also saw its contacts with the Middle East completely cut. Germans could not even travel there without a British or French visa.[58] The idea, an expert explained in 1925, that Germany would one day again have influence in the Middle East seemed doubtful.[59]

Of course, the French and British were determined that Berlin would never return to any important role in an area they sought to monopolize.[60] Wanting to avoid trouble and having other priorities, the Weimar Republic's leaders accepted this fate. Germany only did anything in the Middle East when repeatedly asked to do so by governments there.

The best example was Afghanistan, still trying to use Germany to offset British and Russian domination. In 1921, King Amanullah asked for diplomatic relations, educational exchanges, and German advisers, along with trade and investment. Berlin was so cautious that it immediately informed the British about the exchange and did nothing for more than two years.[61] Only in late 1923 did Grobba, who had led Muslim ex–prisoners of war against the French in World War I, arrive in Kabul with a seventy-man mission, including military officers to train the Afghans.[62] Almost immediately, the Soviets approached him for an alliance to subvert British rule in India, a major theme in von Oppenheim's plan. Grobba turned them down.

With Berlin's government so hesitant, the private sector took the lead. Businessmen began a German-Iranian Society, headed by von Hentig; a German-Turkish Association, led by Deutsch Bank president Arthur von Gwinner together with Jäckh; and an Egyptian-German Chamber of Commerce led by Aziz Cotta Bey.[63] The German Orient Bank reopened in Turkey in 1924 and in Egypt in 1926, with a big effect on both countries. An Egyptian entrepreneur who worked at that German bank's branch in Istanbul, Talat Harb, used this experience to start the first Egyptian-owned bank, Bank Misr, in Cairo. Similarly, Celal Bayar, who had worked in the German bank's branch in Istanbul, founded the Türkiye İş Bankasi in 1924.[64] A dozen years later he became prime minister and would then work closely with Hitler's envoy, von Papen.

Using such old contacts and experiences, Berlin rebuilt its business presence with remarkable speed. By the late 1920s, Berlin was again the region's third largest trading partner, exceeded only by Great Britain and France.

This doesn't mean that there were no political contacts. Many young nationalists from the Middle East saw Britain and France as their enemies. Beginning in 1920, they went to Berlin to study or as a place of exile. As early as 1922, British policymakers were watching this trend. Their Committee on Eastern Unrest pointed to rising anti-European sentiment throughout the region in which nationalists, Islamists, and Communists were ready to cooperate. But the center of action was not the Middle East or South Asia but Europe itself, with many agitators taking refuge in Germany, Italy, and Switzerland.

Radical newspapers like *Azadi ash-Sharq, Liwa al-Islam,* and *Echo de l'Orient* were published in Berlin and smuggled into Egypt, Iran, and India. Pan-Islamic and nationalist clubs in Germany helped build secret organizations back home and plotted revolts. There was no immediate danger, the British concluded, but the spirit of revolution, if unchecked, could burst into flame in the future.[65] During this period, however, Germany was avoiding trouble, focusing on the strategy von Bismarck had recommended: trade, commerce, and culture. Yet what would happen if a new regime came to power to revive the kaiser's approach at a time that the region was far readier to burst into flame than it had been in 1914?

For Hitler at the start of his political career the Middle East posed an emotional and ideological difficulty. As a racist and German nationalist Hitler disdained what he called "colored humanity." Arab and Muslim immigrants to Germany were for him no better than Jews. He had called France, facing a similar influx, a "Euro-African mulatto state," moving toward "Negrification" and "racial pollution," that posed a "danger for Europe's white race." He did not want to associate with "inflated Orientals" from Egypt or India.[66] In 1920 the Nazi Party demanded permitting only immigration by ethnic Germans and expelling all who had arrived since the war's end.

German academics, often von Oppenheim alumni, supplied an idea, though, that Hitler would later accept: Islam's equality as a religion with Christianity. At a September 1921 meeting of Middle East experts, Islam was described as being closely related to Christianity and to European culture, albeit somewhat inferior since the latter had invented individualism and humanism.[67] Humanism did not figure in Hitler's ideology but Islamism as a useful ally would do so.

Meanwhile, Hitler was busy with other issues. In an attempt to emulate Mussolini's successful march on Rome, Hitler tried to start a coup in Munich on November 8, 1923, but was defeated by von Seeckt, the Ottoman army's last and the Weimar Republic's first chief of staff. Ironically, Hitler's later military successes would depend on what von Seeckt did next. After helping throw Hitler into prison, von Seeckt and other Middle East veterans ran a secret operation to bypass the restrictions on Germany's army by cooperating with that other European pariah state, the USSR, to develop new weapons and military technologies. The Germans' go-between, Alexander Parvus, and his Soviet counterpart, Karl Radek, old partners in the wartime German plan to promote Communist revolution in order to push Russia out of the war, again united in this project.

General von Niedermayer, who had been a leading figure in von Oppenheim's operation, ran von Seeckt's Moscow office. In 1912 he had made a dangerous journey of exploration through India and Persia. During World War I, he had led the daring two-year-long wartime expedition to Afghanistan. He then became commander of German troops in the Middle East, following that up after the war by gaining his Ph.D. at Munich University with a dissertation on Iran's geography.

Von Seeckt began supervising a dozen-year-long German-Soviet effort to develop airplanes, tanks, and chemical weapons. This preparation for rearmament later gave the Nazis a huge, modern military far faster than rival powers expected. When World War II began, von Niedermayer would lead an *Ostlegion*, one of four Soviet Muslim units recruited with help from al-Husaini. Having criticized Hitler, however, he was imprisoned. When he sought refuge with his old Soviet friends at the war's end, they threw him into a concentration camp where he died three years later.[68]

But that all lay in the future. In 1925 von Seeckt began phase two of the secret plan, codenamed Alexander, to rebuild and rearm Germany's army for a war of revenge. From just 100,000 soldiers in 1925, he planned to have 3 million by 1939. Raw materials—many bought cheaply in the USSR in exchange for technical aid—were funneled into arms production. And von Seeckt relied on the old von Oppenheim group and his comrades on the Middle East front to implement his rearmament plan.

Every detail was foreseen. Von Seeckt accurately projected that Germany would have 252 generals and eight armies by 1939. The year for going to war was set, with near accuracy, at 1940. France's army was expected to be weakest then, given the country's low birth rate during World War I. Von Seeckt was only wrong in the strategy he foresaw for the new war. Like generals on the other side, he underestimated how new weapons and strategies would give the offense the advantage. According to von Seeckt's original plan the German army would go on the defensive, draw the French onto German territory, and wear them down with a hit-and-run war of attrition. Then, heavier German forces would finish them off. But von Seeckt's miscalculation didn't matter since he gave the German army the tools needed to win that future war. Every possible weapon would be used in what he described as a war of passionate hatred: scorched earth tactics, sabotage, terrorism, poison gas, and germ warfare.[69]

Writing *Mein Kampf* in his prison cell and no doubt cursing von Seeckt as a traitor, Hitler could never have dreamed that the German army was doing his work for him and that he would one day reap the benefit of von Seeckt's labors. In damning Jews and Communists as his enemy, Hitler was unaware that Communists, including such Soviet Jewish officials as Radek, were building his new army.[70]

Just as von Seeckt turned to veterans of the Middle East front and to von Oppenheim's apparatus, so Hitler used them when building his Nazi Party. The future dictator was also already thinking of Arabs and Muslims as reliable allies. In the draft of his book, though this did not make it into the final version, Hitler counted the people of ancient Egypt and India as examples of Aryan cultures.[71] "I am prevented," Hitler explained, "by mere knowledge of the racial inferiority of the so-called oppressed nations from linking the destiny of my own people with theirs."[72] Yet he left room for temporary alliances with those whose help would benefit Germany.

Still, Hitler's romanticism about Arabs, Muslims, and the Middle East would ultimately let him forgive their racial make-up. Germany's past policy in the region also influenced him. Not that he took previous German experience uncritically: he studied Enver's career and praised the Ottoman leader's tactical flexibility.[73] But he concluded that Germany had made a mistake to ally with the declining Ottoman Empire. He wanted to find new, vigorous revolutionary movements, foreign equivalents of his own Nazi Party.

He also noted the failure of the kaiser's policy to promote jihad in

Egypt and India. Even though Hitler was a secularist who distrusted religion in politics.[74] he valued its ability to promote fanaticism in battle.[75] Only after he took power did a meeting with two Turkish generals make him change his mind on the usefulness of jihad.[76] Under the motto "Aryans always used lower races," he opened the door to dealing with people of relatively "lighter skin color"—a category that included Arabs, Afghanis, Armenians, Indians, Iranians, and Turks, in whom he saw "the last visible traces of former master races."[77]

Hitler also began to take an interest in the Zionist issue. The Jews needed no separate state, he claimed, since they were a "colony of parasites" trying to dominate every other nation.[78] Zionism, Hitler said, was merely a cover for the organization described in the *Protocols of the Elders of Zion*. Even if the book itself was a forgery, he explained, it was still an accurate description of what Jews were doing.[79]

Hitler was cautious on the Middle East at first, however, because he hoped for an alliance with Britain. Consequently, he did not want to appear to be coveting British colonies or threatening its sea routes through the Mediterranean and the Suez Canal.[80] He foresaw Germany's expansion as being in Europe itself and the main battle as having to be fought against the USSR and France.

His trial after the attempted coup in Munich had made Hitler a national hero and his party grew quickly after his release from prison. Helped by the economic depression, the Nazis went from 18 percent of the votes in the 1930 elections, to 33 percent in late 1932, and 44 percent in early 1933. On January 30, 1932, Hitler became Germany's chancellor, having gone from prison cell to total power in just seven years.

Far away, one of those celebrating Hitler's triumph was al-Husaini in Jerusalem. The grand mufti visited the German consulate there to send his congratulations to the new chancellor. During the 1920s while Hitler was building the Nazi movement, al-Husaini was constructing a militant network of his own combining Islamism, Pan-Arab nationalism, and Palestinian Arab nationalism. With the open, militant Islamist movement centered in the safe haven of Berlin, al-Husaini had high hopes for his old German comrades as the best future allies.[81] It was in Berlin that radical Islamists for the first time confronted and defeated more moderate Muslims, developed their ideology and propaganda, and constructed international networks. As early as 1920, the London

Times was already warning about Muslim militants in Germany, reporting prophetically, "It is likely that many, if not all, of those returning students shall be a serious danger for peace in North Africa and the Middle East for they will return as pro-German or Bolshevik agents."[82]

When the Nazis came to power and began to formulate their Middle East policy, they found a reliable set of networks and activists right on their front doorstep. Many of the individuals involved—both German and Muslim—were von Oppenheim's veterans. And their postwar effort began in the war's last days. When peace returned in 1918, about sixty people—half of them German experts and half of them Muslims—worked for von Oppenheim's organization in Berlin. Herbert Müller, one of von Oppenheim's deputies, asked the Foreign Ministry to transform the intelligence and subversion organization into the German Orient Institute, founded on November 1, 1918, with Mittwoch, the news organization's last head, as its first director.[83]

Other wartime groups set up for the jihad effort also continued into the postwar years, including German-Egyptian, German-Turkish, and German-Iranian societies;[84] the Indian Independence Committee, the Central Committee of the Indian Nationalists, the Union of India's Friends; the Iranian Committee, the Tunisian Independence Committee, and the Association for Egypt's Liberation.[85] During their stay in Berlin, Talat and Enver, the Ottoman Empire's fleeing former rulers, had set up the Union of the Revolutionary Islamic Societies, which survived their deaths in 1921 and 1922, respectively.

Activists from South Asia also continued old von Oppenheim projects. In 1923, Muhammad Wali Khan, an Afghan, printed his fortnightly magazine *The Crescent* in Berlin. Kabul's ambassador to Berlin, Ghulam Siddiq Khan, a confidant of al-Husaini and later Afghan foreign minister, also promoted Islamist causes against British rule in India.[86]

Representatives of the Indian caliphate movement and the Muslim League organized along the same lines. These included Mahendra Pratap, the brothers Muhammad and Shaukat Ali,[87] and Muhammad Iqbal, the main ideologue for the creation of Pakistan as a Muslim state.[88] British intelligence reports in the 1920s repeatedly associated Muslim communalism in India—which would eventually bring the country's bloody partition—with the von Oppenheim legacy and Berlin-based Islamists.[89]

THE CRESCENT ☾

The Only Muslim Organ in Europe

A paper published twice a month in the interests of the Muslim World

by

M. Walikhan, Berlin—Germany

| No. 2 | October — November 1923 | Vol. |

A Waziri "Mujahid", Holy Warrior, who is fighting heroically for faith and fatherland against heavy British Odds in Waziristan.

Figure 12. The front page of Muhammad Wali Khan's fortnightly *The Crescent,* one of many Muslim journals published in Berlin after World War I, shows a Waziri warrior against the British in the borderland between India and Afghanistan. In the postwar period, the German capital became a magnet for Arab, Afghan, Iranian, Indian, Kurdish, Turkish, and Turkestani nationalists and Islamists.

Another veteran of the von Oppenheim news organization was Shakib Arslan, who had been present at the kaiser's 1898 speech in Damascus that first publicly expressed Germany's Islamist policy.[90] Arriving in Berlin in 1921, Arslan would lead the local Islamist movement, coordinate with al-Husaini, and work closely with the Nazis. Arslan often repeated the von Oppenheim group's mantra that Germans and Muslims were natural allies.[91]

Born in 1869 to a prominent Lebanese Druze family, Arslan had been a member of the Ottoman parliament, supporting the Ottoman Empire on Islamic grounds, helping to begin the Islamic Benevolent Society and Pan-Islamic League on this basis before World War I.[92] He then worked closely with the Ottoman pro-German leader Enver and become part of Oppenheim's network. When the French took over Lebanon and Syria, they exiled him and he returned to Berlin and Geneva.

During the war, von Oppenheim and Arslan set up many Arabic-language newspapers in Europe. Far away from Middle Eastern rulers' repression or colonial powers' control, these publications grew more radical. Arslan, a prolific writer, promoted Islamism through *The Newspaper of the Orient* in Damascus. Beginning in 1930, he edited the monthlies *La Nation Arabe* and *Al-Islam*. Arslan also published a book that year asking how Muslims could reverse their decline. His response has been accepted by Islamists ever since: adopt European technology but reject its values and instead revive Islamism as the way to govern state and society.[93]

In addition to Arslan and his friend al-Husaini, a third key figure was the deposed pro-German Khedive Abbas Hilmi of Egypt, who lived in exile in Geneva.[94] This trio, architects of the international Islamist movement, would all later work with the Nazis.[95] Hilmi subsidized Arslan's papers like the biweekly *Liwa al-Islam,* established in 1921 by Arslan, his Egyptian deputy Abd al-Aziz Jawish, and the Turkish Islamist Ilias Bragon. Jawish had also worked for von Oppenheim and retained good contacts with revolutionary movements in his home country, among them the Muslim Brotherhood leader, Hasan al-Banna.

With Hilmi's financial support, Arslan and Jawish started the Orient Club in 1920 for Muslims living in Germany.[96] In 1924, Arslan moved his base to Switzerland, often visiting Berlin, and keeping al-Husaini well informed. Jawish became the movement's leader in Berlin, ably assisted by the new generation's most dynamic young Islamist, the Syrian-born Muhammad Abd an-Nafi Shalabi.

Still, the movement was tiny at a time when the Ottoman Empire was wrecked, the last sultan deposed, and European colonial control at its height. But these men tirelessly worked to prepare a base for Islamism (the Arabic word for "base" is *al-qaida*) in Europe and a network throughout the Muslim-majority world, from Morocco all the way to India. This was, to say the least, an ambitious program, yet in the long run the plan worked and its results confront the world in the twenty-first century.

The Islamists' first challenge was to seize control of the Muslim community in Germany. During the 1920s, there were only about 2,500 Muslims in all of Germany[97] while in Berlin there were just about 250. The best-organized among them, controlling the city's sole mosque, were 50 members of the Ahmadiyya sect, a nonpolitical group that most Muslims considered to be heretics.[98] Al-Husaini supplied funds for Arslan, Jawish, and Shalabi to start the Islam Institute in Berlin on November 4, 1927, with Shalabi as its leader.[99] Arslan and Shalabi,[100] as well as the fifty-three-year-old Ahmadiyya leader Muhammad Ali, gave the main speeches, but control was firmly in the Islamists' hands. Ironically, given what Arslan would advocate as a Nazi ally in a few years, his theme was that Islam was above all racial quarrels or claims of superiority. As colonialism declined, he predicted, the Arabs would unite and renew their power under Islam's political as well as religious guidance.[101]

The institute worked closely with German sympathizers, many of whom would soon become Nazi officials. Von Papen, head of the institute's honorary board, would be one of the Third Reich's main policy architects for Middle Eastern issues. Another expert, Georg Kampff-meyer of Berlin University and a co-founder of the institute, had formerly served in the German army on the Iraqi front.

Kampffmeyer was also the creator of an early form of "political correctness" and "multiculturalism." While many at the time spoke of the "Europeanization of the Orient"—the title of Hans Kohn's 1934 book[102]—Kampffmeyer criticized that idea. He opposed Turkey's secular orientation and suggested that Islam was a better framework for governing Middle Eastern countries. In his speech at the institute's opening, Kampffmeyer said it should equip Muslim students with modern knowledge so they could return to their homelands as leaders.[103] Since the institute was controlled by Islamists, they would be returning as pro-German Islamist leaders.

The Islamists completed their victory in 1928 by ejecting the Ahmadiyyas from the mosque leadership.[104] On March 3, 1930, they officially took power by registering the newly created German Muslim Community under their control.[105] At that time there were about three thousand Muslims in Germany but the Islamists seized power with only about 10 percent of them.[106] Indeed, the movement's pro-German orientation was so strong that even the London Pan-Islamic society was controlled by advocates of an alliance with Germany.[107]

While al-Husaini operated behind the scenes[108] and Arslan acted as senior statesman, the main credit for this takeover goes to Shalabi, their lieutenant on the scene.[109] Just twenty-nine years old in 1930, he seemed the movement's rising star. Born in Aleppo, then in Ottoman-ruled Syria, he had arrived in Berlin in 1923 to study engineering at Charlottenburg College.[110] The dynamic Shalabi simultaneously led both the Arab nationalist and the Islamist student clubs, a good symbol

Figure 13. The Ahmadiyya mosque in Berlin-Wilmersdorf was inaugurated in 1927. In the 1920s about twenty-five hundred Muslims lived in Germany, 250 of them in Berlin. The mosque itself was nonpolitical, and some of its worshipers became victims of the rising Nazis, but it was also the venue where former "Asian fighters" of World War I like Franz von Papen and Erich Ludendorff joined ranks with the nationalists and Islamists of Geneva under Shakib Arslan, backed by Amin al-Husaini. The grand mufti also had another base in Berlin, a branch of the Islamic World Congress which met in 1931 under his presidency.

of how these movements intertwined. One of his closest colleagues and fellow students was the Egyptian Kamal ad-Din Jalal who would later become a Nazi government official. Remaining in Berlin after graduation, Shalabi edited a monthly, *Contemporary Islam,* and two weeklies, *The Islamic Student,* for Muslims studying in Europe, and *Islamic Echo.*[111] As if that were not enough, he also ran what he called "the news service of the Islamic Liberation Movement."

Shalabi's world view and the movement's political line were described in an article he wrote for General Erich Ludendorff's magazine, *Ludendorff's Volkswarte,* in 1931. The popular general was a notorious anti-Semite who favored Hitler without being a follower. In his article, "Palestine under Jews and Arabs," Shalabi supported al-Husaini. He quoted extensively from the complaints of the grand mufti's uncle, Musa Kazim al-Husaini, about the alleged barbaric crimes of the Zionists and their British supporters in Palestine. Palestine, Shalabi explained, belonged solely to the Arabs who should use terror and boycotts against the Jews until Zionism was destroyed. He advocated, two years before Hitler came to power, an economic boycott and other anti-Jewish actions in Germany, too; proposed a jihad against all Jews, not just Zionists; and asked Germans to support a new war against "world Jewry" and the British.[112] Shalabi's full leadership potential, however, would never be tested. In the summer of 1933, aged only thirty-two, he drowned in a lake in Berlin's Grunewald Park.

Along with control of mosques, the Muslim community, political groups, and publications, the Islamists next sought to create an international coordinating organization, the General European Islamic Congress. This was to be a branch of al-Husaini's General Islamic Congress, established in Jerusalem in 1931 at a meeting of 132 delegates from twenty-two countries. While the ostensible idea was to mobilize support for Palestinian Arabs against the Zionists, the meeting was also part of al-Husaini's larger scheme to become the Muslim world's leader. Among those involved in the European project were Arslan;[113] Abbas Hilmi; Riyad as-Sulh, a leading Lebanese politician;[114] and Mahmud Ibn Salim al-Arafati, an Egyptian living in Paris.[115]

To prepare for this step, an Iranian student, Husain Danish, founded the Berlin chapter of the Islamic World Congress on October 31, 1932, in the mosque's meeting room. The twenty founders from eight countries made Danish their leader and a former Ottoman officer from Syria, Zaki Kiram, his deputy. Shalabi was put on the board of directors. Their platform included the creation of Islamic schools in Germany based on Sharia law. Danish became editor of the Nazi-backed, French-language magazine, *La Jeune Asie*.[116] In September 1935, sixty-six Muslim delegates met in Geneva, home base of both Hilmi and Arslan. Also participating was Bosnian mufti Salim Muftić who would become al-Husaini's representative there.

Arslan had persuaded Mussolini to send representatives.[117] But the potential for a clash between Islamist and fascist interests was vividly shown when an Italian Muslim convert, Laura Veccia Vaglieri, gave a speech praising Italian colonial rule in Libya, setting off a storm of objections from other delegates.[118] The Nazi-Islamist link in Berlin, however, faced no problems. During the 1930s, al-Husaini's and Arslan's Islam Institute flourished.[119] Finally, in 1939 the Nazis completely took over the institute with the help of its leading figures.

Nazi scholars were very much aware of Islamism's potential as a political movement and its parallels with their own world view. For example, Paul Schmitz-Kairo, who lived in Cairo as a reporter for the Nazi newspaper *Völkischer Beobachter*, wrote a 1937 book on the subject, describing Islamism as a movement opposing Western intervention in the lands of Islam. True, Schmitz noted, the movement's first phase was as the Ottoman sultan's instrument and the World War I jihad had failed. But the new, modernized Islamism, blended with nationalism, was far more powerful. Indeed, the blend of religion and peoplehood, promoting both spiritual and ethnic unity against the West, made it stronger than ordinary nationalism. While Schmitz doubted that all Muslims could unite in one state, he thought the "traditional intolerance of Islam" would ensure its victory in war against outsiders. The grand mufti, whom he approvingly called leader of the "Palestinian terror organization," and the Muslim Brotherhood were the main examples of this new type of movement.[120]

But despite the fact that Islamism was an anti-Western movement, Schmitz-Kairo continued, Germany had nothing to fear from it for two reasons. First, the movement was against democracies, not fellow dictatorships, and, second, Germany had no colonies in the region. Schmitz-Kairo was prophetic on several points. He predicted a future Islamist political resurgence in Turkey; that the Soviets would use Islam as a strategic tool; that the Islamists would adapt well to using modern technology; and that they could use their more rapid population growth to subvert the West.[121]

Another important book read by German leaders at the time was the work of the pro-Nazi Hans Lindemann in 1941. It was a knowledgeable summary of recent regional history that spoke of the clash between Islam and the West as well as of parallels between Nazism and Islamism. Lindemann quoted a 1937 British jibe that al-Husaini was the Middle East's "little Hitler" as a positive assessment. He concluded that the vast majority of Arabs would follow al-Husaini. Lindemann even praised Saudi Arabia as the "Third Reich in the Wahhabi style."[122]

Lindemann also saw Islamism and Nazism as natural allies.[123] The Islamists, too, believed in having a strong single leader (Führer).[124] National Socialism and Islamism, according to the author, shared such virtues as enthusiasm, discipline, and a passion for unity. They had experienced traumatic national humiliation and defeat, while both fearing that their own tradition was disintegrating in the face of foreign challenges.[125] Both were united in hatred of the Jews as an "inferior race"[126] and sought to restore their respective peoples as world powers.[127]

The only thing Lindemann criticized in Islam was polygamy, but he concluded this would disappear in time.[128] Like Schmitz-Kairo, Lindemann was also impressed with the Muslims' high birth rate. In Egypt, he noted, half of the population was under eighteen years old whereas the median age in France was thirty-five and in Germany thirty-three.[129] This meant the Nazi influence on Middle Eastern young people continued to reverberate directly for decades afterward. Indeed, such young men as Abd ad-Nasir and as-Sadat; the Ba'th party's founders; Arafat, socialized in the Muslim Brotherhood; and Saddam Husain, trained by a radical uncle—obscure Nazi sympathizers at the time—would be their countries' future rulers.[130]

Before World War II began, then, and even largely before Hitler came to power, al-Husaini and his allies had taken control of Muslim communities in Europe, with Germany and Switzerland as their headquarters. Not only did this movement furnish many of the cadre who would soon work with Germany's effort to gain hegemony in the Middle East, it also formulated the Islamist ideology that remained largely unchanged into the twenty-first century. From the Third Reich's standpoint, the evolving political situation made an alliance with Islamism and jihad an even more attractive strategy than it had been in the kaiser's day. German writers and Nazi ideologues stressed the viability of the Islamist movement; diplomats, military officers, and intelligence officials who had worked with Muslims in World War I and retained good contacts still believed in the strategy originally developed by von Oppenheim and the kaiser.

But now the movement's leader was not some elderly isolated Ottoman caliph but the vigorous, young, worldly, and well-connected leader of the Palestine Arabs, Arab nationalists, and Islamists: al-Hajj Muhammad Amin al-Husaini, about ten years younger than his idol, Adolf Hitler.

5 Al-Husaini's Revolt

Al-Husaini's importance as father of modern Arab and Islamist politics has never been properly understood for three reasons. First, because he was tainted by his connection with the Nazis, the humiliating Arab defeat by Israel in 1948, and his own subsequent political eclipse, al-Husaini's historical role and regional influence have seemed of only limited importance.

Second, al-Husaini has been remembered as just a Palestinian Arab leader. Actually, however, he was the main chief of international radical Arab forces, both Islamist and nationalist, during the 1930s and 1940s. The later conflict between these two groups—when nationalists gained power and suppressed Islamists—hid the fact that they had worked closely together up to then. Al-Husaini was the man who fused that united front and set its strategy.

Third, even after being discredited as Palestinian Arab leader and shunned by the nationalists, al-Husaini played a central role in the Islamist movement's survival during the 1950s and 1960s. This success made possible the movement's revival in the 1970s to gain hegemony in Iran, Turkey, and much of the Arabic-speaking world and Iran by the early twenty-first century.

Why was al-Husaini so successful? Starting in the 1920s, he built his support base among Palestine's Arabs. In the late 1930s, he launched a revolutionary uprising in Palestine and an international campaign to make himself the region's Arab and Islamic leader. By that decade's end, the fascist Italian and Nazi German governments became his patrons.

During these years, al-Husaini seemed to be everywhere and meeting with everyone. From Morocco in the west to India in the east, al-Husaini laid the foundation for a far-flung movement. In Geneva, he worked with Arslan to build a European base.[1] He went to India to see Islamist leader Shaukat Ali and raise funds from Indian Muslims.[2] In 1924 and 1933, al-Husaini was in Iran, where he gained support from both Islamist activists and the government.[3]

The holy city of Jerusalem, his personal base, was a mecca for visiting Muslims who recognized al-Husaini's leadership and made alliances with him. Among them were Pakistan's future founder, Muhammad Iqbal; Egyptian Prince Muhammad Ali Aluba,[4] a sponsor of the Muslim Brothers; and al-Husaini's old teacher, Rashid Rida. One of al-Husaini's most important links was with the Egyptian Muslim Brotherhood, founded in 1928,[5] with Muhammad Mustafa al-Maraghi, al-Azhar University's rector, as his prime contact.[6]

The breakthrough year for al-Husaini's ambitions was 1931, when he organized the General Islamic Congress in Jerusalem.[7] The Islamic World Congress, formed by the meeting, elected him president[8] and created international branches, one-quarter of whose income went to the Jerusalem central office that he ran.[9] Many of the key people in al-Husaini's new radical networks were veterans of von Oppenheim's operation, including the European-based Jawish, Shalabi, Arslan, and Abbas Hilmi, who would bring al-Husaini together with the Nazis.[10] On one point, however, al-Husaini was cautious. Islamists wanted to restore the caliphate, but personal and national rivalries meant that no one could agree on who should be caliph. The rumor that al-Husaini aspired to that post would fuel opposition. To avoid this, al-Husaini neither highlighted the issue nor openly put forward his candidacy.[11]

Al-Husaini's ideology was a modernized version of Islamism. Yet he now used that once conservative doctrine, developed to defend the Ottoman Empire and the social status quo, as a revolutionary instrument. In al-Husaini's version, Islamism was broadened to encompass Arab grievances and, as Rida had taught him, to become a way to battle the West by building a strong, united state that would be simultaneously nationalist and Islamist. In short, al-Husaini would become the very man—the "Greenmantle" figure—whom earlier German strategy sought but never found.

While al-Husaini had strong credentials for leadership and even eventually claiming the caliphate—descent from Muhammad, influential family, and superior education—his personal qualifications at first were weak to be even an Islamic cleric, much less the world's leading Muslim. He did not have systematic clerical training and had embarked on a career as soldier and secret agent. During World War I, he had deserted the legitimate caliph's side to work for the British and French infidels. He had received his appointment as grand mufti from infidel British hands and had used the post for solely political ends.

Nevertheless, he was the right man in the right place and at the right time. His innovative use of Islamism helped him muster mass support from a passive, religious-oriented public that was not ready to accept secular nationalism. Playing both Islamic and nationalist cards, al-Husaini could claim power throughout the Middle East and even beyond to non-Arab, Muslim-majority lands. No Arab or Muslim leader since has come close to making such a serious bid.

Al-Husaini had no shortage of titles to bolster these claims. On the Islamic side, he was grand mufti of Jerusalem, which he soon changed into "grand mufti of Palestine," and president of both its Higher Islamic Council and the Islamic World Congress, the latter giving him an international platform. On the political side, he was head of the Arab Higher Committee and undisputed leader of Palestine's Arabs. Al-Husaini later cited all these positions and impressive networks in letters to Hitler and other Nazi officials, to portray himself as head of the world's Muslims and Arabs. Given such credentials, it is not surprising that the Third Reich agreed.

A second tactic al-Husaini and the radical faction developed, which dominated Arab and Islamist politics thereafter, was to make militancy the test for legitimacy. The most extreme stance became the legitimate mainstream one; anything more moderate was portrayed as treason to Islam and the Arab people. Using this standard, al-Husaini and his allies could blackmail and intimidate Arab governments, threatening to discredit or even assassinate anyone who wanted to compromise with the West or to oppose their goals.[12]

Third, al-Husaini turned the Palestine issue into the trump card of Arab and Islamic politics. By being the man to decide the only proper course on Palestine, he forced stronger parties to bow to his demands. Arab leaders in Egypt, Iraq, Syria, and Transjordan wanted part or all of Palestine for themselves. But by making Palestine a doubly sacred cause embodied in his own person, al-Husaini turned the tables on them, gaining veto power over the direction of Arab and Islamist policy.

A fourth innovation of al-Husaini and his allies was mass mobilization using mosque sermons, demagogic speeches, intimidating mobs, and demonstrations. Previously, Arab politics had been dominated by wealthy families that preferred to keep politics a private affair and had no interest in inflaming the masses. Al-Husaini and fellow radicals, however, inspired large numbers of people to challenge the oligarchical elite's moderate policies though not its wealth.

Fifth, al-Husaini demonized the British, Jews, and Americans. Most Arab leaders had not been militantly anti-Western or anti-Semitic. They were anti-Zionist but often open to some compromise solution, at least a deal with the British to prevent the creation of a Jewish state. In contrast, the nationalists and Islamists insisted that conflict was inevitable with both Britain and the Zionists because they were sworn enemies of Islam and the Arabs. Anyone who did not support this policy was labeled a Zionist and imperialist stooge.[13]

The radicals' stance in the 1930s and 1940s thus made diplomacy or compromise impossible even if a deal might benefit Palestinian or other Arabs. This approach allowed radicals to defeat moderates but failed miserably as an international strategy. Emphasis on hatred and struggle put the radicals on the losing side in World War II and brought the Arabs to defeat in the 1948 and every ensuing war. That orientation worked no better for the nationalist Saddam Husain or the Islamist bin Ladin. And yet its ideological hegemony has never been successfully challenged explicitly since al-Husaini and his allies developed it in the 1930s.

Finally, the radical nationalists and Islamists believed they could defy Britain and the Arab moderates precisely because Nazi Germany and fascist Italy offered alternatives. They could persuade others that total victory was inevitable since Germany would soon dominate the world. And if politicians in other countries wanted to be on the winning side, they needed to buckle under to al-Husaini's demands.

While Palestine's Arabs, Syrian and Iraqi nationalists, Egyptian Islamists, and others forged an alliance with Hitler's new German regime, based on the German-Ottoman cooperation of earlier days, that new alignment was also fundamentally different in content. The German-Ottoman bond had been built on defending the status quo in the Ottoman Empire while destroying their rivals' colonies. The new Nazi–Arab nationalist and Islamist alliance, however, sought revolutionary political and social change everywhere in the Middle East. In the 1950s, radical Arab nationalists would repeat this pattern with the USSR. From an Arab nationalist standpoint, Communism and fascism were equally ready to back revolution, expel the influence of Western democracies, and destroy a Jewish state. Both systems had features in common that Arab nationalist regimes wanted to adapt: statist economies, mobilized societies, intolerant ruling ideologies, and regime monopolies on every aspect of life. Islamists, however, could not embrace atheistic Marxists as partners, and that was one of the factors that split the nationalist-Islamist partnership.

In the 1930s and 1940s, moderate Arab politicians ultimately rejected the radicals' ideas because they doubted a hardline strategy could succeed. They rightly foresaw disaster, based not only on their nonrevolutionary worldview but also on what experience had taught them. To cite only one example, when Faisal fought France to become Syria's king in 1920 he was totally defeated; when he cooperated with Britain he quickly became Iraq's monarch. Thus, they correctly viewed the British as too strong to defeat and preferred to gain as much as possible by step-by-step diplomacy, compromise, and gradual economic development, rather than bet all on total victory and risk losing everything. They also understood how the strategic situation in the late 1930s meant London was ready to give them big concessions to win their help in the coming war. Most importantly, they could have made a deal with Britain over Palestine that would give the Arabs victory if only they were patient.

The radicals' totally different view saw violence and intransigence as the effective political tools. To them, flexibility was merely traitorous and cowardly. Instead, they preferred to make war on Britain, France, the USSR, even the United States, and expected to win. Disregarding the moderates' cautious realism, al-Husaini's Islamist ideology taught him that Allah was on the Muslims' side; his radical nationalism told him that the Arabs united could never be defeated. On top of this, al-

Husaini, the Muslim Brotherhood, and the radical nationalists were convinced that their invincible European protectors, Nazi Germany and fascist Italy, would win and hand them victory.

The Middle East's future was thus determined starting in the 1930s when radicals set guidelines, and was made inevitable by their taking power in the 1950s and holding onto it in one form or other down to the present day. The basic approach of al-Husaini and his comrades continued through the careers of such leaders as Abd an-Nasir, Arafat, the al-Asad family, al-Qaddafi, Saddam Husain, and bin Ladin, as well as with Iranian Islamists like Khomeini and Mahmud Ahmadinejad.

The views of two alternative archetypes as leaders, Abdallah and al-Husaini, perfectly embodied the contrast between moderate and radical Arab camps. Regarding the Palestine Arabs' uprising of the late 1930s, Abdallah concluded, "There is a lesson for men who want to learn" in its defeat by Britain. The Arabs had to make deals because they could not win wars. Al-Husaini's view was the exact opposite, inaccurately claiming the uprising had triumphed. The Arab "terror of 1936 buried the mandate" and the uprising's continuation, he said at the time, would ensure the Arabs would rule all of Palestine and the Zionists would be destroyed.[14]

This approach set the pattern for what might be called the counter-pragmatic tendency of Arab and Islamist politics that prevailed into the twenty-first century. Policies that produced repeated defeats were extolled because they fit the radical ideological template as proper, noble, and bound to succeed. Those urging pragmatism, caution, and compromise were made pariahs or even—as happened with an-Nashashibi, Abdallah, as-Sulh, and as-Sadat—murdered.

In this context, during the 1930s and through World War II, Nazi Germany's ambitions and ideology made it attractive as an ally for radical Arabs. Al-Husaini and his colleagues, like Hitler and his followers, believed they now had a magic formula for victory: mobilizing the masses to a frenzy of passion; invoking unity through discipline, repression, and a compelling ideology; using the Jews, the British, the Americans, and the Communists as scapegoats; and providing infallible charismatic leadership.

Of course, the Axis collaborators were wrong and inflicted devastating damage on their countries and peoples as a result. The Palestine issue provides a good example of this point, as the hardline, inflexible, anti-British policy of al-Husaini and the radicals played a major role in bringing about Israel's creation.

During the 1930s, Palestine's Arabs had four choices:

- They could have made a deal with the British to partition Palestine, with the Arabs getting most of it—80 percent according to London's 1937 Peel plan—and use that as a base to destroy the Jewish mini-state later.
- They could have accepted the 1939 British offer to give them all of Palestine as an Arab state within ten years and taken control gradually during that period.
- They could have worked with Abdallah and the British to get an Arab-ruled federated state of Transjordan-Palestine.
- Or they could have accepted the strategy of al-Husaini and his camp to reject all of these possibilities, believing that an Axis victory (and later an Arab military victory in 1947–48) would get them everything without compromise, conditions, or Jews.

The radicals triumphed over more moderate forces among Palestine's Arabs—the an-Nashashibi, al-Khalidi, and Jar Allah clans—and Arab governments—notably Egypt and Transjordan—that wanted to take advantage of the chance for a good deal. Al-Husain rejected a proposed agreement among Palestinian Arab factions not to use violence against each other,[15] and his forces murdered hundreds of oppositionists. Fakhr an-Nashashibi was the most important moderate leader and victim of these killings.[16] Leading a powerful clan, he was willing to negotiate with the Zionists, organized a counter-meeting against al-Husaini's 1931 Islamic World Congress,[17] worked with Abdallah to create a Transjordan-Palestine federated state, and demanded elections for a new Higher Islamic Council to remove the grand mufti as head.[18]

Success for al-Husaini depended on his alliance with Nazi Germany. But at the start of Hitler's reign there was a potential conflict between them that could jeopardize this goal. Hitler had written in *Mein Kampf* that he wanted to murder all Jews, but in the Nazi regime's first half-dozen years it seemed possible he might merely expel them. The audacity of genocide seemed to have given even the Nazis pause, concerned as they were at the international reaction. Thus, Hitler made a deal with the Zionists in 1933 to let sixty thousand Jews immigrate to Palestine for six years in exchange for receiving one-third of their property.[19]

Perhaps there might have been an entirely different kind of Final

Solution for Germany, with emigration instead of firing squads and gas chambers. But al-Husaini did not want this outcome. He insisted on stopping all Jewish migration to Palestine. And since any European Jews let out of Europe might later go to Palestine, al-Husaini made it clear that if Hitler wanted Muslims and Arabs as allies he must close Europe's exits to Jews. At the same time, al-Husaini and Arab rulers also told Britain that if it wanted to keep Arabs and Muslims from being enemies, it must close entrance to Palestine to all Jews. By succeeding on both fronts, al-Husaini contributed to the Holocaust doubly, directly, and from the start.

Predicting accurately in 1934 that Hitler's "war of vengeance" would begin by 1939 and be more destructive than World War I, Zionist leader David Ben-Gurion tried to make a deal with Palestinian Arabs that would somehow permit Jewish immigration, no matter what other concessions that required.[20] The man Ben-Gurion turned to for this purpose was Musa al-Alami,[21] a man considered the model moderate. Once again, though, al-Husaini's power blocked the way. Al-Alami's sister was married to Jamal al-Husaini, the grand mufti's cousin and chief lieutenant; al-Alami's own wife was daughter to Ihsan al-Jabiri, who had worked closely with al-Husaini by promoting pro-German Islamism in Berlin. Rather than become leader of an alternative moderate faction, the Cambridge University–educated al-Alami threw in his lot with al-Husaini and the radicals. Al-Husaini sent al-Alami to Germany in 1937 to gain the Nazi regime's help in foiling the British plan to partition Palestine into a large Arab and a small Jewish state.[22] Starting in late 1938, al-Husaini sent al-Alami regularly to Europe to collect Nazi money, obtain German weapons for the revolt,[23] and coordinate al-Husaini's network of agents.[24]

As for what should be done to the Jews, al-Husaini was crystal clear, publicly advocating genocide even before the Nazi government did so. His 1937 "Appeal to All Muslims of the World" urged them to cleanse their lands of the Jews, and it was translated into German in 1938.[25] Urging the use of force against all Jews in the Middle East, al-Husaini both gave his parallel version of Hitler's doctrine and laid the foundation for the anti-Semitic arguments used by radical Arab nationalists and Islamists down to this day. A half-century later, every speech and sermon from Hamas, Hizballah, Iran's regime, the Muslim Brotherhood, and al-Qaida echoed all of the grand mufti's main points in his declaration.

Al-Husaini's analysis combined traditional Islamic hatred of Jews with arguments framed by modern political concepts. According to al-Husaini, the Jews were a cursed and evil people. They had exploited Egypt in ancient times and that was why the pharaoh expelled them; an early Muslim historian had accused them of trying to kill Moses; and God had repeatedly punished them for their sins.[26] Yet the Jews, al-Husaini continued, had become even worse. They had spread diseases and murdered Jesus.[27] They had hated Muhammad and tried to poison him;[28] Muhammad had responded by expelling them from Arabia. Even though this plot had failed (he only ate a little of the tainted lamb that the Jews had offered him) the poison had weakened him and led to his premature death.[29] Therefore, al-Husaini concluded, Arabs understood why the Germans hated Jews.

It is wrong to see al-Husaini and his fellow radicals as merely importing European anti-Semitism or being influenced by the Nazis. The two groups' ideas developed in parallel from their own histories and political cultures. Al-Husaini and other radical Arabs and Islamists were not merely seeking to please Hitler but fully believed these doctrines. The two sides came together on the basis of both common interests and similar worldviews.

In April 1936, al-Husaini ordered a general strike to force the British to end Jewish immigration and grant immediate independence to an Arab Palestine. He believed a show of strength, coupled with Arab state intervention and the looming threat from Germany and Italy, would quickly bring British surrender. Decades later, Arafat would launch two losing revolts, the "intifadas" of 1987–91 and 2000–2005, on similar mistaken premises. When the strike didn't bring total victory, the grand mufti escalated to armed warfare in 1937. Arab guerrillas barricaded and mined roads, derailed trains, attacked Jewish villages, and burned crops and forests. The British responded with curfews, searches, and arrests.

Al-Husaini mobilized Arab rulers and radical groups, as well as Italy and Germany's sponsorship, for his intifada. From March 1937 on, he led delegations to Saudi Arabia and other Arab countries for this purpose. Syrian and Transjordanian border guards looked the other way as arms were smuggled into Palestine. Guerrilla forces that retreated into Iraq and Syria were able to cross the border for more attacks.[30]

The grand mufti also made progress in building relations with Berlin and Rome. Starting in 1935, Mussolini financed him.[31] By 1936, al-Husaini was sending envoys to Grobba, then German ambassador to Iraq, to request arms and money. One of them was Fauzi ad-Din al-Qawuqji. Born in Beirut in 1890, al-Qawuqji graduated from the Ottoman Istanbul Military Academy. In 1925 he fought in the Kurdish uprising against the French in Syria, and in 1932 he was a military instructor with Iraq's army. During the revolt he led a two-hundred-man Iraqi-Syrian volunteer unit fighting for al-Husaini. Since Berlin sends Jews to Palestine, he told Grobba, it must also send arms to fight against them.[32]

Step by step, the Germans responded to al-Husaini's courting. To investigate this potential ally, an obscure German official considered a top expert on the Jews, Adolf Eichmann, was dispatched to Palestine to meet al-Husaini. Eichmann arrived at the port of Haifa on October 2, 1937. But despite his having a tourist visa, the British authorities restricted his stay to forty-eight hours, after which he was put on a ship to Alexandria. Eichmann went to the British embassy in Cairo but couldn't persuade that government to change its mind. Instead, Eichmann stayed in Cairo a while and met with the German News Agency man and al-Husaini's representatives, who came from Jerusalem. He produced a detailed report whose theme was that while Arabs knew little about Nazi ideology, their hatred for Jews and other factors made this ideological difference no barrier to an alliance.

Al-Husaini was being hard pressed by the British at that time. They ordered his arrest in July 1937, so he hid in Jerusalem and in October, as police closed in, fled to Beirut. The French who ruled Lebanon did nothing to capture him, probably to discomfit their British rivals and perhaps due to his previous services to their government. The French would again save him from arrest after World War II.

As his rebellion failed al-Husaini's efforts to gain German aid intensified. He was delighted by Hitler's speech to the German minority in Czechoslovakia when he annexed their area following the September 1938 Munich agreement: "Take the Arab Palestinians as your ideal. With unusual courage they fight both England's British Empire and the world Jewry. They have no protector or helper. I give you the means and weapons, and all of Germany is behind you."[33] Couldn't al-Husaini expect that all of Germany would be behind him, too? He sent his nephew Jamal al-Husaini and the important politician Auni Abd al-Hadi to Grobba in Baghdad with a request for guns. Grobba answered that Germany wasn't ready to back armed Arab uprisings lest that bring confrontation with Britain. But al-Husaini had a solution: the guns could go through the Saudis, whose king agreed to be middleman to hide German involvement.[34] The Germans agreed.[35] In September 1938, Wilhelm Canaris, head of the Abwehr (German military intelligence)—and thereafter contact man for al-Husaini's military and espionage activities—provided Berlin's first donation, £1,000 sterling, to Hamza, the Saudi envoy. Al-Husaini invested part of it in starting a new, radical Arab Club in Syria to organize support for him there.[36]

In mid-1939 Canaris provided four thousand rifles as a gift whose use, one of his aides explained, would create a pro-German "fifth column" in Palestine.[37] In the end, the Germans bypassed the Saudis and secretly shipped the rifles through Greece to Lebanon, where they were loaded onto small boats for smuggling into Palestine.[38] German involvement in Palestine quickly became so important that when U.S. intelligence analysts examined captured German records after World War II, they concluded that al-Husaini's revolt was able to continue only because of Nazi funding.[39] These weapons would also later furnish much of the Palestinian Arab arsenal during the 1947–48 fighting.[40]

While the British were, of course, angry about al-Husaini's growing links to Germany, this strategy also gave them an added incentive to appease Palestine's Arabs and Arabs in general. The British knew war was on the horizon. With Germany and Italy challenging their control of the Mediterranean and Middle East, London was ready for massive concessions to ensure the Arabs did not join their enemies. That, however, meant finding a way to undercut the radicals by empowering those who were more moderate. The problem was that the radicals understood this point and successfully countered that strategy.

The first effort was to make Palestine both Arab-ruled and governed by a moderate monarch. Traveling to London in April 1937 for King George's coronation, Abdallah urged the British to give him Palestine. A British officer explained London's ideal scenario. Abdallah would be king; Rajib an-Nashashibi would be his prime minister; the grand mufti would be pushed aside so he could cause no more trouble.[41] Jewish leaders were unenthusiastic but said they could work with Abdallah. When Abdallah returned home on June 13, he received a spirited welcome from those who thought the British would make him king over Palestine.[42]

Even Berlin's Foreign Ministry thought this plan would succeed and that the moderates would make a deal with Britain.[43] Most Arab leaders—aside from al-Husaini and Iraqi leaders—wanted no quarrel with Britain, von Hentig concluded. The Saudis and Egyptians would do nothing; Transjordan would support the British. Thus, it made no sense to support al-Husaini with arms or money in a losing battle. Von Hentig was right in assessing Arab stances but wrong about British determination to impose a solution by force.[44]

The first British plan was based on the official Peel Commission proposal for a two-state solution in which 80 percent of Palestine would become an Arab state federated with Transjordan and ruled by Abdallah, while the remaining 20 percent would be a Jewish state. But most of Palestine's Arabs opposed giving up any part of the country even as the price for getting the rest. Al-Husaini had nothing to gain from an Arab Palestine ruled by his rivals, Abdallah and the Nashashibis, and thus his Arab Higher Committee opposed the plan. Jealous and suspicious of Abdallah, not only Iraq but Saudi Arabia also rejected it.[45]

In contrast, Abdallah and his Palestinian Arab allies were pleased by a plan that would give them most of that land, $10 million from Britain, and a subsidy from the proposed Jewish state. Advocates of the deal whispered that the tiny Jewish state would be annexed when the chance arose. Abdallah's subjects were delighted, while in the Palestinian town of Nablus, the an-Nashashibi stronghold, Britain's flag was pulled down and replaced by Transjordan's. When an Arab Higher Committee meeting rejected the plan, an-Nashashibi delegates walked out.[46] Egypt's moderate government refused to jeopardize relations with London. When several al-Husaini aides traveled to Cairo in October 1937, they were well received but their request to open a supply base for the revolt on Egyptian soil was rejected.[47]

The radicals fought back. Iraq's militant leaders met with Grobba on July 15 to ask Germany for aid so as to escape from British influence and struggle against the Peel Commission plan. From that time on Iraq-German ties tightened. Berlin offered commercial credits, sent in more agents, and stepped up pro-Arab radio coverage.[48]

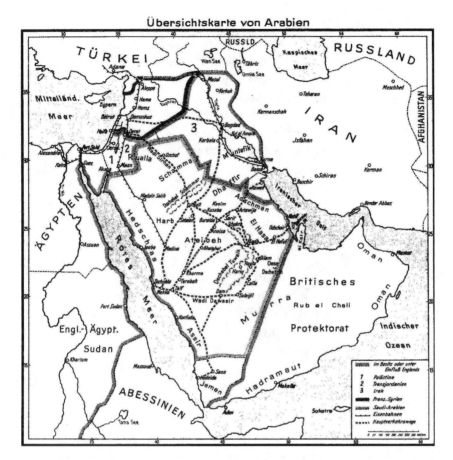

Übersichtskarte von Arabien

Figure 14. A 1942 German map of Arabia showing railroads, other main overland routes, and areas under British and French protection, including Palestine
(1), Transjordan (2), and Iraq (3). But in that very year, Nazi ambitions in the
region were decisively frustrated. Already in 1941, the British had defeated the
Vichy forces in Syria and Lebanon and overthrown a pro-German regime in
Iraq; in 1943, the Allies drove the Germans out of North Africa.

Fearing the radicals' pro-German positions and the militancy of the
Arab masses, the British soon retreated on the political front even as they
increased military pressure on al-Husaini's insurgency.[49] When some of
the grand mufti's forces tried to spread the rebellion to Transjordan—
even daring to place a bomb in Abdallah's palace—the king's well-
disciplined, British-officered army wiped them out.[50] As so often hap-

pened in Arab politics, the next generation of radicals would repeat the pattern. Thirty years later, the PLO would use Jordan as an involuntary Palestinian base to attack its neighbor, try to overthrow the monarchy, and again be defeated by Jordan's army.

In 1938, with the Peel proposal defeated, war approaching, and radicalism growing, the British decided they needed an even more pro-Arab initiative in tandem with the concessions on Czechoslovakia—in effect, the European equivalent of Palestine—to appease Hitler. The same British government was equally ready to turn over Palestine to Arab rule and leave the Jews there to a dismal fate.[51] Secretary of State for the Colonies Malcolm MacDonald and Foreign Secretary Lord Halifax contacted Iraq's Foreign Minister as-Suwaidi, moderate Prime Minister Nuri as-Said, and Egyptian Prime Minister Muhammad Mahmud. If they could moderate the grand mufti's hard line, an Arab-ruled, united Palestine was possible and a major conference would be held in London to discuss a solution.[52]

By this point, however, the grand mufti was even less interested in a deal. As British policy kowtowed to Germany, al-Husaini was even more convinced the Germans would win.[53] He refused even to talk without a prior British guarantee that all of Palestine would become an independent Arab state and that the an-Nashashibi faction would not be allowed to participate in any meetings. Britain refused.

Events in Iraq reinforced al-Husaini's confidence. On December 25, 1938, radical army officers seized power. Minister of Defense Taha al-Hashimi became president of the radical Palestine Defense Committee, whose fund-raising campaigns attained semiofficial status. Anti-Jewish violence escalated. Al-Husaini could fully depend on Iraqi support.[54]

Arab governments put together top-level delegations for the London meeting, sensing that it would be a last desperate attempt to settle the Palestine dispute peacefully. Ibn Saud chose his son and foreign minister, Prince (later king) Faisal and Deputy Foreign Minister Fuad Hamza, himself of Palestinian origin. Transjordan was represented by Prime Minister Taufiq Abu al-Huda, also born in Palestine. Egypt sent Ali Mahir along with al-Husaini's Egyptian ally, Abd ar-Rahman Azzam as an adviser, while Yemen dispatched Prince Saif al-Islam al-Husain.[55]

The conference's timing coincided with the height of Jewish desperation over the fascist persecutions in Europe. No country was willing to take Jewish refugees at a moment when new areas of oppression threatened to open in Italy and the Balkans. The Zionists knew that any Jew prevented from reaching Palestine faced the likelihood of death.[56]

Warning signals of coming war multiplied daily. The London Conference had been planned as Britain was appeasing Hitler. The Germans occupied the rest of Czechoslovakia during its sessions. The opening day, February 7, 1939, was marked by Italian threats to attack Egypt from Libya, coupled with a German general's touring fortifications near the Libya-Egypt border.[57] In this context, the Middle East's immense strategic significance was at the center of British policymakers' thoughts. This meant making the Arabs happy. British forces in the area, no matter how strong, would be insufficient if local populations revolted. But once Palestine was amicably resolved, they reasoned, they need not fear a pro-German Arab fifth column or Islamist rebellion.[58]

Yet the Arab stance made any solution impossible. During pre-conference Arab consultations in Cairo, the states agreed that Palestine's Arabs would have the decisive voice in the London talks and governments would support whatever they—that is, al-Husaini—wanted. That enabled al-Husaini to set the guidelines to ensure that the talks failed. He demanded a total ban on Jewish immigration and land purchases plus rapid creation of an independent Arab Palestine under his rule. For al-Husaini, and thus for all of the Arab leaders, it would be all or nothing.[59]

In London, Prime Minister Neville Chamberlain, Foreign Secretary Lord Halifax, and MacDonald shuttled between Zionist and Arab delegations, which met separately except on three occasions. Making no secret of his desperation for appeasement, Chamberlain assured Arab delegations of Britain's desire to maintain and strengthen friendship with them, while MacDonald noted that trouble in Palestine would echo throughout the region.

MacDonald frankly presented the reasons behind British policy. The likelihood of war necessitated surrender to Arab demands as long as such concessions made London feel more secure. Halifax was blunt: "Gentlemen, there are times when the most ethical consideration must give way to administrative necessity." MacDonald gave the details. Egypt commanded the Suez Canal route to Asia; Alexandria was the only naval base suitable for defending the eastern Mediterranean. Iraq controlled air and land passage to Asia and was Britain's main source of oil. A hostile Saudi Arabia would threaten British strategic routes. In the event of war, all of these places must be on Great Britain's side.[60]

Moshe Sharett, a Zionist leader, tried to counter these arguments. If the Palestine question were settled, he said, Arab governments would merely raise more demands. In the event of war with Germany, Jewish support would be more reliable than Arab pledges. Ben-Gurion added that whatever happened in Palestine, Arab governments would follow their own interests. The Jewish leaders dismissed promises of being protected in an Arab-ruled Palestine, pointing out that the regimes did not even protect Jews in their own countries and insisting that events in Europe made it impossible for them to abandon demands for Jewish immigration.[61]

The British didn't care.[62] Instead, the British government, believing war would begin within months, offered to accept virtually all the Arab governments' demands. It proposed a Palestine constitutional conference be held in six months followed by the creation of a Palestine executive council on which Arabs would have 60 percent of the seats. In addition, the council could stop all Jewish immigration in five years.[63]

While the Zionists considered walking out, Arabs celebrated this news, but that didn't last long. The Palestine Arab delegation quickly rejected this plan. Instead it demanded the immediate establishment of a Palestine government and a ban on all Jewish immigration or land purchases, with full independence to follow within three years. The Arab states were frustrated, and even some of the grand mufti's followers wanted to accept, but al-Husaini wouldn't budge. Trapped by their earlier promises, Arab government delegations fell into line. Indeed, not trusting as-Said to concur, Iraq's government recalled him and sent radical Foreign Minister Taufiq as-Suwaidi instead.[64]

In response to the Arab rejection, MacDonald embarked on another round of concessions to them. Not only would Jewish immigration be under Arab veto after five years, but even before that time it would be limited to a total of seventy-five thousand people. The proportion of Arabs on the executive council would be raised from 60 to 66 percent. There could be no doubt that the result would be an Arab-ruled Palestine. At this point, Ben-Gurion whispered to a colleague, "They have called this meeting . . . to tell us to give up."[65]

The Arab side was on the verge of victory; no Jewish state could ever be created. Yet again the Arabs stood firm on rejection.[66] On March

15, Hitler seized the rest of Czechoslovakia, marking another step toward international confrontation. Two days later the London Conference ended in failure.

Still, the European crisis, wrote British High Commissioner to Egypt Sir Miles Lampson on March 23, "makes it all the more essential that [a] rapid end should be put to disturbances in Palestine." The Arab states, except for Iraq, also still wanted a quick deal.[67] So despite the breakdown, Arab delegations again met in Cairo to propose a new basis for agreement. Arab leaders were still optimistic. How could such a favorable offer be turned down? Egypt's ambassador assured the British Foreign Office that with his country endorsing this plan, the grand mufti could not interfere.

The Arab states proposed some changes in the British plan intended to assure that the result would be an Arab-ruled Palestine as soon as possible. According to this counteroffer, a Palestinian state would be established within ten years and consultations with Arab governments would be held if this schedule could not be met. Jewish immigration would be reduced and the Jewish population of Palestine would be frozen at 33 percent. Palestinian ministers would be chosen to prepare for independence.

The British gave in on almost every point. Chamberlain explained, "We are now compelled to consider the Palestine problem mainly from the point of view of its effect on the international situation. . . . If we must offend one side, let us offend the Jews rather than the Arabs."[68] It seemed as if al-Husaini's radical policy and move toward Germany had succeeded in generating enough leverage to make the British surrender. But London wanted a long interim period. What would be the point of turning over Palestine immediately to al-Husaini only to see him support the Germans? So they wanted to make al-Husaini wait until the European crisis would be resolved. At that point, if he became the head of an independent Arab Palestine there would be little harm to British strategic interests.

On April 28, after talking with Arab negotiators, Lampson reported that the exchanges "are going more favorably than expected."[69] The main point still blocking a deal was the Arab side's demand—which the British knew came from the grand mufti—that an Arab government would start running the country within three years.[70]

C. W. Baxter, head of the Foreign Office's Eastern Department, wrote that the Arab states had come to terms "on all the most difficult outstanding points."[71] Lampson agreed that there was "substantial agreement . . . on all the main issues." But, both men explained, the Arab states must persuade the Palestine Arabs to agree. The Egyptians were confident of success, with Prime Minister Mahmud claiming he would simply invite the grand mufti to Cairo and "make him toe the line."[72]

On May 17, 1939, Mahmud and Ali Mahir, soon to be his successor, met the Palestinian Arab delegation to talk them into agreeing. Mahir told them that they should accept the British plan. The reason the Jews were so much against it was that it so favored the Arab side. This was a tremendous opportunity; the best deal the Arabs could ever obtain. Cooperation with Britain was better than being "at the mercy of the Jews." Once the Palestine Arabs had a state, sympathetic Arab regimes would help ensure their total control.[73]

Winning an independent state, Mahir continued, required training administrators, preparing for defense, and achieving international "legitimacy." A transitional period, Mahir suggested, was an advantage, not a trap. The best way to triumph was to advance step by step, as in a war in which "One army is vacating some of its front trenches. Would you refrain from jumping into them and occupying them?"

But the Palestine Arab leaders retorted, "If we accept, the revolution will end."

So Mahir tried again to explain reality to them. "Do you believe," he asked, "that Great Britain is unable to crush your revolution, with all its modern satanic war inventions?" Mahmud and Mahir knew the Arab revolt in Palestine had been defeated by the British. "Is it not better for you," Mahir continued, "to come nearer to the British authorities and get them to forsake the Jews?" Then the Arabs wouldn't have to ask London to stop Jewish immigration, they'd control it themselves and not even a single Jew could enter the country. Next Mahmud weighed in with a prophetic warning. If the Palestinian Arabs agreed right now, he insisted, they could have their way. But soon there would be a war that would put them in a weaker position. Britain would lose patience and invoke martial law. Arab countries would be too involved with their own problems to help.

Again the Palestine Arabs refused: "When the revolt started, we had aims in view to attain. We cannot now tell our people, 'Stop the revolution because we got some high posts. . . .'"

"You can tell your people," Mahir answered, "that you shall be able to control your country's government; to stop [British] persecution, deportations, and harsh measures. You could set Palestine's budget, limit the Jewish population to one-third, and justify accepting the deal on the basis of the Arab governments' advice." The Palestine Arabs would not even have to sign anything, but merely to agree verbally to cooperate with a British government White Paper setting the new policy. None of his arguments made any headway.

Mahir and Mahmud were right. The British wanted to satisfy Arab demands as much as possible and thus a little temporary compromise and patience would have achieved a total victory for the Arab side. Under these conditions, an Arab Palestine would have obtained independence within a decade, by 1949 and would have ruled the entire country from the Jordan River to the Mediterranean Sea.[74] Once Palestine was independent, the Arabs could do whatever they wanted to Jews there including—as al-Husaini had made clear—killing them all. If the Palestine Arabs had accepted the British proposal, taken over the government, and worked with the British, Israel never would have existed.

Instead, the Palestine Arab leaders rejected the White Paper, sought total victory, collaborated with the Germans against the British, and in the end received nothing. This orientation made inevitable the Arab rejection of partition and a Palestinian Arab state in 1947; Israel's creation in 1948; five wars; the delay of Israel-Palestinian negotiations for forty-five years; and the absence of a Palestinian state well into the twenty-first century, generations after the rejection of the 1939 deal.

But in 1939 it was possible to believe history would take a different course. A like-minded regime in Germany seemed the world's strongest power, supported the radical Arabs, and might soon destroy all of the Arabs' and Muslims' enemies. The growing radical movement believed that millions of Arabs and other Muslims were about to revolt under its leadership, that soon it would seize control of Iraq and Egypt, Palestine and Jordan, Saudi Arabia and Syria. Believing total victory imminent, why should Palestine's Arabs make any deal with the British, even one requiring the smallest compromise? Al-Husaini was set on a revolutionary approach depending on Germany. Already he was for all practical purposes the Arab world's strongest leader. Such was the power of saying "no," a lesson that would be fully absorbed by postwar Arab leaders.

While Arab governments generally understood that Britain's offer was a great opportunity, they also knew that radicals would exploit any sign of compromise to inflame their own people against them. Moreover, they were trapped by their decision to grant al-Husaini total veto power. Indeed, many wondered whether the grand mufti might be right. Perhaps the Nazis were the wave of the future and a more useful ally than the British.[75] As a result, even though all the Arab governments except Iraq wanted a deal with the British, al-Husaini's men walked out of the talks, certain that their ambitions would be met more quickly and fully by violent Arab revolts combined with Axis victory in the coming war.

At long last, it was London's turn to dig in its heels. It told the Arab states that unless further progress in negotiations was made, it would set its own policy. On May 17 the White Paper proposed that a united Palestine—which everyone knew meant an Arab-dominated Palestine —would be established in ten years. Jews could only buy land in a few areas; Jewish immigration would be strictly limited for five years, after which the Arabs would decide how many would be admitted, which meant none. Yet on the Arab side only Transjordan and the an-Nashashibi faction publicly said anything favorable about the White Paper.[76]

The Jewish Agency strongly protested the White Paper as contrary to the mandate's provisions. Even the Soviets accused Britain of selling out the Jews for its own benefit. Despite the refusal of any Arab state to approve it, the British White Paper became the governing document for Palestine during the next six years. The restrictions on immigration would cost hundreds of thousands of Jews their lives.

Instead of making a deal with Britain, by the summer of 1939 virtually every Arab leader except Abdallah of Transjordan had secretly contacted Germany to offer cooperation. Most enthusiastic were the radicals in Iraq. When the relatively moderate Iraqi politician Rustum Haidar said British policy didn't give the Arab side everything from fear of international Jewish financial power, a radical politician responded that it didn't matter. Might made right. Force rather than more talk was the answer.[77]

Egypt's government, the most ardent advocate for accepting the White Paper, was the first to denounce it. In line with the new Arab style of outbidding rivals in militancy, the Wafd Party—even more moderate and pro-British than the government—attacked its rejection as being too mild. The fascist Young Egypt Party started a bombing campaign against Jewish stores.[78]

Iraq and Saudi Arabia also rejected the White Paper. Iraqi Foreign Minister Ali Jawdat neatly showed the Arab governments' ambiguity on the issue. On the one hand, he denounced the White Paper, claiming the transition period was too long and restrictions on Jewish immigration too mild. On the other hand, he called the White Paper a great Arab victory, and confided privately that he and as-Said had tried to convince Jamal al-Husaini to accept it.[79] The Iraqi regime also tried to calm the passions the radicals were fomenting. Instructions were issued to newspapers not to publish anything that might damage Anglo-Iraqi relations. Still, Baghdad would not cooperate with a request from the moderate Palestinian Auni Abd al-Hadi to support a pro–White Paper group of Palestine Arabs.[80] Only al-Husaini and his hardline stance would ever be allowed to represent the Palestine Arabs.

Blinded by bitterness toward the British and overestimating German power, the grand mufti had already taken the road to Berlin. In mid-1939, al-Husaini made his first request to Canaris to visit the German capital.[81] When the grand mufti left Lebanon for Iraq in October 1939, his triumphalism was enhanced by his reception in Baghdad, where he was granted refuge and acclaimed a national hero. Every politician from the prime minister down, as well as all the political clubs and groups, threw parties in his honor, events that turned into Pan-Arab, anti-British demonstrations.[82]

Nor was this support expressed only in words. Iraq's parliament granted the grand mufti £18,000 a month plus £1,000 a month from secret service funds and a 2 percent tax on government officials' salaries. More contributions came from Egypt and Saudi Arabia. Although he promised as-Said not to engage in political activity, the grand mufti played political kingmaker in Iraq, helping first Taha al-Hashimi and then al-Kailani become prime minister. He strengthened the radical faction by placing militant Palestinians and Syrians in teaching jobs and in the government bureaucracy.[83]

The difference between radicals and moderates was well represented by the remark of the Palestinian Arab delegates in their May 1939 meeting with Egypt's leaders, "We cannot now tell our people, 'Stop the revolution because we got some high posts. . . .'" But that was precisely what moderate Arab politicians wanted: not a revolution in Palestine but a solution to Palestine. And they viewed that as having been achieved in the London negotiations because Palestinian Arabs would obtain "high posts" and thus would be running the country. The story of al-Husaini and the 1939 London Conference would be reenacted by Arafat at the Camp David meeting in 2000, when Arafat rejected getting a Palestinian state through negotiations because he preferred the illusory hope of getting it all by violence.

Now, the moment had come for each Arab leader to choose between the Anglo-French alliance and the German-Italian Axis. The radical faction had already decided on Berlin; even moderate leaders sought to hedge their bets in case the Axis emerged triumphant. It seems as if the time of von Oppenheim's old plan had truly come. But once again a world war would determine the outcome.

6 The Nazi–Arab/Islamist Alliance Prepares for Battle

Once again, Germany prepared to battle its British rivals in the Middle East, led by a formidable team of experts made up of von Oppenheim veterans, soldiers who had served there during World War I, career diplomats, and academic experts.

The Nazi regime also had new tactics that made this second effort seem more likely to succeed. Nazi Party branches had been established among Germans living in the Middle East and elsewhere in the world in a project headed by the young Wilhelm Bohle, who became an SS general. By 1938, this Auslands-Organisation had 580 cells in eighty-two lands engaged in spying, propaganda, and covert operations.[1]

Alfred Hess and his brother Rudolf, later Hitler's top deputy, were sons of a wealthy German merchant living in Egypt. Alfred organized the first party cell in Alexandria in 1926 followed by one in Cairo. There were 214 party members in Egypt by the 1930s, representing one-third of the German families in the country. They urged Egypt's elite toward pro-Nazi and anti-Semitic feelings, organized anti-Jewish boycotts, and in 1933 held a mock trial of the Jews.[2]

The party branch in Iran became especially important, running German policy there since the ambassador in Tehran was an apolitical career man. In Beirut and Baghdad, Cairo and Jerusalem, Kabul and Tehran, Tripoli and Tunis, local Nazi Party branches coordinated military and SS intelligence, businessmen, and academics to spread the influence of Hitler's regime. There were also Nazi Party branches in Alexandria and Port Said; Haifa and Jaffa; and Adana, Ankara, Istanbul, and Izmir.[3]

The Nazi Party's branch in Iraq used new strategies to spread German influence. Its leader was the archaeologist Julius Jordan, who had been digging there since before World War I at the ancient city of Uruk, where Gilgamesh had been king forty-five hundred years earlier.[4] In 1928, Jordan returned to Iraq for the German Oriental Society,[5] and attracted others to his party cell like Willi G. Steffen who, heading a Christian mission in Baghdad and Mosul, had joined the party in 1934.[6] Two years later Grobba hired him as an Arabic translator. Steffen became a key figure in planning how to make Iraq into a German client state. Another recruit was the scholar Adam Falkenstein, who joined the Nazi Party and the Abwehr at age thirty-three in 1939, transferring to its Ankara office when the British seized Iraq in 1941.[7]

A second new feature of Nazi policy in the Middle East was to subsidize and use ideologically compatible Islamist and nationalist groups. These included the fascist Young Egypt Party and the Muslim Brotherhood in Egypt; al-Husaini's forces in Palestine; and many groups in Syria and Iraq. Arab nationalist clubs were important—one of the main ones being the Arab Club of Damascus, financed by al-Husaini using German money—that energetically organized meetings, demonstrations, and propaganda campaigns.

Arab radicals also aided German intelligence-gathering, working closely with Abwehr agents like Rudolf Roser in Beirut and Paula Koch in Aleppo.[8] Koch was an important figure, though Allied intelligence sensationalized that middle-aged, gray-haired lady into a supposed Mata Hari. Born in 1900 to a German family in Aleppo, Koch was a highly praised nurse with the German army during World War I. After some years living in Brazil and Indonesia, she returned to the Middle East for the Abwehr, effectively using her long acquaintance with leading Arab families. Her contact man with Palestine's Arabs was the grand mufti's nephew and intelligence chief, Musa al-Husaini.[9]

The Nazis thought al-Husaini's network provided generally accurate information from an estimated thirty-six agents in the Beirut area alone.[10] In Turkey, al-Husaini built his own spying system headed by the Syrian Adil Azma, who became Syria's ambassador there after the war.[11]

But Berlin's good basis for intelligence and covert operations was hindered by competition between Canaris's Abwehr and the Sicherheitsdient (SD), the foreign intelligence unit of Reinhard Heydrich's Security Ministry. The Abwehr looked down on the SD as incompetent; the SD saw the Abwehr as ideologically unreliable. The antagonism was symbolized by their leaders' contrasting backgrounds and personalities. The prematurely gray-haired Canaris, his face weather-beaten from service at sea, was a respected naval officer who had joined Germany's navy at age eighteen. During World War I, his cruiser was scuttled off Chile and, avoiding capture by the British, he escaped and made his way back to Germany. In recognition of his skill and initiative, he was sent on an intelligence mission to Spain, where he recruited seamen to give German U-boats information on Allied shipping. He also befriended a young Spanish officer named Francisco Franco. Caught by the French while trying to return to Germany disguised as a monk, Canaris was released because of poor health, returned to Spain, and was evacuated by a German submarine. After holding several naval commands in the 1920s and 1930s, he became Abwehr chief on January 2, 1936, and built the agency into an organization of fifteen thousand people. It gathered and analyzed reports from military attachés, agents under diplomatic or other cover, and local informants.

The younger Heydrich, in contrast, had been dismissed from the navy for dishonorable conduct. Heydrich, the embodiment of Nazi brutality and fanaticism, was noted for his sadism; Canaris, for his sense of humor. Heydrich served under Canaris in the 1920s and alternated between trying to destroy the admiral and seeking to win his approval.

Canaris was a conservative nationalist who had little love for the Hitler regime and sheltered anti-Nazis in the Abwehr's ranks. In the Middle East, those critical of the Nazis included Paul Leverkuehn, Abwehr station chief in Istanbul, and Günther Pawelke, Grobba's deputy in Baghdad. Before the war, Canaris used back channels, sometimes through the Vatican, to warn the British of Hitler's aggressive intentions.

While von Oppenheim returned to the region to try to implement his World War I strategy, Grobba, who spoke Turkish, a little Arabic, and Persian, was now Germany's leading expert. In March 1916, he had led a thousand former Muslim prisoners of war to Istanbul where they joined the German-inspired, Ottoman-organized jihad. His wide network of Arab friends was especially strong in Iraq, whose king, Faisal, he personally escorted on his trips to Germany in 1921 and 1930. In 1926, Grobba became German ambassador to Afghanistan and stopped in Baghdad to renew his ties. Under Hitler's regime, Grobba became ambassador to Iraq and was later accredited to Saudi Arabia too. When the British seized Iraq in 1941, Grobba returned to Germany to become the regime's top Middle East adviser.[12]

Von Papen, Germany's ambassador to Turkey, was the other key senior figure on the scene. Born in 1879, von Papen became a cavalry officer and joined the army's elite General Staff in 1913. When World War I began, he was made military attaché to Washington, where he organized agents to sabotage or use U.S. shipyards and munitions factories while buying arms for von Oppenheim's planned jihad in India. After his sabotage efforts became public—in part, due to British intelligence—Washington angrily demanded his recall.

Despite his amateurish failure to subvert America, von Papen's adventures made him a hero in Germany. After service on the Western Front, he joined the military mission to Istanbul in 1917. There he met future Turkish President Ismet İnönü, fought the British, and was interned when the Turks surrendered in 1918. After the war, von Papen returned to Germany and went into politics in the Catholic Center Party. In 1932, when von Papen was proposed as Germany's chancellor despite his own party's objections, he falsely told its leader—a priest, no less—that he would not accept the post. The enraged priest later labeled von Papen a "Judas," a significant insult in Catholic circles. Von Papen's defection further divided moderates and allowed Hitler's power to grow.

During von Papen's six months as chancellor, Germany faced economic collapse, growing polarization, and street violence. To win Nazi backing for his cabinet, von Papen ended a ban on Hitler's private army. Weakening the already tottering republic, he purged democratic-minded civil servants He then invited Hitler to become his vice chancellor, but on January 30, 1933, President Paul von Hindenburg made Hitler chancellor and von Papen received the number two spot. When new elections gave the Nazi Party 44 percent of the vote, Hitler seized power completely on March 23 and made Germany a one-party state.

Von Papen miscalculated, thinking he could outmaneuver the Nazis. He made a speech urging Hitler to allow a multiparty state and grant more liberties. Hitler was infuriated and considered having him killed, but instead, the Nazis murdered the aide who wrote the speech. Von Papen became ambassador to Austria in 1934, where he earned a reprieve by helping subvert that country's independence, bringing it under Hitler's control in 1938.

With this achievement under his belt, von Papen was named ambassador to Turkey in April 1939.[13] The Turks agreed only reluctantly, since von Papen's diplomatic record encompassed the attempted subversion of one neutral country and the destruction of another. These precedents of duplicity boded ill for Turkey. "It would have been difficult for the German government to hit upon a more unpopular nominee," wrote British Ambassador Hughe Knatchbull-Hugessen in a secret evaluation of his rival.[14] Yet von Papen defused his hosts' initial misgivings through charm and far-reaching connections among the leading Turks, hints that he was working to moderate Hitler, and threats based on Germany's power.

The Nazis also had able men, both party and non–party members, at midlevel posts, many of them with long experience in the region and speaking its languages fluently. An example of this expertise was Kurt Munzel, who began work at the Foreign Ministry in 1939 supervising Arabic-language broadcasts[15] and advising Grobba's Arabian Committee on operations and propaganda. In 1942, he became head of the ministry's Orient Department.[16] Incidentally, his boss at the radio propaganda office was a Nazi Party member, Kurt Georg Kiesinger, whom al-Husaini knew through wartime cooperation on propaganda and would contact when Kiesinger was West Germany's chancellor between 1966 and 1969.

During the time before the Nazis began preparations for war and revolt in the Middle East, Germany's most effective way of spreading its influence was economic activity. While Middle East trade was an insignificant part of Germany's economy, for the region's countries Germany was the number three trading partner, surpassed only by Britain and France.

Iran, then still called Persia, was the Muslim country Berlin economically courted most in the 1930s as well as the only such country whose inhabitants the Nazis regarded as fellow Aryans. That conclusion was rooted in the writings of German experts and diplomats who traveled there before World War I and in the 1920s, such as Friedrich C. Andreas,[17] Georg Graf von Kanitz, and Rudolf Nadolny.[18]

Walter Hinz, one of these Iran experts, wrote a 1936 book extolling Persians as a superior race. He joined the Nazi Party the next year and served with the Abwehr in Turkey during World War II. In 1974, the University of Tehran gave Hinz an honorary doctorate in recognition of his services to Iran.[19] German-Persian relations were so successful that the shah's decision in 1935 to change the country's name from Persia to Iran—derived from the word Aryan—is often attributed to a suggestion from Iran's ambassador to Berlin.[20]

Ernst Herzfeld, an archaeologist, was another key figure linking the two countries. After serving in Iran in World War I, he returned there in 1923. During the early 1930s, he excavated the ancient Persian capital of Persepolis.[21] Iran's ruler, Reza Shah, and his son the crown prince—the future shah—were impressed by their visit to the site. Sebastian Beck, a Persian language expert and another World War I veteran in the area, joined the Nazi Party in 1932 and returned to Iran in 1934. The shah gave him a medal for his research.[22]

To accelerate its economic development, Iran hired many German advisers in the 1920s and 1930s. Lufthansa, the German airline, opened a direct Berlin-Tehran route. By 1937 there were about six hundred Germans living in Iran. Tehran concluded a new trade agreement with Berlin in 1935. The next year, a dozen big German companies started the Iranian-German Trade Association.[23] Yet with Nazi Germany focusing on rearmament, companies faced difficulties in obtaining financing and foreign exchange at home.[24] The British also countered German economic interests.

The most important event in Nazi-Iranian economic relations was the 1936 visit of Hjalmar Schacht, Hitler's minister for economy and president of the Reichsbank, with a sixty-member delegation. The shah gave Schacht a medal; Schacht saluted the monarch, "completely against protocol"—German Ambassador Johannes Smend disapprovingly noted—with "Heil Hitler." Out of politeness, the shah and crown prince replied the same way.[25]

Among the German businessmen Schacht visited in Iran was his own son-in-law, Lutz Gielhammer, director of Bank Mellié Iran. The thirty-eight-year-old Gielhammer had served in World War I, earned a doctorate, and spent a decade in Tehran. After World War II he became West German ambassador to Iran for a dozen years. Schacht also toured Nazi Party headquarters, the Hitler Youth branch,[26] and the Iranian-German Technical School, where pro-German Iranians received professional training. One of those students, Nawwab Safawi, later became the main radical Islamist leader and al-Husaini's closest collaborator in Iran.[27]

But Iraq was the country where Germany held most influence in the 1930s, especially in the army, many of whose officers had fought in the Ottoman army alongside Germany during World War I. Their pro-German attitude was exemplified by Colonel Salah ad-Din al-Sabbagh, leader of the powerful, pro-Nazi Golden Square faction that would later seize power, who named the three Germans who influenced him as his unit's military adviser in World War I; Major Hans Steffen of the Rheinmetall company, who sold weapons to the Iraqi army; and Grobba.[28]

Iraqi nationalists hoped Germany would help them develop their economy. Despite gaining independence in 1932, Iraq was still tied closely to Britain. The British controlled Iraq's oil and pipelines connecting that country's Mosul fields to the Mediterranean ports of Haifa, in British-ruled Palestine, and Tripoli, in French-ruled Lebanon. By 1939, oil financed one-third of Iraq's budget through the British-controlled Oil Development Company. Hitler had the chance to buy shares in the company in 1936 but refused so as not to antagonize London.[29] Yet this dependence stirred growing anti-British and pro-German passion.[30] The radical faction, mainly nationalists but also Islamists, was more powerful in Iraq than any other Arab state. Sati al-Husri, a leading architect of Arab radical nationalist ideology, was strongly pro-German and used that country as his model as director of Iraq's education system. Iraqi pro-German organizations and individuals cooperated closely with Berlin.[31] Officers like Colonel as-Sabbagh and militant politicians like Yunis as-Sabawi, for example, smuggled German arms to Syria and Palestine.[32]

Yet the two allies did not always perceive their interests in identical ways. In 1936, the anti-British General Bakr Sidqi, a Kurd, seized power and selected as prime minister the radical Hikmat Sulaiman, later replaced by another radical, Jamil al-Midfai, a man close to al-Husaini.[33] Grobba met both of them twice a week. Sidqi hired German Colonel Rolf Heins as his military adviser and Heins surveyed the country, planning border defenses and building up the army. Even more German advisers were brought to Baghdad. The situation looked excellent from Berlin's perspective. But in 1937, Sidqi was assassinated, partly because radical Arab nationalists suspected he was too pro-Kurdish. Ironically, the killer was a pro-German radical who had previously saluted Grobba with an enthusiastic "Heil Hitler" whenever they met.[34] The plot was hatched in the German-subsidized Muthanna Club, whose leaders were on the German payroll and whose members called themselves "national socialists."[35] In other words, pro-German agents motivated by Nazi ideology had assassinated a pro-German leader, thus subverting German influence.

The Germans thought that if their Arab allies became more ideologically Nazified the alliance would be even stronger. One effort was to create groups patterned after the Hitler Youth. In 1937 the thirty-year-old Nazi youth leader Baldur von Schirach visited Baghdad and asked King Ghazi to support the al-Futuwa youth movement instead of the British-based Boy Scouts. A year later thirty young Iraqis from al-Futuwa traveled to Germany as guests of the Nazi Party—along with counterparts from Afghanistan, Egypt, Turkey, and Iran—for the annual Nuremberg rally, met Hitler, and toured the country for two weeks. They returned home fascinated by the new Germany. Al-Husaini's Palestinian Arab Party organized its own al-Futuwa movement.[36]

Beginning in 1936, Berlin also began to sponsor large numbers of Iraqi students to study in Germany. Many became strong supporters of an Arab-Nazi alliance, returning home impressed by the Nazi regime's order, discipline, progress, and unity as a remedy for their own countries' weakness, factionalism, and stagnation. In addition, there were outright fascist movements. In Iraq, led by as-Sabawi and Sami Shaukat, they wore red shirts. The Egyptian equivalent was the Young Egypt Party's green shirt movement. By the time war broke out, these groups had, at least nominally, thousands of members.[37]

The Muthanna Club was just one part of the strong radical, pro-German network of Iraqi groups, which also included the Palestine Defense Committee and the Islamist-dominated Young Men's Muslim Association and Islamic Guidance Association. Such powerful mainstream politicians as Naji as-Suwaidi, al-Midfai, and Sulaiman, all prime ministers, also supported the radical faction. In contrast, as-Suwaidi's brother, Taufiq, who had served as foreign minister, and as-Said held moderate views. They wanted to maintain the alliance with Britain, compromise on Palestine, and use diplomacy instead of force. Yet such men, unlike the radicals, had no mass organizations or systematic ideology, making it hard for them to compete with rivals using sophisticated mobilization methods adapted from European fascist practices.

Grobba led the effort in Iraq. In 1936 and again in 1938, Canaris secretly visited Baghdad to obtain first-hand impressions of Arab politics. On the second trip, Canaris asked Grobba to become Abwehr chief in Iraq, a job he added to his ambassadorial duties. At first, the Abwehr's rival, the SD, resisted his authority but soon Grobba controlled its activities as well.[38]

The ambassador also took the lead in establishing German relations with Saudi Arabia. In 1933, Ibn Saud had proposed giving Germany a concession to drill for oil. Hitler rejected the idea, believing he could not secure the fields in wartime.[39] Watching events in Europe and seeking to counter British influence, Ibn Saud sent his secretary Yusuf Yasin to meet Grobba in Baghdad on November 5, 1937. He requested a new treaty and a German mission to his country, and hinted at an alliance with Berlin, saying he would be a "benevolent neutral, if not more, in case of a war."[40] The king also offered to be middleman for sending German weapons to al-Husaini's Palestine revolt.

Negotiations advanced slowly, however, due to German foreign exchange shortages, debates over how openly to challenge British interests, and suspicions that Yasin might be a British agent. Only in 1939 were talks successfully concluded. On January 13, Grobba was accredited as ambassador to Saudi Arabia. With approval by Hitler and von Ribbentrop, Germany provided a six-million-mark credit for the Saudis to buy weapons.[41]

When the war began, however, and German fortunes flagged in the Middle East, the king, knowing he was surrounded by British-controlled territory, quickly claimed to be for the Allies. He would soon use the United States, rather than Germany, as Saudi Arabia's alternative patron to the British.[42] Unlike the big city, intellectually more sophisticated Palestinian Arab, Iraqi, and Egyptian radicals, the wily old desert

Figure 15. Fritz Grobba was in the course of a quarter-century successively the German envoy to Kabul, Baghdad, and ar-Riyadh, and the senior official for Muslim and Arab affairs within the Foreign Ministry. Interrogated by the Soviets immediately after World War II, he told them about Hitler's plan to deport the Jews of Palestine as soon as the Nazi troops arrived.

chieftain kept his options open and did not commit himself to the losing side from miscalculation or ideological zeal.

In Egypt, too, the Germans built the foundation for an alliance. Wilhelm Stellbogen, press attaché and director of the German News Bureau in Cairo, acting for the Abwehr,[43] paid Muslim Brotherhood leader al-Banna about one thousand Egyptian pounds a month in 1939 and probably before as well.[44] To show how proportionately large were these sums, the Brotherhood's high-priority fund-raising for the Palestine cause that year yielded just five hundred Egyptian pounds.[45] Al-Husaini gave more German money to al-Banna through such intermediaries as Auni Abd al-Hadi, Muhammad Ali Tahir, and Sabri Abd ad-Din.[46]

Some of the key pro-German figures in Egypt made their connections with Germany while in Baghdad. In 1938, Egypt's ambassador to Iraq, Azzam, a close friend of al-Husaini and later Arab League secretary general, along with Major Aziz Ali al-Misri—who fought in World War I on the British side but had now become pro-German—met frequently with Grobba.[47]

An alliance with the Arabs, of course, was not enough for Hitler to start a war. He also needed support from the country that was ostensibly his worst enemy, the USSR. At 1 P.M. on August 22, 1939, two German Focke-Wulf Condor planes landed at Moscow airport. Von Ribbentrop came down the stairs to be greeted by a Soviet military band playing the Nazi anthem. That afternoon, the German and Soviet foreign ministers initialed a treaty of alliance. Ostensibly a nonaggression pact, the accord included a secret plan to invade and partition Poland and defined the two dictators' spheres of influence in the Balkans and Turkey. With everything in place, in September 1939 Germany invaded Poland. The Allies still had substantial superiority in the Middle East but quickly lost the battle for Europe. In 1940, when France, Holland, Belgium, and Norway were conquered by Germany, the British army fled the continent, and Italy entered the war on Germany's side, the Nazis seemed likely victors.

Germany's Arab sympathizers became more outspokenly so. In June 1940, the grand mufti wrote von Papen to offer his services. His vision was to obtain from the Axis in World War II what the Arabs had failed to gain from the Allies in World War I, a huge and fully independent state led by himself and absorbing Syria, Lebanon, Palestine, Jordan, and Iraq. In contrast to the Ottomans, al-Husaini had a popular network extending throughout the Arabic-speaking world and into Muslim countries beyond. Moreover, unlike the Ottoman sultan, he united Arab nationalists and Islamists into one movement.[48]

The radical Iraqi politicians were eager to smash their country's alliance with England. In Syria and Lebanon, an additional pro-German incentive was that their colonial master had been defeated and the way was open to join the victors. When things looked bleakest for the Allies, the cautious Ibn Saud, the moderate Iraqi as-Said, and others considered jumping ship.

But before doing so as-Said made one final bid, based on wishful thinking, to stave off the radical revolt. He urged Britain to make even more concessions to keep Arabs from defecting to the Axis. If, as-Said urged, Britain immediately turned Palestine over to the Arabs with full independence within ten years; obtained Syria's independence from France; and supplied arms, Iraq would enter the war on England's side.[49] Iraq's people and government, wrote as-Said, "are unanimous in seeking the safety of their country before anything else and in following the road which leads to that safety." As-Said was right in saying Iraq would face disaster if it fought Britain but wrong in arguing that the radicals thought the same way. They believed Nazi Germany was the safer bet.[50] Understanding this fact, Prime Minister Winston Churchill, who had so clearly foreseen the failure of appeasing Hitler in Europe, refused any additional concessions.

As-Said then proposed to defect to the Axis camp but was rejected by the grand mufti and his Iraqi ally, Justice Minister Naji Shaukat. Why, they reasoned, let a rival join with them on the eve of their total victory? Thus, the most famous of all Arab moderate politicians did not become a Nazi collaborator only because his application was turned down.

Once the tide turned in the war, as-Said resumed his posture as loyal friend of the Allies in 1941. Thanks to his having joined the actually winning side, his career prospered thereafter. In the short run, he triumphed. But the radicals were to have revenge by taking over the region in the following decade. Eighteen years after rejecting as-Said's effort to join them, the radicals took over Iraq in a 1958 coup and a Baghdad mob tore as-Said to pieces.[51]

As for the British, they knew their appeasement efforts in 1939 had failed and so, in 1940, they turned to pressure. The British demanded that Iraq freeze all relations with Germany, as well as the resignation of radical nationalist Prime Minister al-Kailani, scion of the family von Oppenheim had predicted in 1893 would one day lead a pro-German revolt. Recognizing that Britain still had much leverage in Iraq, on January 31, 1941 the king forced al-Kailani to resign. Taha al-Hashimi's new moderate government tried to purge the radical officers, who responded with an April 3 military coup returning al-Kailani to power. Given the military situation, they had good reason to believe they were right to back Germany, a country whose armies were at that moment victorious everywhere.

Egyptians reached similar conclusions. They saw the Italian army advance eighty-five miles into their own territory from Libya. Prime Minister Mahir rejected British efforts to make him break relations with Italy. The British pushed him from office and forced pro-German General al-Misri to resign as Egypt's army commander. Riddled with pro-German officers, Cairo's armed forces were largely disarmed and demobilized by the British.[52]

At the same time, the British did not neglect offering incentives for Arab cooperation as well. On May 29, 1941, Foreign Secretary Anthony Eden's Mansion House speech catered to Arab nationalist ambitions by endorsing stronger links among Arab countries, a stance that after the war would bring British backing for forming the Arab League.[53] But those placing hopes on the Axis were unimpressed. They looked instead to Iraq's defiance of Britain. Egyptian dissidents, as-Sadat explained, "wanted to attack the British and make Egypt a second Iraq. [Al-Kailani] had given the signal for the war of liberation. It was our duty to rush to his aid."[54] Leaders of the nascent Ba'th Party in Syria felt the same way.

Now battle would be fully joined. Al-Husaini and his colleagues would do everything possible to make the Arab world, Iran, Afghanistan, and even India go up in the flames of a pro-Nazi Islamic revolt.

7 Al-Husaini in Search of an Empire

During World War II, Berlin backed Islamism and militant Arab nationalism. Al-Husaini was its candidate to lead a revolution, rule the Middle East, assist in destroying the British there, kill the Jews, and help ensure that Adolf Hitler ruled the world supreme. The grand mufti was the Nazis' most important nonstate ally, and both sides intended that the radical Arab-Muslim forces, once in control of their countries, become a full partner in the Axis alongside Germany, Italy, and Japan. This alliance between al-Husaini and Hitler, militant Arab nationalist-Islamist forces and Nazis, was vital for waging and winning the war on many levels.

First, al-Husaini pledged to provide tens of thousands of Muslim troops to fight for the Axis. While al-Husaini only recruited a few hundred Arabs, he helped raise more than twenty thousand Soviet and Balkan Muslims.

Second, al-Husaini provided valuable intelligence through networks of contacts and agents stretching from Morocco to Afghanistan and India.

Third, al-Husaini promised to organize uprisings to tie down Allied troops, sabotage enemy installations, and block supply lines. While his successes were limited, the Allies did have to take into account the possibility that revolts might break out, and thus al-Husaini's efforts were somewhat effective.

Fourth, al-Husaini gave good advice on how Axis propaganda could appeal to Arabs and Muslims.

Fifth, al-Husaini and his partners promised to bring Arab countries into the war by either overthrowing or winning over governments. They succeeded in Iraq and came close in Egypt. German forces' failure to conquer more of the Middle East was the biggest factor determining the radical Arabs' failure to recruit more rulers.

Finally, al-Husaini planned to extend the mass murder of Jews to Muslim-populated areas, a genocide that the Nazis considered an integral part of the war effort. This was indeed implemented where German rule extended in the Caucasus, North Africa, and the Balkans.

History could easily have turned out differently, and all these goals could have been achieved, with the Third Reich triumphant, al-Husaini dictator over the Middle East, and all Jews outside of the Americas dead. The radical Arab and Muslim forces tried their best to achieve this result.

When al-Husaini left Beirut and arrived in Baghdad on October 15, 1939, the nationalists there received him as a hero.[1] Al-Husaini knew many of them from Ottoman army days, and others from his first visit to Baghdad in 1932. As they watched World War II begin, al-Husaini's Palestine Arabs and the militant Iraqi nationalists were eager to be Germany's allies. To organize the Arab world as part of the Axis, hardline nationalists and Islamists established the secret Arab Committee for Cooperation among Arabs. Its impressive membership included Palestine Arab, Saudi, and Iraqi leaders along with a strong representation from Syria. Largely thanks to al-Husaini, the committee also had strong contacts among Muslims in Europe, Egypt, Libya, and Lebanon.[2]

The Iraqi participants included Prime Minister al-Kailani, Justice Minister Shaukat, and as-Sabawi, translator of *Mein Kampf* into Arabic. From Syria came forty-nine-year-old Shukri al-Quwatli, a future, postwar president who had attended al-Husaini's 1931 Jerusalem conference, and Zaki al-Khatib, a future prime minister.

Saudi King Abd al-Aziz Ibn Saud sent his trusted private secretary, Yasin, and his political adviser al-Hud, who had visited Hitler the previous year to conclude the secret weapons deal for al-Husaini.[3] The veteran pro-German Islamist Arslan was European representative, and worked closely with von Oppenheim, who called him the "best political head on Middle Eastern affairs."[4]

To cement the alliance, the committee sent Shaukat to Ankara to see von Papen.[5] The conversation went well, and as the next step al-Husaini sent his secretary, Kamal Uthman Haddad, to Berlin to meet with the Foreign Ministry's Ernst von Weizsäcker[6] at his office in a confiscated Jewish home.[7] Al-Kailani spoke with Italy's ambassador in Iraq, who assured him of Mussolini's support for throwing the British and French out of the Middle East.[8]

The Germans, for their part, were also working on an alliance with the Arabs. By summer 1940, when France collapsed, von Oppenheim was already in Syria, traveling frequently to Baghdad to coordinate with al-Kailani and al-Husaini on their plan for pro-German coups in Iraq and Syria.[9] Watching von Oppenheim closely, the then-neutral Americans were impressed with his effectiveness. They wryly claimed that he was so eager to prove his loyalty to the Third Reich that he raised his arm and heiled Hitler even when talking on the telephone. Despite—or more likely because—of his Jewish ancestry, Baron von Oppenheim, as the Americans called him, went out of his way to express his hatred of Jews.[10]

On July 25, 1940, von Oppenheim presented to his government a detailed "Union Jack" plan on how to stir unrest in British-ruled areas. Theo Habicht, the German under secretary who had previously restructured the Austrian Nazi organization; von Ribbentrop;[11] von Papen in Ankara; and von Weizsäcker in Berlin were all consulted. A month later, al-Husaini sent his own proposal to Berlin which was largely a copy of von Oppenheim's version.[12]

Thus, when von Weizsäcker again met al-Husaini's envoy Haddad, on October 18, 1940, the German official said they had a deal. Von Weizsäcker read him the German-Italian declaration of support for the Arabs.[13] It was broadcast repeatedly in Arabic by Radio Berlin and Italy's Radio Bari.[14] On January 14, 1941, the Germans and Italians formally issued a declaration supporting Arab independence.[15]

Six days later, al-Husaini wrote a nine-page letter to Hitler further defining the alliance. The Palestine question, said the grand mufti, united them in their joint hatred against the British and Jews.[16] He asked

Germany and Italy to support the merger of most Arabs into a single state called the Greater Arab Empire, Greater Arabia, or United Arab State.[17] Al-Husaini never mentioned any Palestinian Arab nationalism but instead proposed, faithful to his past Greater Syrian stance, to make Syria, Lebanon, Palestine, and Transjordan a single federated state with a Nazi-style system.[18] Later, he added Saudi Arabia, Iraq, and the Gulf emirates to his projected empire. And later still al-Husaini threw in Egypt, North Africa, and Sudan as well.

The other main demand was Axis help for the Arabs to wipe out all Jews in the Middle East. With Hitler openly declaring that a world war meant the "eradication of the Jewish race in Europe,"[19] al-Husaini sought to do the same thing in his region.

The Arab committee offered to aid Germany with oil and other support for Hitler's war effort. It claimed to have ten thousand men ready for an armed uprising to overthrow Transjordan's pro-British monarch, seize Palestine, and wipe out the Jews there. The committee promised that its nonexistent army and the Arab masses of Palestine would defeat the forty thousand British troops there. The revolt would be carried on with weapons from French stockpiles in Syria which, after France's fall, was now a virtual German protectorate.[20]

Finally, the committee suggested that the pro-German Iraqi regime could block British reinforcements to the Middle East sent from India. And if the British did invade Iraq, the Baghdad government pledged to fight them with help from German advisers.

The Germans completely accepted these claims and saw al-Husaini, according to internal documents, as the legitimate spokesman for the people of Iraq, Palestine, Lebanon, Saudi Arabia, and Syria—the whole Arab east.[21]

Within the German government, though, there were some, especially in the Foreign Ministry, who were skeptical about the ability of al-Husaini and his colleagues to deliver on their promises. Von Hentig favored quiet cooperation with the Arabs, not a publicly declared alliance.[22] German ambassador to France Otto Abetz worried that a pro-Arab policy might push French colonial administrators in Syria and Lebanon into the arms of the Allies. He also warned that toying with Islam could produce Muslim-Christian conflicts in future.[23]

But the outcome was not in doubt. The region's oil was vital for Germany, Grobba argued, and must be denied to the British.[24] Making Iraq into Germany's ally was a great opportunity. As for whether jihad might turn against German interests, Grobba cynically claimed, "The Arabs we use currently in our game do not fight for religious but for political goals."[25] Thus, Berlin decided on an Arab policy based on three main principles.

First, al-Husaini was its main partner in the Middle East, followed by Iraq. Given his primacy, funding should go directly to al-Husaini and through him to others.

Second, German intelligence would organize sabotage operations and promote nationalist-Islamist insurrections in Palestine and Jordan.

Third, Berlin should not rush to support independence for Syria and Lebanon publicly so as not to antagonize the Vichy French rulers there who were also German allies.[26] Nevertheless, the Germans were ready to use France's Middle East colonies, which they controlled,[27] to provide French weapons to Arab allies and as a base for an Arab army to launch what the grand mufti called his war against "the democracies and international Jewry."[28]

Aside from Syria, the pro-Nazi Arabs' main asset was control over Iraq and its army. Pressed by the Axis offensive in North Africa, the British shifted many soldiers from Iraq to Egypt, weakening their garrison and making Baghdad's resistance more likely to succeed. Thus, the Germans concluded that al-Kailani's regime, with relatively little aid, could defeat the reduced British forces in Iraq.

Yet al-Husaini had even more to bring to the bargaining table with Hitler. The kings of Saudi Arabia and Egypt, with whom al-Husaini had close secret links, were ready to collaborate the moment they concluded Germany would probably win the war. With German control over Syria and Lebanon, a victory by pro-German forces in Iraq plus an Islamist-nationalist uprising in Palestine and Transjordan could persuade the kings to ally openly with the Axis. In Egypt, al-Husaini also had many assets cultivated for almost two decades: the monarch himself, top politicians, army officers, the Young Egypt Party, and the Muslim Brotherhood.

There was also a third partner to this German-Arab alliance: the French collaborationist Vichy government and its officials in the Middle East. That regime knew of the plots by al-Husaini and von Oppenheim and were ready to cooperate if the Germans respected, despite Arab demands, future French control over Syria and Lebanon.[29]

Given this situation, al-Husaini seemed the man of the hour, eventually able to deliver the entire Middle East to Hitler. Thus, on March 1, Berlin and Rome decided to work with the Arab Cooperation Committee, as it was now called. At the grand mufti's request, they specified that the Arabs could treat Jews in their own lands as Germany did in Europe.[30]

On March 11, von Weizsäcker informed Haddad of Hitler's personal support for the grand mufti's leadership of the Arabs and Muslims.[31] Within a month, the Germans gave al-Husaini a hundred thousand reichsmarks, with twenty thousand more every month paid equally by Germany and Italy.[32] Hitler wrote al-Husaini on April 3 further confirming his personal support, and praising the Arabs as an ancient civilization quite capable of self-government. He recognized full Arab independence and agreed that the British and the Jews were common enemies.[33]

While it had taken a full year—in retrospect a fatal delay—to confirm the alliance, the partners now moved quickly. Prime Minister al-Kailani made a military pact with the Germans. The plan was for him to be cautious, avoiding confrontation with Britain. The next step was also taken, starting to build a German base in Syria, run by Grobba, to seize control there and then extend the chain of German client regimes to Lebanon, Palestine, and Jordan. The Germans planned to give Arab revolutionaries lavish funding, oust French officials, and install a pro-German Arab government in Damascus. Grobba and his staff created an Arab Legion of 1000 men as the nucleus—"under the green flag of Arab freedom," in a German dispatch's words—for an Arab army.[34] Von Oppenheim praised its commander, al-Qawuqji, al-Husaini's military adviser, as an extraordinary leader.[35]

In May 1941 Hitler met with Admiral François Darlan, Vichy's military commander, and made a deal giving the Germans military facilities in the French colonies of Syria and North Africa. Darlan's commander in Syria, General Henri Dentz, supported the planned insurrections and supplied arms from his depots for the Arab Legion and the Iraqi army.[36] When the Turks refused to let the equipment pass through their country to Baghdad, Dentz pretended it was being shipped through Iraq en route to France's Asian colonies.[37] He obtained Turkish transit permits for two trains and fueled German planes headed to Baghdad.[38] If Germany helped, Dentz was even ready to send his French troops to fight the British in Palestine and Egypt. For all practical purposes, the French authorities in Syria and Lebanon had themselves joined the Axis side.

In retrospect, one may see all of these schemes as inevitably illusory because in the end they did fail. Yet that result was not preordained. After all, Hitler appeared to be the victor in Europe and was now patron of both Islamism and Arab nationalism. Germany's anti-Jewish, anti-British message seemed a match falling on dry tinder, and his impressive array of Arab allies gave lavish pledges of support. Germany was already close to controlling Syria, Lebanon, and Iraq. Given this strong start and apparent widespread Arab support the region could become a battlefield, tying down Allied troops and supplies so that German forces could win the war. A Nazi world seemed within reach.

Von Oppenheim and his colleagues were optimistic. The British, von Oppenheim suggested, might even abandon Iraq to its pro-German regime in order to focus on Egypt's defense. Once the pro-British government was overthrown in Jordan, the Saudi king would be bribed with that country's southern part, with the rest going to al-Husaini's Palestine government.[39]

A German agent in Syria described the mood there by quoting a common saying among Arabs: "No more monsieur and mister [no French or British colonialism]; Allah in heaven, Hitler on earth."[40] Aside from the Muslim Brotherhood, the Young Egypt Party, the monarchs and military officers in Egypt and Iran; the grand mufti as leader of the Palestine Arabs; Iraq's government; and the Saudi monarchy, additional pro-German forces were arising in the region. The most durable of these would prove be the Ba'th, a Pan-Arab nationalist party based on the fascist model. One branch would rule Iraq for forty-five years after the war, brought down only by an American-led invasion in 2003; another would rule Syria for a half-century.

The Ba'th's founders were students who, in the contemporary spirit of radical Arab nationalist thinking, sought a strong leader to achieve for Arabs what Hitler had done for Germans. One of the books that influenced them was an anti-Semitic work by Alfred Rosenberg, the Nazi ideologue who would soon become al-Husaini's friend and supervisor in Berlin.[41] On November 29, 1940, they founded the new party using a word (ba'th means renaissance in Arabic), frequent in Nazi propaganda to the Arabs and with a program paralleling that of the Nazi

Party.[42] Two decades later, after he had been Syria's prime minister, one of the founders, Sami al-Jundi, recalled those early days: "We had been racist admirers of Nazism. We . . . were among the first who liked to translate Hitler's book. In Damascus we felt admiration for Nazism."[43]

The movement soon spread to Iraq, where one of its early adherents was a Nazi-sympathizing officer named Khairallah Talfah. When the pro-German regime fell its pro-British replacement court-martialed Talfah and gave him a five-year prison sentence. After his release, Talfah became surrogate father and political mentor to his young nephew, Saddam Husain, who would marry Talfah's oldest daughter and make his father-in-law Baghdad's mayor.

With so many assets, what went wrong with the German-Arab-Islamist strategy? The answer is that the British were too fast; the Germans too slow and set counterproductive priorities; and the Arabs did not fulfill their promises to Berlin.

One problem was the priority Hitler gave to conquering the Balkans and USSR, unrealistically assuming that this would happen fast enough to permit a quick transfer of German forces to the Middle East. Until that happened, Germany planned a low-cost policy in the region. Local allies would take the lead in subverting the British presence. The Germans would establish intelligence networks, bribe politicians, and subsidize newspapers, while arming and training client Arab military forces.[44]

Instead, German forces were tied up in Yugoslavia and Greece in the spring, delaying invasion of the USSR to June. Then, although the Germans advanced in the Soviet Union they did not do so quickly enough to avoid the harsh winter's effects and growing Soviet resistance. Berlin's timetable was upset. Instead of marching into Egypt, Turkey, and Iran, German soldiers were bogged down in the snowdrifts of the Eastern Front in Russia. German army chief Franz Halder would later complain that Hitler's Arab policy was seriously flawed because of his ignorance of the region and shortcomings in German intelligence, as seen in the Iraq failure. Another mistake was that Berlin was too worried about not offending the French and Italians by pushing harder and more openly for Arab independence and unity.[45]

The second fatal factor was the poor performance of Berlin's Arab allies. Al-Husaini and his allies had promised a hundred thousand Arab soldiers but in the end recruited only about a thousand outside of

Iraq. As for Iraq, the pro-German Egyptian General al-Misri, who had spent years there before the war, was skeptical. "You don't know Iraqi politicians as well as I do," he told fellow Egyptian officer as-Sadat; they would mess up.[46] Al-Misri was right.

On April 1, as the Nazis began their advance into Yugoslavia and Greece, al-Kailani and the pro-German "Golden Square" military faction made their own move without consulting the Germans. When the British asked to bring new troops through Iraq on their way to Egypt, al-Kailani refused and purged all the remaining pro-British Iraqi officials. Skirmishes broke out between arriving British units and the Iraqi army on April 19. Although nine thousand Iraqi troops surrounded the Royal Air Force base at Habbaniyya for an entire month, they made no decisive attack. Al-Kailani and al-Husaini took two weeks after the confrontation began to request German supplies and air support. In early May, attacking British planes broke the Habbaniyya siege.[47]

Caught off guard, the Germans scrambled to send aid.[48] Al-Husaini's aide Haddad, alias Max Müller, traveled between Berlin, Ankara, and Baghdad to coordinate operations.[49] Disappointing his radical friends' expectations, the Saudi king shrewdly decided not to get involved and rejected al-Kailani's request for arms.[50]

Grobba arrived in Baghdad on May 6. The following day, Hitler agreed to send a squadron of German Messerschmitt 110 fighters and one of Heinkel-111 bombers to Iraq.[51] Dubbed the "falcon of Palestine" for his exploits with the Ottomans during World War I, Grobba's brother-in-law, General Hellmuth Felmy, took command of the military effort.[52] By May 16, German planes were battling the British in dogfights over Baghdad. Three trainloads of military equipment were sent from Syria to Iraq on May 12 and 28.

Germany also sought to use a covert asset, the Palestine Germans, Arabic-speaking men who had grown up in German Protestant religious colonies established in Ottoman Palestine during the previous century. Based in Greece and led by Theodor von Hippel, a World War I veteran, about two dozen of them were trained to sabotage Iraqi oil wells and pipelines. But the British moved into Iraq before the team could get there.[53] German propaganda claimed that their measures would liberate the Iraqis from British rule.[54] Yet the Germans were too slow in reacting to events, too far away, and gave Iraq too low a priority to do so.[55]

Even more blame can be put on al-Husaini and his Iraqi allies, who had exaggerated their power, acted too soon, and spent more time talking big than organizing for battle. The Abwehr was shocked to discover that al-Husaini had no plan for actually staging insurrections. The mismanaged Iraqi army lacked fuel for its airplanes despite Iraq being one of the world's main oil producers. Reconnaissance flights and German bombing raids against Habbaniyya failed due to poor coordination with Iraqi ground forces.[56] So incompetent was Iraq's military that on May 12 it mistakenly shot down an arriving German plane, killing Axel von Blomberg, the German military mission's field commander and son of Hitler's former war minister. The fiasco was so embarrassing that Grobba—who witnessed the incident personally—insisted the British had shot down von Blomberg's plane. The pilot said there had been damage in a dogfight but the plane had been brought down by the Iraqis.[57]

The British were also helped by the fact that Italy's North African offensive had stalled. They thus did not need to consider abandoning Iraq and shifting all forces from there to Egypt.[58] Faced with their Italian ally's failure, it was the Germans who had to send more troops to North Africa, leaving them fewer resources to throw into the region's eastern sector.

As a result, the Iraqi revolt became not a triumph but such a disaster for the Germans that it triggered an internal quarrel about who was to blame. Wilhelm Melchers of the Foreign Ministry claimed Grobba had given al-Kailani a green light to rebel without Berlin's authorization. Melchers's colleague von Weizsäcker denied this.[59] Grobba blamed Germany's army. Werner Junck, leader of the military mission in Iraq, asked for a court martial to clear himself of this charge. Göring backed him and rejected Grobba's claim.[60]

When he met al-Husaini six months later, Hitler made some apology for having been unable to give sufficient help; al-Husaini later rationalized the defeat by attributing the revolt's failure to sabotage by a Jewish fifth column of infiltrators and spies.[61]

In contrast to Arab incompetence and German indecision, the British handled the Middle East crisis decisively and reaped total victory.[62]

First, the British invaded Iraq with help from the British-officered Transjordanian army, which crossed the desert from Amman, easily defeated Iraq's army, reached the capital's outskirts on May 30, and installed a pro-British government under as-Said. Al-Kailani and al-Husaini fled. Along with them went al-Qawuqji, on the last train to Tehran full of escaping Iraqi officers. He fought on the Syrian front until he was wounded on a scouting mission and taken to Berlin for treatment.[63]

Before the British could gain full control of Baghdad, pro-German forces launched a pogrom in its Jewish quarter, killing at least 180 people, injuring 1,000 more, and looting thousands of homes and businesses. In honor of this riot, as-Sabawi later took the name by which the massacre was called, the Farhud, as his personal codename.[64]

Second, with help from Free French and Zionist volunteers—including a young Moshe Dayan, who lost an eye in the campaign—the British attacked Syria and Lebanon. Despite resistance from Dentz's much larger force and the German-backed Arab Legion, the British quickly gained control of the country by July 14.[65] Al-Husaini's soldiers fled through Turkey to German-held territory where they joined the Nazi army.

Third, the Soviets, now at war with Germany, and British seized Iran in a three-week operation beginning August 25. The Allies exiled the shah, who had flirted with Germany, and put on the throne his young son, who would rule until overthrown by the 1979 Islamist revolution. With the USSR governing the north and Britain the south, Iran's oil went to the Allies, not the Axis. Military supplies also flowed into the USSR via this back door. The Germans could only rationalize the defeat by claiming that occupation tied down enemy troops.[66]

Within weeks, the threat of a German takeover in the Middle East—seemingly inevitable a few weeks earlier—evaporated. The Arab east was in Allied hands. Still, as the duke of Wellington had remarked of his victory at Waterloo 130 years earlier, it was a close thing. Churchill had already written in his history of World War I that if von Falkenhayn hadn't attacked the srongest enemy at his strongest point, namely Verdun in 1916, but had turned against the softest spots of Germany's weakest foe in Europe and had marched through Egypt and Mesopotamia to India, he might have earned for the German eagle the credit for future changes among the Asian peoples. German diplomats like Fritz Grobba claimed the same in regard to World War II: enemies of Hitler concealed from him the same great opportunity represented by the British Empire's weakest spot in the Middle East.[67] At any rate, the failures in Iraq, Iran, and Syria did not disillusion the Germans and Italians regarding al-Husaini's importance or reliability.

Meanwhile, in Iran, the Allied occupiers rounded up pro-German Iraqi officers hiding there and sent them home to be executed or exiled to Rhodesia. Al-Husaini's own family, including his wife, five daughters, and seventeen-year-old son Salah ad-Din, were permitted to return to Jerusalem.[68] The surviving German agents and Arab allies fled to Turkey, where that neutral country's government interned some of them. The Abwehr subsidized those who weren't captured and in September 1941 organized a conference of Arab nationalist leaders there. Some pro-German Arabs remained in Istanbul to maintain contacts with underground movements in their home countries, collect intelligence, and await the day German troops arrived on their borders.

The grand mufti eluded capture in Tehran despite a £25,000 British reward offered for his capture. Foreign Secretary Anthony Eden called him the British Empire's number-one enemy in the Middle East. Al-Husaini immediately asked Berlin to grant him refuge in the Nazi capital.[69] The Abwehr hid him in Japan's embassy in Tehran since the British couldn't touch the property of that still-neutral German ally.[70] According to a U.S. intelligence report, al-Husaini was disguised as the Italian ambassador's footman and left with the rest of the embassy staff when Iran broke relations with Italy. Al-Husaini arrived in Istanbul on September 23, 1941,[71] and continued on a three-week journey to Berlin.[72] Along the way he reflected on his life and the big political questions facing Arabs and Muslims. Passing through Romania and Hungary, he thought about how these lands had once been, but were no longer, Muslim-ruled, a sign of his civilization's defeat and retreat. In Bulgaria, the food reminded him of the delicious shishkabab at the al-Hati Restaurant in Cairo. As he entered Italy, he recalled his World War I experiences, the battles of Ottoman Arab units under German command, and further back, the German-Arab alliance's start with the kaiser's 1898 trip to Jerusalem.[73]

Al-Husaini stopped off in Venice to visit Mussolini on November 4, 1941. The grand mufti asked Mussolini to urge Hitler to attack Egypt, then seize Palestine, make al-Husaini ruler, and liquidate the Jews there.[74] This was precisely what the Germans planned.

As al-Husaini neared Berlin his ambition grew steadily. Visiting the Vatican set his imagination soaring to imagine himself as ruler of all

Rom, den 28.April 1942.

Herr Reichsminister !

In unseren Besprechungen mit Ihnen haben wir
das Vertrauen des arabischen Volkes zu den Achsen-
mächten und ihren hohen Zielen zum Ausdruck gebracht
und die nationalen Ziele der zur Zeit unter englischer
Unterdrückung leidenden arabischen Länder des vorderen
Orients dargelegt. Wir haben die Bereitschaft des
arabischen Volkes zur Teilnahme am Kampf gegen die
gemeinsamen Feinde bis zum Endsieg erklärt.

Wir bitten Sie nun, dass die deutsche Regierung
ihre Bereitschaft erklären möge, den gegenwärtig unter
britischer Unterdrückung leidenden arabischen Ländern
in ihrem Kampf für die Befreiung jede denkbare Unter-
stützung zu gewähren, die Souveränität und die Unab-
hängigkeit der gegenwärtig unter englischer Unterdrückung leidenden arabischen Länder des nahen Orients
anzuerkennen und ihrer Vereinigung, wenn sie von den
Beteiligten gewünscht wird, sowie der Beseitigung
der jüdisch-nationalen Heimstätte in Palästina
zuzustimmen.

Es besteht Einverständnis darüber, dass der
Wortlaut und der Inhalt dieses Briefes unbedingt
geheimgehalten werden, bis im gegenseitigen Einver-
nehmen etwas anderes bestimmt wird.

Genehmigen Sie, Herr Reichsminister, die
Versicherung meiner ausgezeichnetsten Hochachtung !

Emin El Husseini

Reschid Ali El Gailani

An den Reichsminister
des Auswärtigen
Herrn Joachim von RIBBENTROP
          BERLIN

Figure 16. Letter of April 28, 1942 from Grand Mufti Amin al-Husaini and Iraqi
ex-premier Rashid Ali al-Kailani to Foreign Minister Joachim von Ribbentrop
(and his Italian counterpart Count Gian Galeazzo Ciano). They stress that "the
Arab people are ready to fight the common enemies until the final victory," and
ask the Axis to support the Arab struggle against British oppression, Arab unification, and the abolition of the Jewish national home in Palestine. By May 14 the
two Axis powers had agreed to these requests, thereby making the letter into a
pact to liquidate Jews in the Middle East. The four signatories agreed to keep this
text top secret and still hoped to gain access to Iraq, Iran and the Middle East via
the Caucasus.

Muslims. "How mighty is the Catholic bloc of twenty-six states," al-Husaini thought, dreaming about restoring the caliphate.[75] By the time he came to the German capital, al-Husaini believed he would wield equivalent power over the Muslims and probably thought of himself as the next caliph.

Al-Kailani, too, was on the way to Germany from his refuge in Turkey. He had already been put on Germany's payroll at the rate of fifty-five hundred Turkish pounds a month. The Abwehr considered shipping him to Bulgaria in a packing case left in the consulate's basement from prewar German archaeological expeditions, but then switched to another plan. When a seven-member German press delegation arrived in Turkey, the Germans informed their hosts that an eighth man, Herr Wackernagel, had come with the delegation to Istanbul but was too ill to accompany the others on their tour. The night before the group was to go home, al-Kailani arrived at the German consulate after sneaking away from a dental appointment. A German doctor wrapped him in bandages like a mumps patient, and the next morning al-Kailani was taken to the airport as Wackernagel. The acuity of the Turkish delegation on hand to say farewell was dimmed by hangovers from the previous evening's party. They merely wished the sick man a quick recovery. Certain that al-Kailani would be useful in the future, Grobba urged von Ribbentrop and Hitler to receive him personally.[76]

Back in Iran, about two hundred reliable German residents and agents, led by the intelligence agent Erwin Ettel, waged a rearguard action. The Allies overrated their potential for carrying on subversion there, though even al-Husaini—who often exaggerated—had concluded that the German fifth column in Iran was unimpressive.[77] The British-Soviet forces quickly quashed this underground, and Ettel had to leave on September 17.[78] Moving to Turkey, he continued to direct German operations in Iran through radio broadcasts and infiltrated Iranian agents. Berlin hoped to keep up such operations until a German army advancing from the USSR might persuade Iranian officers to join up with Hitler's imminent victory by rebelling.[79]

Captain Bernhardt Schulze-Holthus, Abwehr chief in Tabriz, went underground, protected by pro-German Iranian nationalists. At one time, he hid in a brothel. One cold night he went out disguised as a mullah, with a henna-dyed beard, dark silk trousers, and Persian clothes, walking along Shapur Street north to the main road and the city's outskirts for a meeting with his chief agent. The man told Schulze-Holthus that one of the shah's top generals, Fazlollah Zahedi, promised, "A large part of Iran's army is ready to rise at a signal from us." But there was no way to communicate this news to Berlin. Schulze-Holthus's wife, the only German available, was sent on the long, dangerous journey across the mountains by donkey and finally reached Istanbul, where she reported to the Abwehr office there. Zahedi, though, did not keep his promise. To avoid capture, Schulze-Holthus had to seek refuge with rebellious tribesman, and in July 1942, four more agents parachuted in to join him. They wore tribal clothes, built landing strips to receive supplies, and told Iranians they were fellow Aryans who wanted to help them rule their own country. Their main mission, never fulfilled, was to destroy oil installations so vital for the Allied war effort.[80]

The British, fearing Schulze-Holthus might sabotage the railroad carrying military supplies from Persian Gulf ports to the Soviet Union, chased him for several months until the tribesmen tired of the game and sold him to them.[81] Thus, the British and Soviets controlled Iran, its oil, and the transport routes to the USSR without German interference. On January 29, 1943, Iran concluded an alliance with the British and Soviets; on September 9 the shah declared war on Germany.

Although Hitler had missed his 1941 chance in the Middle East he would get a second chance in 1942. Since the indirect method of backing Arab and Iranian forces had failed, the 1942 German strategy was to use Arabs and Muslims as auxiliaries awaiting the German armies' advance through the USSR and North Africa. Hitler explained to al-Husaini and al-Kailani several times between November 1941 and July 1942 this plan of enclosing the region between those two pincers.[82]

Rather than fomenting insurrections, al-Husaini's task shifted to providing the Axis with intelligence and propaganda while helping to recruit and train Muslim soldiers for Germany's army.[83] Al-Husaini and al-Kailani were still to be made rulers of their respective domains but only after German armies captured them. Acknowledging his value, the Italians followed Hitler's example of a year earlier by recognizing al-Husaini as sole leader of all Arabs.[84]

In preparation, the Germans printed currency and manufactured uniforms for the projected Iraqi regime.[85] Von Ribbentrop called the projected turning point the "Tiflis moment," named after the Georgian capital. When Rommel's army crossed the Suez Canal and simultaneously German troops reached Tiflis as they advanced through the

Soviet Caucasus, the two Arab leaders plus the Indian nationalist Bose would rush to Tiflis, set up governments in exile there, and order revolts.[86] As Rommel advanced into Egypt in 1942, al-Husaini cabled "the charming leader" Hitler that the big battle would come soon and the Arab people would prove themselves a worthy ally. If that failed, Grobba had warned, the British might flood all Arab lands with millions of Jewish immigrants who would enslave them forever.[87]

How, then, could al-Husaini bring German victory? On the North African front he was relatively weak, but he did have some useful agents. Chief among them was the Moroccan Taqi ad-Din al-Hilali.[88] Born in Casablanca, al-Hilali became an Islamist while studying in Cairo and living in Saudi Arabia. After six years in India and Iraq, the well-traveled al-Hilali was hired to teach Arabic at Bonn University in 1936.[89] Obtaining his doctorate at Berlin University in 1941, the forty-five-year-old al-Hilali became head of the culture section of al-Husaini's Central Islam Institute and a Radio Berlin broadcaster. In 1942, al-Husaini sent him home to organize covert operations. One of al-Hilali's ideas was to persuade Vichy France to release some North African Arab nationalists if they agreed to join the Axis. The French did so, one of those let go being Tunisia's future president, al-Habib Burqiba, though he never actually helped the Germans.[90] Those willing to collaborate were sent for training at the German commando base at Nizza, Italy.[91]

Al-Husaini placed much hope in another prisoner, Muhammad Abd al-Karim al-Khattabi, an old Algerian rebel and German collaborator in World War I who the French had exiled to the Indian Ocean island of Réunion. But Germany's friends, Vichy France and Spain, opposed releasing a man so dedicated to overthrowing their colonial rule in Morocco.[92] U.S. intelligence considered trying to recruit Abd al-Karim and another veteran German collaborator, Libyan leader Idris as-Sanusi, but rejected the idea, fearing that either an American Islamist strategy might trigger future Christian-Muslim war or these two men would desert to the Germans.[93]

Regarding political strategy, al-Husaini suggested Germany recognize Algeria, Morocco, and Tunisia as a Western Arab Union of States that would become part of the Axis. He predicted this new country would furnish 2.5 million Arab soldiers to fight alongside Germany. Nazi Party leaders were enthusiastic, but the army and Foreign Ministry were less so—Hitler had already double-crossed the Arabs by promising North Africa to Mussolini—so nothing was done.[94]

In addition to his political efforts, the grand mufti played an important role in shaping German propaganda directed at North Africa. The best way to win over Muslims there and elsewhere, al-Husaini advised, was to combine promises for independence and wiping out the Jews with large measures of flattery. He used these themes in his own broadcasts on Radio Berlin and the Voice of the Free Arabs station in Rome. The latter was guided by two of his aides, Dhu al-Kuffar Abd al-Latif and Salim al-Husaini, a nephew, and operated by fifteen Arab students.[95]

The single best way to win Arabs' hearts, al-Husaini advised, was to preach hatred of the Jews, or in his words, "The Jewish attack and the plagues they carry." Al-Husaini recommended telling Arabs that President Franklin Roosevelt was a Jew and a slave to Jewish masters. In contrast, the Germans should highlight Hitler's statements dealing with his own religious faith, the certainty of victory, and evil British treatment of the Arabs.[96] The Germans followed his advice. One theme was Islamic-oriented, quoting Muhammad, Islam's founder, to justify Arabs fighting Judeo-Anglo-Bolshevist "infidels" enslaving Muslims. The other focused directly on anti-Jewish propaganda, calling Jews "evil parasites."[97] There was a problem, though, in adapting Nazi anti-Semitic propaganda for Arab audiences. Since unflattering physical descriptions of Jews, including portraying them as having large noses, could also apply to Arabs all of this material had to be dropped.[98]

Anti-Jewish hatred would not be confined merely to words. By May 14, 1942, Germany and Italy had also both formally agreed to al-Husaini's request to liquidate the Jews in Palestine as soon as possible. But while the Germans couldn't murder Jews in areas they didn't possess, al-Husaini repeatedly pressed for quick action in those parts of North Africa they did control.[99] The chance might be short-lived: once America entered the war in December 1941, German military intelligence expected an Allied landing on Morocco's Atlantic coast.[100]

Vichy France and Italy, Germany's allies who ruled North Africa, had already followed Berlin's lead by instituting anti-Semitic regulations. The Italian government ordered all Jews in Libya under age forty-five to be imprisoned. Of 2,500 internees, 562 died in forced labor camps.[101] Jewish properties were systematically plundered by Axis troops, European administrators, and local Arabs.[102] In October 1940, the Vichy government revoked Algerian Jews' citizenship rights.

The Arab rulers in Morocco and Tunisia confirmed discriminatory anti-Jewish laws, further tightened in June 1941.[103]

Anticipating the conquest of Egypt, the thirty-six-year-old Walther Rauff, a naval officer who had helped develop mobile gas vans, went to see Rommel in June 1942, to ask his help in murdering all of Cairo's Jews by such measures.[104] Rommel, a traditional military officer disgusted by Nazi behavior, threw Rauff out.[105] But Rauff didn't need Rommel's permission to operate behind German lines. He was named head of the Gestapo in Tunis and brought in one hundred Arab soldiers,[106] supplemented by local Tunisians, to carry out genocide there.[107] He hoped to build a European-style concentration camp[108] but began by arrests, property confiscations, stealing valuables, and creating thirty forced labor camps.[109]

Rauff managed to kill 2,500 Tunisian Jews and sent 350 French, Arab, and Jewish oppositionists to concentration camps in Europe.[110] Altogether, about 5,000 Jews in French-ruled Morocco, Tunisia, and Libya were murdered.[111] When Rauff was reassigned to Italy in May 1943—where he would kill many Italian partisans and civilians—he received the German Silver Cross medal for his work in Tunisia.[112] After the war, he escaped prosecution and went to work for Syrian intelligence.

Al-Husaini's other priority was getting troops into the field, both to help the Germans and to strengthen his claim to become the Arabs' ruler. He wrote von Ribbentrop on July 26 asking that Arab and especially Palestinian Arab commandos be sent to North Africa.[113] German officials listed the pros and cons of such a step. On the negative side, Arab troops would probably get out of control, loot French settlers, and stage unauthorized pogroms against Jews.[114] On the other hand, they could help win over local people and make them willing collaborators with the Nazis.[115] In the end, German intelligence supported the idea and Hitler approved.[116] Al-Husaini was authorized to establish his own headquarters in North Africa to promote subversion, hunt down anti-German forces, and gather intelligence.[117]

The agreement established the Arab Freedom Corps as the nucleus of new armies for countries ruled by al-Husaini and his colleagues once Germany's army conquered them.[118] Al-Husaini was appointed commander in chief of Arab military forces.[119] In keeping with Hitler's commitments to Mussolini, however, the actual commander was the Italian naval intelligence officer who headed that country's own Arab

Legion.[120] Hitler also asked al-Kailani to raise Arab troops though the Iraqi failed completely at that task.[121] Within its first two months of operation in North Africa, al-Husaini's Freedom Corps recruited two thousand Arabs for separate "Tunisia," "Algeria," and "Morocco" units. Some fought at the front but most were used in rear areas for building fortifications.[122]

Meanwhile, the German army advanced ever closer to Cairo, where Axis supporters included the king and such key politicians as sometime prime minister Ali Mahir, Salih Harb, who had defected to the Germans during the first world war, and Abd ar-Rahman Azzam, a pro-jihad Ottoman officer who now worked closely with al-Husaini.[123] Even Egypt's army commander al-Misri sought German victory. Like al-Husaini, he had defected from the Ottomans to the British and had become a senior officer in the British-sponsored Arab revolt. Such junior officers as as-Sadat, the air force officer Salih Ibrahim, and Abd an-Nasir were also Nazi sympathizers. This trio would later furnish Egypt with two presidents and two of its vice presidents between 1955 and 1981.[124]

"Great Britain stood alone," as-Sadat later wrote. "Her weakness in the Middle East was apparent to everyone," and her military position in the war "had become untenable."[125] On February 3, 1942, as Rommel's army advanced into Egypt, five thousand students took a petition to King Faruq, demanding that three top pro-Nazi politicians form a new government, an idea that the king favored. Otherwise, they threatened a general strike and sabotage. The crowd shouted, "We are all Axis soldiers! Forward, Rommel! Down with Churchill!"[126] Knowing that such a government would deliver Egypt to the Germans, the British surrounded the Abdin Palace with tanks and threatened to unseat Faruq unless he installed a moderate Wafd Party government.[127] The king backed down and complied. The tide had turned. The Wafd took office, German agents were rounded up, and al-Misri was thrown into prison. While angering Egyptian nationalist sentiment, this British near-coup held Egypt politically for the Allies.[128]

But if the Germans actually captured Egypt the issue would be decided otherwise. On June 24, Rommel's tanks crossed the Libya-Egypt border. The next day, al-Husaini's Voice of the Free Arabs told Egyptians to make lists of the home addresses and workplaces of every Jew in Cairo so they could be annihilated at the earliest opportunity. The broadcast promised that the Axis was about to liberate Egypt.[129] Three days later, al-Husaini said he would start an uprising in Egypt soon and sent sabotage teams into Egypt to prepare.[130]

The Germans kept in touch with the king and other supporters through Ettel and Egypt's consul Amin Zaki Bey in Istanbul; the king's uncle, Husain Said, and his aide, Zu al-Fiqar; and Prince Mansur Daud. The Egyptians also reported through al-Husaini, who briefed von Ribbentrop on developments.[131] Meanwhile, pro-German elements in Egypt's army were making their move to link up with the German advance. They sent an envoy to Rommel promising to recruit an army of Egyptians to join him[132] and provide intelligence, including photos of British defensive positions.[133]

The Germans dispatched Abwehr agent Hans Eppler, alias Husain Jaffar, as liaison with the sympathetic Egyptian officers. After a hard ride through the Libyan Desert to the Nile in May, he arrived in Cairo where he contacted as-Sadat and began sending information to Rommel. But the British captured Eppler and many of his contacts on July 23, precisely ten years to the day before as-Sadat and other former collaborators would take over the country.[134]

Secretly and simultaneously, Egypt's king thanked the Axis and al-Husaini for pledging to help Egypt and promised his country would never join the war against Germany. At the end of July, Hitler told Faruq he feared the British might assassinate him, urging the king to flee to Rommel's forces for protection. Faruq, unwilling to put himself in Germany's hands, replied that if necessary he would hide in Egypt until Rommel arrived. But to show support for the Axis cause, the king offered to send two planes to German-held territory with maps showing British troop dispositions. The Germans were to signal readiness to receive these emissaries by broadcasting certain *suras* of al-Qur'an over a three-day period. Mustafa al-Wakil, one of al-Husaini's secretaries and a leader of the Nazi-imitating Young Egypt Party, chose two *suras*: *al-Ikhlas* (Devotion), and *al-Falaq* (Dawn), and Radio Berlin broadcast them.[135]

The two pilots set off. One of them, Ahmad Sayyid Husain, became lost and was shot down by the British. The other, Muhammad Radwan, survived an antiaircraft attack by the British and then another by the Germans before they realized that he was defecting to their side. Unknowingly, Radwan landed in the midst of a minefield and, not knowing his peril, walked straight through it unharmed as astonished

Germans yelled at him to stop. Radwan told his interrogators that he had come from the pro-German underground, hoped to meet Hitler, and was ready to fight for the Nazis on the Soviet front. He also supplied copies of British military plans. Quickly sent on to Berlin, Radwan gave interviews to newspapers and recorded broadcasts for Radio Berlin urging Egyptian soldiers to desert and join the Nazi side.[136]

In Cairo, Faruq patiently waited, expecting, like many Egyptians, the German army's imminent arrival.[137] On July 3, Berlin and Rome had officially declared they were invading Egypt "To liberate the Middle East from the British yoke" and give "Egypt to the Egyptians." Al-Husaini and al-Kailani made radio appeals predicting a glorious Axis victory over the British, Jews, and Communists.[138] The loss of Egypt, they declared, would be the British Empire's end.[139] But that very day, Rommel's offensive stalled at al-Alamain, just three hours from Alexandria. Months of stalemate followed as the British gradually strangled Rommel's supply lines across the Mediterranean.[140]

At the time, of course, neither the Germans nor al-Husaini's supporters knew Rommel would advance no further. On the evening of July 7, the Voice of the Free Arabs broadcast to the Arab world a call to "Kill the Jews before they kill you!" It portrayed this proposed massacre as self-defense, claiming the British had distributed weapons to Armenians, Greeks, Jews, and other minorities in Egypt telling them to kill Muslims—including women and children—and loot their property. The announcer shouted into the microphone:

> Kill the Jews who took your valuables. Arabs of Syria, Iraq and Palestine, what are you waiting for? . . . According to Islam it is a duty to defend your lives. This can only be fulfilled by the liquidation of the Jews. This is your best chance to get rid of this dirty race. Kill the Jews! Set their possessions on fire! Demolish their shops! Liquidate those evil helpers of British imperialism! Your only hope for rescue is to annihilate the Jews before they do this to you.[141]

On the evening of July 17, ten days after his call to kill the Jews of the Middle East, al-Husaini met Canaris at the admiral's Berlin apartment. Al-Husaini offered to deploy all the Arabs at his and al-Kailani's disposal in the Middle East for acts of sabotage and subversion under the Abwehr's auspices.[142] After Canaris consulted with his Italian counterpart, Cesare Amé, they accepted that project, to be carried out once Germany's army broke through into the Nile Valley.[143]

Everything was thus in place for a triumphant German march through the Middle East and the murder of all Jews there. The only missing element was Rommel's victory and a breakthrough by German armies deep inside the USSR across the Middle East's northern frontier. But whereas in September it seemed as if Rommel would win, he was soundly defeated at al-Alamain on October 19. On November 8, furthermore, the U.S. army landed in Morocco and Algeria. Vichy French forces there surrendered.

According to Oscar Reile, a former Nazi intelligence officer close to Canaris, al-Husaini got information about plans for an Allied invasion of North Africa from Morocco's Sultan Muhammad V in October 1942 and passed it on to the Abwehr, but Hitler didn't heed his warning. If the story is true, this might have been al-Husaini's finest moment as an intelligence source for the Germans, but this claim is unconfirmed. At any rate, Hitler expected an Allied attack in Spain instead and Canaris was unable to convince him otherwise.[144]

Despite al-Husaini's propaganda and passionate broadcasts, no Arab revolt materialized either in Egypt or North Africa. The worse Rommel did at the front, the less eager were Arabs to join the Axis cause.[145] For example, Tunisia's ruler, Bey al-Munsif, suddenly decided that he did not want to be Germany's ally, though a few months earlier he had been very friendly to the Nazis. In December 1942, realizing time was running out, al-Husaini made one final attempt to mobilize North African Arabs. He offered to go to Tunis along with Canaris to launch a mighty insurgency through his contacts with the nationalist Islah Party.[146] But Hitler decided against the idea. Al-Husaini would have to await a better opportunity. In Morocco, the Germans could only try with little success to subvert the Allied presence through anti-Semitic propaganda and agents trying to instigate demonstrations, looting, and anti-Jewish pogroms.[147]

The start of 1943 brought no improvement in North Africa for Hitler and al-Husaini. Rommel steadily retreated. Hitler ordered him back to Germany in March, and two months later, on May 13, 1942, all the Axis forces in North Africa surrendered. A quarter-million soldiers became prisoners of war. It was estimated that six thousand men took refuge in Egypt. Faruq let them stay.[148]

Only the Russian front was left to give the Germans and their Arab allies hope that they might return triumphant to the Middle East.

8   Germany's Muslim Army

German strategy in the Middle East had failed twice. Depending on al-Husaini and his radical Arab faction of nationalist and Islamist groups to stage a revolt in Iraq, Syria, and Palestine had fizzled, with the British left in control of all these countries. Equally, the attempt to march through North Africa, capture Cairo, and advance into Palestine, spreading genocide along the way, had been defeated on the battlefield. For the fulfillment of Hitler's and al-Husaini's hopes only the Soviet front was left.

Ironically, the decision to attack the USSR and its timing, in June 1941, had ruined the Nazis' best chance of conquering the Middle East. Hitler's overconfidence about quickly defeating the Soviets had made him believe he could transfer his forces into the Middle East by year's end. At first, though, the Germans advanced so quickly that in September 1941 von Ribbentrop told von Papen that the Soviet army was finished and once this battle was won, Berlin would conquer England and perhaps then America.[1]

The German plan, officially adopted by the military high command six days after the invasion of the USSR, saw that country as the Middle East's back door.[2] If Germany's armies could advance through North Africa and capture Egypt while simultaneously marching through Russia and driving south through the Caucasus, Turkey, and Iran to India, the Middle East would fall into its lap. The two victorious armies would meet in Syria or Palestine. Not everyone in the German hierarchy liked the idea. Von Ribbentrop and navy commander Admiral Erich Raeder wanted to make the priority driving the British from the Middle East before turning to attack the Soviets.[3] They proposed seizing Iraq and the Arab east, then Iran, and next marching through the Persian Gulf and Afghanistan to India.[4] But once Hitler decided, debate was at an end.

Now, however, the situation had changed due to the defeat in Iraq and that of German forces in North Africa. Germany's Muslim allies were still important, but now, instead of using Muslim soldiers in the Middle East, Germany needed Muslim soldiers to fight for the Axis in the USSR and the Balkans. This required recruiting Muslims from those areas and even sending Arab volunteers there.

The Germans organized their own Arab units in early 1941 with General Felmy in command. His Special Command F (for Felmy) was located at Cape Sounion in Greece, an hour's drive from Athens. That July, training was moved to Doeberitz near Brandenburg. It prepared Arabs for small, fast-moving commando units that could sabotage bridges, railroads, and oil wells behind Allied lines while blending in with the local population. Some instructors were Arabic-speaking Palestinian-Germans. On August 24 the first thirty troops were sworn into the German army, wearing a unit patch that said "Free Arabia." After the Allies seized Syria, Arabs from the volunteer forces raised by the Germans there also joined the unit, along with—in early 1942—103 Arab prisoners-of-war who changed sides.[5]

In September 1942, at the peak of the German advance in North Africa and the USSR, al-Husaini promised to raise a one-hundred-thousand-man Muslim force in Iraq and North Africa. He would largely redeem that pledge, except that the Muslims he ultimately recruited for Germany were not Arabs but either Turkic peoples from the Soviet Caucasus or Bosnians and Albanians from the Balkans.[6]

The grand mufti's aide and nephew, Musa al-Husaini, and his Syrian-born secretary Firhan Jandali were sent to Paris to recruit North African Muslims who had been in France's army.[7] There were also recruiting operations opened in Istanbul and Sofia.[8] Still, at the moment that al-Husaini spoke of raising one hundred thousand soldiers, the Arab Freedom Corps comprised only 243 of them: 24 Iraqis, 112 Syrians and Palestinians, and 107 North Africans.[9] Al-Husaini told these men they would be sent to the Middle East. But the Germany army, not himself, was in command and ordered them to the Caucasus, a largely Muslim area but far from their homes. Al-Husaini tried but failed to overturn this decision. In the end, he could only send a liaison officer to the men's base in Stalino as a symbol of his leadership.[10]

The real material support for the German war effort would take place in the German-captured Muslim areas in the USSR. Rosenberg, the Cabinet minister with whom al-Husaini had the best relations, was in charge of ruling these areas, and the Germans made a concerted effort to turn the Muslims there into allies.[11] Nazi broadcasts directed at the Arab world boasted with some truth about how German forces treated these Muslims better than the Soviets had done.[12] Soldiers were told to win trust and sympathy by reopening mosques closed by the Soviet regime, respecting property, safeguarding the honor of women, and paying for any goods taken. If harsh measures were required their motives must be explained to local Muslims.[13]

An example of the success of Germany's Soviet Muslim policy in the Caucasus came in October 1942 when German troops hosted Muslims in the town of Kislovodsk to celebrate an Islamic festival held there for the first time in a quarter-century. With drums and music, prayers in Arabic were said to Allah and for Hitler's victory. Muslim residents treated the elated German soldiers like heroes. The town's two religious leaders, Mullah Ramazan and Qadi Ibrahim, thanked them for the liberation from the Bolsheviks. Muslim peasants declared the hated collective farm system abolished and a 107-year-old man told the crowd that the German troops' arrival had been the best day of his life. The German commander, General Ernst Köstring, thanked the people for their support in the "joint battle." Cheering Muslims lifted him onto their shoulders and tossed him into the air in celebration. As a token of gratitude, they donated a large number of sheep and cattle.[14] Many or most Soviet Muslims preferred the Germans to their Russian masters, as did a dozen Christian peoples, ranging from Armenians to Ukrainians, who also collaborated.[15]

To rule, administer, and exploit these lands, Rosenberg assembled a team of experts. One was Gerhard von Mende, a thirty-seven-year-old German born in the Baltic city of Riga. His father had been killed by the Bolsheviks during the revolution, and von Mende had gone to Germany where he had studied Turkic languages and worked at Berlin's

Economics College. The day before Germany invaded the USSR, on
June 21, 1941, von Mende was hired by the Foreign Ministry. He was
fully briefed on the planned genocide of Jews at the March 6, 1942
follow-up meeting of the Wannsee Conference, since he would help
implement that policy in the Caucasus.[16] Von Mende worked for Otto
Bräutigam in the Department of Alien Peoples. The forty-six-year-old
Bräutigam, who had been German consul in four Soviet cities, was
brought home to prepare for the invasion. He produced a leaflet telling
Turkic peoples that the Germans were coming as liberators from the
Bolsheviks.[17]

At first, though, the Germans viewed Soviet Muslim peoples as inferior races whose support was not needed.[18] During the invasion's early
days, German forces killed many Muslims because they mistook them
for Jews. As a high-ranking SS official told a colleague, his organization hadn't known that Muslims were also circumcised.[19] But as they
swiftly advanced into the Soviet Union, the Germans understood that
many Muslims were ready to collaborate given their grievances against
Communist mistreatment and ethnic Russian domination. One German official wrote of how he witnessed in October 1941 Soviet Muslims, whom he described as endless lines of "brown masses," fleeing to
the German side. By 1942 the Germans were seeking to recruit tens of
thousands of Soviet Turks for their army.[20]

Alim Idris was a leading figure in this effort. Born in Kazakhstan in
1887, he studied Islam and philosophy in Bukhara and Istanbul for a
decade. In the Ottoman capital he also worked with the Young Turk
magazine *Türk Yurdu*, advocating a Pan-Turkish state incorporating
those living under tsarist rule. During World War I, Idris was an imam
for prisoners of war and editor of the Tatar-language edition of *al-
Jihad* magazine when von Oppenheim hired him to recruit Russian
Muslim prisoners. After the war, he stayed in Berlin to build networks
and edit publications for anti-Communist Muslims in the USSR. The
Nazis hired Idris for translation, propaganda, and radio work where he
incited hatred against the "Judeo-Bolshevists" who ruled his people.[21]
Shortly after the invasion, Idris suggested that Berlin create a German-
backed, independent Turkestan.[22]

Von Papen proposed recruiting Soviet Turks in July 1941 and para-
chuting them back to their homelands behind Soviet lines.[23] His proposal was accepted, and Operation Zeppelin, as it was called, recruited

about sixteen hundred Uzbeks, Tadjiks, Kirgiz, Tatars, Turks, Georgians, Azerbaijanis, Chechens, and Kazakhs as fifth columnists.[24] Aside from sabotaging railroads, oil facilities at Ufa, and inciting Islamist uprisings their longer-term task was to prepare bases for larger commando operations in the Soviet hinterland. Another such plan, codenamed Mammut, was to do the same thing in Iraq, possibly with cooperation from the Kurdish leader Mahmud Barzani. In June 1943, a group led by Gottfried Müller set out from the Crimea to land near Mosul, but the British discovered the plan and arrested those involved.[25]

Another German goal was to win over Turkey as an ally or at least gain its cooperation in using its territory to launch covert operations. To further this effort, von Papen encouraged Turkish leaders to visit Berlin. One of the first was ex-general Nuri Killigil, brother of Germany's World War I Ottoman partner, Enver. In September 1941 Killigil offered to organize an anti-Soviet, Pan-Turkish uprising in the Caucasus, but the Germans, uncertain of his loyalties, demurred.[26]

Preferring to make deals with Turkey's military, von Papen got Hitler to invite a delegation to visit Germany's armies in October 1941. It was led by two generals who had fought alongside the Germans in World War I, Ali Fuat Erden and Hüsnü Erkilet. They visited prisoner of war camps, the front line, and newly captured Sevastopol (just across the Black Sea from Turkey). They were warmly received by German officers who had been their comrades two decades earlier. "Everywhere we went," they recounted, "we were greeted with feelings of affection mixed with respect and admiration, which Germans all feel for the Turkish nation." They were impressed by a German army "which has won victory upon victory for three years."[27] The Germans promised Turkey military equipment to compete with U.S. and British aid. At the end of the generals' trip, Hitler hosted them on October 28 at his headquarters near Rastenburg. They urged him to use Muslim prisoners for a jihad against the "godless Soviet regime," and Hitler formally accepted the plan on November 15, 1941.

But dealing with Soviet Muslims also posed a delicate problem for Germany. They might prove useful allies but Hitler considered them racially inferior, preferring to expel all Turkic Muslims from the Crimea and resettle it with Germans.[28] There was also a political problem. Hitler stressed that if Soviet Muslims helped destroy the Communist regime they would make political demands after the war, tying his hands regarding the conquered territory's future. Such recruits did ask some difficult questions, particularly whether the Caucasus would be a German colony and whether Muslims could participate in governing it.[29]

Hitler suggested instead that volunteers become workers, freeing Germans to fight. A good worker in a factory, he explained, was better than an unreliable soldier in battle.[30] But Hitler changed his mind under the pressure of war and mounting German casualties. He decided that "pure Turkic Muslims" had been good soldiers in their nineteenth-century battles against Russians and could be so again in his army.[31] The search for candidates began in the prisoner of war camps, with prospects being sent to Camp Wustrau near Berlin[32] were they were organized by ethnic group.[33] In part of the camp at Luckenwalde, a half-hour south of Berlin, the best recruits were gathered for training by German intelligence.[34] The resulting force, the East Turk Unit, was assigned to rear areas in the USSR.

Once having gone down this road, Hitler became enthusiastic. On December 22 he agreed to create an Indian Legion; an Arab Legion was to come next, but the Italians objected since they had their own unit of that name.[35] So Berlin and al-Husaini instead called it the German-Arab Training Group, later the Arab Freedom Corps, the Arab Brigade, and finally the Islamic Division.[36] With al-Husaini's help, starting in February 1942, six East Turk Units were formed from Muslim and Christian ethnic minorities: the Turkestan, North Caucasus, Azerbaijan, Georgia, Volga Tatar, and Armenian units, each with its own uniform and national insignia. Four of them were made up of Muslims.

This was no marginal effort. By the end of 1942, such units had a total strength of fifty-three thousand men, equal to four German divisions. The list of Muslim units fighting for the Germans included the 162nd Turcoman Division (incorporating the Volga Tatar Legion), the 450th Infantry Battalion (largely Azeri), the Azerbaijani Legion, the Caucasian Muslim Legion (mainly Chechens, Daghestanis, and Ingushes), and the 34th Turkestan Battalion (Uzbeks, Kazakhs, and Turcomans). They fought in the Soviet Union, Italy, and France but never in the Middle East. Al-Husaini established an institute in Dresden to train Muslim chaplains for these units. Graduates were commissioned as Waffen SS captains. Idris worked closely with him and taught courses there.[37]

In May 1942, Bräutigam became the official responsible for governing the Caucasus and nearby regions. The Azerbaijan, Caucasus,

Figure 17. Bosnian Muslim soldiers of the Handžar SS Division reading al-Husaini's "Appeal to All Muslims of the World" of 1937, in which he claimed that the holy texts, al-Qur'an and the hadith, showed that the Jews were Islam's foremost foes, and called on Muslims to fight for their religion and never stop until all Muslim lands were Jew-free: "Palestine, an Arab land, shall remain for ever Arab." The Nazis distributed the appeal to their Muslim troops in the Middle East, Soviet Asia, and the Balkans.

Crimca Tatar, Volga Tatar, and Turkestan departments were all run by people from these areas, such as the Caucasus German Walter Zeitler or the Crimea German Boris Müller. These departments established commissions of former Soviet soldiers that went into prisoner of war camps to recruit for the German occupation government and army.[38] The ministry's long-term plan was to develop German-led governments for new German provinces, including the Caucasus and Turkestan, but not independent states.[39]

On April 5, 1942, Hitler ordered a summer offensive to crush the remaining Soviet forces, reach the Caucasian oil-producing region, and open the way through the mountains into the Middle East.[40] In August, as his troops raised their swastika flag on Mount Elbrus in the borderland between Europe and Asia,[41] Rosenberg led a delegation on a two-week trip to Turkey to investigate how the Middle East and India should be invaded.[42] The result was a plan to establish Iraqi, Palestinian-Jordanian, Iranian, and Indian governments in exile.[43]

Felmy's small Arab military command, formally part of the Abwehr rather than the regular army,[44] would quickly expand to become the German Middle Eastern Formation (Deutsches Orientkorps) consisting of six thousand men, including eight hundred Arabs, and 1,640 vehicles. Al-Husaini's Arab unit, based in the Ukrainian town of Stalino, was to advance through Tbilisi into Iran and then Iraq.[45] Canaris and al-Husaini met monthly to coordinate planning.[46] The Germans as-

Figure 18. Amin al-Husaini inspects a parade of Bosnian SS Handžar troops in Silesia, which he had helped recruit, in November 1943. The twenty-thousand-man Handžar Division became known for atrocities against Jews and partisans in the Balkans and France.

sured al-Husaini and al-Kailani that once Iraq was taken they would cooperate in wiping out the Jews there and everywhere else their armies reached.[47]

Aside from Soviet Muslims, al-Husaini also recruited their Balkan counterparts in Albania and Bosnia. In his role with these Balkan Muslims, as with the Soviet Turkic ones, al-Husaini had moved far beyond being only a Palestine Arab, Arab in general, or even an Islamist leader to project himself as head of all Muslims.[48] His work in Albania yielded the 21st SS Waffen Mountain Division, or Handžar Division, so named after a type of scimitar wielded by Turks in the Balkans. During 1942, al-Husaini twice met with Bosnian Muslims in Rome to discuss recruiting.[49] He predicted to the German government that this group could yield up to twenty thousand volunteers.[50]

On March 14, 1943, al-Husaini traveled from Berlin to Zagreb, Croatia's capital. There, on April 1, he met the head of the pro-Nazi Croatian government, Ante Pavelić, leader of the Ustaša fascist organization. Pavelić, a Christian, welcomed al-Husaini's help to ensure Muslims' loyalty to his pro-German regime.[51]

Al-Husaini was there to recruit Muslims into a new Bosnian SS division and German-controlled police units which, he told them, would lead to a Bosnian Islamist state. His effort succeeded. The Germans in his entourage wrote of the great impression he made on Muslim audiences that saw him as a descendant of Muhammad and the liberating Muslim hero of their era.[52] The result was an impressive twelve thousand volunteers. Al-Husaini told them in his speeches that being in SS units meant they were "better" than ordinary soldiers.[53]

When al-Husaini spoke on April 9 at the Begova Mosque in Sarajevo, a beautiful building dating from 1531, he was protected by two dozen security men because of a rumored assassination plot. But the audience was completely on his side. Many wept with joy at his eloquence.[54] Al-Husaini told listeners they had lost their way but returning to Islam was the compass guiding them to success. He spoke of how the Axis would help them realize their dreams. When a local delegation asked for ten thousand marks a month for *Osvit* (Daybreak), the only Muslim weekly in Croatia, al-Husaini quickly paid them from his German-supplied budget.

On his way back to Berlin, al-Husaini stopped in Vienna where the governor, former Nazi youth leader Baldur von Schirach, had deported 185,000 Jews to the death camps, calling this "a contribution to European culture." Von Schirach gave al-Husaini tickets for the musical *Troubadour*.[55]

Returning to Berlin on April 15, al-Husaini reported on the trip to SS General Gottlob Berger, the official responsible for recruiting non-German volunteers. Berger had already read glowing reports from SS commander Karl-Gustav Sauberzweig, who had accompanied al-Husaini and assured Berger that the grand mufti had stuck to the agreed script.[56] Berger became an admirer of al-Husaini. The forty-seven-year-old Berger had been wounded in World War I and in 1922 was one of the first to join the Nazi Party. Berger told Hitler that al-Husaini had, exceeding all expectations, "rendered us an extraordinary political and military service."[57] On April 19, Hitler received Berger personally to thank him. Within a month, Hitler ordered that al-Husaini be helped to prepare the force and train its imams.

While al-Husaini was championed by Himmler, Berger, Goebbels (who praised his "great work" to Hitler), and the Foreign Ministry generally, some were not so captivated.[58] These officials noted that during World War I al-Husaini had broken his Ottoman officer's oath, changed sides, and fought against the caliph.[59] They feared he would gain too much power, or that a Muslim SS division might become a pan-Islamist force and ally itself with the British or Japanese. Moreover, if war broke out between the Axis powers and Turkey a Bosnian SS division might prove loyal to its Turkic identity.[60]

These warnings were ignored. The grand mufti had the support of all the truly important leaders including Hitler, who took a personal interest in the division's success.[61] As the war went against Germany and casualties grew, the need for such troops became ever stronger. Thus, when al-Husaini asked Berger and Himmler to talk to Hitler about creating an Arab Brigade made up mainly of Palestinian Arabs, Hitler agreed, choosing November 2, 1944, the Balfour Declaration's anniversary, for the announcement.

In recruiting Muslims for the German army, al-Husaini was already thinking of the postwar situation, foreseeing the future battle against the Zionists and wanting Nazi-trained soldiers for his side. He later wrote that the Nazi regime's training and equipment had indeed laid the basis for a Palestinian Arab army.[62] In 1943, al-Husaini had suggested anticivilian commando operations as their main military tactic, a strategy later adopted by the PLO. His recruitment of Arabs for German commando operations marked the first step in the new war the grand mufti would begin less than a year after World War II ended.

The elite of that nascent army was a commando paratrooper unit. In August 1943, al-Husaini visited the sabotage school in The Hague for a week, meeting sixty Arabs there,[63] including defected Soviet Turkic officers training to parachute into the USSR.[64] Three of these Arab units would be deployed for combat missions.

The first was led by Hasan Salama. Born near Ramla, Salama had fought in the Palestine Arab uprising under the nom de guerre Abu Ali.[65] He trained with al-Husaini's men for the 1941 Iraqi revolt, and then fled through Turkey to Germany where he attended the commando course before going on to the sabotage school. On October 6, 1944, his five-man team took off in a German plane from Rhodes and parachuted over Jericho to wage war on the Jews and the British, but they were dropped into a heavy wind, scattered, lost their equipment, and landed in an area heavily patrolled by the British.[66] Ten days later, three of them were caught: the commander, Lieutenant Kurt Wieland, another German, and Dhu al-Kuffar Abd al-Latif, one of al-Husaini's aides.

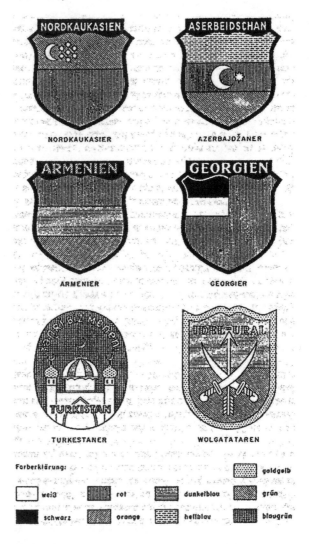

Figure 19. Insignia of Germany's six so-called Eastern Legions, in four of which—those of Azerbaijan, the North Caucasus, Turkestan, and the Volga Tatars—Muslims served. Al-Husaini trained imams and mullahs for these German units.

The British interrogated them in Cairo. Since they were all wearing German uniforms under Arab clothing, the British decided they could not be prosecuted as spies. From the interrogations, the British concluded that the team's mission was to gather intelligence, raise Arab guerrilla bands, and launch terror attacks on Jewish civilians. There was suspicion, never confirmed, that the team was to be supplied with ten containers of toxin to poison Tel Aviv's water system.[67]

Two others escaped, the Palestinian-German Friedrich Deininger-Schaeffer and Salama, who broke a leg in the jump.[68] Deininger-Schaeffer eventually made his way to Australia after Germany's defeat while Salama would be one of the main organizers of the grand mufti's army in the 1948 war.[69]

The second Arab commando unit's assignment was to set up a weapons depot in the Egyptian desert—according to the grand mufti, with thirty thousand rifles, but this seems exaggerated—for the planned uprising in Cairo against the British and to massacre the Jewish and Christian minorities there.[70]

The third unit, wearing German uniforms, landed at Tall Afar in northern Iraq on November 28, 1944. Local police quickly captured the three Iraqis and a Palestinian Arab. They carried, among other things, German soldiers' identification books; swastika badges; small al-Qur'ans with magnifying lenses; Zeiss cameras; German rifles; loaves of "ever-fresh" bread; and French, British, and Belgian gold coins worth £12,000 sterling to pay those willing to join an anti-British revolt.[71]

Given the success of the Bosnian SS and Soviet Turkic units, al-Husaini also worked with SS and Foreign Ministry support to develop Soviet Muslim SS units, too. In January 1944, the Turkestan unit, led by an SS officer Reiner Olzscha, was established in Dresden. The Germans had some problems with it due to factional infighting. Consequently, on July 20, 1944, Himmler ordered the unit merged into the SS East Turk Armed Formation. By the end of 1944 this formation included three thousand Muslim SS men.[72]

Al-Husaini opened two schools for training imams to serve both SS and regular Muslim units: one in Dresden for Soviet Turkic recruits, and another in Guben for those from the Balkans. Among the teachers in Dresden were Professors Richard Hartmann, sixty-three, of Berlin University and Munich University's Bertold Spuler, thirty-three. They trained forty Turkic Muslim imams at a time for both SS and regular units in six courses lasting two to four weeks each.[73]

The Guben imam school opened on April 21, 1944, in ceremonies presided over by al-Husaini and Berger. Al-Husaini spoke about the common fight of Nazism and Islam against world Jewry and the Bolsheviks who had subjugated forty million Muslims. The graduates were told to preach Islam in their units, bond Germans and Muslims together, and make their soldiers into good SS men.[74] The teachers were four more senior Bosnian clerics, the best-known being Husain Sulaiman Djozo, and seventeen younger men. Three of al-Husaini's aides—Shaikh Hasan, Abu as-Saud, and Mustafa al-Wakil—helped with the courses and al-Husaini himself often lectured there, too.[75] The school trained fifty SS imams in two courses of four months each.[76]

Djozo, thirty-two years old at the time and an al-Azhar graduate, became the SS division's chief imam. In 1943, Djozo had published a pro-Nazi text entitled *The Anticapitalist Views of Islam*. Ironically, when he later served a Communist regime, this booklet came in handy to prove his socialist credentials. In his classes, Djozo described Islam's "deep enmity toward Jews," who were rightfully excluded from society because of their "materialism and infidelity." In another article, Djozo explained that the SS soldier must "eliminate from life all negative forces" in order to create a new world.

So important had volunteer, and especially Muslim, units become for the German army on the Eastern Front, that when Hitler asked for two more divisions to operate in the Balkans he was told that one unit was only 60 and the other just 30 percent German citizens. The rest were either ethnic Germans from other countries or foreign—largely Muslim—volunteers.[77]

The basis for successful recruitment was propaganda, and due to al-Husaini's helpful advice, Germany's effort was about as effective as it could have been. The most ambitious project was launched in May 1943 when Himmler ordered Berger to find Qur'anic verses that seemingly predicted Hitler's role as an Islamic hero. Two academics, Johannes Schubert and Otto Rössler, were assigned to this task with al-Husaini as consultant. Schubert, then forty-seven years old, was a librarian at Leipzig University. In 1951, he was promoted to professor and later taught at the Free University of Berlin. Rössler, thirty-six years old, was an Africa expert who worked for the SS and had a successful academic career for two decades after the war ended.

Their recommendation was to focus on the belief that at the end of time there would be a great battle between Muslims—one of whose leaders would be an anti-Christian Jesus—and infidels. The current war was to be portrayed in that framework. Rössler's boss, Ernst Kaltenbrunner, the SS's Berlin chief, objected to Hitler being portrayed as an Islamic messiah but would agree to Hitler being identified with Jesus.

The evil forces' leader, the one-eyed false messiah, would be equated with world Jewry.[78] Kaltenbrunner suggested that this story be used for leaflets in the Balkans and Middle East. Himmler and al-Husaini agreed, as did SS adviser Walther Wüst, a forty-two-year-old professor at Munich University, who also had a successful postwar academic career. After opening with the appropriate Qur'anic quotation,[79] the leaflet told the story of the curly black-haired giant, the "Jewish" king Dajjal who steals all the Arabs' land, then asks the Arabs to recognize him as their ruler. Then Jesus/Hitler emerges, fights Dajjal, kills him, and sends the demon, the Jews, and all of their allies to Hell.[80]

In a real sense, al-Husaini's allies were already sending the Jews of Europe into a replication of the Hell on earth he also wanted to create in the Middle East: the Nazi death camps. Although details of what was going on in such places and the mass shootings of Jews in Eastern Europe were secret, the Germans kept al-Husaini briefed on their progress. On July 4, 1943, Himmler hosted al-Husaini at his private spa in East Prussia and told him that three million Jews had already been killed. He added that the Germans hoped to get the atomic bomb "three years before the Allies." Al-Husaini prominently displayed in his apartment the photo taken of himself and Himmler on that occasion, telling visitors of his close friendship with Hitler's SS leader. A few days later al-Husaini wrote Himmler, praising him as an "understanding, generous and energetic man."[81]

After the war, al-Husaini wrote of his reverence for Germany because it had "fought our enemies, the colonialists and the Zionists. For the enemy of your enemy is your friend." He was convinced that if the Axis powers had won the war, "No trace would have been left of Zionists in Palestine and Arab areas."[82]

While al-Husaini's opposition to Zionism was understandable, his anti-Jewish hatred—like Hitler's—went beyond any rational calculation of self-interest into the realm of the pathological. Yet that was due not to some psychological malady but to the centrality of Jews in his worldview, a point that also applies to radical Arab nationalists and Islamists of later times who held the same ideology. For them, as in Nazi doctrine, Jews were the villains of all history, the eternal enemy without whose extinction salvation and a proper world were impossible.

In November 1941, al-Husaini, accompanied by Grobba, had a medical exam with the Nazi physician, Pierre Schrumpf. According to

Schrumpf's account, the three men conversed about Turkey. Al-Husaini said he didn't like the Turkish government. The reason, he explained, was the evil influence of Tevfik Rüstü Aras, a former Turkish foreign minister and wartime ambassador to Britain. Aras was clearly an ethnic Turk and a Muslim, but al-Husaini claimed Aras was one of many disguised Jews in the Turkish government. Grobba, who was never a Nazi Party member, responded that not all Jews were bad and that he had met many pleasant ones in Iraq.[83] Angrily, al-Husaini replied that he'd never met a good Jew. They were all equally bad.[84]

Like many Muslims and Arabs, al-Husaini often asked himself why his communities had fallen behind the West in wealth and power. This question paralleled that asked by Hitler and his comrades regarding Germany. They found the same answer, one al-Husaini later summarized as "as-Sudma al-Kubra," the "Big Clash."[85] To the Nazis, that clash was between Jews—who might take on the guise of British or Bolsheviks—and Aryans; for al-Husaini's comrades and successors it was the battle between the Jews and the Muslims, democracies and dictatorships, moderates and militants. For Islamists, hostility to Jews and other infidels was rooted in their reading of Muslim texts but they identified the modern turning point as the 1924 Turkish decision to abolish the caliphate. Ignoring the fact that this system had not functioned for centuries, al-Husaini argued that to dissolve Islam's unique global bond was suicidal, especially given its clash with Anglo-American democracies and their "Jewish advocates."

In immediate terms, al-Husaini blamed the British, but behind this stab in the back were the Jews. This is precisely how the Nazis saw their equivalent betrayal, Germany's defeat in World War I. Both of these events related to the downfall of the German-Ottoman alliance partners, for whose cause both Hitler and al-Husaini had fought. Al-Husaini claimed that in the 1921 negotiations securing Turkish independence London insisted on abolishing the caliphate and creating a secular republic. One of his sources for this belief, al-Husaini said, was a 1943 meeting with General Kemal Dogan Bek, who had been an aide to Atatürk.[86] In fact, though, it was Atatürk's choice to take that course because he believed it the only route to modernity.[87]

For al-Husaini, though, this was not a sufficient explanation. He quoted a poem by Ahmad Shauqi who asked why Atatürk, victor in the post–World War I battle to expel the occupying Allied armies, abolished the caliphate and so injured Islam. Al-Husaini's answer was that a Jewish conspiracy lay behind Atatürk's policy. Just as Hitler saw Jews who were Communists, Social Democrats, or liberals as plotting against his people, so al-Husaini identified as master manipulator in this plot a man named Haim Nahum.

Born in 1872 in Izmir, Nahum studied Islamic law in Istanbul and linguistics in Paris. Back in Istanbul he taught at the military academy where he met many cadets who would become Young Turk leaders. In 1909, he became the Ottoman Empire's chief rabbi and in 1923 a member of Turkey's delegation that signed the Lausanne peace treaty. That year he then became chief rabbi of Egypt and senator in that country's parliament. There was, of course, no evidence that Nahum played any wider role. But al-Husaini claimed that Nahum had coordinated with Jewish leaders in London and New York as well as with a small group within Turkey who pretended to be Muslims but were really secret Jews. They worked to corrupt the Ottoman Empire, organize the 1908 Young Turk revolution, and turn Turkey into a secular state.

According to al-Husaini's story, once Turkey came under Jewish control, Nahum went to Cairo to destroy Islam and ensure the victory of Zionism there.[88] So while Hitler and the Nazis blamed the Jews for the fate of Germans and "Aryans" generally, al-Husaini and the radical nationalists and Islamists did the same thing regarding the fate of Arabs and Muslims. They did not need the Nazis to teach them this idea. They had already invented stories using elements from their own religious, cultural, and historical traditions.

But the Jews were not the only leaders of the alleged conspiracy to destroy Islam. For al-Husaini, Nahum's partner was nineteenth-century British Prime Minister William Gladstone. Al-Husaini said that Gladstone wanted to destroy Islam so Christians could permanently dominate the Middle East.[89] Today, such groups as al-Qaida, the Muslim Brotherhood, Hamas, Hizballah, and the Iranian government have built further on such material.

Al-Husaini had no proof for any of this tale except for the tsarist Russian forgery, *The Protocols of the Elders of Zion*.[90] He also claimed that an unidentified 1936 article in the Zionist newspaper *Haaretz* revealed the secret plan.[91] He added that Britain's part in the conspiracy was confirmed to him by the Egyptian Abd al-Wahhab Azzam, cousin of al-Husaini's agent and future Arab League head, Abd ar-Rahman Azzam.[92] Abd al-Wahhab's grandson and Abd ar-Rahman's nephew, Aiman az-Zawahiri, would later be one of al-Qaida's top leaders and a planner of the September 11, 2001, terror attack on the World Trade Center and the Pentagon.

Due to his worldview, al-Husaini advocated genocide against the Jews as passionately as did Hitler and his involvement in the Holocaust was quite extensive. In 1937, al-Husaini had urged all Muslims to rid their lands of Jews. That same year he proposed a deal to Hitler in which the Arabs would support German aims if the Germans would stop Jews from leaving their country and help him destroy the Jewish home in Palestine "by all means."

It is logical to believe that the Holocaust was a decision based on fanatical ideology rather than on German self-interest. Of course, Hitler's virulent hatred of Jews and talk of wiping them out had begun in the 1920s. If al-Husaini or some counterpart had not existed, the Nazis would probably have acted in a similar fashion. But the influence of al-Husaini, al-Kailani, and their movements also reinforced, made more necessary, and accelerated a policy of genocide in Europe that the Axis's partners intended to spread to the Middle East.

Al-Husaini's relationship to the timeline of Nazi decision making on the Holocaust was revealing. Despite Hitler's hatred of the Jews, given international concerns and other priorities his government embraced the idea of deportation. Between 1933 and 1941, the Nazi government allowed about 537,000 Jews to leave, receiving in return $9.5 million from the émigrés themselves and from foreign Jewish donors paying ransom.[93] Hitler might have been satisfied if Germany and the lands it ruled—but not the world—would be cleansed of any Jewish presence.

By closing this escape route for the Jews and discouraging any alternative strategy al-Husaini helped make the "Final Solution" inevitable.[94] Before 1941 imprisoning and murdering Jews in concentration camps did not benefit Germany. That changed as the alliance with Arabs and Muslims became important, Al-Husaini's and al-Kailani's stance and the advantage of a Muslim-Arab alliance turned Hitler's personal obsession from a handicap for German foreign policy into a valuable geopolitical strategy, mobilizing Muslim military units at the fronts and Islamist commandos in the enemy's rear, and raising hopes that jihad mobs might disrupt Allied colonies.

In February 1941 Hitler had received al-Husaini's proposal for an alliance of which one condition—paragraph seven—was that Germany stop Jewish emigration from Europe.[95] After Hitler promised al-Husaini on March 11 to do so, Germany's expulsion of the Jews was impossible and only mass murder remained. After agreeing in early June to meet al-Husaini to discuss the issue, Hitler ordered SS leader Reinhard Heydrich on July 31, 1941 to prepare an "overall solution for the Jewish question in Europe."[96] On October 31, he ended the legal emigration of Jews from German-ruled areas.[97] But the specific final decision had not yet been taken.

At four P.M. on Friday, November 28, Hitler met with al-Husaini, beginning the occasion with a warm on-camera handshake. Their talk in the Nazi leader's office in the presence of von Ribbentrop, Grobba, and the French-language translator Paul Schmidt lasted one hour and thirty-five minutes, ending just after 5:30.[98] Behind closed doors, Hitler promised al-Husaini that Arab aspirations would be fulfilled. Once "we win" the battle against world Jewry, Hitler said, Germany would eliminate the Jews in the Middle East, too.

According to the official record of the meeting, Hitler explained:

> Germany stood for uncompromising war against the Jews. That naturally included active opposition to the Jewish national home in Palestine, which was nothing other than a center, in the form of a state, for the exercise of destructive influence by Jewish interests. . . .
>
> Germany was now engaged in very severe battles to force the gateway to the northern Caucasus region. At some moment which is impossible to predict exactly today but is not distant, the German armies would reach the southern exit of the Caucasus Mountains. The moment that Germany's tank divisions and air squadrons had made their appearance south of the Caucasus, the public appeal requested by the grand mufti could go out to the Arab world.[99]

The Führer would announce that the Arab world's hour of liberation had arrived and the grand mufti, the Arab world's new leader, would implement the task, already secretly prepared, of eliminating all the Jews in his domain.

In his account of the conversation, the grand mufti echoed this theme, recalling that Hitler told him: "The road from Rostov [in southern Russia] to Iran and Iraq is shorter than the distance from Berlin to Rostov. . . . When we shall have arrived in the southern Caucasus, then the time of the liberation of the Arabs will have arrived. And you can rely on my word." Hitler asked al-Husaini to keep this confidential declaration secret—to lock it deeply in his heart—until the time was ripe.[100]

After the meeting, Hitler called in Foreign Ministry official Emil von Rintelen, to whom he dictated "four points following the reception of the grand mufti," including a brief press release on his "important talk" with al-Husaini "about the future of the Arab people" and co-ordination of the next steps with Mussolini in regard to al-Husaini.[101] Hitler fulfilled that last provision in a meeting with Rome's foreign minister Count Galeazzo Ciano, whom he told that the war against Russia was in principle won, so that now German troops would march across the Caucasus to conquer Iraq and Iran, followed by Syria and Palestine.[102]

At this same moment, Hitler made a fifth decision that would end millions of lives. He ordered Heydrich to organize a conference within ten days to prepare the "final solution of the Jewish question." Thus, Hitler made his key decision to start the genocide with al-Husaini's anti-Jewish rhetoric and insistence on wiping out the Jews fresh in his ears.

The next day Heydrich signed invitations for thirteen high-ranking Nazis to meet at the Berlin suburb of Wannsee on December 9. Just two days before that gathering, however, an event disrupted the time-table. On December 7, Japan attacked Pearl Harbor, bringing America into the war. From Japanese Ambassador Hiroshi Oshima, Hitler had known about this in advance. But the fallout from Japan's attack gave so much more work for officials involved in the Wannsee meeting that on December 8 the conference was postponed to January 20, 1942.[103]

The day after the conference's postponement, December 9, al-Husaini witnessed Hitler's declaration of war on America at Berlin's Kroll Opera House.[104] Later he was an honored guest at the Sport Palace to hear Hitler's speech proclaiming that while Britain now had America on its side, Germany, too, had new, equally important allies in the Middle East to match that. To underline the point, that same day the Germans published for the first time the photo of the al-Husaini–Hitler meeting as confirmation of Hitler's claim. This sequence shows how much importance the Germans gave to al-Husaini and the alliance with his forces.

Another significant link was that Adolf Eichmann, who had prepared the background briefing for the genocide discussion at Wannsee, was ordered to give al-Husaini a preview before any high-ranking Germans had heard the briefing. Probably on Thursday, December 4, Eichmann took al-Husaini into the map room at the Reich Main Security Office's Jewish Affairs division to explain how Germany would "solve the Jewish question." Al-Husaini was so impressed that he asked to have one of Himmler's aides—likely Dieter Wisliceny—sent to Jerusalem after Germany won the war in order to make a similar plan for wiping out the Middle East's Jews. Both men expected this to happen in 1942 or, at the latest, in 1943.

Meanwhile, Hitler told Nazi leaders on December 12 that he was determined to "solve the Jewish question now."[105] When the Wannsee Conference met in January 1942 it concluded with the decision to deport all Jews under German control to concentration camps where they would be murdered.[106] Eichmann told his aide Wisliceny that the Final Solution meant the "biological extermination of the Jewish race."[107] Wisliceny's story, including his statement that Hitler gave an oral order for implementing the mass murder, is supported by other sources,[108] including Eichmann himself during his interrogation.[109]

One of the items discussed at the meeting was a memorandum of "wishes and ideas for an overall solution of the Jewish question in Europe" that included the list of countries whose Jews would be murdered. Franz Rademacher, von Ribbentrop's "officer for Jewish affairs," had prepared this at the request of Luther, who would be al-Husaini's liaison on Holocaust-related matters. At the meeting, four countries with large Muslim populations and in which al-Husaini would soon be active—the USSR, Croatia, Bosnia, and Turkey—were included in the list.[110] Just a dozen years later, when Rademacher was a fleeing war criminal, al-Husaini helped arrange for him to find a safe haven in Syria.

The relationship between Martin Luther and al-Husaini was another sign of the grand mufti's involvement in the genocide project. Luther was the Foreign Ministry official responsible for the Final Solution and for liaison with the SS. After the Wannsee Conference he coordinated the involvement of Germany's allies and client states in the genocide plan. In virtually every case other than that of al-Husaini and his colleagues, the Nazis had to apply force or heavy pressure—including on

Mussolini and Vichy France—to get anti-Jewish measures carried out, let alone mass killings. Aside from local fascist movements in other places, only the Arab and Islamist allies were eager supporters. And this policy was politically beneficial for the Nazis above all in Muslim regions.

Once the Wannsee meeting ended and other attendees left, Heydrich, Heinrich Müller, head of the Gestapo, and Eichmann had a glass of cognac and spoke of the "killing, elimination, and annihilation" to come.[111] The following day, Grobba met al-Husaini to brief him on what had been decided. Al-Husaini must have been pleased that his request had been so speedily fulfilled by Hitler, but nonetheless asked for written agreement to create a Jew-free Greater Syria consisting of Syria, Lebanon, Palestine, and Transjordan that he would rule. He reminded Grobba that Hitler had already promised this to him.[112]

Hitler fulfilled al-Husaini's request. On April 28, the German government sent secret letters to al-Husaini and al-Kailani agreeing to their wish to liquidate the Jews living in Palestine. The pledge to kill all of the Jews in the Middle East was repeated on July 15 when Hitler met al-Kailani in his Russian front headquarters and offered him rule over Iraq.[113]

Thus, the visits of Germany's Arab allies to extermination camps were a first step toward instituting a Middle Eastern Holocaust.[114] According to Wisliceny, the aide whom al-Husaini wanted to employ for this project, Eichmann personally took al-Husaini to visit the Auschwitz and Maidanek concentration camps.[115] The Hungarian Jewish leader Rudolf Kastner testified that Wisliceny told him in 1944—when he would have had no motive to make such a story up—about al-Husaini's visit to the Auschwitz gas chambers.[116] The story seems credible, especially after the discovery of pages in Himmler's office calendar that prove beyond reasonable doubt that the two men met in the Ukrainian town of Zhitomir, near Auschwitz (see Figure 22). And al-Husaini was traveling back and forth through Poland in June and July 1943.

Al-Husaini had also already chosen his own future Eichmanns: three Iraqis—Naji Shaukat, Muhammad Hasan Salman, and Kamil al-Kailani—along with one of his nephews, probably Safwat al-Husaini, his security expert.[117] He had sent men to the SS training course to be instructed by the world's leading experts on mass murder.[118] Al-

Husaini's men also participated in killing Jews in North Africa, and would have been ready to do so in other countries if they had had the opportunity.

As it became obvious that they weren't winning the war, some German officials began to worry about facing punishment for their crimes following defeat. A few sought to help some Jews escape as insurance for their own futures, but al-Husaini saw this self-interested mercy as a threat to be blocked. No Jews must escape at all. Whenever the prospect arose of Nazis letting some Jews go free, al-Husaini campaigned to stop it. At the end of 1942, ten thousand Jewish children were to travel via Romania to Palestine in exchange for the Allied release of interned German civilians. With Himmler's consent, Eichmann ordered that they be kept at Theresienstadt, least oppressive of concentration camps, until they were deported. The first group had already arrived. Suddenly, Wisliceny was called to Berlin. Eichmann told him that al-Husaini had heard of the plan and protested to Himmler, who had then reversed his decision and sent them back to almost certain death.[119]

The same pattern prevailed on other occasions. Al-Husaini helped convince Mussolini to persecute Italian Jews, in 1942 to hand over Croatian Jews living under Italian control to Germany, and to give Germany a free hand to imprison and kill Jews in his colony of Libya.[120]

Likewise, in May 1943, al-Husaini wrote von Ribbentrop warning that the Americans and British were talking secretly with some of Berlin's Balkan clients about releasing a few Jews. The British colonial secretary Oliver Stanley unwisely told Parliament publicly that four thousand Jewish children and five hundred accompanying adults were being let go by Bulgaria to go to Palestine. He hoped, Stanley said, similar deals could be worked out with Romania and Hungary. Al-Husaini told von Ribbentrop that this threatened Arab interests. Many Arabs had taken the Axis side, expecting Germany "to solve the Jewish problem globally by taking Jews under their closest control." He asked von Ribbentrop to ensure Jews didn't get away,[121] reminding him of Germany's commitment to ensure there would never be a Jewish state in Palestine.[122] Al-Husaini also visited the Bulgarian ambassador to Germany, SS headquarters, and Germany's Foreign Ministry to complain. In the end, the Bulgarian government stopped the plan, dooming the forty-five hundred Jews to death.[123] Al-Husaini thanked the ambassador for his cooperation.[124]

Al-Husaini's strategy generally worked. When 1,681 Hungarian Jews were allowed to leave that country in 1944 as a trial balloon to see if the Allies might make deals with Nazi Germany,[125] Eichmann insisted that they not go to Palestine since this would anger the Arabs and also violate a personal promise to his friend al-Husaini.[126]

Another time, in July 1944, al-Husaini learned that some Jews might be exchanged for Germans interned by the British in Palestine. He protested to Himmler and to the Italian, Hungarian, Rumanian, and Turkish foreign ministers, urging them to let no Jews leave or pass through their countries. Jews were responsible for the war, he told them, and intended to use Palestine as a base to dominate the world.[127] Letting Jews escape Europe would "not solve the Jewish problem." Rather they would link up with "racial brethren" in enemy lands to continue their war against civilization. If forced to stay in Poland, the mufti added, Jews would be better supervised; he knew full well that this meant the death camps.[128]

After the war, al-Husaini recalled that his attempts to keep Jews from escaping had a "positive effect" for the Palestinian cause.[129] But when, after the war, Zionist groups charged that his letters and actions had helped condemn hundreds of thousands of Jews to death, al-Husaini reversed course.[130] He challenged the testimonies of two Eichmann aides, Hermann Krumey and Wisliceny, that detailed his discussions with their chief. Although he called Eichmann a "noble-minded and honest man," al-Husaini claimed never to have met him.[131]

Al-Husaini claimed that Krumey had been lying in an attempt to save his own life but was executed anyway. In fact, Krumey was spared the death penalty precisely because he had helped free several hundred Hungarian Jews despite al-Husaini's attempts to block the operation. Released from prison in 1948, Krumey was returned to jail with a life sentence only in 1969 when new information surfaced about his involvement in killing eighty-one Jewish children and others.[132] He died in prison in 1981.

The SS men had no motive to drag al-Husaini into the story falsely. The Allies were simply not after al-Husaini. They never even made any attempt to discredit him after the war and in the almost three decades he lived after Hitler's fall, no Western government agency tried to bring him to justice or to document his war crimes. Further, the two SS men were consistent; Wisliceny—who described al-Husaini as Eichmann's colleague, partner, and adviser—repeated his same story on at least four occasions over the years.[133] Both were in a position to know first-hand the information they imparted.[134] Finally, the report that al-Husaini and Eichmann met on November 9, 1944 is supported by the fact that al-Husaini's personal diary for that day contained one word: "Eichmann."[135] Other documents show he was in Berlin that day, also meeting with Wilhelm Melchers, head of the Foreign Ministry's Middle East desk.[136]

When al-Husaini asked Eichmann as a personal favor to set free a Muslim being held at the Mauthausen camp, he complied, referring to their personal friendship, as he did when al-Husaini asked him to send Jews to concentration camps—or keep them there. Al-Husaini's advocacy of the mass murder of Jews convinced the Nazi leadership this would be popular among Muslims not only in the Middle East but also in the USSR and the Balkans. In light of all of his actions, nothing could sum up the situation better than the SS officer Wisliceny's remark about al-Husaini to Kastner in 1944, that he "surpassed us in anti-Jewish attacks."[137]

While genocide against the Jews was a high priority for al-Husaini and his radical nationalist and Islamist colleagues, their main goal was to help Germany win the war. Al-Husaini gave extensive aid and comfort to the Nazi cause, raising forces that delayed the war's end and thus increased the number of victims. Aside from his activities in the USSR, Balkans, and Middle East, al-Husaini's effort to help Germany extended into India and the Far East. India was often on the Nazis' mind, though distance made it hard for them to do anything effective there. Still, attempts were made to stir revolt among the subcontinent's Muslim population. In May 1941, the high water mark of German influence in the parts of the Middle East closest to it, Hitler thought often of establishing an Indian government in exile in Berlin.[138] Another plan was to instigate an Indian revolution from bases in Afghanistan and Tibet, an idea the Germans had tried during World War I.[139] From Tibet, Ernst Schäfer, an SS man and explorer, had just returned to Germany with his four-man expedition in 1940, when he offered to go back to prepare a revolt in neighboring India.[140] But as preparations dragged, Ribbentrop dropped this project.[141]

A new twist was added, however, to the old idea of using Afghanistan as a base against British India. The Soviet-German Nonaggression

Pact of 1939 was in fact an alliance that Stalin was prepared to continue infinitely. If Hitler had delayed attacking the USSR or had never done so, the Germans might have captured the Middle East and won the war. As late as April 1941, according to German reports, Stalin told Berlin's military attaché that Russia and Germany would march forward together.[142] Only Germany's invasion disrupted this alliance.

While the alliance was in effect, the German government approached Soviet foreign minister Vyacheslav Molotov for a partnership to help exiled Afghan King Amanullah and his foreign minister, Ghulam Siddiq Khan, launch a jihad against India.[143] Two decades earlier, the Soviets had asked Berlin to do precisely the same thing; now it was Germany's turn. When Italy, under whose protection Amanullah lived in Rome, discouraged him from participating, the Germans revised the plan to base it on local tribes and an Indian government in exile in Afghanistan. The Soviets would provide supply lines and bases; the Germans, troops and weapons.[144] Hitler showed no interest when he reviewed the idea on November 1, 1939, but in a meeting with a German foreign official Molotov told the Germans he liked the idea but needed more information. The project remained mired in rivalry between Rosenberg, who opposed it, and von Ribbentrop, who supported it, and by the time von Ribbentrop's envoy returned to Moscow for more talks in February 1940, the Soviets had lost interest.[145]

During the period of rapid German advances inside the USSR, Berlin's thoughts again turned to India. As its troops approached the Caucasus and thus the Persian Gulf, the German military discussed airlifting troops into India to kindle a revolt. In February 1941, Hitler ordered General Walter Warlimont, deputy chief of operations, to make preliminary studies for an invasion of Afghanistan and then India after the Soviets were defeated.[146]

The Germans hoped that supporting independence could persuade many Indians in the British army to desert and Indian prisoners of war to join the Axis forces. To further this goal, the Nazis backed the idea of an Indian Legion to be deployed as close as possible to India.[147] In 1940, there were about eighty million Muslims in India. The German assessment—proven correct just two years after the war—was that they would ultimately rebel against Hindu rule, seize the country's northwestern part, and create a Muslim state.[148] In this strategy, al-Husaini was to play an important role. Whether true or not, the Nazis reported that he controlled seventy-two revolutionary cells in India.[149]

Besides working secretly with his network of Islamists in India, in mid-1942 al-Husaini used German and Italian transmitters to make a personal appeal for Indian Muslims to revolt. He spoke of the alleged historical unity of Arabs and Indians. To arouse religious passions, al-Husaini claimed the Jews would steal the al-Aqsa Mosque unless Muslims united against British oppressors, fought for liberation, and won.[150]

One of al-Husaini's most promising contacts was his counterpart, India's mufti Kifayatullah Dehlavi, a supporter of the caliphate, the Muslim Brotherhood, and al-Husaini's Palestine Arab movement. The British Indian government acted decisively to block al-Husaini's influence by arresting Dehlavi's aide and intermediary with al-Husaini, Muttahida at-Tarrazi.[151] They also refused an entry visa in 1943 to al-Husaini's own emissary, Salih Mustafa Ashmawi, editor of a Muslim Brotherhood publication. Ashmawi had previously carried messages and propaganda materials from al-Husaini to Islamists in the Punjab region.[152] Ashmawi's reaction showed why some Germans didn't want to use Islamists in India. In addition to complaining about the British Indian government, he also condemned the Hindu majority there as anti-Arab and anti-Muslim.[153]

Did Germany need to choose between Hindu Indian nationalists and Muslim Islamists, or could it support both sides despite their growing rivalry? Foreign Ministry Under Secretary Wilhelm Keppler favored a Hindu strategy and opposed using al-Husaini or supporting the Muslim League secessionists and their leader Muhammad Ali Jinnah.[154] However, another under secretary, Theo Habicht, whose task was to subvert the British Empire from within,[155] and Erwin Ettel, German intelligence's Istanbul-based coordinator for Asian issues, backed al-Husaini's effort to encourage a jihad against the British Raj.[156]

The man who might have bridged this gap for the Germans was Subhas Chandra Bose, the Hindu organizer of the Free India movement. The forty-five-year-old Bose met Hitler on May 27, 1942, and offered to recruit an Indian Tiger Legion from prisoners of war. Friendly toward al-Husaini, Bose proposed a joint Arab-Indian Committee to incite uprisings. In addition to Bose, it would include the Abwehr, al-Husaini, and al-Kailani.[157] To Canaris, Germany's military intelligence chief, Bose confided that he thought Germany would lose the war but that his movement's collaboration would pressure the British to keep their promise of granting full independence afterward. In 1943, he formed a Provisional Indian Government in exile in Japanese-occupied Singapore and named himself its head of state. Bose proposed to base the operation in Basra, southern Iraq's port which had close trade ties with India. Of course, the Germans would have to capture Iraq first.

While this plan never came close to fruition, Bose's longer-term assessment proved correct. Just four years later some of his former soldiers marched in India's Independence Day parade.[158] By that time, though, Bose was dead, killed in a 1945 plane crash off the China coast. What might have been was depicted in a blockbuster Indian movie a half-century after his death, showing Hitler as sympathetic and Bose leading an expedition by a forty-thousand-strong army to free India.[159]

There were many marginal schemes in which al-Husaini was eager to participate to spread Germany's, and his own, influence eastward. In 1943 he exchanged letters with the Faqir of Ibi whose real name, according to Grobba, was Saadi al-Kailani, a German-subsidized Islamist from Afghanistan who lived in Damascus, urging him to get Indian Muslims to rise in jihad.[160] Al-Husaini assured him of assistance in his fight against the British and other "foes" of Islam.[161]

Another German connection was with al-Mashriqi, the Islamic alternative to Bose as pro-German leader in South Asia. Although generally forgotten today, al-Mashriqi was one of the first to advocate a separate Muslim state of Pakistan carved from India. One German expert on the region suggested that al-Mashriqi was a great leader like Hitler, whose troops supposedly numbered in the hundreds of thousands, including men ready to undertake suicide missions.[162]

Sultan Muhammad Shah, better known as the Aga Khan, a cofounder of the Indian Muslim League that favored the creation of Pakistan, was a key contact for Hitler with Shia Muslims in India and Iran. He visited the Führer in 1937 for a cup of tea at Hitler's vacation home near Berchtesgaden. The visitor was impressed by wonderful views of the Untersberg Hill, dark woods, and lush meadows. Hitler openly explained his plans for conquering Europe. The Aga Khan liked him very much and told him that if the Christians had not defeated invading Arab Muslims in 732 at the battle of Tours, in what is now France, Europe would have become Muslim and thus have enjoyed peace and unity.[163] Hitler was equally impressed with his visitor.[164] In mid-1942, Hitler returned to the same theme. Extolling Islam as a religion glorifying heroism and promising warriors great rewards in heaven, Hitler said that if the Germans had become Muslims—rather than being restrained by Christian morality—they would have conquered the world.[165]

Hitler and the German Foreign Ministry maintained links with the Shiite leader in later years.[166] They viewed him as a good source of information on what was happening in London (where he knew Churchill and many other leaders), as a Muslim leader of some value to their plans to gain influence in India, and as a possible agent.[167]

The Aga Khan's personal politics were relatively liberal. He had opposed the Ottoman jihad during World War I and his son served in the British army.[168] His motives toward the Germans were opportunistic. He seemed mostly interested in getting them to lend him money to support his gambling, and of course there was always the chance Germany would win the war.[169] He also had an idea that he might serve as a peacemaking intermediary between Germany and Britain. A few days after Paris fell to the Germans in June 1940, he proposed that plan to Hitler, who was not interested in pursuing it.[170]

Through one of his German friends, Prince Max Hohenlohe, with whom he met frequently in Switzerland, the Aga Khan passed to Hitler his views on what was happening in Britain.[171] He told Hitler that the British were not the Führer's enemies but were fighting only because Churchill was in the pay of the Jews.[172] Although annoyed at the German confiscation of some of his French racehorses, the Aga Khan offered Hitler his services to help if Germany conquered India but urged the German leader in 1940 to put a priority on taking Egypt and the Middle East. If Hitler ever did arrive as victor in London, the Aga Khan offered to share a bottle of champagne with the two pro-Nazi Egyptian royals, the exiled Abbas Hilmi and Faruq.[173]

While adventurers like the Aga Khan produced little of value for the Germans, al-Husaini genuinely tried his best to advance an Axis victory even in East Asia. There were sixty million Muslims in Dutch-ruled Indonesia, seized by al-Husaini's ally Japan in 1942, and about fifty million in western China, territory Japan hoped to conquer.[174] Al-Husaini had good relations with Japan's ambassador in Berlin Hiroshi Oshima,[175] and was in contact with Japanese Muslim leader Muhammad Abd al-Hai.[176]

Al-Husaini sought to ensure that a Japanese-ruled Asia had some Islamist flavor. During the war, he praised Japan for its policies, including support for Indian independence. Repeatedly, he urged the Japanese to ally themselves with Muslims against what he called the outside imperialist powers. In February 1943, he proposed that Japan establish an "Islamic Army" to fight against America.[177] In mid-1944, he personally signed—both as grand mufti and as president of the World Islamic Congress—an Islam-Japan pact that included a call for this army's creation.[178]

His other pet project was asking the Japanese to recognize Indonesia as an independent Muslim republic. The Japanese answered by proposing autonomy, but nothing ever came of it.[179] Despite its polite responses Tokyo never had much interest in these ideas since, like the Germans in the USSR, it wanted to rule and exploit conquered lands, not create potentially troublesome client states.

For any of al-Husaini's dreams to come true, however, all depended on Axis victory. By 1944—as even some of al-Husaini's fanatical Nazi colleagues were recognizing—this wasn't going to happen. A few tried to save themselves by cutting personal deals involving saving some Jews. Several courageous German officers tried to assassinate Hitler and paid with their lives. Al-Husaini, however, remained loyal to the end. He and his colleagues believed that their cause required a total Axis victory or else the British would still control the Middle East and the Jews might get their state. Yet al-Husaini and the other Arab and Muslim collaborators would emerge from the war not only unscathed but with their political careers intact. Indeed, their prospects actually improved.

In 1944 and 1945, of course, nobody knew this would happen. As the vice closed on Germany's ever-shrinking empire, al-Husaini became increasingly desperate for an Islamic uprising. But why should others —even those eager to rebel in 1940—want to leap aboard a sinking ship? Al-Husaini kept issuing repeated appeals for all Muslims to drive the Jews and British from their countries.[180] He wrote leaflets to Arab soldiers in the Allied armies urging them to desert from the side of the Muslims' enemies and the Jews' protectors. Only a martyr's death or joining the Germans, he wrote, could save their souls.[181] But like many of those—including modern-day Islamist leaders—who urge others to become martyrs, al-Husaini had no intention to become one himself. This led to another seemingly fantastic—but by no means inconceivable—turn history might have taken.

Goebbels was one of the Nazis al-Husaini had charmed. The Third Reich's propaganda genius was so taken with his Arab ally that he told Hitler, the day after their May 1944 meeting, what a great asset al-Husaini was. In response, Hitler ordered Goebbels to support all of al-Husaini's activities.[182] The Führer's renewed backing was timed perfectly to protect al-Husaini against the mounting German suspicion that he was jumping ship. Just two days earlier, SS troops had captured a Yugoslav Communist guerrilla camp where they found letters al-Husaini had written to the Communist leader, Tito, asking the latter to put him in touch with the Soviets. Having concluded that Germany might not win, al-Husaini was exploring options, despite the fact that he'd always decried the Communists as part of the international Jewish conspiracy.

After receiving this information Himmler, one of al-Husaini's strongest backers, distanced himself from the Arab cleric.[183] When al-Husaini asked for permission to send his two secretaries on a trip to Switzerland in early 1945, Himmler refused, expecting he was plotting to meet with Germany's enemies.[184] The Germans made clear to al-Husaini that they knew of his back-channel communications and demanded that they cease. Al-Husaini gave up this effort. But while he never switched from German to Soviet patrons many of his Egyptian, Iraqi, and Syrian allies did so in the 1950s and 1960s, with Arafat, his anointed successor as Palestinian Arab leader, among them.

The end was drawing near. On November 24, 1944, U.S. intelligence began hunting for al-Husaini and al-Kailani, as well as their archives. In early December, security officers of the 12th U.S. Army were told to search for al-Husaini in the villas of Bad Gastein, Austria. Their orders said: "He should be arrested and this Headquarters notified immediately." By early 1945 many of his papers had fallen into U.S. hands and reports on their contents had been written, including documentation of his close collaboration with the Nazis and German intelligence.[185] As late as January 20, 1945, as Germany crumbled, al-Husaini was still supervising the training of soldiers for a projected Arab Brigade headquartered at the Adolf Hitler School in Dresden.[186] This priority reflected the fact that he was preparing for what he rightly expected would come next: an Arab and Islamist war against the Jews.[187]

But it was not the Americans who finally caught al-Husaini. In February 1945, Eichmann and al-Husaini met in Linz, where Eichmann had gone to high school and begun his Nazi career. The likely topic was how to survive the war's end and what to do afterward.[188] Many plans were made and abandoned. In April, for example, German officers proposed that al-Husaini travel by submarine to Libya. The Nazis paid al-Husaini's salary for the last time on April 5.[189] On May 4, he crossed into Switzerland, where he had previously stored ample funds with German permission. But for some reason, perhaps because he needed to make more arrangements, al-Husaini returned to Germany. At last, on the very day Nazi Germany surrendered, May 8, al-Husaini took one of the last planes to Berne. When he came down the stairs, Swiss officials told al-Husaini that he was on a list of thirty-two men, including Hitler himself, to whom Switzerland had decided not to give asylum. Al-Husaini boarded a train back to Germany and was taken into custody by the French army in Konstanz.

Al-Husaini was hosted in a villa near Paris until the French decided what to do with him. Well guarded but free to receive guests, he stayed there for a year. But just as they had employed him after World War I to subvert British influence in the Middle East, the French again played that game. And so he was simply freed.

9 A Bid for Partnership in the Axis

Both before and during World War II, al-Husaini and the Arab nationalist-Islamist faction stood at the very center of Germany's strategy. In effect, they sought to become the Axis's fourth member, alongside Germany, Italy, and Japan. But how did that group promote its interests and build its ideology in the collaborationist era, and what other nationalist and Islamist forces developed during the war?

In their September 27, 1940, agreement that al-Husaini and al-Kailani had originally proposed they were granted admission into the Axis as a full partner with Germany. The plan was that once Egypt, Iraq, and al-Husaini's personal empire made up of Lebanon, Palestine, Transjordan, and Syria were under German allies' control these states would enter into such a formal alliance. Ultimately, the Islamists and radical Arab nationalists did not achieve this status because they were unable to deliver the armies, uprisings, and territory they had promised. If not for German military failures and clever, energetic British strategies the grand mufti would have become ruler of a substantial state and the region's leading figure.

Nevertheless, al-Husaini and his colleagues were treated as highly important for the Axis's interests. Al-Husaini regularly met with the

Nazi regime's highest-ranking figures: Hitler, Himmler, von Ribbentrop, Rosenberg, Göring, and Goebbels. They listened to him and usually followed his advice on propaganda, recruiting Muslim soldiers,
and other matters. The Germans and Italians both viewed him as the
most important figure among Arabs, among Muslims in general—including in the USSR, the Balkans, and India—and in the Middle East
region.[1] So highly did Hitler value him that Grobba was fired when he
displeased the grand mufti.[2] The Germans also sidelined al-Kailani, his
sole rival. Al-Husaini was the single most important foreign collaborator with the Nazis and certainly the most prized non-European one.

Yet al-Husaini was no mere puppet of the Germans but had his own
strong support base. Indeed, he had a better chance of becoming caliph
than any other individual since the old Ottoman line ended in 1924.
His qualifications included his descent from Muhammad lineage; high
religious office as grand mufti of Jerusalem, generally considered by
Muslims as a holy site ranking alongside Mecca and Medina; connections with every corner of the Muslim world; a charismatic personality
and excellence as a speaker and writer; the ability to combine Islamism
and nationalism; lack of any serious competitor; possession of the Palestine card; and Axis backing.

In 1942, German military intelligence agreed that al-Husaini would
take the lead on a wide range of espionage activities including information gathering, propaganda, sabotage, managing Arab intelligence
agents, and organizing uprisings.[3] On December 2, German military
intelligence and the SS discussed taking supervision of the grand mufti
away from the Foreign Ministry and making him their official chief
agent in the region. The file of these exchanges is entitled "The Mufti
as co-worker" (*Mitarbeiter*), less than a colleague but far more than a
simple employee.

When Grobba was fired to please al-Husaini, he was replaced by
Curt M. Prüfer. Sixty-one years old in 1942, Prüfer was well qualified
to be the grand mufti's handler. Speaking Arabic, Turkish, and French,
he had served the German Foreign Ministry for thirty-five years as a
Middle East linguist and expert. During World War I, Prüfer had been
stationed in Istanbul where he headed von Oppenheim's operation, and
had later fought alongside the Ottomans in Palestine. In his work for
von Oppenheim, Prüfer had helped organize several jihad congresses.[4]
He joined the Nazi Party in 1937.

Prüfer had the perfect argument to assure al-Husaini of Berlin's reliability for his cause. Germany, he said, had studied empires having distant colonies—the British and French model—and concluded that this type of imperial system didn't work. Consequently, Nazi Germany "only intends to expand in Europe and not to have any colonies [abroad]."[5] Al-Husaini was convinced that the Germans would support Arab independence rather than seek to replace the old colonial masters.

Despite the failures of his 1941 Iraqi and 1942 North African campaigns, in September 1942 al-Husaini developed an even more ambitious proposal that he presented to Walther Schellenberg, an intelligence official whom al-Husaini described as "Himmler's well-known deputy."[6] Calling himself, "One of the most influential Arab freedom fighters," al-Husaini bragged that he had fought the Jews long before the Nazis took power.[7] Having already put himself up as future leader of a Greater Arab Empire including Palestine, Transjordan, Syria, Saudi Arabia, and Iraq, he now added Egypt, Libya, and French North Africa to his projected domain.[8] The basis for this Pan-Arab, Pan-Muslim grand unity scheme came from Islamic doctrine, regional history, and Hitler's own strategy of uniting all Germans in one great empire.

While sometimes giving preference to Vichy French or Italian demands, Hitler generally supported al-Husaini, treated him as a virtual head of state, and funded him lavishly. Even before the war al-Husaini had been receiving German subsidies to pay to various groups including the Muslim Brotherhood.[9] The Germans gave him 150,000 marks in foreign currency every month just to subsidize between 125 and 150 Arab students in Paris.[10] One of al-Husaini's agents there was Maruf ad-Dawalibi, later prime minister of Syria and al-Husaini's successor four decades later as president of the World Islamic Congress.[11]

Al-Husaini's immediate entourage, financed by the German government, included about sixty officials. His monthly payroll for the most important aides totaled 11,450 marks paid to twenty-three people, each receiving 200 to 700 marks a month.[12] To put this amount in perspective, al-Husaini's German liaison Grobba, a high-ranking official, earned 1,000 marks a month.[13]

Among the entourage were at least three nephews: Musa, the intelligence and security chief; Salim; and Safwat, the liaison with students. Others were senior members of al-Husaini's Higher Arab Committee who had fled to Berlin. Some were involved in military activities, like Fauzi al-Qutb, his explosives expert. Dhu al-Kuffar Abd al-Latif was trained in sabotage and parachuted into Palestine with an elite German-Arab military unit.[14]

Not all the Germans' propaganda, intelligence, and military assets among Arabs and Muslims worked for al-Husaini. While accepting al-Husaini's primacy, Hitler wanted to leave the door open for Arab monarchs to join him. His dream was a Berlin-based Council of Arab Leaders including Egypt's King Faruq and King Ibn Saud.[15] There would also be separate groups representing non-Arab Muslims from the Soviet Union, the Balkans, and India.

A good example of one of the many Arab collaborators independent of al-Husaini or other groups was Yunus Bahri, the most popular Arab broadcaster. In 1931 he had traveled to Berlin and met Goebbels, and in 1939 he began radio work for the Germans. His opening line, "This is Berlin" (*Huna Barlin*) became famous in the Arabic-speaking world, as did his oft-repeated slogan, "Hayy, ja aiyuha al Arab!" urging the Arabs to "get ready" to launch a revolt. Aside from on-air activity, Bahri worked for the SS to build spy rings.[16]

But the only potential competitor for al-Husaini was Rashid Ali al-Kailani, whose separate operation focused on Iraq. This was no ideological dispute, merely a battle for personal rank and power. Al-Kailani contested al-Husaini's primacy but never with any real success. He was the one who signed the September 1941 agreement to create an Arab Freedom Corps, but it was al-Husaini who led it.[17] Al-Kailani repeatedly failed with proposals for a German-Arab pact to make himself leader of the whole Middle East.[18] The Germans' preference for the grand mufti was understandable. Al-Husaini had a wide international reach while, at best, al-Kailani only had support in Iraq. Moreover, al-Husaini had impeccable Muslim credentials and, as World Islamic Congress president,[19] he assured Hitler that hundreds of millions of Muslims would cooperate closely with Germany.[20] Al-Kailani's effort to strike back was restricted to petty maneuvers. He ordered his entourage to address him by the same title used for Hitler, as their "Führer."[21] He also called himself the United Arab States prime minister.[22] In retaliation, al-Husaini successfully campaigned for Berlin and Rome to recognize him as head of the multinational Arab Nation Party.[23] The Iraqi scored a point on July 15, 1942, getting a personal meeting with Hitler at his headquarters near the Russian front. The grand mufti retaliated by putting a Pan-Arab flag on his car to show that he represented the whole Arab world.[24]

In September 1942, the Germans and Italians brought al-Husaini and al-Kailani together with their own respective spy chiefs in Rome. Al-Husaini emerged the victor in the encounter and the Italians officially recognized him as the main Arab leader.[25] The four parties agreed that if Axis troops reached Syria, Lebanon, Palestine, and Jordan, they would create a Pan-Arab army for al-Husaini and a separate Iraqi army for al-Kailani. Both would have Arab generals but would be under the German military's overall command. Within six months after the war's end Axis troops were to leave all Middle Eastern lands.[26]

Al-Husaini was never shy about reminding the Germans of his real or alleged help for their cause and, on that basis, asserting his primacy as the Arab and Muslim leader. In a late 1943 letter to the Foreign Ministry, for example, he claimed to represent all Arabs and Muslims, taking credit for organizing revolts against the Jews and British while leading his people into an alliance with Germany.[27] When the BBC condemned al-Husaini as a Nazi collaborator, he went on Radio Berlin and quoted the 1936 British government's Peel report on Palestine which described him as a powerful figure who had 150,000 people within his network of charities and clerical institutions.[28]

That doesn't mean that al-Husaini always got his way with the Germans. He unsuccessfully suggested at least four times that the Foreign Ministry start a Department of Islamic Affairs, proposing as its chief Ettel, who had rescued him in Iran and from Turkey.[29] This was a political miscalculation since Ettel was really an intelligence man under cover as a diplomat, and the Foreign Ministry would never have accepted him in such a post. The Foreign Ministry also rejected al-Husaini's idea of building a large separate army of Muslims from French colonies, since Germany had given primacy in that area to Italy. Germany also used Muslim troops to suit the Reich's immediate needs, ignoring al-Husaini's pleas to send them to North Africa.

Still, al-Husaini obtained most of what he wanted. One of the main institutional bases the Nazis gave him was Berlin's Central Islamic Institute. Founded in 1927, this was largely Goebbels's project. After briefly visiting Egypt three years earlier, Goebbels became fascinated by Islam and, later, with al-Husaini personally.[30] Goebbels saw in al-Husaini a fellow master propagandist with a similar worldview who spoke in the name of millions of Muslims and Arabs.[31] Al-Husaini, Goebbels wrote in his diary, was intelligent and had good judgment. If the Nazis worked properly with him they would win over four hundred million Muslims.[32]

Under al-Husaini's guidance, the Islamic Institute became a network for propagandists, diplomats, military officers, and intelligence agents. The institute steadily expanded, establishing branches in Göttingen, Dresden, Guben, and Radom.[33] The Italians started a similar project in 1942 and invited al-Husaini to its opening in Rome, along with al-Kailani and Afghanistan's exiled former King Amanullah.[34]

The Institute's secretary, the Egyptian Abd al-Halim Najjar, an employee of German Arabic-language radio, was a figurehead. The real chief was the journalist Kamal ad-Din Jalal, who worked with both Goebbels and von Ribbentrop.[35] At the December 18, 1942 opening ceremony in Berlin, which took place in the Air War Ministry building, al-Husaini said the Institute would serve not only the two thousand Muslims living in Germany but all of the world's four hundred million Muslims, who were with Germany in the fight against their joint enemies: Jews, Bolsheviks, Great Britain, and America. He quoted al-Qur'an as showing that Jews were terrorists, the Muslims' most spiteful enemies, and haters of Muhammad.[36]

Next to the "Jews, with their race-hatred and capitalism," al-Husaini continued, the British were the worst enemies, who crushed Arab protests by terror, blood, and fire. Such a brutal foe must be fought with brutality. His audience would have recognized the last phrase as a variation on Hitler's "Terror can only be broken by terror."[37] Al-Husaini added that he was personally doing his best for the cause by convincing Muslims to join the German army and the SS. Already, he continued, there were twelve thousand volunteers in Bosnia, many of them with military experience. And if the Allies invaded the Balkans, up to fifty thousand Muslims might rise to fight against them.[38] Goebbels was very impressed with al-Husaini's speech, and German newspapers covered it with such headlines as "This War Can Bring Freedom to Islam" and "Against Terror and Slavery," because the war was a fight to the death between Islam and the Jews.[39]

A few months later, Rosenberg invited al-Husaini to see his Institute for Research into the Jewish Question in Frankfurt. Al-Husaini admired the Nazis' chief ideologue as a great philosopher. They agreed on every point, including viewing the *Protocols of the Elders of Zion* as the core document explaining world history. Al-Husaini's visit to Rosenberg's institute lasted for three full days starting April 12, 1943, and both sides were quite pleased with the result. The institute, founded in 1939, had seventy researchers and six hundred employees studying Europe's Jews, including academics from Germany, Austria, Hungary, and France. The director, Hans Hagemeyer, flattered al-Husaini, calling him a pioneer in the struggle against Zionism, a man from whom the Nazis could learn much about Jewish perfidy.[40]

As a result of these meetings, al-Husaini decided that he wanted his own Jewish institute. He sent an aide, the Syrian Adil Maski, to work for Rosenberg's institute to gain experience, his main task being to translate its fortnightly anti-Semitic magazine, *Weltkampf: Die Judenfrage in Geschichte und Gegenwart* (Battle for the World: The Jewish Question Past and Present), into Arabic.[41] With three thousand marks a month from the German government, al-Husaini began his own Jewish Institute in Berlin, mixing hatred of Jews with promoting Islamism. He specifically requested and received a confiscated Jewish apartment to house the institute.[42]

Al-Husaini wrote Rosenberg, thanking the Nazi ideologue for showing how the "democracies consider the protection of the Jewish parasites as their holy duty." He commended Rosenberg for revealing that the Jews wanted a state as a base for subordinating and destroying all the other peoples of the world, and concluded, "Our common fight against world Jewry makes the Germans and Arabs allies."[43]

There was no clearer proof of how the radical Arab nationalist and Islamist worldview paralleled that of the Nazis than al-Husaini's "stump speech," written in 1943 and used in his talks to SS soldiers and imam training courses.[44] One of his translators, Zvonimir Bernwald of the Bosnian SS Hanžar Division, testified that he heard al-Husaini give this speech to classes of Muslim SS soldiers in Zagreb and Banja Luka in occupied Yugoslavia, and later in an imam training course at Potsdam near Berlin.[45] Al-Husaini made a similar speech to Bosnian SS division imams in October 1944.[46]

Nazi Germany, said the grand mufti, was the Muslims' natural ally. It had never invaded an Islamic land; it fought world Jewry, the archenemy of Islam; and it battled against England, the power that had destroyed the caliphate and the Islamic empire in India. Nazi Germany also fought against Communism, which tyrannized forty million Muslims and tried to destroy Islam.

These things would be sufficient to justify a strong Nazi-Muslim alliance, al-Husaini continued, but there was something else that brought the two sides together: the parallels between the Islamic world view and National Socialism. He gave a long list of such parallels, backing each assertion with quotes from al-Qur'an and Muhammad's sayings:

- Belief in one God taught the need for a single, all-powerful leader. When Muhammad died, a caliph was chosen as sole ruler whom all Muslims must obey. Order, discipline and obedience were central to Islam: the imam led the prayer; the commander led the soldiers. This leader makes decisions alone, not bound by anyone else including voters or a parliament. National Socialism was built on this same principle, with Hitler as the German equivalent of the caliph.
- Islam saw its people as a single global community (*umma*) that should live within a single powerful state. The Nazis had the same view of the Germans.
- Jihad was one of Islam's main duties. Every Muslim saw jihad and martyrdom as the crown to his deeds of faith. Many verses of al-Qur'an asked Muslims to fight and to sacrifice their livelihoods and blood. Nazism also stressed struggle, battle, and self-sacrifice.
- Islam put the community of believers first, with the common good being more important than any individual's welfare. A Nazi Party motto, directed against the "Jewish materialistic spirit"—and even appearing on coins after 1934—was "The common good comes before the private good."[47]
- Islam dealt with family as society's basic organizational group. The father ruled the family; children must obey parents. Motherhood was revered. Having children was good; abortion was prohibited. This approach echoed Hitler's doctrines including the idea—popular among Islamists—that a woman's main job was to produce future soldiers.
- Islam and National Socialism both fought the Jews. Almost one-third of al-Qur'an deals with the Jews, warning Muslims to distrust and battle them, said al-Husaini. The Jews tried to poison Muhammad several times and thus the prophet had no choice but to kill them or drive them from Arabia. Al-Husaini drew up a detailed program from his reading of Muhammad's example that paralleled Hitler's policy: Step 1: Stop tolerating Jews. Step 2: Drive out as many as

possible. Step 3: Kill all the males and enslave the rest, eventually annihilating them entirely.

- Reverence for labor. Islam protected and esteemed work so that everyone gave according to his ability. This argument was the kind of claim later made by radical Arab nationalists in the postwar era when they decided that they were "Arab Socialists" and aligned themselves with the Soviet Union.

- Finally, an Allied victory would be a triumph for the Jews and a disaster for Muslims and Islam. Since the war was a jihad, all Muslims must fight alongside the Germans. If they did so, the radical Arabs' program would succeed: the war would be won, Islam saved, the Arabs united, and the Jews destroyed.[48]

Islamist and Arab nationalist ideology also paralleled that of the Nazis in being racialist. Al-Husaini rejected the claim that Jews and Arabs had common ancestors. No, he said, the two groups were totally different. Arabs were generous and courageous; Jews were greedy and cowardly. He and al-Kailani protested the Nazi use of the phrase "anti-Semitism" lest people think it included the Arabs, also Semites, as well. Hitler and Rosenberg ordered German propagandists not to use that term[49] and instead refer only to being "anti-Jewish."[50] Al-Husaini also encouraged the airing of a radio broadcast in late 1942, written with Grobba's supervision, saying that the Germans viewed the Arabs as a worthy race equal to the Aryans.[51]

The differences between the Arab and Jewish races, al-Husaini explained, were the reason for the eternal hostility between them. The conflict had intensified with the advent of Islam because the Jews plotted against Muhammad. This enmity had continued as Muslims recognized they must liberate themselves from the Jews. The struggle "between two races" was rooted in religion and would continue until "one race" was destroyed.[52] Thus, genocide against the Jews was a necessity in al-Husaini's own ideology, not an idea borrowed from Hitler or abandoned once the Third Reich fell.

This basic approach was echoed and amplified by the forty-four-year-old Egyptian Muhammad Sabri, who had edited the German translation of al-Husaini's prewar appeal for Muslims to cleanse their lands of Jews, to which Sabri added his own thoughts.[53] The Nazis distributed the booklet as widely as possible in several languages.[54]

In explaining why Muslims were uninterested in Communism, Sabri

Figure 20. Heinrich Himmler and Amin al-Husaini meet on July 4, 1943 near the Ukrainian town of Zhitomir. On that occasion, as al-Husaini admitted in his 1999 memoirs, Himmler confided to him that he had killed three million Jews.

pointed out that their society lacked both proletarians and industry, while Islam as a religion was at odds with atheistic Communism. Indeed, the Communists, guided by the Jews, had decided to destroy Islam. In this conspiracy, Sabri provided the enemy with a surprising ally: African-Americans from Harlem—presumably American Communists studying in the USSR—were allegedly training to destroy Islam in Africa.

Muslims know, continued Sabri, that "as Muhammad said: 'You will never see a Jew and a Muslim together without the Jew trying secretly to destroy the Muslim.'" Even before Nazism, Arabs and other Muslims had placed restrictions on the Jews who lived among them. God had revealed Islam; Jews had created Communism.[55] Sabri even adapted the Nazi term of Jews as subhuman, *Untermenschen.* Consequently, he concluded, "The German steps against the Jews nowhere found so much sympathy and support as with the Muslim people."[56]

While there were many later attempts to revise or explain away the rhetoric of al-Husaini and his colleagues, they were always totally unrepentant. For al-Husaini, the Arabs and Muslims were engaged in a "struggle for liberation [against the] dirty race" of Jews.[57] In his memoirs, al-Husaini recalls telling the students at the imam school that the Jews were full of greedy egoism and feelings of superiority, hatred, and self-hatred. All attempts to educate or improve them had failed. Consequently, the only solution was extermination.[58]

It was at the site of such an extermination campaign, in the village of Zhitomir, just east of Kiev, where Himmler and al-Husaini met on July 4, 1943. The previous year Jews in the area had been wiped out by the

وقد كنت أسمع من هملر كل مرة ما يدل على شدة حقده على اليهود، يتهمهم
بأنهم ظالمون، ويزعمون أنهم مظلومون، ويقول أنهم موقدو نيران الحروب، وأنانيون
ونحو ذلك، ويبين مقدار الأذى الذي انزلوه بالمانيا في الحرب الماضية، وأنهم دائماً
يوقدون نار الحرب ثم يستغلونها لمصالحهم المادية، دون أن يخسروا فيها أي شيء،
ولذلك فإننا صممنا في هذه الحرب على ان نذيقهم وبال اعمالهم مقدماً، فقد أبدنا
حتى الآن حوالي ثلاثة ملايين منهم. (وكان حديثه هذا في صيف عام ١٩٤٣)

—————————————— ١٢٦ ——————————————

Figure 21. On page 126 of his memoirs, al-Husaini reveals Himmler's remarks at their meeting in Zhitomir on the Jews and the Final Solution. "Every time I heard of his deep hatred of the Jews. He accused them of being offenders who allege that they are ill-treated. He said they are igniters of the fire of war. In doing so, they are selfish, as shown by the scope of harm done to Germany in the past war. They always stoke the fire of war and use it for their material interests though without injuring themselves a bit. Therefore, we have decided in this war to make them suffer and to pay attention to their activities in advance. Thus, up to now we have liquidated about three million of them (this conversation was in the summer of 1943)."

Germans. Now the village had been renamed Hochwald and was the site of Himmler's field headquarters. He traveled there on his own private train named "Heinrich," after himself, managed by an SS officer, Josef Tiefenbacher.

The story of this meeting between Himmler and al-Husaini can only be told now, using materials from Russian archives.[59] Al-Husaini mentions it vaguely in his memoirs.[60] Along the way, al-Husaini visited some places in Poland and the USSR that the Germans had captured. There is an interesting mystery here. Simon Wiesenthal, who conducted the most thorough contemporary research on al-Husaini's wartime activities, thought the grand mufti had visited Auschwitz or other German death camps in May.[61] It is also possible, however, that al-Husaini did so, accompanied by Eichmann and his aide Alois Brunner, on his way to Zhitomir.[62] Also conveniently located for a possible visit along the route were the Treblinka and Majdanek concentration camps.[63]

Once he arrived in Zhitomir, al-Husaini saw, according to Himmler's diary, the SS model colony, one of twenty-seven organized by Rosenberg in the plan to Germanize large areas of western Russia.[64] The

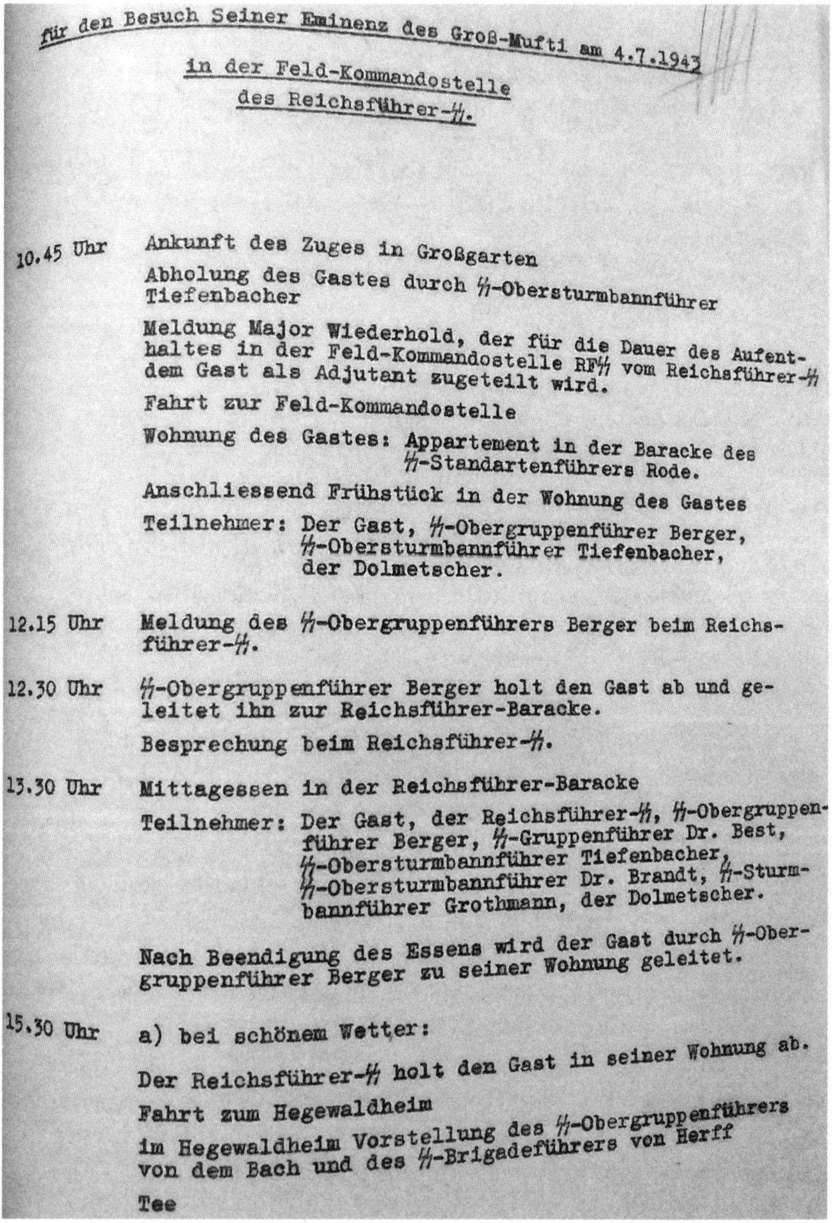

<u>für den Besuch Seiner Eminenz des Groß-Mufti am 4.7.1943</u>

in der Feld-Kommandostelle
des Reichsführer-ℋ.

10.45 Uhr   Ankunft des Zuges in Großgarten

Abholung des Gastes durch ℋ-Obersturmbannführer
Tiefenbacher

Meldung Major Wiederhold, der für die Dauer des Aufent-
haltes in der Feld-Kommandostelle RFℋ vom Reichsführer-ℋ
dem Gast als Adjutant zugeteilt wird.

Fahrt zur Feld-Kommandostelle

Wohnung des Gastes: Appartement in der Baracke des
ℋ-Standartenführers Rode.

Anschliessend Frühstück in der Wohnung des Gastes

Teilnehmer: Der Gast, ℋ-Obergruppenführer Berger,
ℋ-Obersturmbannführer Tiefenbacher,
der Dolmetscher.

12.15 Uhr   Meldung des ℋ-Obergruppenführers Berger beim Reichsführer-ℋ.

12.30 Uhr   ℋ-Obergruppenführer Berger holt den Gast ab und geleitet ihn zur Reichsführer-Baracke.

Besprechung beim Reichsführer-ℋ.

13.30 Uhr   Mittagessen in der Reichsführer-Baracke

Teilnehmer: Der Gast, der Reichsführer-ℋ, ℋ-Obergruppenführer Berger, ℋ-Gruppenführer Dr. Best,
ℋ-Obersturmbannführer Tiefenbacher,
ℋ-Obersturmbannführer Dr. Brandt, ℋ-Sturmbannführer Grothmann, der Dolmetscher.

Nach Beendigung des Essens wird der Gast durch ℋ-Obergruppenführer Berger zu seiner Wohnung geleitet.

15.30 Uhr   a) bei schönem Wetter:

Der Reichsführer-ℋ holt den Gast in seiner Wohnung ab.

Fahrt zum Hegewaldheim

im Hegewaldheim Vorstellung des ℋ-Obergruppenführers
von dem Bach und des ℋ-Brigadeführers von Herff

Tee

Figure 22. The program of al-Husaini's visit to Himmler at Zhitomir planned
every activity down to the minute, including morning and afternoon refresh-
ments, a one-hour conversation followed by a luncheon with the Reichsführer-SS,
alternative clement and inclement weather afternoon activities, and exactly which

17.30 Uhr   direkte Fahrt vom Hegewaldheim zum Bahnhof
                Begleitung durch SS-Brigadeführer von Herff,
                SS-Obersturmbannführer Tiefenbacher

                b) bei schlechtem Wetter

15³⁰ Uhr   Abholung des Gastes durch den Reichsführer-SS in
                seiner Wohnung

                Filmvorführung "Der unendliche Weg" (List-Film)
                Am Beginn des Filmes Vorstellung des SS-Obergruppen-
                führers von dem Bach und des SS-Brigadeführers von
                Herff

17.50 Uhr   Fahrt von der Feld-Kommandostelle zum Bahnhof.
                Major Wiederhold begleitet den Gast bis Berlin.

----

leading SS officers (mostly known as mass murderers of Jews) were to attend at
each stage. Copy of Heinrich Himmler's office calendar, 1943–44, in the possession of the German Historical Institute, Moscow.

8089

14,00 Uhr   Essen mit Großmufti von Jerusalem
und Begleiter
ℋ-Obergruppenführer   B e r g e r
ℋ-Standartenführer   W a g n e r
ℋ-Sturmbannführer   W e i b r e c h t
ℋ-Gruppenführer   J o h s t
ℋ-Sturmbannführer   G r o t h m a n n

16,00 Uhr   Besprechung mit
Großmufti von Jerusalem
und Begleiter
ℋ-Obergruppenführer   B e r g e r

18,00 Uhr   Tee mit Großmufti und Begleiter
ℋ-Obergruppenführer   B e r g e r
ℋ-Brigadeführer   F e g e l e i n

18,30 Uhr   ℋ-Obergruppenführer   B e r g e r
General   R e i n i c k e

Oberst   W e s t h o f f

20,15 Uhr   Essen mit ℋ-Obergruppenführer   B e r g e r
ℋ-Gruppenführer   J o h s t
ℋ-Standartenführer   W a g n e r

21,40 Uhr   ℋ-Standartenführer   W a g n e r

23   ℋ-Obergruppenführer   B e r g e r

Arab guest was given the apartment next to the rooms of SS General Ernst August Rode, who had been leading the forces pursuing partisans in the German-occupied areas with great brutality.[65] The visit was marked by two receptions, where Himmler and al-Husaini dined with the SS generals Berger, Fritz von Scholz, Rudolf Brandt, and Werner Best. Brandt would become notorious for ordering eighty-six Jews to be killed in order to create a collection of their skeletons for research.[66] Best had been instrumental in persuading French officials to implement anti-Jewish measures, and would soon become German commander in Copenhagen.

After dinner and a stroll around the grounds, al-Husaini, Himmler, Berger, Best, and von Scholz went to Himmler's home at Hegewaldheim.[67] They watched a film, Walter von Molo's *The Never-Ending Way*, about the life of the German economist Friedrich List, who a half-century earlier had argued that Germany didn't need colonies in the Middle East.[68] Himmler told al-Husaini, not so tactfully it seems, that the Germans had played the leading role in defeating Muslim invasions of Europe in the past, referring to the battle at Poitiers that stopped them in 732 and the two sieges of Vienna in 1529 and 1683. Al-Husaini replied that this was a pity as it "took away from Europe the spiritual light [of Islam] and the blooming Islamic civilization."[69]

As if to make up for this potential discord, the Germans asked al-Husaini to tell them more about Islam and Arab history. They praised the religion, and Himmler told him that SS men, like Muslims, were not permitted to drink alcohol.[70] Getting down to business, Himmler informed al-Husaini that the Nazis had already killed three million Jews and were making great progress on developing nuclear weapons. He was trying to persuade his guest that Germany would win the war and make him ruler over much of the Middle East.

This argument was harder to make when Himmler and al-Husaini met again on May 8, 1944 in Germany, near the town of Oybin in Sax-

Figure 23. The program of the Oybin meeting between Himmler and al-Husaini once again included many SS officers known as perpetrators of genocide. Given that al-Husaini traveled widely in occupied Poland, the Oybin and Zhitomir meeting schedules make Simon Wiesenthal's findings on al-Husaini's visits en route to the death camps of Auschwitz, Maidanek, and Treblinka all the more plausible. Copy of Heinrich Himmler's office calendar, 1943–44, in the possession of the German Historical Institute, Moscow.

ony where al-Husaini was living. By this point, the Allies were bombing Germany daily and the Red Army was advancing on the eastern front. Just ten days earlier, Eichmann had begun the deportation of Hungarian Jews to Auschwitz.

In the afternoon, al-Husaini met SS leader General Hermann Fegelein, brother-in-law of Hitler's companion Eva Braun.[71] According to al-Husaini, they spoke about horses and the grand mufti recited some Arabic poetry.[72] Al-Husaini does not record whether he discussed Fegelein's experience leading his men in their murder of about fourteen thousand Jews in the area between Brest and Pinsk. Before dinner, al-Husaini talked with General Hermann Reinecke and Colonel Adolf Westhoff for two hours. The two men had been involved in organizing and leading the Muslim units al-Husaini had helped raise.[73] This included the Hanžar Division, which had participated in massacring thousands of Bosnian Jews, Christian Serbs, and Roma ("Gypsies").[74]

Attending the two sessions of discussion held that evening were Berger; SS Sturmbannführer Grothmann; Sturmbannführer Hans Weibrecht, who had commanded units executing Jews in Poland and Russia and had been appointed al-Husaini's personal aide for the occasion; Horst Wagner from the Foreign Ministry, who had worked with al-Husaini on Balkan issues; and Hanns Johst, a friend of Himmler and one of Hitler's favorite writers.[75]

All of these interactions showed that both sides in the alliance saw their relationship as a true partnership and not merely a minimum cooperation conducted for convenience. This was made possible by the fact that the worldview and ideology of the Nazis and their radical Arab and Islamist allies was so compatible.

Still, their utmost efforts and mutual help could not bring victory. Yet while the Nazi ideology collapsed in 1945 and virtually vanished from German and European life, the radical Arab nationalist and Islamist ideologies flourished thereafter. Their basic concepts changed surprisingly little despite the passage of decades, events, and generations. Often the word "Israel" was substituted for the word "Jew." Nevertheless, the profoundly doctrinal hatred for Jews and the belief in the necessity of destroying them remained the core reason for the Arab-Israeli conflict's enduring and irresolvable nature.[76]

While these ideas and activities would continue to be powerful in the Middle East, Berlin would no longer be at their center. SS Hauptscharführer Erich Mansfeld did not know, on April 30, 1945, that this would be his last day of work. The thirty-two-year-old German policeman was a guard at Hitler's Berlin bunker. The main entrance was through a tunnel from Hitler's offices on the Wilhelmstrasse. But there were also an emergency exit and an escape hatch behind the building, a few yards from Hermann-Göring-Strasse. That day, Mansfeld was assigned to a small concrete tower next to the escape hatch when another guard dropped by at 4 P.M. to borrow a gun. As Mansfeld leaned out the tower's window to hand it down, he saw four members of Hitler's bodyguard run out the emergency door ten yards away.[77]

He went over to see what was happening. Out came Hitler's personal aide followed by two SS men carrying the Führer's body wrapped in a carpet. Immediately behind came another guard holding the body of Hitler's companion, Eva Braun. Accompanied only by Goebbels and Hitler's secretary, Martin Bormann, they walked a few steps from the exit. An officer ordered Mansfeld back to his post. He complied but continued watching through the observation slit. He saw men pour gasoline onto the two bodies and set them aflame.

But the Third Reich's Arab and Islamist allies were just getting started in conducting what would become the longest war of all.

10 The War After the War

By 1943, the British controlled the regimes ruling every Arab country, or at least could depend on their support for the war. Britain had returned as-Said to power in Iraq; installed the moderate nationalist Wafd Party in Egypt; backed the loyal Abdallah in Transjordan; taken over the French colonies of Lebanon and Syria; ruled Palestine; captured—along with the Americans—Morocco, Tunisia, and Algeria; and also occupied Iran, along with the Soviets and Americans. In contrast, their Arab enemies were either in Allied prisons or in Berlin. The same situation of moderates displacing radicals happened briefly in Palestinian Arab politics. The absence of the grand mufti and his closest supporters gave a chance for more moderate men to fill the vacuum. Musa al-Alami, who had previously collaborated with al-Husaini and the Nazis, changed sides and persuaded five anti-Husaini Palestine Arab parties to make him their joint representative at the October 1944 Arab summit conference in Alexandria.[1]

At first, al-Alami was seated at a small side table but then his credentials were accepted and Arab leaders welcomed him with kisses and embraces. No doubt they were relieved not to have to deal with al-Husaini.[2] The meeting's tone was moderate. Al-Alami proposed accepting the British White Paper, reversing al-Husaini's 1939 rejection of it. Egypt even suggested offering some compromise to the Jews. The

Saudi king warned against too strong a resolution on Palestine during the U.S. election campaign. In the end, the conference backed the 1939 White Paper.[3] Of course, Arab countries and al-Alami wanted to prevent the creation of a Jewish state. But, in contrast to al-Husaini and his pro-German allies, they hoped to do so through diplomacy rather than violence, and possibly make some deal with the Zionists rather than murdering all of the Jews.[4]

Since the grand mufti's strategy had clearly failed, Transjordan's ruler Abdallah argued, someone else should be given a chance to solve the issue. Only he accurately gauged the Zionists' power and organization. He pulled no punches in describing the Palestine Arabs' "backward state of development" while, in contrast, the Jews, "Are constantly increasing their hold on the country. . . . Cultivating the sandy areas, boring wells, recovering dead lands and converting them into gardens of paradise. Arab parties are still fighting over the claims to leadership of those men who were responsible for the ruin of their country."[5]

As the war came to an end, some portents seemed to favor the Arab side in the dispute: Western desire for Arab friendship, relative unity, the Arab states' bigger role in international politics, and Arab oil's growing importance. But in fact, largely due to the radicals' disastrous strategy and the war itself, the Arabs had lost ground since 1939. U.S. involvement in the region provided additional support for the Zionists. The Holocaust had brought not only international sympathy for the Jews but made hundreds of thousands of European Jewish survivors desperate to immigrate to Palestine.

Yet the key question remained: Was the surest way to Arab victory through diplomacy and compromise or was total triumph the only acceptable outcome and war the only proper method?

In 1939, the radical nationalists and Islamists had chosen the path of violence and extremism, a story that would repeat itself in 1947–48. Yet that outcome was not inevitable and in 1945 even seemed unlikely. Al-Alami tried to prevent the grand mufti's return by obtaining the Arab states' backing for himself. He even courted Jamal al-Husaini, just released from his wartime exile in Southern Rhodesia. As-Said and the British also hoped Jamal would participate in a new, more moderate Palestinian Arab leadership. Instead, Jamal remained loyal to his brother Amin al-Husaini rather than join his brother-in-law al-Alami.

The Arab states lost their nerve and Jamal al-Husaini, leading Amin al-Husaini's forces, outmaneuvered the smaller parties. Instead of imposing al-Alami and less extreme forces as the new Palestine Arab leadership, an Arab League–appointed commission appointed a twelve-man Palestinian leadership group, with five seats given to al-Husaini's Palestine Arab Party and the presidency left open for Amin al-Husaini. Al-Alami was merely given one seat as an independent while the other smaller parties got one place each. The prewar radical nationalist, Nazi collaborationist and Islamist leadership had been restored. What followed—war, defeat, Israel's creation, and a seemingly endless Arab-Israeli conflict—was thus largely inevitable.

How did al-Husaini so easily escape punishment for his war crimes? After the world war ended, even ordinary concentration camp guards were charged, tried, and convicted of acting as accessories to mass murder. They had done far less than the man who had been Germany's leading non-European accomplice. Among his deeds had been launching a bloody revolt in Palestine; assassinating British officials; killing hundreds of other Palestine Arab and Jewish civilians; fomenting a pro-Axis revolt and a massacre of Jews in Iraq; collaborating with Hitler; gathering intelligence for the Germans; recruiting Muslim army units for the German army and SS; preparing a Middle East Holocaust against the Jews; promoting pro-Axis revolts in Egypt and elsewhere; and conducting pro-Nazi propaganda by every means at his disposal.

Al-Husaini's denials of the charges against him were not very credible. On August 26, 1946, he claimed that Zionists had inserted forged statements about him in captured German records. A year later he promised to produce documents disproving his "alleged pro-Axis activity as claimed by the Jews" and proving his "innocence," but he never did so.[6] To neutralize any U.S. effort to go after him as a war criminal, al-Husaini lied by claiming he had "never spoken against America" in his Berlin radio talks. In fact, from the time America entered the war in December 1941 he had constantly charged it as being the Muslims' enemy and the slave of world Jewry.[7]

During Eichmann's trial, he lied at a May 4, 1961 press conference, saying he had "never met Eichmann" and claiming, "The Nazis needed no persuasion or instigation either by me or anybody."[8] Trying to conceal how decisions to commit genocide coincided with his agreements and meetings with Hitler, al-Husaini added that he had arrived in Germany only "after the Nazis had adopted their measures against the Jews."[9]

Yet on other matters, he boasted of complicity. In his memoirs, al-Husaini bragged about how he had blocked Jewish escape from Europe, and made clear that he understood that this was why he was considered to be responsible for the death of so many Jews.[10] He mentioned his many interventions to stop releases, including those of children.[11] Al-Husaini justified this behavior at the time and later by saying that these people would have helped build and maintain a Jewish state in Palestine, the same rationale the PLO and Hamas would use for killing Israeli civilians, including children, decades later. Eichmann himself identified the al-Husaini–Hitler meeting as the turning point in setting off the implementation of genocide.[12]

The Germans also kept him better informed than anyone else about the planned and ongoing mass murders. Of course, this was because they knew he favored them, furthered them in every way in his power, and planned to initiate his own genocide in the Middle East. The only thing that stopped him was the German army's failure to conquer that region. And where the Nazis ruled and al-Husaini had influence—in the Balkans, Tunisia, and Soviet Muslim areas—he supported their policy and trained people to implement it.

For this and many other reasons, al-Husaini was a war criminal and should have been tried as such. The grand mufti was so unrepentantly pro-Nazi that in his memoirs he attacked as a traitor and sell-out his old espionage handler, Canaris, who had turned against Hitler and tried to overthrow the Nazi regime.[13] Some German counterparts noted that he was more fanatical than they were.

The Allies knew all of these facts, and began hunting Eichmann and al-Husaini as war criminals in late 1944.[14] It was an American officer who seized al-Husaini's archive in Berlin. Prior to this, al-Husaini had one of his aides, Mustafa al-Wakil, photograph his papers, and used parts of them in his memoirs.[15] But most of the materials fell into Allied hands and ended up in the State Department's basement.[16]

In mid-1945 Simon Wiesenthal, an Austrian Jew who had spent four and a half years in concentration camps[17] and had thereafter worked for U.S. and Israeli intelligence and war crimes investigators, began researching the close ties between Eichmann and al-Husaini.[18] He published his conclusions in early 1947 and later testified about al-Husaini at the Eichmann trial.[19]

The State Department considered the idea of trying al-Husaini as a war criminal at the Nuremberg trial, while the CIA produced a dozen reports on al-Husaini's involvement in war crimes. But in 1950, it decided to let al-Husaini escape justice, concluding that to do otherwise would stir up trouble for the United States in the Middle East. The British and French had already reached similar conclusions. As would happen in later decades with many terrorists—especially the PLO—Western inaction was justified by political considerations.[20]

Equally, while much of the Arab-Israeli conflict's ensuing history might have happened anyway, if al-Husaini had been kept in custody or tried for war crimes, thus allowing more moderate leaders to emerge, it is conceivable that Palestine might have been partitioned into two states in 1948. The flight of Palestinian Arab refugees might never have happened. Tens of thousands of people who died over decades of continuing conflict might have lived.

This, of course, involves speculation. Yet it is a reasonable assertion that this history would have been less bloody than what actually happened. Certainly, the radical nationalists' and Islamists' post-1948 domination of both the Palestinian movement and most Arab states, whose view of Jews was comparable to that of their former Nazi allies, made it all the more certain. Western inaction against al-Husaini's Islamist ideology and role as an accomplice to genocide made it harder for a self-critical climate in the Arab world, or any international soul-searching that might have brought the region alternative policies and rulers.

In the war's closing days, the Germans had tried to spirit al-Husaini to a neutral country, but Switzerland refused him entry and the French captured him. The only country that ever demanded his prosecution was Yugoslavia, because of the atrocities committed by the Muslim units al-Husaini had recruited and helped train. On July 10, 1945, Tito's government put his name on the international list of wanted war criminals.

Ironically, al-Husaini was saved by two other former Nazi collaborators who had worked for him during the war. One was Husain Sulaiman Djozo, whom al-Husaini had hired as an instructor at his SS imam training school and who went on to be the Bosnian SS division's chief imam. Tito's Communist government pardoned Djozo because it needed a Muslim leader who it knew would follow orders. As an ex-collaborator Djozo was too vulnerable not to obey. If al-Husaini was a war criminal for raising the SS units, Djozo was, too, for helping to lead them. Thus he had a strong incentive to persuade Tito to leave al-Husaini alone.[21]

The grand mufti's other savior was Abd ar-Rahman Azzam, the post-war Arab League's secretary general. Azzam threatened an Arab boycott against Yugoslavia unless al-Husaini was taken off the list. Since the deposed Yugoslav royal family had taken refuge in Cairo, Egypt's government hinted that it would retaliate by letting them organize an opposition center there. Consequently, the Yugoslav government quietly removed al-Husaini's name in August 1945.[22]

Meanwhile, al-Husaini enjoyed relative freedom in Paris. The French let him direct aides, seek Arab League support, and order arms purchases for the next battle against the Jews. He authorized Saad ad-Din Arif, his main arms smuggler, to draw money from funds supplied by Nazi Germany. Ahmad Hilmi, his banker, and Ishaq Darwish, his secretary, signed the checks.[23] While in French custody for crimes committed during the last war, al-Husaini was permitted to start fighting the next one, using Nazi-supplied money and guns.

When al-Husaini's arrest was reported in late May 1945, it was widely expected that the French would turn him over to the British, who had been chasing him for the last seven years. While the Anglo-French extradition treaty related to criminals not politicians, al-Husaini worried that he would end up in British hands and be tried as a war criminal, but neither country took any serious action against him.[24]

On the contrary, the French protected him.[25] On August 28, 1945, the French government elevated the captured man's status to "privileged" because it was negotiating politically with him.[26] U.S. intelligence knew by May 1946 that al-Husaini had secretly instructed old comrades to prepare for his arrival, saying that the French had no objection to his returning to the Middle East.[27] As would happen with Khomeini, whom it would help more than thirty years later, the French government reasoned that it could help a dangerous radical in exchange for his promising to respect French interests in the future whatever he did to the British, Americans, or anyone else. In both cases, the French were deceived.

The British government said that the offenses with which al-Husaini might be charged were "not extraditable" and he was "not a war criminal in the technical sense, not a person who served in enemy forces."[28] Yet, of course, he had done far more damage than any private in the ranks of an Axis army. At the time, London was sponsoring the Arab League and seeking to develop postwar strategic ties with the region's countries. One can only conclude that the British thought prosecuting al-Husaini would cause revolts, resentment, and retaliation in the Arab and Muslim world.[29]

In June 1946, Acting Secretary of State Dean Acheson announced the issuing of a White Paper on al-Husaini's war record based on captured files, but the report never appeared. Supreme Court Justice Robert H. Jackson, chief prosecutor at the Nuremburg war crimes trials, said that since the court's jurisdiction was only to try war criminals in Axis Europe, al-Husaini could not be tried there, disregarding the fact that his activities in the Balkans and USSR fit the requirements for prosecution.[30]

While some American Jewish groups proposed that al-Husaini be tried for his role in the Holocaust, they received no cooperation from the U.S. government.[31] At the end of the war, the government stopped New York's *Morgen Journal* from publishing material about al-Husaini and demanding his trial as a war criminal.[32] The liberal magazine *The Nation* called him an accomplice in the Holocaust, suggested he was only being treated leniently so as not to hurt Muslim feelings, and charged him with directing a movement in Palestine that echoed Nazi slogans.[33] The liberal *New York Post* added new information by publishing extracts from British interrogations of the Arab paratroopers al-Husaini had sent to Iraq. The grand mufti, it said, "organized Axis activities in the Middle East" and was a war criminal being spared punishment because the British and French had agreed to use him as a political instrument.[34]

Since there were no charges against al-Husaini and the Yugoslavs had dropped him from the wanted list, however, the French released him in May 1946 and he quickly went to Egypt. Following the principle al-Husaini had done so much to introduce—that the most radical was always the most legitimate—no Arab leader tried to block al-Husaini's return despite all the problems he had caused them. In the Arabic-speaking world he was a hero.

The Muslim Brotherhood campaigned for al-Husaini's return precisely because of his past radicalism and intransigence, which it defined as Islamist heroism. His old ally Hasan al-Banna wrote:

> Great welcome should be extended to him wherever he goes, as a sign of appreciation for his great services for the glory of Islam and the Arabs. . . . What a hero, what a miracle of a man. We wish to know what the Arab youth, cabinet ministers, rich men, and princes of Palestine, Syria, Iraq, Tunis, Morocco, and Tripoli are going to do to be worthy of this hero. Yes, this hero who challenged an empire and fought Zionism, with the help of Hitler and Germany. Germany and Hitler are gone, but Amin al-Husaini will continue the struggle.[35]

Al-Husaini did continue the struggle, in the same spirit as he had done when allied with Hitler. Most of those who worked with him did the same. Al-Husaini's top military commanders in the new war against the Jews—al-Qawuqji, Abd al-Qadir al-Husaini, and Salama—had all been Nazi collaborators. Practically the first thing al-Husaini did on arriving in Cairo was to meet Salama and Abd al-Qadir al-Husaini to plan his attack.[36]

Abd al-Qadir had fought alongside the other two men in defense of Iraq's pro-Nazi regime. But in a June 1941 battle at Sadr Abu Ghraib he was captured and imprisoned in Iraq for three years. After being released, Abd al-Qadir spent the rest of the war as a guest of the Saudi king in Mecca, where the al-Husaini clan had temporarily moved its headquarters. In January 1946 he arrived in Cairo to go back to work for his uncle.[37]

Their first task was to retrieve the Nazi arms al-Husaini's men had hidden in Egypt's desert for use in the projected 1942 pro-German revolt, a task carried out with help from the Muslim Brotherhood and the Young Egypt Party. The rifles sent directly to them by the Nazis in 1939 for their own revolt were also utilized in the new battles. Salama's men used them, for example, in the December 8, 1947 attack against Tel Aviv's Hatikva quarter.[38]

Al-Husaini had called the SS units he recruited for the Germans "as-Sa'iqa," ("lightning storm"), named after the Nazis' stormtroopers. Later, he would use the same name for his Syria-based Palestinian army fighting in the 1947–48 war, which was commanded by al-Qawuqji, still another collaborator with the Germans.[39]

As leader of the Holy Jihad Troops, *al-Jihad al-Muqaddas*, Abd al-Qadir drilled his men in a secret training camp near Egypt's border with Libya. He then led al-Husaini's main army until he was killed.[40] Salama commanded on the key central front where he was mortally wounded by grenade fragments at the battle of Ras al-Ain in 1948.[41] There are reports that the Palestinian Arab forces also had ex-Nazi advisers in the field.[42]

Between arriving in Cairo in May 1946 and launching his war about a year later, al-Husaini worked to muster Arab and Muslim state support, pressuring and blackmailing those—especially in Transjordan and Egypt—who were not eager to fight. As had happened in the late 1930s, Arab governments once more had to take into account the grand mufti's charisma, ability to incite their own people to violence, and determination to veto any concessions, as well as internal pressures from Islamist and nationalist radicals who incited flammable public opinion.

It might seem excessive to assert that there would have been no 1948 war and no Arab-Israeli conflict without al-Husaini and his allies. Yet no one individual made this outcome more likely than him. While pressures from the public and militant groups between 1946 and 1948 made war seem inevitable, without al-Husaini's presence as the Palestinian Arabs' and a transnational Islamist leader there might have been other options. And al-Husaini was well funded by money and well-armed with rifles that had been provided by the Nazis.

With a moderate Palestinian leadership, partition might have been accepted and a Palestinian state created in 1948 or a deal worked out at some point during the half-century that followed.[43] Certainly, if the radical faction had not triumphed so thoroughly both politically and ideologically, such an outcome would have been far more possible. Transjordan's ruler Abdallah was interested in annexing the West Bank and making some deal with the Jews. The Egyptian government was eager to avoid war, and there were other relatively moderate Arab and other Muslim leaders.

One should not oversimplify these complex issues, but the retrospective view that everything was inevitable overstates the case. Once al-Husaini was allowed to reestablish himself as unchallengeable leader of the Palestinian Arabs, this ensured that no compromise or two-state solution would be considered, while making certain that Arab leaders would be intimidated and driven to war. Al-Husaini's and the radical legacy has continued to dominate the Palestinian national and the Islamist global movement down to the present day.

Like al-Husaini and his own movement, most of the other forces pushing for intransigence and war over the Palestine issue also came from the same radical Arab and Islamist faction that had cooperated with the Nazis: the Muslim Brotherhood in Egypt and Syria as well as militant nationalists and Islamists in Syria and Iraq. Again, while it might seem obvious that what happened was inevitable, a study of the records and secret discussions among Arabs and between Arab leaders and the West during that period—just as with the 1938–1939 events—makes that conclusion far less certain.

During the first phase, between the November 1947 UN partition vote and the end of the mandate accompanied by Israel's declaration of independence in May 1948, al-Husaini's men and foreign volunteers from formerly pro-Nazi radical groups fought the Jews. One of those volunteers was a resident of Egypt whose family had emigrated from Palestine named Yasir Arafat, a distant relative of al-Husaini. Arafat claimed that his mentor was Abd al-Qadir al-Husaini, who had fought for the Nazis, and that he had served in a unit under Abd al-Qadir's command. That unit was a Muslim Brotherhood one and Arafat was at that time either a member of that organization or at least very close to it.[44]

Among those offering al-Husaini help were Egyptian officers who just five years earlier had collaborated with the Nazis. They called themselves the Free Officers and their ranks included as-Sadat, who had been expelled from the army for his pro-German activities and jailed in 1942. He escaped in October 1944, hiding out as a laborer and truck driver, and then returned home in September 1945, though he was only allowed to rejoin the army five years later.

Immediately after the November 29, 1947, UN partition vote, Free Officers leader Abd an-Nasir, another member of the pro-Nazi faction during the world war, visited al-Husaini at his home in Cairo to explain that his group wanted to support the "resistance movement in Palestine" as volunteers. Al-Husaini requested government permission and was turned down. The moderate Egyptian regime didn't want to turn over its soldiers to al-Husaini's control.[45]

The failure of al-Husaini's local forces to destroy the Jews in 1947

and early 1948 led to the regular Arab armies' intervention, finally getting Abd an-Nasir into the fighting. But they, too, were defeated. Israel
survived the onslaught, though this was not the conflict's end but only
its beginning.

After the lost war, al-Husaini was desperate. The Jewish state was
established despite his four-decade-long struggle from Istanbul, Jerusalem, Beirut, Baghdad, Tehran, Berlin, Paris, and Cairo to stop it. The rest
of Palestine was also lost to him. Egypt seized the Gaza Strip; Transjordan annexed the West Bank and the eastern part of Jerusalem. On
December 20, 1948, Abdallah even took away the grand mufti job,
appointing in al-Husaini's place his old rival Hisham ad-Din Jar Allah,
and al-Husaini's effort to create—at last, when too late—a Palestinian
government in exile went nowhere.

Habib Hasan, his bodyguard for many years, left him.[46] Al-Husaini,
clearly under psychological stress, became irritable and antagonistic
toward people. Trusting no one, he carried two guns and slept in a different place each night.[47] He certainly could not depend on Arab governments, which had finally succeeded in shutting him out of regional
politics. Publicly and officially, however, nobody blamed al-Husaini for
having thrown away the prewar opportunities to get all of Palestine,
betting on the Nazis to win the war, rejecting a UN-created Palestinian
state, losing the remaining territory to his supposed Arab allies, and
leading his people into a disastrous, avoidable war that resulted in so
many of them becoming refugees.

Instead, the radical nationalists and Islamists blamed the disaster—the
nakba, in Arabic—on Israel, the West, and Arab state leaders rather than
on al-Husaini's radicalism, intransigence and Islamism. And when they—
like Abd an-Nasir—condemned governments of the time as incompetent,
weak, and corrupt, they were complaining that those rulers had been
too moderate. What was needed, the revolutionaries concluded, was
not rethinking but revenge.

It would be easy to assume that al-Husaini's career as an important political figure was finished in 1948, but that was not at all true.
Instead, he devoted the remaining quarter-century of his life in seeking to ensure that radical Islamism would have its revenge on Western
democracies, Israel, and Arab nationalists alike. During the years of
Islamism's eclipse, supplanted and repressed by its former radical nationalist partners, al-Husaini kept the movement alive. Arab regimes,

VI. THE MUFTI ATTEMPTS TO BROADEN HIS SUPPORT

A. The Islamic Congress for the Palestine Cause

By the autumn of 1953, Hajj Amin had reached the conclusion that the time had come to give formal organization of his supporters and program in Jordan. Although he attempted to gain entry into Jordan, reportedly with the assistance of Syrian President Shishakli, he failed. In creating this organization, he planned to establish it on as broad a base as possible and to constitute it principally of Moslem religious personalities; the latter device was designed to appeal to the religious sensibilities of the West Bank masses and also to make it more difficult for the Jordanian Government to attack the group. Furthermore, in order to give the impression that his organization had backing from the Moslem world at large, he adopted the technique used earlier by the Pakistanis for gaining additional support for their cause in Kashmir and their leadership in the Islamic world. He assembled, on December 3-9, 1953, an "Islamic Congress" in Jerusalem, Jordan, with delegates ostensibly representing as many Moslem countries and organizations as possible.

Most of the delegates were from the Moslem Brethren, with whom Hajj Amin had established a close working agreement at the time of the Palestine War and in the course of his activities at various Islamic conferences in Karachi. Other delegates included exiled North African nationalist leaders in Cairo and a representative of the Iranian extremist leader Ayatollah Kashani. The resolutions adopted by the conference were as follows:

1. All Moslem must work for the liberation of Palestine.

2. The Israeli occupation of Palestine is invalid and Israel's displacement of the Palestine Arabs and usurpation of their rights is an aggression against every Moslem.

3. Consideration of peace with Israel or dealing with Israel is treason.

4. The proposed internationalization of Jerusalem is a conspiracy against the Moslem world.

5. There should be popular mobilization for an active struggle to help the refugees regain their homes. Until this is achieved the refugees' condition must be improved.

6. A Moslem Palestine fund of $5,000,000 should be established to finance plans for economic revival in Jordan and financing the general struggle.

Figure 24. A CIA report from 1953 describes al-Husaini's Islamic Congress in Jerusalem, his outreach to the West Bank Palestinians, and his cooperation with the Muslim Brothers and other Islamists, among them Said Ramadan in Karachi and Ayatullah Kashani in Tehran. Note the congress's resolutions that "all Muslims must work for the liberation of Palestine" and that "dealing with Israel is treason." The report is testimony to the survival of international Islamism at a time that it was being suppressed by nationalist regimes in many Middle Eastern countries.

aside from the pious Saudis, wanted nothing to do with al-Husaini. Jordanian and Iraqi leaders were angry at al-Husaini's past subversive efforts against them. Egypt and Syria wanted no interference by al-Husaini or the Islamists with their radical nationalist agenda and the Palestinian issue. Given this enmity, al-Husaini had ample reason to end his attempt to balance nationalism and Islamism in favor of becoming a purely Islamist revolutionary.[48]

At the time, al-Husaini's plan for a worldwide radical Islamist movement seemed utmost fantasy, yet today that dream has come true. His first step was an attempt to unite the movement in 1951 by founding the League of Jihad Call at his Cairo residence. Mostly, however, it just brought together his old Egyptian allies, the Muslim Brotherhood, whose leader Hasan al-Hudaibi participated, and the fascist Young Egypt Party.[49]

But al-Husaini would not confine his new campaign to mere words. On July 16, 1951, he met al-Qawuqji in a Lebanese village. They had received reports that former Lebanese Prime Minister as-Sulh was visiting Abdallah to discuss making peace with Israel. According to a CIA investigation at the time, al-Husaini gave the order and, the next day, al-Sulh was assassinated. Three days later, one of al-Husaini's men, a member of his Holy Jihad militia, killed Abdallah.[50] The Jordanians captured Musa Abdallah al-Husaini, who had planned the attack for his boss and relative, and hanged him the following year.

Al-Husaini also kept up his contacts with old German comrades, many of them now escaped war criminals. In Cairo, Damascus, and other places he helped ex-Nazi officials obtain new identities and jobs, and even converted several of them to Islam. His most notable convert, Johann von Leers, would lead the Nazi underground in the Middle East.[51]

Shut out of Middle East politics, al-Husaini developed a broader Third World orientation, finding a political home in the growing "nonaligned movement" of countries trying to stake out an independent position in the Cold War. He was personally admitted to participate in the organization of nonaligned countries despite the fact that he had only recently been aligned with the Axis and led no country. Al-Husaini took part in the 1949 New Delhi and 1954 Colombo conferences of Asian nations, making sure the Palestine question was always included in discussions. In 1955 he attended the Bandung summit in Indonesia, where the nonaligned movement became a significant force. Arriving with two aides, Muhammad Ishaq Darwish and Emil al-Ghuri, al-Husaini met with leaders of twenty-nine countries, including India's Jawaharlal Nehru, Indonesia's Ahmad Sukarno, and Egypt's Abd an-Nasir. He was also at the Belgrade session six years later where his host was Yugoslav dictator Tito, who had once added him to and then removed him from the list of war criminals for his involvement in massacring Tito's countrymen during World War II.

While Abd an-Nasir continued to consult with al-Husaini through the 1950s, the former grand mufti's main sphere of activity was in non-Arab Muslim countries, especially Pakistan and Iran. He cultivated such figures as Ghulam Siddiq Khan in Berlin, Mirza Ali Khan in Waziristan, and, continuing old efforts to foment Muslim revolts in India, with Ghulam Abbas, head of the Kashmir Liberation Front.[52] In Pakistan, al-Husaini organized annual meetings from 1949 to 1952 of his Islamic World Congress, whose services he had offered Hitler a few years earlier, thanks to the hospitality of the Pakistani government, Egypt's ambassador to Pakistan Muhammad Ali Aluba, and Shaudri Khaliq az-Zaman, head of Pakistan's Muslim League.[53]

Early in 1951, al-Husaini visited Tehran to renew his acquaintance with Abd al-Qasim al-Kashani, the leading Islamist cleric, and Nawwab Safawi, the ex-Nazi agent who headed the radical Islamist group Fidaiyyun al-Islam. Tehran was then in turmoil due largely to Safawi's group which committed six political assassinations that year. On March 7, it killed pro-British Prime Minister Ali Razmara. U.S. intelligence reported, whether accurately or not isn't clear, that the Soviets were now funding the Iranian Islamists and al-Husaini, too.[54]

Al-Husaini next sent two of his Egyptian agents—Abd al-Jalil Sukkar and Said Ramadan—to meet with al-Kashani, offering him an alliance. Al-Kashani agreed, and at the Islamic World Congress's next session, al-Kashani became a board member of al-Husaini's secret terrorist group, Jamiyyat Fidaiyyun al-Filastin.[55] While few of the plans made by this Palestinian Sunni and his Iranian Shia partner were implemented, the two men kept Islamism going through its leanest years. In 1952 they met in Beirut, and al-Kashani brought up his idea of creating a Brothers in Peace group to defend Muslim holy places from foreign imperialism.[56]

Al-Husaini proposed blocking West Germany's decision to pay compensation to Israel for Nazi persecution of Jews and confiscation of their property.[57] He also suggested getting the Arab League to threaten a boy-cott of West Germany. His old colleague Azzam, the Arab League's chief, unsuccessfully sent a joint Arab delegation to Bonn to protest such compensation. No one seemed to notice the irony of two former Nazi collaborators who had been paid some of that confiscated wealth—al-Husaini and Azzam—fighting to deny compensation to the victims. Indeed, that was still the source of the funds that al-Husaini was using to finance his anti-Jewish campaign.

At the December 1953 Islamic World Congress session in east Jeru-salem, al-Husaini again cooperated with al-Kashani and Safawi. Also participating were Ramadan, who worked for both al-Husaini and the Muslim Brotherhood, and Sayyid Qutb, the Brotherhood's leading ideo-logue.[58] Ramadan would become leader of Islamism in Europe while Qutb would be the father of modern Islamist ideology.

In the short run, however, Islamism's fortunes declined. Safawi was executed in 1955 by Iran's government for his terrorist deeds, while al-Kashani withdrew from politics and died in 1962. As a result, al-Husaini's connections with Iranian Islamists were almost extinguished. The Abd an-Nasir regime's ferocious persecution of the Egyptian and Syrian Muslim Brothers in the 1950s, closing down the organization entirely, was also a setback for his Islamist alliance. Qutb was arrested in 1954, spent most of the next decade in prison, and was executed in 1966. Yet the seeds for future revolution and violence had been planted: one of al-Kashani's disciples was Khomeini; Safawi's example inspired revolutionary terrorist Islamist groups in Iran. Both legacies would be critical in the future Islamic revolution there. The Muslim Brotherhood, its many even more radical spin-offs, and indeed all the revolutionary Islamist groups of the late twentieth and early twenty-first centuries would owe a big debt to al-Husaini's and Qutb's innovative thinking.

Why did the United States and its European allies never see the dan-ger posed by al-Husaini and the other Islamists? Of course, at the time they were focused on the Cold War with the Soviet Union. Since the Islamists were anti-Communist, as well as being so weak, they were not perceived as a threat. Indeed, Islamist defectors from the USSR were useful intelligence assets, while Islamism seemed a way to counter the radical secularist Arab nationalists aligned with Moscow.

In part, though, U.S. policymakers were deliberately misled. In 1949,

U.S. intelligence was alarmed by al-Husaini's attempts to set up an intelligence service in partnership with Egypt,[59] his efforts to create terrorist groups and foment a new war to destroy Israel, and the chance that he might align himself with the USSR.[60] But they soon decided that he was harmless because this was what Arab and German sources told them. Arab contacts and allies asked about the issue by the State Department and CIA assured the Americans that they need not worry because al-Husaini was discredited—for losing Palestine, not as a Nazi accomplice—and would no longer be a problem. West Germany's Foreign Ministry told the State Department the same thing: Israel considered him a war criminal but this was wrong. Al-Husaini had never been interested in Nazism and had not worked well with the Hitler regime.[61] It is easier to understand this assessment when one knows that those making this claim were often themselves ex-Nazi diplomats who had worked with al-Husaini during the war. They now had to clear the former grand mufti in order to clear themselves.

Instead, American policymakers should have been listening to Musa Ali Bigiyev. During the war, he was a Soviet fighter pilot, and was shot down and captured by the Germans. Bigiyev was an ethnic Tatar, son of a distinguished Muslim cleric named Musa Jarullah Bigiyev who lived and taught in Cairo.[62] The elder Musa met al-Husaini in the early 1930s at one of the international meetings hosted by the grand mufti. Apparently, after his son was shot down and captured Musa asked al-Husaini to get him released from the Mauthausen camp. Al-Husaini approached Eichmann but Musa Ali refused to join the German army units the grand mufti was forming and so remained a German prisoner.[63] Freed at the war's end, Musa Ali remained in Germany.

In 1949 the younger Bigiyev joined the German Muslim League in Hamburg.[64] Members of the group admired al-Husaini.[65] Although he remained opposed to the radical Islamists, Bigiyev's activities made al-Husaini think he was a supporter and thus he tried to use Bigiyev as an agent. What al-Husaini didn't know, however, was that Bigiyev was passing information to Wiesenthal.[66] From Cairo, al-Husaini wrote asking Bigiyev to help establish contacts with Eichmann and other high-ranking Nazis.[67] When that plan didn't work, al-Husaini sent his emissary, Husain Haurani, in October 1949 to give Eichmann's wife, Veronica, money so she and their three children could join her husband in Argentina.[68]

As for al-Husaini himself, he never had to flee anywhere. The man whose miscalculations did the most to prevent a Palestinian Arab state's creation was the one the Nazis would have made the Arabs' monarch and perhaps even the Muslims' caliph. The decades of war, blood, and conflict that followed—while obviously the result of wider decisions and forces—were set in motion by a man who should have been in prison as a war criminal yet who most of the world was ready to make a head of state in 1948 if only he would take the invitation.

Al-Husaini lived unvexed in Lebanon until his death by natural causes there in 1974.

11 The Arab States' Useful Nazis

Many Nazi war criminals evaded justice, but only in the Middle East did this fact have major political implications, and almost exclusively in that region were they able to continue their careers in government, the military, and propaganda work. No Arab country ever expelled any of them for their past war crimes or views, but instead shielded from prosecution all of the German war criminals who fled to them.

South America was also a destination for Nazis to flee and flourish but they were only able to do so in smaller numbers and generally for shorter periods of time than in the Middle East. Indeed, while Argentina's president Juan Perón invited some to settle in his country, his reign did not last long. When he fell in 1955, a number of those fugitives also moved to the Middle East.[1] Outside cooperating Arab countries it was hard for Nazis to keep their presence a secret or to rely on government protection. In effect, old Arab nationalist and Islamist allies functioned as part of the international Nazi underground in helping such people escape and find safe haven. Even Eichmann's escape to Argentina was largely due to al-Husaini's help.[2]

The number of former German officials or officers involved in the war or war crimes who went to the Middle East was over four thousand. In comparison, it is estimated that only between 180 and 800 Nazis escaped to Latin America, mostly Argentina.[3] Wiesenthal estimated in 1967 that there were between six and seven thousand ex-Nazi regime officials and officers living in Arab lands.[4] For those who still sought to carry out Hitler's genocidal project or create an ideal totalitarian state, Arabs were the obvious allies and Muslim countries the indispensable refuge.[5]

Former Nazi government officials and foreign collaborators who worked on Middle East issues were able to revive their fortunes in postwar West Germany after the first wave of prosecutions ended by 1950. In their revived careers, they continued to be sympathetic to other former Nazis, Nazi-era officials, radical Arab nationalists, and Islamists. One of the most influential of these was Hans Globke, Chancellor Konrad Adenauer's national security adviser who had helped write the laws giving Hitler unlimited power and denying citizenship to Jews.[6] Reinhard Gehlen,[7] head of West Germany's Federal Intelligence Service, was the most important ex-Nazi official working with Western intelligence.[8] His operation was mainly directed against the USSR but he also did some work involving the Middle East, where Grobba became one of his main agents.[9] During the war, Gehlen had been on the staff of army General Staff chief Franz Halder, who also worked for U.S. army intelligence starting in 1946, debriefing captured German officials including Grobba.[10]

West Germany's employment of former Nazis, especially SS men and those accused of war crimes, was a source of friction with the United States. The CIA worried about embarrassing public exposure of this fact, and CIA officials discussed as early as May 1950 how to persuade West German intelligence to limit the practice. The CIA proposed to infiltrate Gehlen's operations to get rid of ex-Nazis there, but in the end, Gehlen was deemed too valuable to sacrifice.[11]

Another career survivor was Fritz Grobba. Released from a Soviet camp in 1956 after a decade of imprisonment,[12] the seventy-year-old Grobba restarted his career, working for both West Germany and the Saudis, beginning with a visit to Baghdad that year.[13] The Saudi envoy Midhat al-Ard, a former al-Husaini aide, met Grobba in Berne in 1957 and asked him to set up a West German–Arab Friendship Society. He also invited Grobba to meet Saudi King Khalid, whose kingdom Grobba as ambassador had tried to persuade to join the Axis. After seeing the king, Grobba went to the Middle East to recruit sponsors for the friendship society.[14] The plan failed because of Arab anger at West Germany's decision at the time to pay compensation to Israel for losses and suffering during the Holocaust.[15]

Aside from hiring Grobba, Gehlen also reportedly consulted with ex-SS officer Otto Skorzeny, who visited Cairo frequently in his job representing Austrian steel companies.[16] There he met al-Husaini in early 1953. The two men shared such mutual friends as Eichmann and François Genoud, the Swiss Nazi banker.[17] Skorzeny may have later spied for Israel's Mossad and the CIA against ex-Nazi circles in Cairo.[18]

Gehlen's was not the only West German operation based largely on ex–World War II agents. Leverkuehn, a von Oppenheim veteran from World War I and Abwehr chief in Istanbul during World War II, maintained a Lebanon-based network with the help of the Christian Democratic Party, the Foreign Ministry, and the prime minister's office.

A former Nazi in a particularly key position to help Islamists was Adenauer's minister of refugees, Theodor Oberländer. A history teacher, Oberländer had joined the Nazi Party and worked in military intelligence. In 1940 he had urged the elimination of all Polish Jews and the next year helped round up and kill seven thousand Jews in Lvov. Later, Oberländer led Abwehr teams in Caucasian Muslim units, recruited with al-Husaini's help, which committed atrocities in Poland. In his postwar work for the West German government, Oberländer employed other ex-Nazis and assisted Muslim collaborators to remain in the country.

East Germany waged periodic campaigns to discredit West Germany by exposing the Nazi background of government officials there,[19] and on November 12, 1958 it released a book that documented Oberländer's involvements.[20] In 1960, he resigned, one of the few former Nazis in key positions who lost their jobs.[21]

Those who did face prosecution were often able to escape, helped by an underground railroad of sympathizers and former colleagues. The most important such group was ODESSA—Organisation der ehemaligen SS-Angehörigen (Organization of Former Members of the SS), founded by 1947. Another organization, Stille Hilfe (Silent Aid), was set up in Munich by Helene Elizabeth von Isenburg in 1951. On the board were two bishops, Theophil Wurm of Württemberg and Johannes Neuhäusler of Munich, as well as ex-SS men like Wilhelm Spengler and

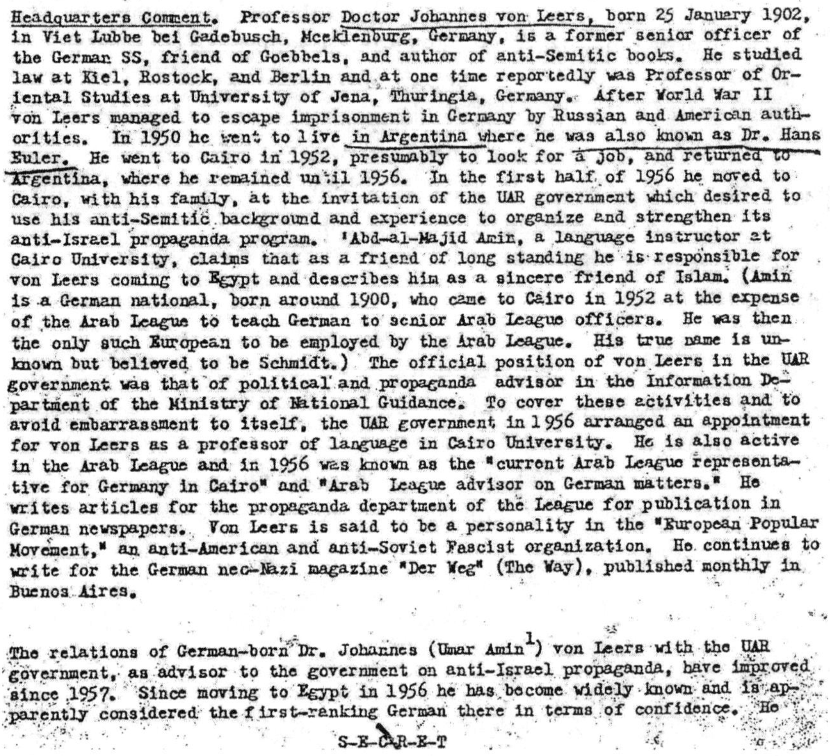

Headquarters Comment. Professor Doctor Johannes von Leers, born 25 January 1902, in Viet Lubbe bei Gadebusch, Mecklenburg, Germany, is a former senior officer of the German SS, friend of Goebbels, and author of anti-Semitic books. He studied law at Kiel, Rostock, and Berlin and at one time reportedly was Professor of Oriental Studies at University of Jena, Thuringia, Germany. After World War II von Leers managed to escape imprisonment in Germany by Russian and American authorities. In 1950 he went to live in Argentina where he was also known as Dr. Hans Euler. He went to Cairo in 1952, presumably to look for a job, and returned to Argentina, where he remained until 1956. In the first half of 1956 he moved to Cairo, with his family, at the invitation of the UAR government which desired to use his anti-Semitic background and experience to organize and strengthen its anti-Israel propaganda program. 'Abd-al-Majid Amin, a language instructor at Cairo University, claims that as a friend of long standing he is responsible for von Leers coming to Egypt and describes him as a sincere friend of Islam. (Amin is a German national, born around 1900, who came to Cairo in 1952 at the expense of the Arab League to teach German to senior Arab League officers. He was then the only such European to be employed by the Arab League. His true name is unknown but believed to be Schmidt.) The official position of von Leers in the UAR government was that of political and propaganda advisor in the Information Department of the Ministry of National Guidance. To cover these activities and to avoid embarrassment to itself, the UAR government in 1956 arranged an appointment for von Leers as a professor of language in Cairo University. He is also active in the Arab League and in 1956 was known as the "current Arab League representative for Germany in Cairo" and "Arab League advisor on German matters." He writes articles for the propaganda department of the League for publication in German newspapers. Von Leers is said to be a personality in the "European Popular Movement," an anti-American and anti-Soviet Fascist organization. He continues to write for the German neo-Nazi magazine "Der Weg" (The Way), published monthly in Buenos Aires.

The relations of German-born Dr. Johannes (Umar Amin[1]) von Leers with the UAR government, as advisor to the government on anti-Israel propaganda, have improved since 1957. Since moving to Egypt in 1956 he has become widely known and is apparently considered the first-ranking German there in terms of confidence. He

S-E-C-R-E-T

Figure 25. The postwar Nazi Middle Eastern network: A CIA report from 1959 gives the basic "curriculum vitae" of the ex–SS officer and anti-Semitic propagandist Johann von Leers, including his journey from defeated Germany via Argentina to Egypt to become adviser on propaganda to an-Nasir's regime.

Heinrich Malz, the latter an aide to Gestapo chief Ernst Kaltenbrunner. The complex network involved anti-Communist Catholics, the International Red Cross, and also its Islamic equivalent, the Red Crescent.

The Middle East escape route ran through Italy, Spain, or Portugal, usually ending in Algeria, Egypt, or Syria. ODESSA's goal was not merely to rescue Nazis but to rebuild the Nazi movement and work to create a Fourth Reich.[22] ODESSA's regional headquarters was in Cairo where it was directed by Johann von Leers.[23] In hundreds of dispatches American agents reported regularly about ODESSA activities starting February 26, 1948. Wiesenthal heard about it for the first time in No-has never been officially received by UAR President Jamal 'Abd-al-Nasir, but is persona grata with the following officials:

(a) Ali Sabri, Minister of State for Presidential Affairs, UAR, who has granted him several interviews.

(b) Anwar al-Sadat, president of the Afro-Asian Solidarity Council.

(c) Muhammad 'Abd-al-Khaliq Hassuna, secretary-general of the Arab League.

(d) Former Grand Mufti of Jerusalem, Haj Amin-Al-Husayni, through whom von Leers was initiated into Islam and with whom he wants to make a pilgrimage to Mecca.

(e) Brigadier General 'Abd-al-Azim Ibrahim Fahmi, Director of General Investigations Department of UAR Ministry of Interior.

(f) Sayed Hafez 'Abd-al-Karim, secretary-general of Ministry of Economy and Commerce, UAR (Egyptian Region).

2. Von Leers assumes that he is under observation by the West German government. Knowing that the UAR values the maintenance of good relations with Bonn, particularly in the economic field, von Leers now limits his calls at government offices and occasionally sends instead his daughter, Gesine, or his wife to make them for him.

3. To lessen the possibility of surveillance by phone-tapping, von Leers planned to move on 1 October 1958 from his former address (#21 rue 83, Cairo-Ma'adi) to a larger house at #52 rue 11 in the same suburb, where he could have a direct telephone line. The Arab League will pay the costs of this move. For his services to the League he receives between 80 and 100 Egyptian pounds per month.

4. The Algerian resistance movement is also of interest to von Leers, and he advises 'Abd-al-Karim of information he receives on developments relating to it. He helped German journalist Erich Kernmayer (who writes for "Deutsche Soldatenzeitung," Munich, under the pen name Erich Kern) to compile material for his book "Algerien in Flammen" (Algeria in Flames).

5. Von Leers is writing a book, tentatively entitled, "Der Freiheitskampf der Kolonialunterdrückten Völker" (The Fight for Freedom of the Peoples Repressed by Colonialism). This will present the history and problems of the peoples of Asia and Africa formerly or still under colonial domination. The book will conclude with a discussion of the occupied countries of Europe.

6. Von Leers's hatred of the West German government and its policies is increasing. He speaks only in terms of contempt of Bundestag President Eugen Gerstenmaier and Foreign Minister Heinrich von Brentano. He is slightly less bitter toward President Theodor Heuss. His letters are full of disparagement of that government. He is constantly pressing for the West German nationalist opposition to come to an agreement with the Soviet Union, on the theory that the Soviets should be brought in to clean up the West. To arguments that such measures would result in great loss of life and freedom he replies that in view of West Germans' conduct since 1945 they deserve nothing better. He believes that after such a clean-up the Soviets could be removed by anti-colonial pressure and the Reich restored.

Figure 26. The postwar Nazi Middle Eastern network: A CIA report describes von Leers's contacts and activities in Cairo. Note his close relationship with al-Husaini, his precautions against West German surveillance, and his hatred of that country's democratic government.

ATTACHMENT #10   "\ RANDOM NOTES /\
                                        /\ \lambda M/

        ODESSA's latest planned escape was for HANS WALTER ZECH-
NENNTWHICH, Ex-Capt. SS. This man was up for trail for the
mass murder of 5,200 Polish Jews at PINSK. His escape to
Egypt from BRUNSWICK PRISON.

        ODESSA - its initials are for Organization DER ENEMALIGEN
S. S. ANGEHORIGEN (organization of former members of the SS.

        This Organization is also known as the "Spider's Web".

        Head of ODESSA in Spain is former SS Colonel Otto "Scar-
face" SKORZENY of resc (?) Mussoline fame.

        Of the 2,000 odd ex-members of Hitler's SS Gestapo & SD
members I list some of the most important on the wanted list
and also active members of ODESSA: at present in Lima is OMAR
AMIN VON LEERS who is Johann (or Jahannes) von Leers - has
made contact with Federico Schwend for the buying of queer
dollar bills. The amount to be bought will be that of the equivalent of $100,000 real monies. The price set is at 47 on the
dollar - the plates made for "Operation Berhardt" of $10, $20,
$50 and $100 are now in Sao Paulo, Brazil.

        This queer monies are said to be sent to Cuba and then to
find its way to the US. The $100,000 in this writing is being
given by the Egyptian Government.

        One of ODESSA's main contact here is Baron Von Sothen at
present second to the German Ambassador in Peru. At present
he is now in Rio de Janeiro apparently on a month's vacation
with wife and children - it is known the Baron von Sothen is
still an ardent NAZI.

Figure 27. The postwar Nazi Middle Eastern network: A 1964 CIA report details
some of the activities of ODESSA, the Organization of Former SS Members, in
helping wanted Nazis escape from Europe and establish themselves overseas.
Note the cooperation of a German prison guard in helping the SS officer Hans
Zech-Nentwig make a successful jail break, and of an official at the West German
embassy in Peru in transmitting forged dollar bills to von Leers.

vember 1950, from a former Abwehr man operating under the alias
"Hans."[24]

    The case of Hans Walter Zech-Nentwig is a good illustration of how
Nazis went to work for Western intelligence agencies and the West
German government, evaded punishment for many years, reestablished
links to Islamists, were helped to escape when facing prosecution, and
ended up in Arabic-speaking countries.

    Born in 1916, Zech-Nentwig was a German official in Poland whose
activities were so brutal that in April 1943 the Nazis put him in a
Warsaw prison charged with rape and smuggling. Escaping to neutral

Sweden using the alias Hermann Böttcher, Zech-Nentwig claimed that
he had been jailed because he was helping the resistance. British intelligence hired him and Zech-Nentwig plied them with fantastic stories
like that of an alleged opposition group led by relatives of SS General
Fegelein, brother-in-law of Hitler's girlfriend, Eva Braun.[25]

Zech-Nentwig was put to work for the British agent Sefton Delmer's
group in Soldier's Radio, supposedly located in German-occupied
France but actually broadcasting from northern England.[26] Pretending
to be a genuine German station, it provided doctored news to undermine Axis morale. One of Zech-Nentwig's colleagues there, Otto John,
whom the Allies put in charge as first chief of Bonn's Federal Office for
the Protection of the Constitution in 1950, turned out to be a Soviet
agent, and he defected to East Berlin in 1954.

After the war, British intelligence helped Zech-Nentwig—now living
under the alias Sven Nansen—to find work as an aide of Robert Lehr,
later West German minister of interior. But Zech-Nentwig also maintained secret ties with Nazi underground groups. In 1954, fired by the
British and by Lehr, Zech-Nentwig became director of a department in
Bavaria's Ministry of Labor and Social Affairs in Munich. Among his
duties was dealing with Soviet and Middle Eastern Muslims who had
collaborated with Germany during the war and wanted to stay in the
country.

One of Zech-Nentwig's colleagues was Gerhard Wolfrum, another
former SS member.[27] Wolfrum told Zech-Nentwig in 1957 about the
establishment of an "Islamic community" in Munich that had two secret goals. One was to help former Nazi allies; the other was to rebuild
the radical Islamist movement in Europe created by al-Husaini and
his colleagues before the war. The community's leader was Nur ad-
Din Namanjani, who had fought in both world wars on the German
side and became an associate of al-Husaini. "If we succeed in building
a true religious community," wrote Wolfrum to Zech-Nentwig, "we
succeed also in gaining political sway." The result was a renewed partnership. Former Nazis provided financial help and, as West German
officials, assisted in dealing with their own government. For their part,
al-Husaini and the Muslim Brotherhood cooperated in taking over the
Munich mosque.[28]

Wolfrum was correct. As Ian Johnson shows in his detailed study, *A
Mosque in Munich*, this mosque created by former Nazi collaborators

helped by unrepentant Nazis would be the base for an Islamist movement that largely dominates the ever-growing Muslim communities in
Europe today.[29] At times, this Munich group also worked with U.S.
intelligence, for example by providing Muslims to go to Mecca on the
1956 pilgrimage and find out from Soviet counterparts about conditions behind the Iron Curtain.[30]

Zech-Nentwig, however, did not fare so well personally. Losing his
government job, he tried journalism, business, and even asked the East
Germans if they would like to buy his services. Finally, some SS men
turned him in for the reward. Even Zech-Nentwig's connections with the
powerful Globke couldn't save him from a trial for the murder of two
Jews in Poland.[31] Though Globke himself took the witness stand, saying, "It was impossible to reject the order to kill Jews," Zech-Nentwig
was sentenced to four years in prison. But the courts were not yet finished with him. A second trial was scheduled on charges that he had
killed fifty-two hundred Polish Jews in Pinsk.[32] The ODESSA network
engineered his escape from Braunschweig prison to Egypt on April 22,
1964,[33] made possible by the fact that a prison guard, Dietrich Zee-
mann, was a fellow Nazi.[34]

Not only did the effort to capture war criminals basically end by
1950, but many such people received pardons and some returned to
old jobs in government, the police, and other influential positions.[35]
Efforts to investigate war criminals and put them on trial were ham-
pered by competition between East and West Germany, sabotage by
Nazi sympathizers, and bureaucratic infighting. While monitoring their
activities closely—in 1956 the CIA compiled a list of the one hundred
most wanted Nazis and there was a global watch list of two thousand
former SS men—the victorious Allies were unenthusiastic about catch-
ing war criminals.[36]

The only ones who seemed to be avidly seeking to find Nazi war
criminals were Arab governments that wanted to offer them jobs. Von
Leers was the most important of these men. Born in 1902, von Leers
had been one of Goebbels's most prolific propagandists.[37] After imprisonment by the U.S. Army for eighteen months at war's end, von Leers,
like Eichmann, fled from Hamburg to Argentina. In Buenos Aires he edited pro-Nazi texts for the monthly magazine *Der Weg* (The Way) and in
1954 published a booklet, entitled *Imperial Traitors,* condemning those
Germans who had opposed Hitler's regime.[38] He wrote articles prais-

ing Juan Perón's dictatorship and expressing passionate anti-Semitism under such pen names as Hans A. Euler, Karl Neubert, Felix Schwarzenborn, and Fritz Büttner.[39]

Finally the Egyptian embassy in Argentina hired von Leers for a 1956 anti-Jewish campaign. The military attaché, General Hasan Fahmi Ismail, was so pleased with his work that he offered von Leers a well-paid job in Egypt.[40] In April 1956, von Leers moved to Cairo. His wife and daughter followed on June 21. Soon after his arrival, al-Husaini converted him to Islam, and in honor of his patron von Leers took "Amin" as part of his own Muslim name, Umar Amin von Leers.[41]

One of von Leers's first tasks, in June 1956, was to provide information about which West German government officials were Jews. He worked with another ardent Nazi supporter, Paul Schmitz-Kairo. Von Leers obtained credentials as a journalist, attended the Afro-Asian conference in Bandung—where al-Husaini was also present—and unsuccessfully proposed a resolution there designating Allied-occupied Germany as a colonial area that should be liberated.[42]

Moving to Egypt's Ministry of Information and Voice of the Arabs radio station, von Leers carried on his mission of spreading anti-Semitism.[43] The CIA reported that he was becoming a religious zealot advocating Islam's expansion into Europe.[44] He founded a publishing company, Umar's Sword,[45] and tapped into al-Husaini's network through the latter's associate Mahmud Salih, self-styled head of the anti-Zionist movement in Cairo. He met with Egyptian dictator Abd-an Nasir and made a good impression on that former collaborator with Germany.

One scheme von Leers was involved in was a plan to create an Amnesty International–type group on behalf of ex-Nazis, neo-Nazis, and Third World nationalists, or in his words, a German "national aid society to support the members of nationalist groups imprisoned by courts or prosecuted for their beliefs."[46] And to tie everything together he became the head of ODESSA's Middle East branch.[47]

While a February 1959, U.S. intelligence report exaggerated in saying von Leers was "chief propaganda adviser" to Abd an-Nasir, another such evaluation accurately depicted his excellent access to the president.[48] Abd an-Nasir certainly saw him as a respected counselor.[49] In October, perhaps at von Leers's suggestion, the Egyptian president read the *Protocols of the Elders of Zion,* which von Leers tirelessly promoted. Thereafter, Abd an-Nasir echoed the book's themes, telling an Indian interviewer, for example, that "Europe was in the hands of three hundred Zionists" and calling the Holocaust a lie.[50] His brother Shauqi translated the *Protocols* into Arabic and championed its message for decades.[51]

Von Leers's other high-level Egyptian contacts included as-Sadat; Ali Sabri, state minister of presidential affairs; Muhammad Khaliq Hasuna, Arab League secretary-general; General Abd al-Azim Ibrahim Fahmi, director of general investigations for the Ministry of Interior; and Hafiz Abd al-Karim, secretary general of the economics ministry.[52] For his work, von Leers received a good salary of eighty to a hundred Egyptian pounds monthly.[53]

One mission von Leers undertook for Abd an-Nasir in October 1957 was to locate former German tank officers to work in Egypt and other Arab countries.[54] The Arab League's representative in Bonn, Hasan Fakhusa, came to Cairo to ask von Leers's advice on how to effectively lobby West Germany for Arab interests. The Egyptians also used von Leers for anti-British counterintelligence operations.

Von Leers also became an employment agency for escaped Nazis. For instance, he helped Schmitz-Kairo, now known as Abd al-Majid Amin, get an Arab League job. In October 1958 the forty-five-year-old Nazi concentration camp physician Hans Eisele—who had tortured inmates at Buchenwald, Mauthausen, Natzweiler, and Dachau—was a guest at von Leers's house after fleeing Germany. Eisele, alias Carl Debouche, nursed an ailing von Leers back to health. Cairo granted Eisele asylum, licensed him to practice as a physician, and rejected German attempts to extradite him for trial. After surviving an assassination attempt, in which an Egyptian postman was killed, Eisele died on May 3, 1967 due to unknown causes.[55]

Von Leers also worked with al-Husaini and his secretary, Hasan Kirkut, on a joint book, *The Truth about the Palestine Question,* which was to be published in West Germany in a series, "The World Fight against Imperialism and Colonialism," by the ex-SS man and neo-Nazi publisher Karl-Heinz Priester of Wiesbaden. The book, serialized in the Egyptian newspaper *al-Misri* in 1954, appeared in Arabic and quickly went through three printings.[56]

Von Leers's cover was blown when he ran into a Canadian journalist, William Stevenson of the *Toronto Star,* who promptly reported on

July 3, 1956 that this "former propaganda adviser to Hitler and Perón, now in Cairo, advises Nasser and the Arab League." Von Leers told him that in postwar Germany, "Americans were Jews running the concentration camps." He added that Israel must be destroyed because it caused trouble, was not a proper state, and was behind all opposition to Abd an-Nasir and Egypt.[57]

The British journalist Anne Sharpley also interviewed von Leers in his Ministry of Information office where he poured out his anti-Jewish hatred. She counted two hundred ex-German officers working for the Egyptians.[58] Embarrassed, the Egyptians expelled the two Western journalists. Al-Husaini's Jerusalem daily newspaper *al-Jihad* reported as well that von Leers was doing propaganda work for Egypt.[59] To conceal his government activities, von Leers took a nominal post as German language instructor at Cairo University.

American intelligence discussed the possibility of exploiting "the role of von Leers and other ex-Nazi advisers" to subvert the Egyptian regime. Might Arabs and Muslims be persuaded that Abd an-Nasir was a new Hitler who intended to terrorize and enslave them? But the idea was dropped since, U.S. officials concluded, associating Abd an-Nasir with the Nazis was likely to make him more, not less, popular in the Arab world. [60]

Meanwhile, von Leers held court in Cairo, bringing together Nazis with important Arab and Islamist figures, some of whom they had worked with during the war. Among von Leers's many visitors was Vagner Kristensen, an SS man who had helped him escape in 1946.[61] Von Leers also met regularly with other ex-Nazi converts to Islam like Ahmad Huber and helped the unrepentant Nazi Ludwig Zind to flee from West Germany to Egypt in 1958. Zind had openly continued to advocate Hitler's ideas in Germany, including claiming the Jews were guilty for the loss of World War I and Germany's decline thereafter. Zind even defended the gassing of Jews. When this became known, he was prosecuted.[62] During the proceedings, Zind said Israel was a "plague spot" that had to be wiped off the map. He was sentenced to one year in prison but fled on November 28, 1958 to Cairo, then Tripoli, Libya, where the authorities offered him asylum and a teaching post.[63] He was later twice briefly arrested during trips to Europe but got off due to technicalities.

Von Leers also dealt with Algerians; with Salah Ben Yusuf, leader of the radical nationalist forces in Tunisia; and the old Moroccan rebel Abd al-Karim. He helped the Algerians in their independence war against France by discouraging West Germans from joining the French Foreign Legion,[64] and did research for a book about the conflict, *Algeria in Flames*.[65] Abd an-Nasir also sent ex-Nazis as advisers to the Algerians.[66] The story of one such Nazi, who had participated in the Final Solution, was the model four decades later for Algerian writer Boualem Sansal's book, *The German's Village*, which showed how Nazi, Soviet, and Islamist influences would blend together to create so much bloodshed in his country.[67]

The news of Eichmann's capture, announced by Israel on May 23, 1960, worried von Leers and his colleagues, who discussed the matter extensively, but he continued to live unmolested in Cairo until his death there on March 5, 1965. Among his close friends was Ludwig Heiden, alias Louis al-Hajj, and John W. Eppler alias Husain Jaffar. Eppler had been a spy for Rommel in Cairo, who had been captured by the British in 1942 when he was liaison to the pro-German underground. One of his main contacts, as-Sadat, was now Egypt's vice president.[68]

Heiden worked with both von Leers and al-Husaini.[69] He produced a new translation of *Mein Kampf* into Arabic. In the 1950s it was published in five installments, then in 1963 it appeared as a book that sold well over a million copies. It was so popular that by 1999 the seventh edition appeared, edited by no less than Mustafa Tlass, Syria's veteran defense minister.

One of the other Nazis who went to Egypt was Ferdinand Heim, a doctor on the Wiesenthal Center's list of the ten most-wanted war criminals for having tortured concentration camp prisoners.[70] Born in 1914, Heim joined the Nazi Party and SS and then, starting in 1940, worked in the Sachsenhausen, Buchenwald, and Mauthausen camps. After two years' incarceration in U.S. custody, he returned to Germany to work as a physician in 1947. When Eichmann was on trial in Israel in 1961, Vienna issued an arrest warrant for Heim, who fled via France, Spain, Morocco, and Libya to Egypt. Although he was one of the world's most-wanted war criminals, efforts to trace his whereabouts repeatedly failed. In fact, having converted to Islam and acquired the name Tariq Farid Husain, Ferdinand Heim lived for decades hidden in Cairo. Reportedly, he died in 1992.

Many of the Germans who moved to the Middle East were ex-soldiers who worked for Egypt's government in training, intelligence, prison administration, and propaganda. Some were from among the six thousand German prisoners of war who stayed in Egypt after the war.[71] Starting in mid-1947, the Egyptian government began to hire them. Recruiters like Haddad Said, a German with a Syrian passport, with help from the Red Crescent, systematically recruited German prisoners from camps in Germany and Cyprus.

After the 1948 war with Israel began, Arab recruitment of German military advisers moved to Turkey.[72] Between 1948 and 1956 the Egyptians had two units of German military advisers. Ex-general Wilhelm Fahrmbacher led the Armed Forces group with thirty-one men, while Wilhelm Voss of the Nazis' wartime Škoda factories led the Research Center for Explosives and Weapons unit, with fifteen. Their Egyptian counterparts later judged them superior to the Soviet technicians who eventually replaced them.[73]

The Americans received reports in 1952 that Voss had helped Otto Ernst Remer to escape to Cairo. Remer had been a key figure in blocking the anti-Nazi coup against Hitler following the attempted assassination of the dictator on July 20, 1944, and denouncing those involved, who were executed as a result. In Cairo, the adviser for Egyptian paratroops, Gerhard Mertens, who was paid 144 Egyptian pounds a month, helped Remer get on the Egyptian payroll at 50 Egyptian pounds a month. Remer met al-Husaini and worked with the Muslim Brotherhood as a military adviser until he returned to Germany under a 1954 amnesty. There, he became a leading Holocaust denier.[74]

German war criminals were also important as advisers to the Egyptian secret police. Gleim, the former SS commander in Poland, and his aide, Bernard Bender alias Ben Salam, held leading posts in the security police and greatly assisted Abd an-Nasir in gaining and holding power. Another SS official in Poland and Ukraine, the physician Heinrich Willermann alias Naim Yachim, supervised jails in Alexandria and ran the Samara concentration camp in the Western Desert.

Joachim Doemling of the SS became police adviser Ibrahim Mustafa.[75] He had joined the main office of the security police in Berlin in 1939 and, in March 1943, became an adviser to al-Husaini's Muslim troops in Croatia. In 1957 he returned to Germany. Ten years later he was jailed on charges of having murdered 3,823 people, but he escaped and fled to Egypt. There, one of his aides was Heinrich Sellmann, formerly head of the secret police in Ulm who, as Hamid Sulaiman, became political chief of Egypt's secret police.

On one occasion, Israel was able to exploit these networks through the work of Max Bineth.[76] Born in 1917 in Hungary, Bineth grew up in Cologne, but in 1935 his family moved to Palestine. In 1949 he joined Israeli intelligence and served on a secret mission in Iraq, and in 1952, under cover of being a German salesman and engineer sympathetic to Nazism, he moved to Cairo.[77] In this guise, he met many Egyptian leaders and obtained much information from German advisers on Egypt's army and military industries. Bineth was so successful that the Egyptians even offered him a job. In 1954, though, Bineth was arrested but committed suicide before his trial.[78]

German advisers also managed Egypt's highest-priority military projects. Abd an-Nasir hired Willy Messerschmitt, the aircraft designer and manufacturer, and Wolfgang Pilz, a missile expert who had worked for the Nazi regime. In 1964, Messerschmitt produced Egypt's first jet fighter, the Hulwan 300. Eventually, however, the Egyptians ran out of money and Israeli threats discouraged German scientists from working there. Cairo dropped the plan. The same pressure was applied against the missile project. Pilz, working under the name Ben Amman, designed two missiles, al-Qahir and as-Safir, first shown publicly in a 1962 military parade. That July, Abd an-Nasir announced that Egypt had made four successful tests of missiles capable of striking anywhere "south of Beirut"—that is, in Israel. Israel's military intelligence quickly learned that Egypt had built a secret facility in the desert known as Factory 333, staffed by German scientists who had built the V1 and V2 rockets that had devastated London. Even the project's security chief was an SS veteran.

The Egyptians planned to build some nine hundred missiles, which posed a major security threat to Israel. Israeli intelligence focused on the program's weakness, Egypt's need for help from German scientists, and the Mossad initiated Operation Damocles. The missiles were indeed a sword of Damocles hanging over Israel, but Israel would turn the tables on the German scientists, who would be made to choose between quitting and risking death. In September 1962, Heinz Krug, head of a Factory 333 front company called Intra, vanished in Munich. In November, two parcel bombs arrived at Pilz's office, maiming his secretary and killing five Egyptian workers. In February 1963 another Factory 333 scientist, Hans Kleinwächter, narrowly escaped an ambush in Switzerland. In April of that year, two Mossad agents in Basel accosted Heidi Goerke, the daughter of project manager Paul Goerke, and threatened to kill both her and her father. The two agents were briefly jailed. The West German government was upset about the Israeli operations so Israel shared its intelligence, and Bonn then pressured the scientists to quit, offering them jobs at home instead. Nearly all accepted and Egypt abandoned the project. Pilz returned to West Germany in 1965.

Many other Nazis went to Syria. Franz Rademacher, alias Tomé Rosello, is a good example of this group. Born in 1906, during the Nazi era he was an aide to Under Secretary of State Luther, al-Husaini's liaison in the Foreign Ministry. He had close ties to Eichmann and was probably the one who handled al-Husaini's request for an Arab delegation to visit the Sachsenhausen concentration camp.[79] Rademacher had also signed the Foreign Ministry's position paper for the Wannsee Conference, supporting mass deportations of Jews to be murdered and, as al-Husaini had requested, barring them from immigrating elsewhere.[80] On March 6, 1942, Rademacher attended the Wannsee Conference's follow-up meeting, reporting the next day to his superiors on further steps planned against "mongrels" and later on the sterilization of seventy thousand people.[81] On March 20, 1942, he approved Eichmann's request to deport six thousand French and stateless Jews to Auschwitz.[82]

Rademacher was in American hands in 1947 and 1948 and was then turned over to German custody. In 1952, convicted for involvement in murdering thirty-two hundred Jews in Serbia, he fled to Spain and then to Syria. In Damascus he worked first in a foreign trade business but fell out with the Syrians and was imprisoned by them. He returned to West Germany in 1966 and was due to be tried for war crimes when he died in 1973.[83]

Walter Rauff was the most notorious of the Nazis who went to Syria. He had been involved in developing mobile gas vans, and had killed Jews in Tunisia and Italian civilians in Milan, Turin, and Genoa. After being hidden by Bishop Giuseppe Siri of Genoa, he fled to Damascus in 1947. For the next two years he worked with at least forty-seven other ex-Nazis in reorganizing Syrian intelligence.[84] When their patron, President Husni az-Zaim, was overthrown in 1949, his German mercenaries were all fired.[85] but Rauff was allowed to leave the country and used Red Cross papers under the alias of Bauermeister to flee through Genoa to Ecuador where he worked for the Bayer Company. In 1960 he returned to his homeland under his real name and lived unmolested. When the Eichmann trial began, however, Rauff's many murders were also remembered. Indicted for crimes against humanity, he fled through Italy, Ecuador, and Argentina to Chile where he was protected by the government.

According to newly released records, the West German secret service, the Bundesnachrichtendienst, hired Rauff in 1958. It was a sign of the BND's continuity from the Nazi era that the men who gave Rauff a job were two former SS officers whom he had known during the war. Wilhelm Beisner had been a member of Rauff's commando in Athens and was considered an expert on the Balkans and the Middle East. Rudolf Oebsger-Roeder had served Eichmann in deporting Hungarian Jews to the death camps in 1944. He wrote for such prestigious newspapers as the *Süddeutsche Zeitung* and the *Neue Zürcher Zeitung* on Islamic subjects, and during the 1960s, he served the BND as an adviser to Indonesian dictator Muhammad Suharto and also worked in Bangkok.[86]

One of Rauff's tasks was to gather information on Fidel Castro and how far he had moved toward the Soviet bloc. Although a West German court issued a federal detention order against Rauff in 1960, he visited the country several times secretly to participate in study courses of the secret service. Rauff's alias was Enrico Gomez, his agent number was V-7.410, and his monthly pay was two thousand marks. The service even paid part of his lawyer's fees as it tried to keep him from being indicted in Germany. All in all, he received seventy thousand marks by the time he was arrested in Chile in 1963. According to Chilean law, however, his crimes were not prosecutable because of a sixteen-year statute of limitations,[87] so he remained free and became a wealthy man after founding a fish-processing factory. When he died a natural death in 1984, his funeral turned into a Nazi rally.[88]

But the Syrians' longest-running Nazi associate was Alois Brunner, born in 1912 in the Austro-Hungarian town of Nádkút. Eichmann called Brunner the "best man" on his staff; Wiesenthal dubbed him "Eichmann's right-hand man with brains."[89] He was held responsible for deporting one hundred thousand European Jews to their deaths.

Brunner also led commandos in France to hunt down the Reich's enemies and deliver them to concentration camps. There was a good reason that al-Husaini did not mention Brunner in his memoirs, as he was the German officer who—along with Eichmann—reportedly accompanied al-Husaini on his tour of the Auschwitz concentration camp around June 1943. But they encountered each other a number of other times, for example in mid-September 1943 at the Hotel Excelsior in Nice and in mid-October 1944, when al-Husaini visited Budapest.[90]

After the war Brunner worked under a false name for the unknowing Americans in Munich. From 1947 to 1954, using the alias Alois Schmaldienst, he was a miner in Essen. That year, a French tribunal sentenced him to death, but Brunner escaped to Egypt, allegedly with Gehlen's help. There he met von Leers and al-Husaini, who advised him to go to Syria.[91]

Despite the fact that Brunner gave interviews in Damascus and was seen living in one of the government's official guest houses, the Syrians always insisted they knew nothing about his whereabouts and refused Interpol's extradition request. In fact, under the name Georg Fischer he was working for Syrian intelligence. On the side, he made money with foreign trade companies in Austria and Germany. His brother-in-law, Rudolf Schneeweiss, worked as his agent in Vienna.

During the Eichmann trial, Brunner and his fellow ex-Nazi officials plotted to kidnap the Jewish leader Nahum Goldmann to exchange him for Eichmann. The action, to be carried out by veterans of the elite German Brandenburger unit, was to take place in late 1960 when Goldmann was going to meet Adenauer in Bonn. Some Algerians were also recruited and, according to Wiesenthal, Arab sources collected 300,000 marks to pay for the operation, but they never went through with it because former Brandenburger commander Arthur Meichanitz refused to be involved.[92] One of those Brunner asked to participate was a Lebanese Arab secretly working for Wiesenthal,[93] and Brunner later confirmed in an interview that this man was one of those he tried to recruit.[94]

In 1977, Israeli Prime Minister Menachem Begin reactivated the campaign against escaped Nazi war criminals. An attempt was made to kill Brunner with a letter bomb but though badly injured, Brunner survived.[95] A decade later, American politicians became aware of Brunner's presence in Damascus. Now seventy-five, he lived quietly at

7 rue Haddad, protected around the clock by Syrian government bodyguards. In a brief phone conversation, reported an American newspaper, Brunner said of the Jews he had killed, "All of them deserved to die because they were the devil's agents and human garbage."[96] In other talks he showed no remorse about his role in the Holocaust.

These events, and a Canadian official's encountering Brunner in October 1987 led to the Canadian government's briefing U.S. Secretary of State George Shultz, who also gathered information from German prosecutors and Israeli intelligence reports. But no U.S. government found any effective pressure to use against Syria to obtain Brunner's extradition.[97] At the end of 1987, when East German head of state Erich Honecker wanted to visit the United States to obtain financial assistance, the Israelis secretly told Honecker that if he used his ties to Syria to extradite Brunner and free some captured Israeli soldiers they would support his efforts in Washington. As a result East German Foreign Minister Oskar Fischer almost succeeded in getting Brunner, but the East German regime's rapid decline and fall ended this effort.[98] In 1991, French, German, and Austrian extradition requests to Syria backed by the United States had no effect either.[99] Nor did a European parliament resolution.[100] Brunner reportedly died in 1999.[101]

Soviet Turkic Muslims who had fought for Germany and escaped deportation to the USSR also flourished. They formed committees in Berlin to carry on their nationalist battle against the Soviets. These people were useful Cold War assets for the West and many also remained connected with al-Husaini as well. Those who built the foundation for Islamism and the Muslim Brotherhood in Europe came from this group.

The most important of them to flee to the Middle East was Abd ar-Rahman Fatali Beyli-Dudanginsky. Born in 1908 in Azerbaijan, he attended military schools in Baku, Leningrad, and Moscow, graduating as an officer in 1933. Having distinguished himself in battle and won the Red Star medal, he was promoted to deputy chief of staff of the 27th Soviet Army. On September 28, 1941 Beyli-Dudanginsky was captured by the Germans and spent eight months in a prisoner of war camp. Recruited to the German army's new Turkic units in mid-1942, he became commander of the Azerbaijan Legion fighting the Soviets.[102] In late 1943, he was elected president of the Azerbaijan National Committee in Berlin. During this period, Beyli-Dudanginsky developed close relations with al-Husaini. Both pushed the Nazis to recognize Azerbaijan's independence, which happened only on March 17, 1945.

Fearing what would become of himself and his men if taken by the Soviets, Beyli-Dudanginsky managed to transfer his Muslim troops to Denmark and Italy in 1944. There they surrendered to the Americans and the British on the understanding that they would not be forcibly returned to the Soviets. This promise was broken and most were shipped back to the USSR in September 1945, though many escaped en route. While working from Italy in 1947 with refugees from Azerbaijan and other Turkic Muslims from the Caucasus, Beyli-Dudanginsky reconnected to al-Husaini in Cairo. On January 29, 1948 he visited Egypt as al-Husaini's personal guest and, in effect, employee. Fearing that a Jewish state would become a Soviet colony in the region—a common misperception at the time—Beyli-Dudanginsky offered his military expertise to al-Husaini for raising an Arab army.

The Egyptian government, which had always opposed letting al-Husaini organize any independent military force in the country, vetoed the plan but let Beyli-Dudanginsky remain in the country along with about one hundred followers trying to create their own organization to fight the Soviets. A U.S. intelligence report described him as a "fanatical Caucasian patriot with no scruples of any kind."[103]

All these efforts, of course, required money. At the war's end some Nazis managed to hide funds for later use, and with Hitler's consent, al-Husaini had sent a large amount to Switzerland during the war to fund his operations in other countries. His main banker was François Genoud, who had known the grand mufti since 1933. Born in 1915, Genoud worked with German military intelligence in World War II and thereafter as financier, benefactor, and literary executor for Nazis on the run in the ODESSA network. In 1958, he founded the Arab Commercial Bank in Geneva, specializing in lending for political rather than—despite its name—commercial purposes. In 1960, he bankrolled Eichmann's legal defense in Jerusalem, in 1962, he became director of the Arab Peoples Bank in Algiers, and in 1965, he sponsored a meeting between Swiss convert to Islam Ahmad Huber and al-Husaini. In the late 1960s he promoted weapons deals to Palestinian terror groups, especially George Habash's Popular Front for the Liberation of Palestine. He was also secretary general of the International Organization of Friends of the Arab World.[104]

In February 1943, al-Husaini, through Göring as trustee, invested about 18.4 million marks (about $920,000 at the time) through a Berlin branch of the Handels-Gesellschaft in Swiss banks and German companies.[105] After being rejected for Swiss asylum on May 8, 1945,[106] al-Hasaini destroyed the investment agreement and receipts lest the British capture it and demand the money. And there matters rested until February 26, 1959 when, his financial resources drying up, al-Husaini launched a lawsuit to reclaim the funds. He worked with François Genoud who, if successful, would get 75 percent after paying all costs. The total value of al-Husaini's shares was estimated that year at about 150 million marks, approximately $60 million. A victory at the time the case ended in 1974 would have brought al-Husaini a fortune. But the case dragged on for years.

The Berlin court asked al-Husaini for witnesses to prove his claim. His attorneys produced Hans Rechenberg, a former Nazi official; Göring's wife, Emma; and Walter Funk, Hitler's economy minister and president of the Central Bank who was released from prison on health grounds in 1957, all of whom testified that al-Husaini had made such a deal with Göring.[107]

In 1970, al-Husaini and his aides Munif al-Husaini and Saad ad-Din Abd al-Latif said they had discovered a notebook in which they had noted the shares supposedly purchased during the war. It showed an investment of almost half a million dollars in eight companies including the automaker Daimler Benz and the chemical company I. G. Farben. But since the evidence was far from complete, on June 25, 1971 the court decided against al-Husaini[108] and on April 3, 1974 it finally rejected al-Husaini's appeal.[109]

During the fifteen-year legal battle, the West German Foreign Ministry debated whether it would be in the country's interest to pay the money. One of al-Husaini's most active advocates in this struggle was Hans-Ferdinand Linsser of the Legal Department, who had served in the Middle East. He and others argued in 1967 that helping al-Husaini would improve West Germany's influence because many Muslims held him in high esteem. Moreover, Germany should not show people in the area "that we let down this best-ever friend of Germany." In their arguments, officials used the word "reparations" for the return of al-Husaini's funds, equating them with Bonn's payments to Jews and Israel for property confiscated by the Nazis.[110] Linsser added that even while it was difficult legally to justify paying al-Husaini the funds, the government might as a good will gesture give some money to pay for a Sunni mosque in West Germany.[111]

Those opposed argued that al-Husaini had continued his anti-Jewish activities and had no real influence in the Arab world that might benefit Bonn. In the end, the Foreign Ministry faction that opposed payments won and no money was handed out. Yet nobody noted the profound and revealing irony that most of the money given to al-Husaini by the Nazis had come from looted Jewish gold and the possessions of those sent to the death camps.

The Americans kept a close eye on Genoud. In the mid-1970s, the CIA noted that he still had close ties to Nazi circles and escaped war criminals living in Arab countries.[112] He was barred from the United States after Secretary of State Henry Kissinger wrote to the U.S. embassy in Switzerland about Genoud's "long and unsavory record of Nazi and Fascist associations."[113] Genoud's career also demonstrated the continuing alliance between neo-Nazi forces and radical Arab nationalist and Islamist ones. He worked with the radical French lawyer Jacques Vergès, who defended the Palestinian terrorist leader George Habash, the Nazi Klaus Barbie, and the ex-Communist convert to Islam and Holocaust denier Roger Garaudy. He always retained his close association with al-Husaini, visiting him in Beirut in October 1970. Genoud also helped bankroll Khomeini when he was in France during the 1970s before his victorious return to Tehran as leader of the Iranian Islamist revolution. By 1994, Genoud was financing the courtroom defense of Ilich Ramírez Sánchez, the forty-five-year-old Venezuelan terrorist known widely as Carlos the Jackal, who worked with Habash in various terror attacks including the raid on the OPEC headquarters in Vienna and the bombing of cars, banks, and El Al airplanes in Paris in 1975. In 1997 Carlos was found guilty of the murder of two policemen in Paris and sentenced to life in prison.

The main constant in Genoud's life was his passionate hatred of Jews and Israel.[114] Swiss authorities claimed that Genoud built the Lugano-based At-Taqwa Bank, which helped fund al-Qaida and Hamas, and was shut down after the September 11 attacks. In 1996, as the Swiss authorities were reportedly about to arrest him for hiding Nazi gold, he committed suicide at age eighty-one.[115] Such was the man who was al-Husaini's main banker. His Arab Commercial Bank in Geneva became a focal point for Islamist networks in Europe in the years before Ramadan and others succeeded in building their own banking system. Al-Husaini also sent his men, in this case his Egyptian aide Ahmad Husain, from the fascist Young Egypt Party, as far away as America to raise money.

Later, the Islamists built their own banking system, partly based in their Munich headquarters. Among the key Muslim Brotherhood bankers were Ghalib Himmat and Yusuf Nada, both named as financiers of terrorism in the post–September 11 investigations.[116] When Munich became too hot for him, Himmat left the Islamic Center there and moved to the secondary center in Switzerland to become head of the Lugano Islamic Center in 2004, and was thereafter not bothered by the authorities.

In sharp contrast to the former Nazi officials and SS men, Germany's Hitler-era diplomats did not have to go underground. Many of them continued their professional careers, like von Hentig, who worked from 1954 as King Saud's adviser and accompanied him to the Bandung Conference, once again meeting up with al-Husaini. Grobba also worked for the Saudi king. But most entered West Germany's service. Adenauer declared that their expertise was indispensable despite their past, and by October 1952, there were 195 former Nazi Party members in West Germany's Foreign Ministry, of whom 106 had served under von Ribbentrop. Of these, fifty-seven, more than half of the veteran diplomats, had been involved in the Middle East and Islamic matters. Thus, a large proportion of the new government's Middle East expertise, responsible for devising policy toward the Arabs, Muslims, and Israel, had been enthusiastic supporters of Hitler.[117]

One of al-Husaini's foes in the wartime Foreign Ministry had been Wilhelm Melchers. Born in 1900 in Bremen, he studied law and fought briefly in World War I. Joining the Foreign Ministry, he served in Ethiopia, Japan, Iran, and just before World War II, as consul in Haifa where he joined the Nazi Party. During the war he led the ministry's Middle East section and afterward was promoted to head the all-important personnel department where he could help former comrades obtain jobs. He became successively West German ambassador to Iraq, Jordan, India, and Greece until his retirement in 1965.

Of particular importance was Hermann Voigt, who grew up in the German Templers' religious settlement near Tel Aviv where he was born in 1889.[118] Voigt studied law and Turkish, serving as a translator at the German embassy in Istanbul during World War I. He joined the Nazi Party and served in the Foreign Ministry during World War II. In 1953 he began a decade-long posting as Adenauer's desk officer for the Middle East.[119]

Germany's ambassador to Turkey in the early 1970s was Gustav Adolf Sonnenhol. Born in 1912, Sonnenhol joined the Nazi Party as a student in 1929. In 1939 he joined the Foreign Ministry and then worked in Paris for a time in the section coordinating the deportation of Jews. Between 1942 and 1944 he served in the North African cities of Casablanca and Tangiers where Berlin and al-Husaini were planning the murder of all of the Jews. Beginning in mid-1943, while in Tangiers, he also worked for Himmler in SS intelligence.[120] Sonnenhol had good relations with Kurt Georg Kiesinger, who headed von Ribbentrop's radio propaganda section where he worked with al-Husaini promoting anti-Jewish agitation.[121] This link helped to ensure Sonnenhol's rise in the postwar Foreign Ministry, especially during Kiesinger's years as West Germany's chancellor from 1966 to 1969.[122]

The case of Günther Pawelke was more complicated. A World War I veteran, he studied afterward in Berlin, Paris, Rome, and Washington, earning a doctorate. Pawelke entered the Foreign Ministry in 1927, served in Baghdad between 1934 and 1937 as Grobba's deputy, but was forced out when he refused to become a Nazi Party member. Joining the army when the war broke out, he flew bombing missions over Britain and France but, given his knowledge of Arabic, was sent as part of the military aid mission to help Iraq's 1941 revolt. While Pawelke's plane was coming in for a landing in Baghdad, it was mistakenly shot down by the Iraqis, but he survived. From 1952 to 1955, Pawelke became West German ambassador to Egypt and Yemen.[123] He was denounced in the Israeli media, inaccurately, as a Nazi and a former paymaster for the grand mufti.[124] In later years he served as ambassador to Saudi Arabia and Yemen.

While virtually none of those who had helped Hitler's Foreign Ministry in its many deceptions and conquests paid for their deeds, the situation was even worse in academia.[125] Professors who had enthusiastically participated in Nazi Middle East efforts flourished in the postwar years. Berthold Spuler, a Nazi Party member since 1933 who had helped manage Muslim SS units, continued at Göttingen University. When information about his Nazi past began to surface in the late 1960s and some students criticized him, he shouted back, "You all belong in a concentration camp."[126]

This tirade illustrated the broader problem of these postwar Nazis and Hitler-era officials. While the West German government as a whole made a break with the past, these individuals in its ranks continued to hold their pre-1945 views and to advocate similar Middle East policies. They remained hostile toward a Jewish state and soft on radical Islamism and Arab nationalism.

12 How the Axis Legacy Shapes Today's Middle East

Hitler committed suicide, Nazi Germany disappeared. But the era's legacy continued to shape Middle East events long afterward through their allies in the region. Al-Husaini emerged as Palestinian Arab and Islamist leader; many of the collaborationist nationalists and Islamists became top officials or leading forces in their countries; and there was continuity between the Arab nationalist and Islamist ideologies that had led them to collaboration with Nazi Germany and those that dominated the Middle East during the seven decades after Hitler's fall.

While greatly diminished in importance, al-Husaini remained the historic Palestinian Arab leader until he was able to anoint Arafat as successor during meetings between them in 1968, and selected Said Ramadan as his successor to lead the European-based Islamist movement. Even more important was al-Husaini's role as leader of the international Islamist movement, ensuring that it survived the lean years of the 1950s and 1960s. When Islamism revived in the 1970s, its ideology bore the mark of al-Husaini and the other wartime collaborators, especially the Muslim Brotherhood.

There was similar continuity with the radical Arab nationalist forces. In Egypt, Abd an-Nasir, as-Sadat, and other wartime collaborators seized power in 1952. They gave refuge to escaped Nazis who worked for them as advisers, intelligence operatives, and weapons developers. The Muslim Brotherhood, emerging as the most powerful force in Egypt after the 2011 revolution, was rooted in the German-Ottoman alliance in its ideological approach and its enthusiastic participation in the Nazi-Islamist alliances. In Syria and Iraq, the Ba'th party, which ruled both countries for decades, was created—as its founders later acknowledged—as a pro-Nazi party. It took many fascist elements into its ideology, structure, worldview, and propaganda. There were also connections with the Islamist revolution and the subsequent regime in Iran, whose two leading forerunners had worked closely with al-Husaini.

Of course, the Arabic-speaking world's historical connection with Nazi Germany was not solely responsible for the existence of radical forces, anti-Western sentiments, terrorism, conflict with Israel, anti-Jewish hatreds, and repressive dictatorships. Yet this historical relationship, along with the ideas and motives prompting it, does help explain that history in all its deviations from what might otherwise have been expected.

It is precisely because of this tremendous influence that the history of this process remains so controversial in the West and ignored in the Middle East. At the moment the Muslim Brotherhood was beginning its takeover of Egypt, in February 2011, Tariq Ramadan, a respected Islamist intellectual who had held Western academic posts, wrote a *New York Times* op-ed article denying altogether that the Muslim Brotherhood and its leader, his grandfather, had been Nazi collaborators.[1] On the contrary, he claimed that the Brotherhood was an antifascist organization opposed to violence and admiring "the British parliamentary model" in the 1930s and 1940s.

Actually, as demonstrated here, the Brotherhood was clearly well financed and armed by the Nazis before and during World War II.[2] Collaborating with the Germans and al-Husaini, it planned an uprising to support the German army's conquest of Egypt as well as to kill Cairo's Jews and Christians. The only reason this plot failed was that the British stopped the German advance and forced King Faruq to replace pro-German politicians in the government. One aspect of the Brotherhood's campaign to portray itself as moderate in the early twenty-first century was to rewrite its history.

Another controversy arose around a September 2009 exhibition in Germany organized by Karl Rössel, entitled The Third World in the Second World War, for Werkstatt der Kulturen, a publicly funded multicultural center in Berlin's heavily Turkish and Arab neighborhood of Neukölln. A small part of the exhibition recounted Arab and Islamist involvement in Nazi crimes. The center's director, Philippa Ebéné, canceled the project lest it produce German-Arab tensions. Berlin's integration commissioner, Günter Piening concurred but eventually, following media criticism, let a smaller version of the exhibition to be shown. Angry at censorship of his work, Rössel charged that German historians and Middle East experts had misrepresented historic truth. Daniel Schwammenthal wrote about the affair in the *Wall Street Journal:* "What Mr. Rössel says about Germany applies to most of the Western world, where it is often claimed that the mufti's Hitler alliance later discredited him in the region. Nothing could be further from the truth."[3]

Why is the alliance of Middle Eastern political movements with Nazi Germany so many decades ago more than a mere historical footnote today? Because the forces that forged this partnership returned, after a brief interruption, to help shape the course of Middle East history ever since. In the Middle East, and nowhere else in the world, the Axis's local supporters won political power in many countries and exerted significant ideological influence over many of the institutions and public debate.

Not just the doctrines but in many cases the very same individuals responsible for the Middle East's post-1945 course had direct links to the German-Ottoman-Islamist and Nazi-nationalist-Islamist eras. These ideologies would also contribute to the ways in which Middle Eastern countries were governed. Militant nationalist and Islamist forces chose Germany's side before and during World War II because that country's system mirrored their own beliefs and desires. They were wrong in thinking that an autocratic state organized according to their preferred system would achieve rapid development and foreign conquests, but they were right in expecting it would ensure their power for a long time.

Comprehending this fact is the starting point for understanding modern Middle East history, its turbulence, tragedies, and its many differences from other parts of the world. Few people in 1945 would have believed that the militant Arab nationalism that found Nazi Germany so congenial could seize power in the main Arab countries within a few years and hold it for six decades. Fewer could have thought that it would totally dominate debate on every issue and wipe out the pro-Allied Arab moderates who'd been on the winning side in the war. And by the mid-1950s, with the nationalists victorious and their opponents in flight, hardly anyone would have seen Islamism as the successor to that political and intellectual power. Yet so thoroughly did first nationalism and, much later, Islamism triumph that these outcomes came to be taken for granted and made it seem impossible that history might ever have taken a more moderate direction.

Since 1945, Arab or Muslim collaborators with Nazism were not criticized, punished, or discredited at home for their actions. While Western societies agonized over the Nazi era's lessons, in the Middle East these were regarded as Western problems. If discussed at all, the Holocaust was either dismissed as a Zionist fabrication—despite the fact that al-Husaini knew it was happening before most Nazi leaders did—or as an event that victimized Arabs and other Muslims who were forced to pay for Germany's behavior toward the Jews despite having no role in it.[4]

In contrast to the laudatory treatment given Nazi Germany's allies, moderate Middle Eastern leaders who opposed al-Husaini and alliance with the Axis were driven from public life and demonized as both failures and collaborators with imperialism. Yet in the 1930s and 1940s, those politicians had presided over institutions developing toward their own versions of parliamentary democracy, giving citizens and especially women more rights than the same countries offered a half-century later. Wealthy and from long-established families, the moderate elites were pragmatists, not ideologues. They were indeed corrupt and oligarchical but did not go in for mass murder, ruthless repression, systematic indoctrination, and foreign aggression.[5] The revolutionary groups asserted that national success would come from copying Nazi Germany or fascist Italy and, later, Soviet Russia; moderate leaders believed progress required borrowing from Western democratic societies that had succeeded. They were willing to work with Britain or France but sought full independence. While opposing Zionism they did not want to sacrifice unlimited treasure and blood to the extent that the most damage would be inflicted on their own societies.

Since the old moderate leaders and parties were so thoroughly destroyed and their ideas so completely forgotten, liberal forces had to restart from scratch in the 1990s, and at an added disadvantage since their views were so discredited. Weak, facing fearful obstacles, and with a base limited to a small part of a proportionately tiny urban middle class, they could not compete with determined, organized, popular, and united Islamists. In the 2011 "Arab Spring," just as in the competition of the 1930s and the battles of the 1950s, moderate forces were for a third time overwhelmed by radicals.[6]

Compared to the moderates' broken history, the militant nationalists and Islamists remained firmly linked to the heritage of the Ottoman and Axis eras. For them, such connections became a source of strength not delegitimization as they boasted of having never compromised with imperialism or Zionism but of having fought bravely in a noble cause.

The Palestinian movement was particularly plagued by this cult of honorable defeat and by the continuity of Axis-style ideology, embodied in an event never before documented. On December 29, 1968, at a meeting in the ex–grand mufti's home near Beirut, al-Husaini anointed Arafat as his successor. The movement would be directed by these two sequential leaders and their similar philosophy and methods for an astounding eighty-three years, from al-Husaini's becoming grand mufti in 1921 to Arafat's death in 2004.

In December 1968, the thirty-nine-year-old Arafat, leader of the Fatah guerrilla group, was about to take over a PLO hitherto dominated by the Nazi collaborator Abd an-Nasir. But Arafat's success would be all the more secure if he received the seventy-one-year-old al-Husaini's endorsement. Al-Husaini gave it after lecturing Arafat for several hours on how he should go about destroying Israel and replacing it with a Palestinian Arab state.[7] Within a few weeks Arafat controlled the movement as thoroughly as al-Husaini had ever done.

It may seem peculiar that al-Husaini was revered rather than discredited among Palestinian Arabs and that the movement remained loyal to the same ideas, methods, and goals. Al-Husaini had rejected compromise before World War II then joined what turned out to be the losing side. Next he had rejected partition in 1947, throwing away the chance of establishing a Palestinian Arab state, and instead launched a war against the new Jewish state. Al-Husaini was personally responsible for the death of several hundred of Palestine's Arabs, including the moderate leader an-Nashashibi, sentenced to death "for violating the national consensus."[8] Indeed, part of the projected war crimes indictment of al-Husaini included a list of thirty Palestine Arabs, in some

DOI Late December 1968

SUBJECT Meeting Sponsored by Hajj Amin
Husayni to Discuss the Formation
of a Palestinian State

ACQ Lebanon, Beirut (Mid-January 1969) FIELD NO NLB-9221

SOURCE A Lebanese security official who has continuing and direct
access to Lebanese security documents and who provided a
copy of the report translated below without the knowledge
of his government. The documents he provides are
considered to be authentic.

1. (Field Comment: The following is a summary translation of a Lebanese Sureté Generale report dated 31 December
1968, and classified SECRET. A copy of the report was sent
to the President of the Republic and to the Army G-2.)

2. On the evening of 29 December 1968, a meeting was
held at the home of Hajj Amin Husayni to discuss the concept
of a Palestinian state which would be defended by an army
composed of al Fatah commandos, under the command of al Fatah
leader Yasir Arafat. Participating in the 29 December meeting were Assistant Saudi Military Attache in Lebanon (Major
Muhammad al Qadi, one Hisham Awdi from Ain al Hilwi Camp,
one Ali Qasim from al Bashiryah Camp, one Musa Alami and al
Fatah representative (Captain Ahmad al Husayni. (Field
Comment: According to another security service official,
the Alami family member present was one Sami al Alami, an
influential and wealthy Palestinian.)

3. The meeting lasted several hours, during which Hisham
Awdi and Ali Qasim were delegated to discuss this project in
the Palestinian refugee camps in Lebanon, to make a note of
reactions to the project and to assess what must be done to

S-E-C-R-E-T/NO FOREIGN DISSEM   PAGE 2 OF 2 PAGES

bring it to fruition. Hajj Amin Husayni proposed that the
West Bank be considered a base for the Palestinian state.
He suggested that cooperation with conservative Arab
leaders such as King Faysal would be necessary to the success
of the project. He commented that the King had never
exploited the Palestinian problem for his own ends, in
contradistinction to UAR President Nasir, who was no more
than a Middle Eastern pawn in the hands of the USSR.

4. (Field Comment: According to an independent and
reliable source, a Lebanese businessman with good contacts
in Lebanese political circles, the meeting was called to
discuss al Fatah's position at the Palestine National Council,
scheduled to open in Cairo 1 February 1969. Husayni is the
liaison officer between King Faysal and al Fatah, and he is
the channel for money contributed to al Fatah by King Faysal.
Those present at the meeting were pessimistic about the
outcome of the Council meeting because al Fatah would try
to dominate it and the other Palestinian organizations were
bound to try to resist.)

cases entire families, whom his forces murdered in the late 1930s.[9] Then, too, al-Husaini had assassinated the leaders of two Arab states, Lebanon and Jordan. The latter victim was King Abdallah, the man whom al-Husaini described in a wartime letter to the German Foreign Ministry as a "traitor, agent in the British service, and friend of the Jews who was rejected by God."[10]

Yet Arafat would repeat these themes from al-Husaini's career: choosing to ally with the USSR, which would turn out to be the losing side in a global conflict, missing chances to create a Palestinian state, slaying moderate Arabs, embracing anticivilian terror as a strategy, and launching unsuccessful battles against Israel. Al-Husaini and Arafat met on several occasions in late 1968 and early 1969. Yet within a year of their friendly meetings, Arafat did three things that turned al-Husaini bitterly against him.

First, Arafat disregarded al-Husaini's advice that the Palestinian movement should become the client of conservative, Islamic-oriented Saudi Arabia and not of nationalist Egypt which, al-Husaini warned, "Exploits the Palestinians as a pawn of the Soviets." The Saudi king had let down al-Husaini by not following him into an alliance with Berlin but nevertheless proved a faithful friend in protecting and financing the grand mufti and the Islamist movement after the war.[11] In the 1960s, the Saudis were the last bastion of Islamism. Like al-Husaini, they were virulently anti-Semitic, passionately supported the Palestinian cause, and opposed Abd an-Nasir. So close were al-Husaini's relations with the Saudis that U.S. intelligence thought the ex–grand mufti was in effect the kingdom's "liaison officer" for paying Saudi money to Arafat.[12] One of al-Husain's main Saudi supporters was the king's adviser Khalid al-Qarqani, an admirer of Hitler who had advocated a pro-Nazi policy in the 1930s.

In 1948, Abd an-Nasir had wanted to cooperate with the grand mufti and offered to fight in Palestine under his command, but things changed when that young officer became Egypt's ruler five years later

Figure 28. A Lebanese intelligence report obtained by the CIA describes a meeting at al-Husaini's home in Beirut, at which leading Palestinian figures discussed the formation of a Palestinian state on the West Bank that would be "defended" by an "army" of Fatah fighters, commanded by Yasir Arafat—an important stage in the emergence of Arafat as the leader of the Palestinian movement.

Figure 29. Abd an-Nasir and Amin al-Husaini greet each other. In early 1948 the Egyptian idolized al-Husaini as a hero of the anti-British struggle. He offered to the grand mufti his troops belonging to a secret organization attached to the Free Officers movement. Al-Husaini misread this potential and asked an-Nasir to obtain the permission of King Faruq, so that the offer came to nothing. After an-Nasir took power and turned against the Muslim Brotherhood, in 1956 the two men's ways parted and al-Husaini moved to Beirut.

and suppressed the Muslim Brotherhood. Al-Husaini sided with his old Islamist comrades and became Abd an-Nasir's enemy. Arafat correctly gauged the contemporary power balance and in 1969 joined forces with Egypt which, in turn, gave him control of the PLO.

Second, while al-Husaini hated the Communists, Arafat went to Moscow and took the USSR as a superpower patron. Despite distinctions between Nazi Germany and the USSR, the two great powers embraced, respectively, by al-Husaini and Arafat, they were also parallel in significant ways. Both opposed Western democratic states and the status quo in the Middle East, and both provided the model of a totalitarian state as the best way to achieve national strength and socio-economic progress. While formerly pro-Nazi Arab nationalists chose Moscow in the 1950s and 1960s, Islamists refused to do so and were further marginalized.

The third dispute arose precisely because the two men's worldviews were so much alike. Both rejected any dissent in Palestinian ranks, but now it was Arafat who was leader and al-Husaini who was the one to be silenced. When Arafat clashed with Jordan's monarchy, as al-Husaini had so often done, he sought the ex–grand mufti's help, visiting him for this purpose on February 20, 1969. Jordan's King Husain,

Abdallah's grandson, had threatened to use his army against Arafat's guerrilla forces that were destabilizing his country and threatening to drag it into war with Israel.[13]

Since Jordan's regime was al-Husaini's traditional enemy, Arafat expected that al-Husaini would back him. Instead, however, al-Husaini sided against Arafat, even writing the king to urge that he press Arafat harder.[14] In the short time since he had humbly sought al-Husaini's endorsement, Arafat had become confident that Cairo's and Moscow's backing meant he no longer needed the old man.[15] Arafat's forces attacked the headquarters of al-Husaini's small Islamic Conquest group in a refugee camp near Amman, killing five men, and the survivors joined Arafat's Fatah.[16] Al-Husaini's career in Palestinian politics was now truly at an end.

These clashes, however, do not negate the fact that in many ways Arafat was continuing the policies of his distant relative and discarded mentor. Just as al-Husaini had done in the late 1930s (forcing an Arab consensus against accepting British offers) and in the late 1940s (rejecting the UN partition plan), Arafat would also use the Palestine card to blackmail Arab leaders into yielding to his demands for no compromise.

Equally, as in al-Husaini's day, the PLO made itself part of a wider "anti-imperialist" Arab nationalist struggle that saw Western democracies as its enemy. Accepting al-Husaini's concept that militancy was always superior to moderation, Arafat concurred with the idea that defeat, no matter how devastating, was never a good reason for altering goals or principles.

Like al-Husaini, Arafat was determined that there be no compromise with the Zionists, no acceptance of a Jewish state in any form, and no moral limit on the violence used against the Jews. Al-Husaini had originated the movement's deliberate use of anticivilian terror, believing it would defeat the Zionists. The 1944 Salama commando that had parachuted into Palestine under German command was intended as the first terrorist operation of this new conflict. Arafat also deliberately targeted Jewish civilians as an important military strategy.

Al-Husaini had successfully used threats of terror against the British and his alliance with Germany to stop Jews from leaving Europe or arriving in mandatory Palestine, but now it was too late to keep them out. They were already there. Arafat's problem was to force on them a choice between fleeing and dying. As he explained: "[Violence will] create and maintain an atmosphere of strain and anxiety that will force the Zionists to realize that it is impossible for them to live in Israel. . . . The Israelis have one great fear, the fear of casualties [and such attacks will] prevent immigration and encourage emigration. . . . A quick blow by the regular armies at the right moment [will finish Israel off]."[17] To gain total victory, al-Husaini had hoped to "combine Palestinian armed struggle with regular armies," too: first with an advancing German army in 1941 and 1942, later alongside victorious Arab armies in 1948. Arafat adopted the same strategy and also failed when the armies of allied states were defeated in 1967, 1973, and 1982.

However, al-Husaini also gave Arafat an important new idea in their secret meetings. He suggested that Arafat adopt a two-stage strategy. First, the movement should gain control of the West Bank and Gaza Strip, captured by Israel in 1967, and transform it into a Palestinian state. Next, it should use this land as a base for destroying Israel. Ironically, this was precisely the option al-Husaini had lost by rejecting partition in 1947 but now returned to in his discussions with Arafat.[18]

Arafat did not take this advice in formulating his plan for the upcoming February 1969 Palestinian National Council meeting in Cairo,[19] but five years later he did accept this approach as the centerpiece of PLO strategy and it remained so ever after.[20] Yet despite giving lip service to the two-stage notion, Arafat behaved in practice like the pre-1948 al-Husaini, rejecting proposals that might have given him control over a state he could have used this way. Only a quarter-century later did Arafat sign the 1993 "Oslo Accords" and even then, at the moment of truth in the 2000 Camp David summit, he repeated al-Husaini's 1939 and 1947 error of rejecting compromise—even as camouflage for a two-state strategy—and instead opted for another war.[21]

Aside from the al-Husaini–Arafat connection, there were many other examples of individual, cross-generational, and organizational continuity between the Nazi and contemporary eras. One such story is that of the soldier in the German and al-Husaini armies, Hasan Salama, and his son Ali, the Fatah and PLO commando leader. Hasan was among al-Husaini's top gunmen in the 1937–39 Palestine Arab revolt. He joined the German army, was trained as a commando, and parachuted into Palestine in 1944. Escaping the British, Salama rejoined al-Husaini in 1946 and became one of his top military commanders in a new war, only to be killed in the 1948 fighting.

Figure 30. Arafat looks "over the Wall" from East Berlin to West Berlin, November 2, 1971. As the sway of the ex-Nazis receded, the Soviets and their East European satellites gained influence over radical states and the Palestinian movement, and the Palestinian as-Saiqa organization in Syria received East German arms for five thousand troops. Nazi, Fascist, and Soviet influences inspired the rigid Arab dictatorships that were brought down in the revolts of 2011, mainly to the benefit of Islamists who thereby turned Islamism into an official state ideology. This was as decisive an event as the German-Ottoman jihad of 1914, the emergence of Saudi Arabia in 1932, Iran's Islamist revolution in 1979, and Egypt's elections that led to the former Muslim Brother Muhammad Mursi assuming in mid-2012 almost total power—for a year.

His son, Ali Hasan Salama, was born in 1940. Joining Arafat's Fatah group, Ali received military training in Egypt, Moscow, and Beirut. He, too, was an ally of Germany, though in his case, it was Communist East Germany. Known as the Red Prince, he became operations chief for Fatah's Black September terrorist group, hijacking airplanes and killing both Israeli civilians and moderate Arab officials. In 1972, Salama planned and coordinated the Munich Olympic Games operation that killed eleven Israeli athletes and a German policeman. So close was Ali Salama to Arafat that he founded and led the Palestinian leader's Force-17 bodyguard, which also carried out terrorist attacks. Salama's career finally ended on January 22, 1979, when an Israeli raid assassinated him in Beirut.

Organizational links to the Axis-era past continue to the present day. The West Bank is ruled by the Fatah-dominated Palestinian Authority, created by Arafat, al-Husaini's heir and a former Muslim Brotherhood activist. This regime's chief executive was Mahmud Abbas, successor of Arafat and al-Husaini in leading the Palestinian national movement. Abbas wrote a Moscow University dissertation asserting that the Zionists, not Arabs, had been the Nazis' ally, while contradictorily asserting that a Zionist "declaration of war" on Germany in May 1942 had been the main factor convincing Hitler to wipe out the Jews. Thus, according to Abbas, the Zionists were responsible for the Holocaust; al-Husaini and the Palestinian Arab leadership had nothing to do with it.[22]

In 2007, Fatah and the PLO lost the Gaza Strip to a coup by Hamas, the Muslim Brotherhood's Palestinian branch, whose worldview is indistinguishable from that of al-Husaini and the Brotherhood in the 1930s and 1940s. Thus, each of the two wings of the 1930s radical faction ruled its own Palestinian entity. This continuity extends further. Remarkably, almost six decades after Hitler died in a Berlin bunker, the Middle East's four most important Muslim countries—Egypt, Iran, Iraq, and Syria—are run by leaders politically descended from al-Husaini's and Berlin's allies.

In Egypt, officers who collaborated with Germany came to power in the 1952 Free Officers' coup, and the new regime renewed that association by employing hundreds of former German Nazis. Indeed, in September 1953, when there was a rumor that Hitler was still alive and living in Brazil, as-Sadat wrote an open letter to the dictator in an Egyptian newspaper:

> I congratulate you with all my heart, because though you appear to have been defeated, you were the real victor. You were able to sow dissension between Churchill . . . and his allies on the one hand and their ally, the devil, on the other. . . . I think you made some mistakes, such as opening too many fronts or Ribbentrop's short-sightedness in the face of Britain's . . . diplomacy. But you are forgiven on account of your faith in your country and people. That you have become immortal in Germany is reason enough for pride. And we should not be surprised to see you again in Germany, or a new Hitler in your place.[23]

Although as-Sadat later dramatically changed his country's policy, this new approach did not result in an explicit renunciation of the Axis-era past. And when the Egyptian regime was overthrown in February 2011 and the one-time nationalist collaborators' heirs fell, the Muslim Brotherhood, their Nazi-era ally which had never changed its ideology, filled the vacuum.[24]

Iran was ruled by an Islamist regime based on the ideology of al-Husaini's old allies, al-Kashani and Safawi, who energetically denied that the Nazis had committed the Holocaust and at the same time evinced a Nazi-style anti-Semitism. Khomeini, the Islamist revolution's leader, had studied in pro-Nazi Iraq in the 1930s among teachers influenced by the German-directed World War I jihad and amidst a new wave of German-promoted Islamism.

In Iraq, pro-Axis forces returned to power when a Baghdad mob murdered Prime Minister as-Said, the pro-British rival of al-Kailani and al-Husaini, in 1958. Abd al-Karim Qasim, one of the pro-Nazi nationalists who fought for al-Kailani against the British in 1941, ruled Iraq from 1958 to 1963. His coup allowed al-Kailani himself, who had been living in Saudi Arabia since 1945, to return home. Once again, however, al-Kailani made a too daring bid for power that failed. Sentenced to death, he fled. Later pardoned, he settled down in Lebanon, not far from al-Husaini, and died there in 1965.

Shortly thereafter, in 1968, the Ba'th Party, in effect an Arab version of National Socialism, came to power in Baghdad. The new regime was soon to be led by Saddam Husain at-Tikriti, nephew and virtually adopted son of another al-Kailani supporter. His dictatorship ruled Iraq for thirty-five years and fell only to a U.S-led invasion in 2003. Even seventy years after the events and under a U.S.-installed regime, the errors of Iraq's pro-Nazi past could still not be openly and honestly discussed inside the country.[25]

In Syria, Maruf ad-Dawalibi, one of al-Husaini's wartime aides and postwar allies,[26] founded the Islamic Socialist Front in 1949. He became Syria's prime minister for a single day in 1951 and again for four months in 1961–1962.[27] When the Ba'th Party came to power in 1963, ad-Dawalibi went into exile and, like most Islamist leaders of that era, became part of al-Husaini's network. But the Ba'th Party, which would rule Syria for the next fifty years, had the same worldview, policies, and methods, namely those of a repressive, one-party dictatorship, as those it had had during the pro-Nazi era.[28] Party members, wrote Michel Aflaq, a founder and chief ideologue of the party,

> must be imbued with a hatred unto death, toward any individuals who embody an idea contrary to Arab nationalism. Arab nationalists must never dismiss opponents of Arabism as mere individuals. . . . An idea that is opposed to ours . . . is the incarnation of individuals who must be exterminated, so that their idea might in turn be also exterminated. Indeed, the presence in our midst of a living opponent of the Arab national idea vivifies it and stirs the blood within us.[29]

Saudi Arabia was governed by a dynasty that didn't join the Axis when the king concluded that Berlin would lose the war,[30] but after 1945, Saudi Arabia became the main patron of al-Husaini and the Islamists who had been collaborators. Saudi money and protection ensured the movement's survival until it revived in the 1970s and began to scare even the Saudi monarchy due to its revolutionary ambitions.[31]

The Arabic-speaking world's umbrella organization, the Arab League, established in 1946, was also filled with ex-Axis collaborators. Abd ar-Rahman Azzam, its first secretary general, had been one of al-Husaini's agents working with the Nazis, and still pursued the Jewish genocide implemented in Europe, which he and al-Husaini hoped to spread to the Middle East. What they once expected German armies to accomplish was now to be fulfilled by Arab ones. At the start of the fighting in late 1947, Azzam told a press conference, "This will be a war of extermination and a momentous massacre which will be spoken of like the Mongolian massacres and the Crusades."[32]

Abd ar-Rahman's brother, Abd al-Wahhab Azzam, a Muslim cleric who had not been a Nazi collaborator, was nonetheless a major source for al-Husaini's anti-Semitic conspiracy theories. Aiman az-Zawahiri, Abd al-Wahhab's grandson and Abd ar-Rahman's grandnephew, would become one of al-Qaida's main leaders and an architect of the September 11, 2001 attacks, almost exactly sixty years from the day al-Husaini arrived in Berlin to join the Third Reich's war. And just as al-Husaini had applauded the 1941 Japanese attack on Pearl Harbor, a large number of radical Arab nationalists or Islamists as well as the governments of Iran, Syria, and Iraq cheered the September 11 attacks as a new phase in the war against liberal Muslims, Western democracy, and the Jews.[33]

The Arab League's most important intellectual figure was Sati al-Husri, its cultural director for two decades starting in 1947. He had been a major architect of radical Arab nationalism, a key supporter of the pro-German al-Kailani regime in Iraq, and a Nazi sympathizer. In his Arab League office, al-Husri frequently met with unrepentant Nazis, among them fellow Arab League employee von Leers. In the postwar period, former collaborators like al-Husri had tremendous influence on the next generation. Extremist nationalists set the tone for most of the media and schools; Islamists did so for religious education and mosques. Decades of indoctrination even before World War

I, coupled with the predispositions of traditional society, ensured that large numbers of people held similar ideas.

The career of Kamil Muruwwa provides a good example of how veteran pro-Nazis shaped public thinking. In 1933, as a young editor of the Beirut newspaper *an-Nida,* he wrote von Ribbentrop that all Arab youth were enthusiastically pro-Hitler. Muruwwa translated parts of *Mein Kampf* into Arabic in 1934 and published it in daily installments. A German official recommended putting him on the payroll.[34]

As a German agent, Muruwwa received twenty-five hundred marks monthly, the equivalent of about one thousand dollars a month at the time and more money than many senior German civil servants were paid.[35] He built intelligence-gathering networks in Lebanon and in 1940 became the German News Bureau's Beirut correspondent. The following year, when the British captured Lebanon, he fled to Berlin where von Ribbentrop asked him to start his own Arab News Service. At al-Husaini's recommendation, however, the Shiite Muruwwa was posted to Sofia to run a listening post that analyzed Arabic radio broadcasts and newspapers.

After the war, Muruwwa returned to Lebanon and founded the *al-Hayat* newspaper which became very influential[36] and gave al-Husaini and his allies good press.[37] Muruwwa falsely claimed, for example, that al-Husaini had never been a Nazi collaborator and instead had bravely rejected a German demand in 1942 to start a revolt in Palestine. In *Al-Hayat,* Muruwwa also followed the line on the Holocaust that prevailed in the Arab world from the 1950s onward. The Nazis had been right, merely and understandably reacting to the fact that "half a million Jews enslaved 80 million Germans," and from this arose parallel conclusions for the Arabic-speaking world regarding the Jewish threat to dominate and destroy Arab civilization. In his newspaper as in much of the Arabic mass media, the continuing line was, as in the 1930s, that everything wrong in the Arab world was the fault of Western democracies and the Jews. Muruwwa was murdered in 1966 but the newspaper continued in family hands until purchased by a Saudi prince in 1990.[38]

The World Muslim Congress, the Islamist movement's main international group, had been founded and led by al-Husaini, who offered its support to the Germans. After 1945 al-Husaini moved its headquarters to Karachi, and he selected Inamullah Khan, one of the co-founders, to be secretary-general in 1949. Khan received the 1988 Templeton

Prize for Progress in Religion—previously given to Mother Teresa, the Reverend Billy Graham, and Aleksandr Solzhenitsyn, and carrying a $370,000 award—to honor the Congress's work.[39] When accused of hating Jews, Khan said he merely opposed racist Zionists. This was also a favorite argument of the PLO, which often used using the word "Zionist" instead of "Jew."[40]

The Syrian Islamist and former Nazi collaborationist agent Maruf ad-Dawalibi became al-Husaini's successor as the group's leader. In 1984, as Saudi Arabia's delegate at a UN seminar on religious tolerance and freedom in Geneva, ad-Dawalibi explained: "Why did Hitler want to exterminate them?. . . It is because they call themselves the chosen people and allege they were chosen by God from among all the peoples. . . . The Talmud says if a Jew does not drink every year the blood of a non-Jew, then he will be damned for eternity."[41]

Islamism's successful remaking of its image and its sweeping under the rug its old participation in the German-Ottoman and Nazi-Islamist alliances was demonstrated by the continuity of institutions, ideology, and personnel. Al-Husaini's personal heir in the global Islamist movement was Muhammad Said Ramadan. He was the son-in-law and aide of Hasan al-Banna, the Muslim Brotherhood's founder and leader until his assassination in 1949. Like Arafat, al-Husaini's other political heir, Ramadan fought with Brotherhood forces in the 1948 war. He then moved to Pakistan to represent the group.

Thereafter, Ramadan's career largely depended on al-Husaini's patronage, and he would inherit the ex-grand mufti's Islamist network, financial base, and institutional assets in Switzerland and elsewhere.[42] At the 1951 World Muslim Congress meeting, al-Husaini made his young protégé a member of its secretariat,[43] and two years later Ramadan became the congress's secretary general. He moved to Damascus where he worked for both al-Husaini and the Brotherhood.[44] Al-Husaini financed their joint magazine, *al-Muslimin* (The Muslims),[45] which Ramadan co-edited with Mustafa Husni as-Sibai, the Syrian Muslim Brotherhood leader.[46]

In 1958, when Syria merged temporarily with Egypt and Abd an-Nasir extended his repression of the Muslim Brotherhood there, Ramadan fled to Geneva where he became the Muslim Brotherhood's and al-Husaini's European representative.[47] That post as the chief Islamist in Europe was previously held by Shakib Arslan, the kaiser's and the Nazis' most consistent Arab ally who up to 1945 had been subsidized by Hitler's regime.[48] Arslan's views remained unchanged until his death in 1946.[49] In 1959, Ramadan finished his dissertation on Islamic law at Cologne University, which urged Muslims to fight against Europe's secular societies.[50]

Repressed by Arab nationalist regimes, the Islamists, like their Axis partners after 1945, fled into exile or went underground. Led by al-Husaini and the Muslim Brotherhood, they returned to their 1920s and 1930s strategies, when the Ottoman Empire's collapse had destroyed their Young Turk patrons and Anglo-French rule had made it too hot for them at home. Retreating to Europe, the Islamists began building or taking over mosques, setting up student and other front groups, and creating or gaining control of Muslim associations and journals.[51] Said Ramadan spent four decades on that task. The Brotherhood also founded Islamic institutes and built new mosques. By 2000, many of the Islamic communities throughout Europe adhered to Brotherhood ideology and were led by Brotherhood members.[52]

The focal point for much of this work was the mosque built in Munich by an Egyptian, Ali Ghalib Himmat, and an Uzbek, Nur ad-Din Namanjani. The fifty-eight-year-old Namanjani had been imam of a Turkic SS unit and was close to al-Husaini. Funds for the mosque were raised by al-Husaini in Lebanon and Saudi Arabia in 1961 as well as by contributions from German ex-Nazis.[53] While other Munich Muslims at first resisted Ramadan's and the Brotherhood's control, in the end the group's ability to provide funds carried the day.[54]

In 1961, Ramadan founded the Islamic Center in Geneva with Saudi money. He also took over the Islamic Center of Munich and, two years later, the Islamic Center of London as well. After Ramadan's death, the Geneva center was led by his oldest son, Hani. Himmat became Ramadan's successor in 1973 as leader in Munich, which remained the most important center for Islamism and the Brotherhood in West Germany.[55]

The Syrian Yusuf Mustafa Nada Ibada worked with Himmat, and during the 1980s, Himmat and Ibada also built the Muslim Brotherhood's global financial network. For example, they founded the at-Taqwa Bank in 1988. After the September 11, 2001 attacks on Washington and New York, international investigations named Himmat and Ibada as major financiers of terrorism.[56] Himmat left the Islamic Center of Munich in 2004 to become head of the Lugano Islamic Center in Switzerland.[57]

So Ramadan, leader of the new Islamist generation in the post-Nazi era, who had no publicly expressed opinion on the events of that time, was nevertheless the lieutenant of the ex–Nazi ally al-Husaini as well as son-in-law and aide of another collaborationist leader, al-Banna, and led the international expansion of a group, the Muslim Brotherhood, that had collaborated with the Nazis.

Many of his older colleagues were also Muslims who had been Nazi collaborators (Namanjani, ad-Dawalibi), assisted by German ex-Nazis concealed in West Germany's government (Zech-Nentwig, Wolfrum). They used institutions created and subsidized by the Nazi regime (the Geneva center, the Central Islamic Institute of Berlin) and funds that Hitler's government had paid al-Husaini for his collaboration, now managed by a Nazi banker (Genoud). And Ramadan's protégés would become key financiers of the modern Islamist terrorist movement.

Yet at some point these factors ceased to affect Western perceptions of the Brotherhood. At a critical moment in the 2011 "Arab Spring," as the Brotherhood moved to take control of Egypt and Tunisia, the director of U.S. defense intelligence, James Clapper, told Congress in February 2011 that the Brotherhood was a moderate, secular group that opposed violence.[58]

Such ideas were shaped and encouraged by the Brotherhood's own campaigns. For example, the *New York Times* article by Tariq Ramadan, Said's son, earnestly claimed that the Muslim Brotherhood was a pro-British, anti-Nazi organization.[59] Born in Geneva in 1962, raised in Switzerland, and groomed for leadership from childhood, Ramadan would be Islamism's best-known spokesman in the West, becoming professor of contemporary Islamic studies at Oxford University.

Any effort to persuade the West that it should tolerate or even assist the Muslim Brotherhood requires erasing its legacy of cooperation with the Nazis and, of equal importance, the ideological parallels between the Nazis and the Brotherhood, as well as with Islamism generally. Thus, Islamist organizations fail to acknowledge, much less explicitly reject, their pro-Axis past because of the potential damage to their interests and image. Yet the ideologies and concepts of the movement still largely parallel those of the Ottoman Empire during World War I; of Nazi Germany and al-Husaini in World War II; of Abd an-Nasir, Ba'thists, and the PLO during the Cold War; and of al-Qaida, Iran, the Muslim Brotherhood, and Hizballah thereafter. A few examples are offered here.

Ayman al-Zawahiri, the Egyptian Islamist who became a top al-Qaida leader, explained the mobilization for jihad in terms that sound as if they came from von Oppenheim's memos and the Ottoman declarations or al-Husaini's advice to Nazi Germany. In other words, hatred against Jews and the West would be stirred up, thus generating mass support and leading to a jihad:

> The one slogan that has been well understood by the nation and to which it has been responding for the past 50 years is the call for jihad against Israel [and] against the U.S. presence. . . . The jihad movement has moved to the center of the leadership of the nation when it adopted the slogan of liberating the nation from its external enemies and when it portrayed it as a battle of Islam against infidelity and infidels.[60]

In 1942, al-Husaini had advised the Germans that the most effective propaganda would be to preach hatred of the Jews, or in his words, "The Jewish attack and the plagues they carry."[61] He had also made this idea the centerpiece in his lectures to SS units and imams.[62] This theme was echoed during the following decades. Here, for example, is Sayyid Qutb, the Brotherhood's key theoretician and al-Husaini's friend, in 1950 using almost precisely the same words:

> The Jews did indeed return to evil-doing, so Allah gave to the Muslims power over them. The Muslims then expelled them from the whole of the Arabian Peninsula. . . . Then the Jews again returned to evil-doing and consequently Allah sent against them others of his servants, until the modern period. Then Allah brought Hitler to rule over them. And once again today the Jews have returned to evil-doing, in the form of "Israel" which made the Arabs, the owners of the land, taste of sorrows and woe.[63]

Similarly, Hamas, the Palestinian Muslim Brotherhood, in its Covenant at the end of the 1970s quoted al-Banna, drew heavily on the *Protocols of the Elders of Zion* as did al-Husaini, and echoed the radical Arab-Nazi line that went far beyond opposition to Zionism to portray the Jews as the world's main evil force, the creators of Communism, cultural modernism, and Western imperialism in almost precisely the same words used in al-Husaini's wartime speeches and German propaganda.

> With their money, they took control of the world media. . . . They were behind the French Revolution, the Communist revolution, and

most of the revolutions we heard and hear about, here and there. . . .
With their money they were able to control imperialistic countries and
instigate them to colonize many countries in order to enable them to
exploit their resources and spread corruption there.

They were behind World War I, when they were able to destroy the
Islamic Caliphate. . . . They were behind World War II, through which
they made huge financial gains by trading in armaments, and paved the
way for the establishment of their state . . . to enable them to rule the
world. . . .[64]

Hamas's Deputy Minister of Religious Endowments Abdallah Jarbu
in a February 2010 television interview also spoke in terms parallel
to Nazi and contemporary Islamist propaganda, calling Jews "subhu-
mans," and urging that they be "annihilated." "The Jews," he said,

are thieves and aggressors. . . . They want to present themselves to the
world as if they have rights, but, in fact, they are a microbe unparalleled
in the world. It's not I who say this. The Koran itself says . . . "You
shall find the strongest men in enmity to the believers to be the Jews."
May He annihilate this filthy people who have neither religion nor
conscience. I condemn whoever believes in normalizing relations with
them, whoever supports sitting down with them, and whoever believes
that they are human beings. They are not human beings. They are not
people.[65]

The language az-Zawahiri and Usama bin Ladin employed in their
February 28, 1998 jihad declaration against Jews and Crusaders
(Christians) also closely paralleled al-Husaini's speeches and Muslim
Brotherhood materials of the 1930s and 1940s.[66] Al-Husaini spoke of
a Zionist-British conspiracy to destroy Islam. Al-Qaida and other Is-
lamists in the post-1945 world—no longer needing to excuse fascist
Italy and Nazi Germany as "good" Christians—broadened the enemy
into a Jewish-Christian-American conspiracy.

Similar ideas came from the leading Muslim Brotherhood ideologue
Yusuf al-Qaradawi. As al-Qaradawi put it:

Throughout history, Allah has imposed upon the [Jews] people who
would punish them for their corruption. The last punishment was carried out by Hitler. By means of all the things he did to them—even
though they exaggerated this issue—he managed to put them in their
place. This was divine punishment for them. Allah willing, the next
time will be at the hand of the believers.[67]

Like other nationalist and Islamist commentators, al-Qaradawi attributed the Holocaust solely to Hitler. Yet he showed his support by claiming the genocide enjoyed divine sanction and by predicting that Muslims would implement the next round.

In his October 2010 speech that called for and indeed predicted the revolution in Egypt a few weeks later, Muhammad al-Badi, the Muslim Brotherhood's supreme guide, expressed a vision that mirrored that of von Oppenheim and al-Husaini:

> Waging jihad against both of these infidels [Israel and the United States] is a commandment of Allah that cannot be disregarded. . . . All Muslims are required by their religion to fight: They crucially need to understand that the improvement and change that the [Muslim] nation seeks can only be attained through jihad and sacrifice and by raising a jihadi generation that pursues death just as the enemies pursue life.[68]

The copious references to holy texts in the statements above show that Islamists did not need to take ideas from German Nazis or Italian fascists. As al-Husaini had argued in the 1930s and 1940s, they had a parallel yet symbiotic world view, drawn from their own societies' political traditions, history, and religion.

The common themes tying together Middle Eastern and European extremists included hatred of democracy (as distinct from merely holding elections); glorification of dictatorship; deification of the dictator-leader; organizing society by a systematic ideology that suppressed liberty and debate; and using Jews and the Western democracies as scapegoats whose destruction would bring peace and plenty.[69]

Of course, radical nationalists and Islamists drew inspiration from European partners. But those who worked directly with the Nazis as their comrades inherited the Middle East long after their counterparts in Berlin were reduced to ashes. The resulting history simultaneously realized von Oppenheim's vision of transnational jihad and Hurgronje's warning that this would produce a nightmare of bloody confrontations and out-of-control hatreds. As a consequence, the lasting influence of this worldview and strategies diverted Middle Eastern societies from better alternatives. Even the presence of so much valuable oil and gas did not keep the Middle East from falling behind Asia and South America in almost every index of political freedom, technological progress, and social well-being.

All of these facts do not make al-Husaini or al-Qaida—or for that matter Iran's Islamist regime, the Ba'th governments in Iraq and Syria, Hamas, the PLO, Hizballah, the Muslim Brotherhood, or the dominant exponents of the Arab world's mainstream discourse—into Nazis or fascists. But these groups demonstrated how the same radical vision that had once found the Nazis to be congenial, right-thinking allies had such a powerful, long-lived effect in shaping the contemporary Middle East. This is the terrible secret of modern Middle Eastern history.

Notes

CHAPTER 1. FROM STATION Z TO JERUSALEM

1. ParchAA, R100702. From a July 28, 1942, note by Fritz Grobba we infer that the visit described here took place between June 26 and July 17, 1942.

2. According to one document, the visitors were "three of al-Kailani's men." Grobba said it was "three staffers of al-Kailani and one of al-Husaini" and on a third occasion the document referred to "four Arabs." PArchAA, R100702, F1784–85, Zu Pol VII 6447g II, B611978, "Notiz für Gesandschaftsrat Granow, drei Begleiter al-Kailanis, bedauerlich, zumal Herr RAM sich angeschlossen hat, solche Einrichtungen nicht zu zeigen, Berlin, 06.06.1942, gez. Gödde." PArchAA, R100702, F1784–85, Zu Pol VII 6447g I Metropol: I, B611979.

3. Günter Morsch and Astrid Ley, eds., *Das Konzentrationslager Sachsenhausen 1936–1945* (Berlin: Metropol, 2008), 170, 176, 178.

4. "On the visit of four Arabs to the concentration camp 'Sachsenhausen' near Oranienburg," Berlin, July 17, 1942. See also Wolfgang G. Schwanitz, ed., *Germany and the Middle East, 1871–1945* (Princeton: Wiener, 2004), 218–220.

5. Morsch and Ley, *Das Konzentrationslager Sachsenhausen*, 101–110.

6. Amin al-Husaini, *Mudhakkirat al-Hajj Muhammad Amin al-Husaini* [The memoirs of al-Hajj Muhammad Amin al-Husaini], ed. Abd al-Karim al-Umar (Damascus: Al-Ahali, 1999), 74.

7. PArchAA, R100702, F1784–85, "Wunsch Kailanis ein KZ zu besichtigen, Berlin, 6/26/42, gez. Grobba."

8. PArchAA, R100702, F1784–85, "Wunsch Kailanis ein KZ zu besichtigen, Berlin, 6/26/42, gez. Grobba."

9. PArchAA, R100702, F1784–85, Zu Pol VII 6447g II, B611976, "Notiz für

Herrn Grobba (im Auftrag von U.St.S. Martin Luther), Geheim, Berlin, 7/24/1942, gez. Gödde."

10. Adolf Hitler, *Mein Kampf* (Boston: Mariner, 1999), 307; al-Husaini, *Mudhakkirat*, 94, 414–415.

11. Hitler, *Mein Kampf*, 610, 619.

12. Al-Husaini, *Mudhakkirat*, 73.

13. "Ein Angebot an die zuständigen Stellen in Deutschland," *Akten zur Deutschen Auswärtigen Politik*, 63 vols. (Baden-Baden: Imprimerie Nationale, 1950–1996), ser. D, 5:655–656 (offer for agreement, nine points by the Grand Mufti and Syrian Arabs); "Islam und Judentum," in *Islam—Bolschewismus*, ed. Muhammad Sabri (Berlin: Junker und Dünnhaupt, 1938), 22–32 (grand mufti's call to the Islamic world of 1937).

14. PArchAA, N6, R104795, "Aufzeichnung, Empfang des Sondergesandten von König Abdul Aziz Ibn Saud auf dem Berghofe des Königlichen Rats Khalid Al Hud al-Qarqani, Berlin 20.06.1939, gez. Hentig."

15. PArchWGS, Jewish Question, Hermann Göring to Reinhard Heydrich, Berlin, July 31, 1941, signed Göring.

16. PArchWGS, Office Of Chief Of Counsel For War Crimes, Doc. No. NG-5462–5570, Eidesstattliche Erklärung (sworn statement on financial affairs of Germany's Arab guests), Carl Rekowski, Bremen, October 5, 1947, 1–10.

17. Wolfgang G. Schwanitz, *Gold, Bankiers und Diplomaten: Zur Geschichte der Deutschen Orientbank 1906–1946* (Berlin: Trafo, 2002), 100, 113, 148, 299.

18. Al-Husaini, *Mudhakkirat*, 104.

19. Ibid., 107.

20. Ibid., 105.

21. USArchII, T120, R901, F61123, "Entwurf eines dem Sekretär des Großmuftis mitzugebenden Schreibens im Namen des Führers als Antwort auf den Brief vom 20.01.1941, geheim, Berlin, März 1941 [later dated April 8, 1941], gez. Weizsäcker."

22. German-Italian broadcast declaration on Arab independence, aired October 21, 1941.

23. USArchII, T120, R901, F61123, "Die Person des Großmufti, geheime Reichssache, Berlin, März 1941," 72–73.

24. H. R. Trevor-Roper, *Hitler's Table Talk, 1941–1944*, rev. ed. (New York: Enigma, 2008), 412.

25. USArchII, RG165, B3055, OSS code cablegram, "Grand Mufti, Cairo, confidential," May 19, 1941.

26. USArchII, T120, R63571, R50682, "Der Großmufti von Jerusalem," Berlin, 11/28/41"; al-Husaini, *Mudhakkirat*, 108.

27. Al-Husaini, *Mudhakkirat*, 113.

28. Ibid.

29. Trevor-Roper, *Hitler's Table Talk*, 412.

30. BArchPAA, F56474, Bericht, 351003–351007.

31. Corry Guttstadt, *Die Türkei, die Juden und der Holocaust* (Hamburg: Assoziation A, 2008), 248, 256.

32. Ibid.

33. PArchWGS, protocol of the Wannsee Conference, Berlin-Wannsee, January 20, 1942, online at http://www.ghwk.de/fileadmin/user_upload/pdf-wannsee/protokoll-januar1942.pdf.

34. "Betr. Grossmufti von Jerusalem," written statement by Wisliceny at Nuremberg, July 26, 1946, in Wolfgang G. Schwanitz, *Amin al-Husaini und das Dritte Reich* (Lawrenceville, N.J., 2008), http://www.trafoberlin.de/pdf-Neu/Amin%20 al-Husaini%20und%20das%20Dritte%20Reich%20WGS.pdf, 1–10.

35. Wolfgang G. Schwanitz: "Amin al-Husaini and the Holocaust: What Did the Grand Mufti Know?" *World Politics Review Exclusive*, May 8, 2008, http://www.trafoberlin.de/pdf-Neu/Amin%20al-Husaini%20and%20the%20Holocaust.pdf, 1–10.

36. Schwanitz, *Germany and the Middle East*, 218–220.

37. Morsch and Ley, *Das Konzentrationslager Sachsenhausen*, 174.

38. PArchAA, R100702, F1784–85, Zu Pol VII 6447g II, B611976.

39. PArchAA, R100702, F1784–85, Zu Pol VII 6447g II, B611977.

40. Astrid Ley and Günther Morsch, eds., *Medizin und Verbrechen: Das Krankenrevier des KZ Sachsenhausen 1936–1945* (Berlin: Metropol, 2007), 391–392.

CHAPTER 2. A CHRISTIAN IMPERIAL STRATEGY OF ISLAMIC REVOLUTION

1. "Bismarck im Reichstag, 06.02.1888," in *Otto von Bismarck: Dokumente seines Lebens,* ed. Heinz Wolter (Leipzig: Reclam, 1989), 401–403. See also Friedrich Scherer, *Adler und Halbmond: Bismarck und der Orient 1878–1890* (Paderborn: Schöningh, 2001); Konrad Canis, *Bismarcks Außenpolitik 1870–1890: Aufstieg und Gefährdung* (Paderborn: Schöningh, 2004).

2. Bismarck quoted in Gregor Schöllgen, *Imperialismus im Gleichgewicht: Deutschland, England und die orientalische Frage 1871–1914* (Munich: Oldenbourg, 2000), 16.

3. M. Şükrü Hanioğlu: *A Brief History of the Late Ottoman Empire* (Princeton: Princeton University Press, 2008), 78–83.

4. Ernst Jäckh, ed., *Kiderlen-Wächter: Der Staatsmann und Mensch,* vol. 2 (Berlin: Deutsche Verlags-Anstalt, 1924), 20; John C. G. Röhl, *Wilhelm II* (Munich: Beck, 2009), 784.

5. Karl Wippermann, *Deutscher Geschichtskalender für 1897* (Leipzig: Grunow, 1898), 135–136.

6. Wilhelm van Kampen, "Studien zur deutschen Türkeipolitik in der Zeit Wilhelms II" (Ph.D. diss., Kiel, 1968), 58.

7. Arkadi S. Jerussalimski, *Die Außenpolitik und die Diplomatie des deutschen Imperialismus Ende des 19. Jahrhunderts* (Berlin: Dietz, 1954), 160–161.

8. Van Kampen, "Studien zur deutschen Türkeipolitik," 58.

9. Max Freiherr von Oppenheim, *Vom Mittelmeer zum Persischen Golf durch den Hauran, die Syrische Wüste und Mesopotamien,* 2 vols. (Hildesheim: Olms, 2004), 1:74–76.

10. John Buchan, *Greenmantle* (New York: Oxford University Press, 1999), 13–14.

11. Salvador Oberhaus, *Zum wilden Aufstande entflammen* (Saarbrücken: Müller, 2007), 92.

12. Lieutenant Kannenberg in *Die Naturschätze Kleinasiens,* quoted in Hugo Grothe, *Deutschland, die Türkei und der Islam: Ein Beitrag zu den Grundlinien der deutschen Weltpolitik im islamischen Orient* (Leipzig: Hirzel, 1914), 273–275.

13. ArchSalOppCo, Oppenheim 25/10, Max Freiherr von Oppenheim, "Denkschrift betreffend Die Revolutionierung der islamischen Gebiete unserer Feinde, Berlin, 1914," 85.

14. Gerhard Keiper and Martin Kröger, eds., *Biographisches Handbuch des deutschen Auswärtigen Dienstes 1871–1945,* vol. 3 (Paderborn: Schöningh, 2008), 408–409.

15. Von Oppenheim, *Vom Mittelmeer zum Persischen Golf,* 2:259, 260.

16. Wolfgang Michal, "Der Spion des Kaisers," *National Geographic Deutschland,* February 2008, 90.

17. ArchSalOppCo, "An Reichskanzler Fürsten zu Hohenlohe-Schillingsfürst, Bericht No. 48, Die Panislamische Bewegung, Kairo, 5.07.1898," 3; attachment to No. 48, Singapore, May 2, 1898.

18. Van Kampen, "Studien zur deutschen Türkeipolitik," 363.

19. Ernst Jäckh, "Jihad," *Die Hilfe* 37 (October 9, 1914).

20. Friedrich Rosen, *Aus einem diplomatischen Wanderleben,* vol. 3 (Wiesbaden: Limes, 1959), 140.

21. Fritz Fischer, *Griff nach der Weltmacht: Die Kriegszielpolitik des kaiserlichen Deutschland 1914/18* (Düsseldorf: Droste, 1962), 136.

22. Cornelia Essner and Gerd Winkelhane, "Carl Heinrich Becker (1876–1933), Orientalist und Kulturpolitiker," *Die Welt des Islams* 28 (1988): 155–177. See also Carl Heinrich Becker, *Christianity and Islam* (New York: Harper & Brothers, 1909), 114; Carl Heinrich Becker, "Ist der Islam eine Gefahr für unsere Kolonien?" (1909), in *Islamstudien: Vom Werden und Wesen der islamischen Welt,* vol. 2 (Hildesheim: Olms, 1967), 156–186.

23. Carl Heinrich Becker, "Der Islam und die Kolonisierung Afrikas" (1910), ibid., 210.

24. ArchSalOppCo, "An Reichskanzler Fürsten zu Hohenlohe-Schillingsfürst, Bericht No. 48, Die Panislamische Bewegung, Kairo, 5.07.1898," 3, Attachment, Singapore, May 2, 1898.

25. Karl Wippermann, *Deutscher Geschichtskalender für 1898* (Leipzig: Grunow, 1899), gives a step-by-step description of the Kaiser's journey to and within the Ottoman Empire, 12–31.

26. USArchII, M453, RG59, Roll 5, Vol. 9, January 3, 1898, August 20, 1906, from Consul Selah Merrill, "The Visit of the German Emperor to Palestine, Jerusalem, Syria, 12.11.1898," 1–4.

27. Erich Lichtheim, *Das Programm des Zionismus* (Berlin: Scholem, 1911; 2d ed., 1913), 3–7, 42–43.

28. Ernst Berner, "Kaiser Wilhelm II," in *Hohenzollern Jahrbuch,* ed. Paul Seidel (Berlin: Giesecke, 1898), 3, 8–10; Lichtheim, *Das Programm des Zionismus,* 20–21.

29. Wolfgang G. Schwanitz, "A most favourable impression upon all classes:

Wilhelm II, Sozialdemokraten, Muslime und Nordamerikaner 1898," in *Des Kaisers Reise in den Orient 1898*, ed. Klaus Jaschinski, Julius Waldschmidt (Berlin: Trafo, 2002), 37–60; Theodor Herzl, *Theodor Herzls Tagebücher 1895–1904*, vol. 1 (Berlin: Jüdischer Verlag, 1922), 27, June 2, 1895.

30. Stefan Wild, "Die arabische Rezeption der 'Protokolle der Weisen von Zion,'" in *Islamstudien ohne Ende: Festschrift für Werner Ende zum 65. Geburtstag*, ed. Rainer Brunner et al. (Würzburg: Ergon, 2002), 520.

31. Hannes Möhring, *Saladin* (Munich: Beck, 2005), 122.

32. Gregor Schöllgen, *Imperialismus im Gleichgewicht: Deutschland, England und die orientalische Frage 1871–1914* (Munich: Oldenbourg, 2000), 107.

33. PArchWGS, "Memorandum of the India Office by Request of the Prime Minister, A: German Influence in Turkey" (London: Department Press, May 1, 1917), 3.

34. Sabine Mangold, *Eine "weltbürgerliche Wissenschaft": Die deutsche Orientalistik im 19. Jahrhundert* (Stuttgart: Steiner, 2004), 289.

35. For the meaning of *Legationsrat* in this case, see also Martin Kröger, "Mit Eifer ein Fremder im Auswärtigen Dienst," *Fascination Orient: Max von Oppenheim*, ed. Gabriele Teichmann and Gisela Völger (Cologne: DuMont, 2001), 114–115.

36. John C. G. Röhl, *Wilhelm II: Der Weg in den Abgrund 1900–1941* (Munich: Beck, 2009), 125.

37. "Beziehungen zum türkischen Reiche," in *Norddeutsche Allgemeine Zeitung*, September 30, 1898, in Wippermann, *Deutscher Geschichtskalender für 1898*, 136.

38. Joseph Pomiankowski, *Der Zusammenbruch des Ottomanischen Reiches* (Graz: Akademische Druck- und Verlagsanstalt, 1969), 41, 51–52, 98, 102; Robert-Tarek Fischer, *Österreich im Nahen Osten: Die Großmachtpolitik der Habsburgmonarchie im Arabischen Orient 1633–1918* (Vienna: Böhlau, 2006), 248, 255.

39. Niles Stefan Illich, *German Imperialism in the Ottoman Empire* (College Station: Texas A&M University Press, 2007), chap. 8.

40. Jürgen Kloosterhuis, *Friedliche Imperialisten: Deutsche Auslandsvereine und auswärtige Kulturpolitik, 1906–1918* (Frankfurt am Main: Peter Lang, 1994).

41. Dirk van Laak, *Über alles in der Welt: Deutscher Imperialismus im 19. und 20. Jahrhundert* (Munich: Beck, 2005), 92.

42. PArchWGS, "Bagdad-Bahn-Projekt, Orientalisches Büro. Bericht von der Anatolischen Eisenbahngesellschaft im September 1899 ausgesandten Studienexpedition" (manuscript, Berlin, 1900), 1–91.

43. Wolfgang G. Schwanitz, *Gold, Bankiers und Diplomaten: Zur Geschichte der Deutschen Orientbank 1906–1946* (Berlin: Trafo, 2002).

44. Karl Wippermann, *Deutscher Geschichtskalender für 1897* (Leipzig: Grunow, 1898), 54.

45. Graf Johann-Heinrich Bernstorff, *Deutschland und Amerika: Erinnerungen aus dem fünfjährigen Kriege* (Berlin: Ullstein, 1920), 11–20, 46.

46. PArchWGS, Karl Emil Schabinger Freiherr von Schowingen, "Weltgeschichtliche Mosaiksplitter: Erlebnisse und Erinnerungen eines kaiserlichen Dragomans

(manuscript, Baden-Baden, 1967), 22; 50–52, eyewitness account by Schabinger, consul *ad interim*, of the kaiser's visit to Tangier on March 31, 1905.

47. Röhl, *Wilhelm II*, 742–745.

48. Ibid.

49. Pomiankowski, *Der Zusammenbruch des Ottomanischen Reiches*, 53.

50. Adolf Hitler, *Mein Kampf* (Boston: Mariner, 1999), 19.

51. Brigitte Hamann, *Hitlers Wien: Lehrjahre eines Diktators* (Munich: Piper, 2004), 21; Karl May, *Durch Wüste und Harem* (Herrsching: Pawlak, 1990), 229.

52. May, *Durch Wüste und Harem*, 172–173.

53. Hitler, *Mein Kampf*, 75, 79.

54. Ibid.; Hamann, *Hitlers Wien*, 334.

55. Hamann, *Hitlers Wien*, 191–192.

56. Ibid., 56.

57. Ibid., 239–242, 498, 87–88; Ralf Georg Reuth, *Hitler, eine politische Biographie* (Munich: Piper, 2003), 32.

58. Hitler, *Mein Kampf*, 151.

59. Ibid., 13, 64.

60. Ibid., 347.

61. May, *Durch Wüste und Harem*, 143.

62. Hamann, *Hitlers Wien*, 544–548.

63. Ibid., 548.

64. Hartmut Schmidt, "'Will ganz für mich allein bleiben . . .': Karl Mays Begegnung mit Max von Oppenheim in Kairo," *Karl-May-Haus Information*, no. 16 (2003): 15–21.

65. Hans Rühlmann: "Karl May in Kairo (1899)," *Karl-May-Jahrbuch* (Radebeul: Karl-May-Verlag, 1923), 123–130.

66. USArchII, T120, R3230, Serial 8362H, Frames 590592–95 (PArchAA, PAVII, Politische Beziehungen, Saudisch Arabien Deutschland 1935–1939, vols. 1–2, 385457), "Empfang des Sondergesandten von König Abdul Aziz, Königlicher Rat Khalid Al Hud al-Qarqani, vom Führer auf dem Berghofe, am 17.06.1939, Berlin 20.06.1939, gez. Werner Otto von Hentig."

67. May, *Durch Wüste und Harem*, 275.

68. Amin al-Husaini, *Mudhakkirat al-Hajj Muhammad Amin al-Husaini* [The memoirs of al-Hajj Muhammad Amin al-Husaini], ed. Abd al-Karim al-Umar (Damascus: Al-Ahali, 1999), 15.

69. USArchII, Office of Strategic Services, No. 9677, October 30, 1943, "Hajj Amin al-Husaini, Grand Mufti of Jerusalem, seen against the background of recent Palestine history," 1.

70. Ibid., 24.

71. Tilman Nagel, *Mohammed: Leben und Legende* (Munich: Oldenbourg, 2008), 370, 389, 399.

72. Ibrahim Abu Shaqra, *Al-Hajj Amin al-Husaini mundhu wiladatihi hatta thaurat 1936* [Amin al-Husaini from his birth until the revolution of 1936] (Latakia: Al-Manara, 1998), 21.

73. Ernst Jäckh, *Der aufsteigende Halbmond* (Stuttgart: Deutsche Verlags-Anstalt, 1915), 40–41.

CHAPTER 3. A JIHAD MADE IN GERMANY

1. Fritz Fischer, *Griff nach der Weltmacht: Die Kriegszielpolitik des kaiserlichen Deutschland 1914/18* (Düsseldorf: Droste, 1962), 133–134.

2. PArchAA, R1535, "An Wesendonk, Anschreiben, Deutsches Orient Institut aus NFO, Berlin, 09.08.1918, gez. Müller," 5.

3. Wilhelm van Kampen, "Studien zur deutschen Türkeipolitik in der Zeit Wilhelms II" (Ph.D. diss., Kiel, 1968), 363.

4. PArchWGS, Karl Emil Schabinger Freiherr von Schowingen, ed., "Weltgeschichtliche Mosaiksplitter: Erlebnisse und Erinnerungen eines kaiserlichen Dragomans, hg. von Karl Friedrich Schabinger von Schowingen" (manuscript, Baden-Baden, 1967), 126; Max Freiherr von Oppenheim, *Vom Mittelmeer zum Persischen Golf durch den Hauran, die Syrische Wüste und Mesopotamien,* 2 vols. (Hildesheim: Olms, 2004), 1:130-131.

5. Hugo Grothe, *Deutschland, die Türkei und der Islam: Ein Beitrag zu den Grundlinien der deutschen Weltpolitik im islamischen Orient* (Leipzig: Hirzel, 1914), 27–28.

6. Cited in George Griffin, "Ernst Jäckh and the Search for German Cultural Hegemony in the Ottoman Empire" (M.A. thesis, Ohio University), http://etd.ohiolink.edu/send-pdf.cgi/Griffin%20George%20William%20III.pdf?bgsu1245518955.

7. Aaron Rakeffet-Rothkopp, *The Rav: The World of Rabbi Joseph B. Soloveitchik,* 2 vols. (New York: Ktav, 1999), 225–234.

8. Holger Afflerbach, *Kaiser Wilhelm II. als Oberster Kriegsherr im Ersten Weltkrieg* (Munich: Oldenbourg, 2005), 137–138.

9. Ibid., 76.

10. Friedrich Freiherr Kreß von Kressenstein, *Mit den Türken zum Suezkanal* (Berlin: Schlegel, 1932), 11.

11. Karl Kautsky, ed., *Die deutschen Dokumente zum Kriegsausbruch,* vol. 2 (Berlin: Montgelas, 1919), 171–72, No. 733, French cable, Wangenheim to Saiid Halim, Constantinople, 02.08.1914.

12. Afflerbach, *Kaiser Wilhelm II. als Oberster Kriegsherr,* 138.

13. ArchSalOppCo, Oppenheim 25/10, Max Freiherr von Oppenheim, "Denkschrift betreffend Die Revolutionierung der islamischen Gebiete unserer Feinde (Berlin, 1914)."

14. Carl Heinrich Becker, *Deutschland und der Islam* (Berlin: Deutsche Verlags-Anstalt, 1914); Grothe, *Deutschland, die Türkei und der Islam;* Eugen Mittwoch, *Deutschland, die Türkei und der Heilige Krieg* (Berlin: Kameradschaft, 1914).

15. Becker, *Deutschland und der Islam,* 24.

16. Mittwoch, *Deutschland, die Türkei und der Heilige Krieg,* 25.

17. Von Oppenheim, "Denkschrift betreffend Die Revolutionierung," 89.

18. Becker, *Deutschland und der Islam,* 19–20.

19. Von Oppenheim, "Denkschrift betreffend Die Revolutionierung," 76, 98, 132, 134.

20. Grothe, *Deutschland, die Türkei und der Islam,* 30, 42.

21. ParchAA, NL, vol. 157, report by Gustav Stresemann, 58.

22. Franz von Papen, *Der Wahrheit eine Gasse,* 2 vols. (Munich: List, 1952), 1:89.

23. Von Oppenheim, "Denkschrift betreffend Die Revolutionierung," 8, 53.

24. Gotthard Jäschke refers to the "Bureau for the Revolutionizing of the Middle Eastern Lands to which Baha ad-Din Shakir, Ömer Naci and Hilmi belong," *Der Turanismus der Jungtürken: Zur osmanischen Außenpolitik im Weltkriege* (Leipzig: Harassowitz, 1941), 15.

25. Grothe, *Deutschland, die Türkei und der Islam*, 12; Donald McKale, *War By Revolution: Germany and Great Britain in the Middle East in the Era of World War I* (Kent, Ohio: Kent State University Press, 1998), 47–50; Tilman Lüdke, *Jihad Made in Germany: Ottoman and German Propaganda and Intelligence Operations in the First World War* (Münster: Lit, 2005), 113.

26. Joseph Pomiankowski, *Der Zusammenbruch des Ottomanischen Reiches* (Graz: Akademische Druck- und Verlagsanstalt, 1969), 88.

27. Fischer, *Griff nach der Weltmacht*, 93, 133–137.

28. Von Oppenheim, "Denkschrift betreffend Die Revolutionierung," 49.

29. Von Oppenheim, "Denkschrift betreffend Die Revolutionierung"; Tim Epkenhans, "Geld darf keine Rolle spielen," pt. 2, *Archivum Ottomanicum* 19 (2001): 121–163; Wolfgang G. Schwanitz, "Max von Oppenheim und der Heilige Krieg: Zwei Denkschriften zur Revolutionierung islamischer Gebiete 1914 und 1940," *Sozial.Geschichte* 19, no. 3 (2004): 28–59. See also McKale, *War By Revolution*, 108.

30. Martin Kröger, "Mit Eifer ein Fremder im Auswärtigen Dienst," in *Fascination Orient: Max von Oppenheim*, ed. Gabriele Teichmann and Gisela Völger (Cologne: DuMont, 2001), 106–139, 126–128.

31. USArchII, M1107, R31, 4.

32. Gerhard Höpp, *Muslime in der Mark: Als Kriegsgefangene und Internierte in Wünsdorf und Zossen, 1914–1924* (Berlin: Arabisches Buch, 1997), 23–24.

33. USArchII, M1107, R31, Tekin Alp, *The Turkish and the Pan-Turkish Ideal* (Weimar: Kiepenheuer, 1915), 40 (written in Istanbul); for a 1914 "Turan pamphlet" by Teken alias Moiz Cohen see Jäschke, *Der Turanismus der Jungtürken*, 8, 12. See also Jacob M. Landau, *Tekinalp, Turkish Patriot, 1883–1961* (Istanbul: Nederlands Historisch-Archaeologisch Instituut, 1986), 313.

34. USArchII, M1107, R31, "Report on Tekin Alp," Istanbul, February 15, 1915, 1 (Inquiry Document 579).

35. USArchII, M1107, R31, Tekin Alp, *The Turkish and the Pan-Turkish Ideal*, 40.

36. Ibid.

37. Bernard Lewis, *The Emergence of Modern Turkey* (New York: Oxford University Press, 2002), 326–327; Fischer, *Griff nach der Weltmacht*, 138.

38. Amin al-Husaini, *Mudhakkirat al-Hajj Muhammad Amin al-Husaini* [The memoirs of al-Hajj Muhammad Amin al-Husaini], ed. Abd al-Karim al-Umar (Damascus: Al-Ahali, 1999), 166–167.

39. C. Snouck Hurgronje, *The Holy War, Made in Germany* (New York: G. P. Putnam's Sons, 1915), 2.

40. Wolfgang G. Schwanitz, "Jihad Made in Germany: Der Streit um den Heiligen Krieg 1914–1915," *Sozial.Geschichte* 18, no. 2 (2003): 7–34.

41. Henry I. Morgenthau, *Ambassador Morgenthau's Story* (New York: Doubleday, 1918), chap. 14.

42. Von Oppenheim, *Vom Mittelmeer zum Persischen Golf*, 1:41–42.

43. McKale, *War By Revolution*, 68.

44. USArchII, R21028, Acten betreffend den Krieg 1914, 070814–071214, "Überblick über die in der islamischen Welt eingeleitete Agitationstätigkeit, Berlin 160814, Section II, Israelitische Welt, Zionistenbund, Agenten, Wolff'sches Büro."

45. McKale, *War By Revolution*, 166, 177, 205.

46. Höpp, *Muslime in der Mark*, 19–33.

47. Gottfried Hagen, *Die Türkei im Ersten Weltkrieg* (Frankfurt am Main: Peter Lang, 1994), doc. 8.4 includes both speeches.

48. Schabinger, "Weltgeschichtliche Mosaiksplitter," 102.

49. Quotations are from the translation in Rudolph Peters, *Islam and Colonialism: The Doctrine of Jihad in Modern History* (The Hague: Mouton, 1979), 90–91. See also Ernst Wiesener, *Adler, Doppel-Aar und Halbmond: Der Verbündeten Siegeszug nach dem Orient mit vielen Kriegs- und Landschaftsbildern* (Hamburg: Hansa, 1916), 16–21, and Rudolph Peters, *Jihad in Classical and Modern Islam* (Princeton: Wiener, 2005), "Ottoman Jihad Fatwa, November 11, 1914," 55–57.

50. "Kriegsurkunden: Fatwa über die Freundschaft der Muslime mit den Deutschen von as-Saiyyid Hibat ad-Din ash-Shahrastani an-Nadjafi mit Erläuterungen von Muhammad Farisi," *Die Welt des Islam* 4 (1917): 218–226.

51. Morgenthau, *Ambassador Morgenthau's Story*, chap. 14.

52. Schabinger, "Weltgeschichtliche Mosaiksplitter," 107–108; Morgenthau, *Ambassador Morgenthau's Story*; Pomiankowski, *Der Zusammenbruch des Ottomanischen Reiches*, 59, 65.

53. Schaich Salih Aschscharif Attunisi, *Haqiqat al-Jihad* (Berlin: Islamkunde, 1915), 18, signed in the afterword by Salih on November 3, 1914.

54. Schabinger, "Weltgeschichtliche Mosaiksplitter," 110–114.

55. PArchWGS, "Memorandum by the India Office as requested by the Prime Minister, an Inner View of the Predominant Intellectual and Political Forces in the Ottoman Empire," London, May 1, 1917, 4–5.

56. Kröger, "Mit Eifer ein Fremder im Auswärtigen Dienst," 115.

57. Max von Oppenheim, "Die türkische Nachrichtensaal-Organisation der Nachrichtenstelle der Kaiserlichen Botschaft," in *Konstantinopel im Dienste deutscher Wertarbeit im Orient* (Constantinople: Deutsches Wirtschaftsbüro, 1916), 7.

58. Morgenthau, *Ambassador Morgenthau's Story*, chap. 8.

59. As-Sayyid Hibat ad-Din Muhammad ash-Shahrastani an-Nadjafi, *Al-Haya wa al-Islam* (An-Najaf, about 1910).

60. Lüdke, *Jihad Made in Germany*, 50.

61. Morgenthau, *Ambassador Morgenthau's Story*, chap. 14.

62. Von Oppenheim, "Denkschrift betreffend Die Revolutionierung," 44, 90.

63. Ibid., 20, 23.

64. Ibid., 21–23.

65. Ibid., 22.

66. Pomiankowski, *Der Zusammenbruch des Ottomanischen Reiches*, 162.

67. Ibid.; Peter Jung, *Der k.u.k. Wüstenkrieg 1915–1918: Österreich-Ungarn im Vorderen Orient* (Graz: Styria, 1992), 23–27.

68. PArchWGS, "Memorandum by the India Office as requested by the Prime Minister, An Inner View of The Predominant Intellectual and Political Forces in the Ottoman Empire," London, May 1, 1917.

69. Von Oppenheim, "Denkschrift betreffend Die Revolutionierung," 26–27, 101, 116.

70. McKale, *War By Revolution*, 88–91, 191.

71. Von Oppenheim, "Denkschrift betreffend Die Revolutionierung," 91.

72. Martin Kröger, "Revolution als Programm: Ziele und Realität deutscher Orientpolitik im Ersten Weltkrieg," in *Der Erste Weltkrieg*, ed. Wolfgang Michalka (Munich: Piper, 1994), 382.

73. Pomiankowski, *Der Zusammenbruch des Ottomanischen Reiches*, 171–172; Robert-Tarek Fischer: *Österreich im Nahen Osten* (Vienna: Böhlau, 2006), 255.

74. USArchII, RG256, M1107, R1, digest of the remarks of Aaron Aaronson on conditions in Turkey and Asia Minor prior to September 1916 as he left the country (conveyed by Walter Lippmann), December 28, 1917: Aaronson said that Jaeckh had instigated Pan-Turkism after the Young Turk coup of 1908, 7.

75. Von Oppenheim, "Denkschrift betreffend Die Revolutionierung," 18, 82.

76. Ibid., 19–20, 93.

77. Ibid., 91.

78. Manabendra Nath Roy, *Memoirs* (Bombay: Allied, 1964), 3–4.

79. Von Papen, *Der Wahrheit eine Gasse*, 1:74.

80. Pomiankowski, *Der Zusammenbruch des Ottomanischen Reiches*, 276.

81. Wolfgang G. Schwanitz: *Gold, Bankiers und Diplomaten: Zur Geschichte der Deutschen Orientbank 1906–1946* (Berlin: Trafo, 2002), 62–64, 85–107.

82. Werner Ende, "Iraq in World War I: The Turks, the Germans and the Shi'ite Mujtahids' Call for Jihad," in *Proceedings of the 9th Congress of the Union Européenne des Arabisants et Islamisants*, ed. Rudolph Peters (Leiden: Brill, 1981), 57–71.

83. PArchWGS, "An Reichskanzler Bethmann Hollweg, Telegramm 187, Fritz Klein in Kerbala, Bagdad, 08/03/16, gez. Hesse."

84. Paul Leverkuehn, *German Military Intelligence* (London: Weidenfeld & Nicolson, 1954), and *Der geheime Nachrichtendienst der Wehrmacht im Kriege* (Bonn: Athenäum, 1964).

85. Von Oppenheim, "Denkschrift betreffend Die Revolutionierung," 62–66.

86. Dagobert von Mikusch, *Waßmuß, der deutsche Lawrence* (Leipzig: List, 1937), 195.

87. PArchWGS, "News From Herat," spy report on Germans of August 28, 1915, Khorazan, signed T. W. Haig, Consul General.

88. PArchWGS, report by Hentig and Niedermayer, Vienna, December 13, 1916, signed B. Graf Wedel.

89. Hans-Ulrich Seidt, "'When Continents Awake, Island Empires Fall!': Germany and the Destabilization of the East, 1919–1922," in *Germany and the Middle East, 1871–1945*, ed. Wolfgang G. Schwanitz (Princeton: Wiener, 2004), 84–85.

90. PArchWGS, translation of Afghan draft of Alliance Treaty with Germany, January 24, 1916, signed by the amir, Niedermayer, and Hentig; annotation by

Niedermayer, January 25, 1916, on the amir's statement about when the war was to begin.

91. Seidt, "'When Continents Awake, Island Empires Fall!'" 89.

92. USArchII, RG256, M1107, R1, digest of the remarks of Aaron Aaronson on conditions in Turkey and Asia Minor prior to September 1916 as he left the country (conveyed by Walter Lippmann), December 28, 1917, 6.

93. Pomiankowski, *Der Zusammenbruch des Ottomanischen Reiches*, 158–165.

94. Paul Leverkuehn, *Posten auf ewiger Wache; Aus dem abenteuerreichen Leben des Max von Scheubner-Richter* (Essen: Essener, 1938), 34.

95. Report to von Oppenheim, October 8, 1915, in *Die Armenier-Frage und der Genozid an den Armeniern in der Türkei, 1913–1919,* ed. Wardges Mikaeljan (Yerevan: Institut für Geschichte der Akademie der Wissenschaften Armeniens, 2004), October 8, 15, 225.

96. Von Oppenheim to Foreign Ministry, October 29, 1915, ibid., 284.

97. PArchWGS, "Memorandum by the India Office as requested by the Prime Minister, an Inner View of the Predominant Intellectual and Political Forces in the Ottoman Empire," London, May 1, 1917, 24.

98. See also documents by Wolfgang Gust online, among them "The Armenian Genocide 1915/16 from the Files of the German Foreign Office," Edition I, http://www.sci.am/downloads/musgen/WolfgangGust.pdf.

99. ParchAA, Nachlaß Stresemann, Abschrift aus dem Tagebuch des Stresemann, Balkanreise 1916, 5–10. See also PArchAA, Nachlaß Stresemann, vol. 157, Balkanreise 1916, 5–6.

100. Afflerbach, *Kaiser Wilhelm II. als Oberster Kriegsherr*, 408–409.

101. M. Şükrü Hanioğlu: *A Brief History of the Late Ottoman Empire* (Princeton: Princeton University Press, 2008), 182.

102. Pomiankowski, *Der Zusammenbruch des Ottomanischen Reiches*, 158–165; Klaus Kreiser, *Atatürk: Eine Biographie* (Munich: Beck, 2008), 99.

103. PArchAA, Nachlaß Stresemann, vol. 157, Balkanreise 1916, 5–6. See also USArchII, RG256, M1107, R41, Department of State Weekly Report, Near Eastern Affairs, Interview by Talat Pasha, March 7, 1918, 11–12.

104. Ralf Georg Reuth, *Hitler, eine politische Biographie* (Munich: Piper, 2003), 45.

105. See the kaiser's letter on his insights into Zionism and anti-Semitism in Max Bodenheimer, *Henriette Hannah Bodenheimer: Die Zionisten und das kaiserliche Deutschland* (Bensberg: Schauble, 1972), 82–84.

106. Leonard Stein, *The Balfour Declaration* (New York: Simon & Schuster, 1961), 290–295; Chaim Herzog, *Heroes of Israel: Profiles of Jewish Courage* (Boston: Little, Brown, 1989).

107. Palestine Report by the Twelfth Zionist Congress, 1921, 19–39, in Schabinger, "Weltgeschichtliche Mosaiksplitter," 190. See also *Palestine during the War: Record of the Preservation of the Jewish Settlements in Palestine* (London: Zionist Organization, 1921) (covers the years 1914–1917, report approved by the Twelfth Zionist Congress, 1921).

108. Al-Husaini, *Mudhakkirat*, 201, 216, 388.

109. Robert-Tarek Fischer, *Österreich im Nahen Osten*, 43; Schabinger, "Weltgeschichtliche Mosaiksplitter," 179–208.

110. Stein, *The Balfour Declaration*, 208–209.

111. Palestine Report, in Schabinger, "Weltgeschichtliche Mosaiksplitter," 191.

112. Al-Husaini, *Mudhakkirat*, 94.

113. Ibid., 158–159.

114. Stein, *The Balfour Declaration*, 521, 544–547.

115. USArchII, CIA, Arab Informant, Balfour Declaration 1917, Grand Mufti, secret, Cairo, October 30, 1943, 10.

116. Stein, *The Balfour Declaration*, 537.

117. Ibid., 541–542; Johann-Heinrich Graf von Bernstorff, *The Memoirs of Count Bernstorff* (London: Heinemann, 1936), 171; Bernard Lewis, *A Middle East Mosaic* (New York: Random House, 2000), 420–421.

118. USArchII, RG256, M1107, R41, "Department of State Weekly Report, Near Eastern Affairs, Interview by Talat Pasha," March 7, 1918, 11.

119. PArchAA, R14144, Konstantinopel 394.

120. PArchAA, B Konstantinopel, 394, "An Reichskanzler Grafen von Hertling, Jüdische Palästina-Bestrebungen," Istanbul, July 20, 1918.

121. *Jewish Chronicle*, July 19, September 6, September 30, 1918; Stein, *The Balfour Declaration*, 604.

122. "Aufzeichnung über eine Besprechung Adolf Hitlers mit Reichsminister Speer, 5/24/1942," in Hans-Adolf Jacobsen, *Der Weg zur Teilung der Welt: Politik und Strategie von 1933 bis 1945* (Koblenz: Wehr & Wissen, 1977), 139, doc. 71.

123. *Welt am Montag*, November 21, 1898, quoted in Hagen, "German Heralds of Holy War," *Comparative Studies of South Asia, Africa, and the Middle East* 24, no. 2 (2004): 149.

124. Ibid., 159.

125. Johannes Lepsius, "Vorwort vom August 1896 nach seiner Reise durch Anatolien und Syrien im Mai 1896," in *Eine Anklageschrift wider die christlichen Großmächte und ein Aufruf an das christliche Deutschland* (Berlin: Akademische Buchhandlung Faber, 1897), 7; Lepsius, *Der Todesgesang des Armenischen Volkes: Bericht über das Schicksal des Armenischen Volkes in der Türkei während des Weltkrieges* (Potsdam: Tempelberg, 1919), 129, 156, 199–230.

126. Schabinger, "Weltgeschichtliche Mosaiksplitter,"149.

CHAPTER 4. AN ISLAMISM SHELTERED IN BERLIN

1. Eberhard Kolb, *Der Frieden von Versailles* (Munich: Beck, 2005), 64.

2. Manabendra Nath Roy, *Memoirs* (Bombay: Allied, 1964), 238–241.

3. USArchII, RG59, General Records DA, 1910–29, B9887, Lewis Heck to Department of State, Istanbul, February 6, 1919.

4. Adolf Hitler, *Mein Kampf* (Boston: Mariner, 1999), 195–201; Brigitte Hamann, *Hitlers Wien: Lehrjahre eines Diktators* (Munich: Piper, 2004), 502–503.

5. Hamann, *Hitlers Wien*, 679.

6. Volker Ullrich, *Die Revolution von 1918/19* (Munich: Beck, 2009), 15.

7. "The King-Crane Commission: Recommendations" (August 28, 1919), in

The Israel-Arab Reader: A Documentary History of the Middle East Conflict, ed. Walter Laqueur and Barry Rubin (New York: Penguin, 2008), 23–25.

8. Michael B. Oren, *Power, Faith, and Fantasy: America in the Middle East, 1776 to the Present* (New York: Norton, 2007), 392.

9. USArchII, RG263, CIA Records, Ent ZZ-18, Box 58 (2nd rel.), "Arab Informant, Chapter II, The Palestine Riots and Their Cause, Secret," Cairo, October 30, 1943, 11.

10. Joseph Pomiankowski, *Der Zusammenbruch des Ottomanischen Reiches* (Graz: Akademische Druck- und Verlagsanstalt, 1969), 91, 196, 445.

11. Amin al-Husaini, *Mudhakkirat al-Hajj Muhammad Amin al-Husaini* [The memoirs of al-Hajj Muhammad Amin al-Husaini], ed. Abd al-Karim al-Umar (Damascus: Al-Ahali, 1999), 337.

12. USArchII, RG263, CIA Records, Ent ZZ-18, Box 58 (2nd rel.), OSS, U.S. Army Forces in the Middle East, Report No. 9677, "Hajj Amin al-Husaini: Grand Mufti Of Jerusalem, Secret," Jerusalem, November 12, 1943, 2.

13. PArchAA, B Konstantinopel, 394, "An Reichskanzler Grafen von Hertling, Jüdische Palästina-Bestrebungen," Istanbul, July 20, 1918, signed Bernstorff.

14. Philip Mattar, *The Mufti of Jerusalem: Al-Hajj Amin al-Husaini and the Palestinian National Movement* (New York: Columbia University Press, 1992), 12–13.

15. Ibid., 15. See also Ibrahim Abu Shaqra, *Al-Hajj Amin al-Husaini mundhu wiladatihi hatta thaurat 1936* [Amin al-Husaini from his birth until the revolution of 1936] (Latakia: Al-Manara, 1998), 358.

16. Al-Husaini, *Mudhakkirat,* 358.

17. James Gelvin, "The Ironic Legacy Of The King-Crane Commission," in *The Middle East and the United States: A Historical and Political Reassessment,* ed. David W. Lesch (Boulder: Westview, 1996), 11–27.

18. Oren, *Power, Faith, and Fantasy,* 386.

19. "The General Syrian Congress: Memorandum Presented to the King-Crane Commission (July 2, 1919)," in Laqueur and Rubin, *The Israel-Arab Reader,* 21–23; Abu Shaqra, *Al-Hajj Amin al-Husaini,* 27.

20. Abu Shaqra, *Al-Hajj Amin al-Husaini,* 25–27.

21. "Al-Fidaya Arabischer Geheimbund in Jerusalem zum Kampf gegen Juden mit terroristischen Mitteln gegründet," *Der Asienkämpfer* (Berlin) 2, no. 8 (January 8, 1920): 8.

22. Efraim Karsh, *Islamic Imperialism: A History* (New Haven: Yale University Press, 2006), 138; for Emir Faisal's letter of sympathy with the Zionist movement to W. Frankfurter of Paris, "Arabs and Jews Are Cousins" (January 3, 1919), see Martin Gilbert, *The Story of Israel* (London: Deutsch, 2011), 18–19.

23. USArchII, RG263, CIA Records, Ent ZZ-18, Box 58 (2nd rel.), Office Memorandum: "Hajj Amin al-Husaini, Secret," Jerusalem, November 14, 1951, 1; Biographic Sketch No. 60, "Hajj Amin al-Husaini," April 14, 1951, 1.

24. Abu Shaqra, *Al-Hajj Amin al-Husaini,* 38–41.

25. Ibid., 29.

26. PArchWGS, SIS, Mustafa Fevzi Pasha on Iran and the Islamic United States of the Orient, London, July 6, 1921.

27. PArchWGS, Foreign Office, Turko-Afghan-Persian Treaty, Muslim Countries and Russia, secret, London, January 26, 1923.

28. PArchWGS, Turko-Afghan Treaty, March 1, 1921, SIS, Treaty, Appendix A, 4 pages.

29. PArchWGS, SIS, Afghan envoy to Ankara, Sultan Ahmad Khan, on Indian revolution, London, April 19, 1921.

30. PArchWGS, Turkish Nationalist Intrigue in Central Asia and Afghanistan, Abd ar-Rahman Peshawari, ambassador for Kabul, SIS, Geneva, March 11, 1921.

31. PArchWGS, SIS, Muhammadie Jemiete, Mustafa Kemal, Ahmad as-Sanusi, Abd al-Halim Celebi, Ankara, July 18, 1921.

32. PArchWGS, SIS, "Great National Assembly LT 5 million for pan-Islamic and anti-British propaganda, Ahmad as-Sanusi and his pan-Islamic centers to fight for the crescent against the cross in the new holy war," Istanbul, November 14, 1921.

33. PArchWGS, SIS, Ahmad as-Sanusi, Pan-Islamic Conference March 15, and Mustafa Kemal, Istanbul, January 14, 1922.

34. PArchWGS, SIS, "Speech Extract Mustafa Kemal on Shaikh Ahmad as-Sanusi," Ankara, December 16, 1921.

35. PArchWGS, SIS, "Turkish Pan-Islamic Policy, Council of Ulama, Abd al-Aziz Jawish, Rauoul Bey, Jamiet ul-Islam," Ankara, January 22, 1923.

36. PArchWGS, Interim Report of Inter-Deptl. Committee on Eastern Unrest, London, Most Secret, May 24, 1922, 16, 5–6.

37. "Mustafa Kemal: Die Islamische Politik der Türkei: Kein Islamreich mehr," *Der Asienkämpfer* 4 (January 5, 1922): 5.

38. Tom Reis, *Der Orientalist: Auf den Spuren von Essad Bey* (Berlin: Osburg, 2008), 142–149.

39. PArchWGS, SIS, "Ahmad as-Sanusi prepares Pan-Islamic congress, Istanbul," March 30, 1921; "Appointees in Ankara for pan-Islamic affairs, Farid Bey, Hamdullah Subi, Adnan Bey, Bolshevists promised weapons," Istanbul, April 22, 1921.

40. PArchWGS, Foreign Office, "Turko-Afghan-Persian Treaty, Muslim Countries and Russia, Secret," London, January 26, 1923.

41. Kreiser, *Atatürk: Eine Biographie* (Munich: Beck, 2008), pp. 174–175, 126–127; Jacob M. Landau, *The Politics of Pan-Islam: Ideology and Organization* (New York: Oxford, 1994), 218.

42. Norbert Schwanke, *Deutsche Soldatengräber in Israel: Der Einsatz deutscher Soldaten an der Palästinafront im Ersten Weltkrieg und das Schicksal ihrer Grabstätten* (Münster: Aschendorff, 2008), 25.

43. "Palästina-Mandat und Völkerbund, Lord Balfour hat US-Bedenken behoben," *Der Asienkämpfer* 4 (January 6, 1922): 5.

44. Hans-Ulrich Seidt, "'When Continents Awake, Island Empires Fall!' Germany and the Destabilization of the East, 1919–1922," in *Germany and the Middle East, 1871–1945*, ed. Wolfgang G. Schwanitz (Princeton: Wiener, 2004), 64–84.

45. PArchWGS, "Lebenslauf, 8 Anlagen, Fürstenberg/Mecklenburg, 07.06.44, gez. Harun ar-Raschid Bey," 4: "Leiter der Exekutive der Militär-Polizei, die dem

Reichsschatzministerium angeschlossen war." "Konflikte Enver Pascha und Kemal Pascha," *Der Asienkämpfer* 4 (January 5, 1922): 5.

46. Taner Akçam, *The Young Turks' Crime Against Humanity* (Princeton: Princeton University Press, 2012), 1–25.

47. USArchII, RG256, M1107, R41, Department of State, Weekly Report, "Near Eastern Affairs, Russian Pan/Turanian Movement and Manifesto of Bolsheviki Government of 12/12/17," "Baku and Moscow conferences, 01/17/18," 5–7.

48. Speech of Grigory Zinoviev, *Congress of the Peoples of the East, Baku, September 1920: Stenographic Report,* trans. Brian Pearce (London: New Park, 1977), 33–36.

49. Speech of Karl Radek, ibid., 51–52.

50. Discussion by Efendiev, ibid., 54–55, 57.

51. Roy, *Memoirs*, 417–418, 420, 439–440.

52. Ibid., 444.

53. PArchWGS, SIS "Sources Only, Eastern Summary No. 638, Enver's Activities in Turkestan, Secret," London, April 21, 1922, 1.

54. PArchWGS, "11 Seiten Lebenslauf, 8 Anlagen, Fürstenberg/Mecklenburg, 07.06.44, gez. Harun ar-Raschid Bey"; see also his book, *Marschall Liman von Sanders und sein Werk* (Berlin: Eisenschmidt, 1932).

55. *Die Rote Fahne* (Berlin), November 9, 1918, 1.

56. John C. G. Röhl, *Wilhelm II: Der Weg in den Abgrund 1900–1941* (Munich: Beck, 2009), 1239.

57. Kolb, *Der Frieden von Versailles*, 94.

58. *Der Asienkämpfer* 2, no. 3 (January 3, 1920): 3; "Asien den Asiaten," ibid., no. 7 (January 7, 1920): 2.

59. Werner Steuber, *"Jildirim": Deutsche Streiter auf heiligem Boden* (Berlin: Stalling, 1925), 174.

60. Jehuda L. Wallach, "The Weimar Republic and the Middle East: Salient Points," in *The Great Powers in the Middle East, 1919–1939,* ed. Uriel Dann (New York: Holmes & Meier, 1988), 271–273.

61. USArchII, FMS, P-207, Fritz Grobba, "Supplement des Gesandten a.D. Dr. Fritz Grobba," 14–15. USArchII, RG 338, FMS, P-207 consists of four documents by persons closely involved in German-Arab relations during World War II, composed at different times and bound together under the English title "German Exploitation of Arab National Movements in World War II." The authors, titles, dates, and pagination of each document are as follows. "Vorbemerkungen von Generaloberst a.D. Franz Halder" (1955, x–xiv); General der Flieger a.D. Hellmuth Felmy, "Die deutsche Ausnutzung der arabischen Eingeborenenbewegung im zweiten Weltkrieg" (1955, 1–124); General der Artillerie a.D. Walter Warlimont, "Die deutsche Ausnutzung der arabischen Eingeborenenbewegung im zweiten Weltkrieg" (1955, 125–211); "Vorbemerkungen von Generaloberst Franz Halder zu Fritz Grobbas Supplement" (1956, ii–iv); "Supplement des Gesandten a.D. Dr. Fritz Grobba" (1956, v–ix, 1–82); addendum to "Supplement des Gesandten a.D. Dr. Fritz Grobba" (1957, 1–3). Subsequent citations of these documents will refer to the details in this note.

62. Ibid., 16–24.

63. Wolfgang G. Schwanitz, "Aziz Cotta Bey, Deutsche und ägyptische Handelskammern und der Bund Ägypter Deutscher Bildung (1919–1949)," in *Fremde Erfahrungen,* ed. Gerhard Höpp (Berlin: Arabisches Buch, 1996), 359–382.

64. Camilla Dawletschin-Linder, *Diener seines Staates: Celal Bayar (1883–1986) und die Entwicklung der modernen Türkei* (Wiesbaden: Harrassowitz, 2003), 24.

65. PArchWGS, SIS, "Report of the Inter-Departmental Committee On Eastern Unrest" (War Office, Home Office, Colonial Office, India Office), plus Appendix A, "Terms of Reference, Most Secret," London, February 24, 1922, 16, 6.

66. Hitler, *Mein Kampf,* 644, 655.

67. Carl Heinrich Becker, "Der Islam im Rahmen einer allgemeinen Kulturgeschichte," in *Carl Heinrich Becker: Islamstudien,* vol. 1 (Leipzig: Quelle & Meyer, 1924), 24–32.

68. Hans-Ulrich Seidt, *Berlin, Kabul, Moskau: Oskar Ritter von Niedermayer und Deutschlands Geopolitik* (Munich: Universitas, 2002), 162–166.

69. Walter Dirks and Karl Heinz Janßen, *Der Krieg der Generäle* (Berlin: Propyläen, 1999); Karl-Heinz Janßen: "Der große Plan," *Die Zeit* (July 3, 1997): 11, 15–20.

70. Hitler, *Mein Kampf,* 117–118.

71. Florian Beierl and Othmar Plöckinger, "Neue Dokumente zu Hitlers Buch *Mein Kampf,*" *Vierteljahreshefte für Zeitgeschichte* 43 (2009): 292.

72. Hitler, *Mein Kampf,* 659.

73. Ibid., 676.

74. Ibid., 170–173, 351.

75. Ibid., 116, 267.

76. Ibid., 658.

77. Ibid., 292, 610, 619.

78. Ibid., 150.

79. Ibid., 57, 207, 325.

80. Ibid., 140.

81. RGVArkhM, 7-1-368, Haut-Commissariat de la République Française en Syrie et au Liban, "Liste des Associations et Parties contre le Mandat de la France en Syrie, Comité Supérieur Islamique de Jérusalem, Président Amin al-Husaini," Beirut, January 4, 1926, 2.

82. "Egyptian Students at University of Berlin and Abd al-Aziz Jawish," *Times* (London), August 4, 1920. See also "Jawish und die Vorliebe der ägyptischen Studenten für Berlin," *Mitteilungen des Bundes der Asienkämpfer* 2, no. 5 (January 5, 190): 3.

83. PArchAA, R1535, "An Wesendonk, Anschreiben, Deutsches Orient Institut aus NFO, Berlin, 09.08.1918, gez. Müller"; F28184, "Mittwoch, Deutsches Orient Institut," 114, 116, 121.

84. PArchAA, R1535, "An Wesendonk, Bericht," 2–3.

85. Ibid., 2–3.

86. Al-Husaini, *Mudhakkirat,* 206.

87. Kurt Fischer-Weth, *Amin al-Husayni, Grossmufti von Palästina* (Berlin: Titz, 1943), 87–89.

88. Muhammad Iqbal, *Wiederbelebung des religiösen Denkens im Islam* (original English ed., Lahore, 1930; 2d German ed., Berlin: Schiler, 2004).

89. See also the grand mufti's and his aides' articles on India in the journal *Barid ash-Sharq* [Orient Post], especially "Wathia'q an mauqif muslimi al-Hind" [The truth about Muslims of India], ibid., 47 (1943): 18.

90. William L. Cleveland, *Islam Against the West: Shakib Arslan and the Campaign for Islamic Nationalism* (Austin: University of Texas Press, 1985), 141.

91. Gerhard Höpp, "Araber im Berlin der 20er Jahre," in *Araber in Berlin*, ed. Ausländerbeauftragte des Senats (Berlin: Verwaltungsdruckerei, 1992), p. 35.

92. Landau, *The Politics of Pan-Islam*, 92, 344–345.

93. Shakib Arslan, *Limaza takhkhara al-Muslimun wa taqaddama ghairuhum?* [Why did the Muslims slow down while the others advanced?] (1930; reprint, Beirut: Al-Hayat, 1965).

94. Al-Husaini, *Mudhakkirat*, p. 74.

95. USArchII, FMS, P-207, Fritz Grobba, "Supplement des Gesandten a.D. Dr. Fritz Grobba," in "German Exploitation of Arab National Movements in World War II" (see above, Chapter 4, note 61), 31–32.

96. Nadi ash-Sharq or Orient-Klub e.V., Berlin, Humboldt-Haus, Kalckreuthstraße. See also Gerhard Höpp, *Arabische und islamische Periodika in Berlin und Brandenburg* (Berlin: Arabisches Buch, 1994), 25.

97. *Moslemische Revue* (Berlin), various issues, 1924–1940.

98. "Moslems unterm Hakenkreuz, Islam-Archiv schließt Lücken," ibid., April 13, 1993, 26–27.

99. Klaus Gensicke, *Der Mufti von Jerusalem und die Nationalsozialisten* (Darmstadt: Wissenschaftliche Buchgesellschaft, 2007), 93; Jennie Lebel, *The Mufti of Jerusalem: Hajj Amin al-Husaini and National Socialism* (Belgrade: Čigoja Stampa, 2007), 224.

100. *Die Islamische Gegenwart* (1927): 2.

101. Ibid.; "M. Muhammad Ali und unsere Moschee," *Moslemische Revue* 4 (1929): 45–46.

102. Hans Kohn, *Die Europäisierung des Orients* (Berlin: Schocken, 1934).

103. Georg Kampffmeyer, speech at Islam Institute, Berlin, December 1927, in Ausländerbeauftragte des Senats, *Araber in Berlin*, 39.

104. "Der Fürst der Drusen [Shakib Arslan] und die Ahmadija Anjumat Islam Ish'at-i-Islam Lahore," *Moslemische Revue* 6, no. 3 (1930): 56–59.

105. "Satzungen der Deutsch-Moslemischen Gesellschaft, Berlin e.V.," ibid., 6, no. 3 (1930): 53–56.

106. "Moslems unterm Hakenkreuz, Islam-Archiv schliesst Lücken," 26–27.

107. Ibid., 109.

108. "Al-Hajj Nafi Shalabi, muassis al-Mahad al-Islami fi Berlin" [Al-Hajj Nafi Shalabi, founder of the Islamic Institute in Berlin], in Al-Husaini, *Mudhakkirat*, p. 205.

109. "Der Fürst der Drusen [Shakib Arslan] und die Ahmadija Anjumat Islam Ish'at-i-Islam Lahore."

110. Philip S. Khoury, *Syria and the French Mandate* (Princeton: Princeton University Press, 198/), 401–402.

111. *Die Islamische Gegenwart, Der Islamische Student, Sada al-Islam* [Islam Echo]. See also Höpp, "Arabische und islamische Periodika," 103.

112. Mohammed Nafi Tschelebi, "Palästina unter Juden und Arabern," *Ludendorff's Volkswarte* 3, no. 14 (1931): 2–3.

113. Al-Husaini, *Mudhakkirat*, 132.

114. Reinhard Schulze, *Islamischer Internationalismus im 20. Jahrhundert* (Leiden: Brill, 1990), 102.

115. Landau, *The Politics of Pan-Islam*, 243.

116. Bernd Bauknecht, *Muslime in Deutschland von 1920 bis 1945* (Cologne: Teiresias, 2001), 99–106; Muhammad Asad, *Der Weg nach Mekka* (Düsseldorf: Patmos, 2009), 7–9.

117. Landau, *The Politics of Pan-Islam*, 246.

118. Schulze, *Islamischer Internationalismus im 20. Jahrhundert*, 102.

119. See also Gerhard Höpp, *Muslime in der Mark: Als Kriegsgefangene und Internierte in Wünsdorf und Zossen, 1914–1924* (Berlin: Arabisches Buch, 1997), 35, 37, 47, 74, 106.

120. Paul Schmitz-Kairo, *All-Islam: Weltmacht von morgen?* (Leipzig: Goldmann, 1937; 2d ed., 1942), 106–107, 109–110.

121. Ibid., 115, 130, 170–172, 184, 186, 207.

122. Hans Lindemann, *Der Islam im Aufbruch, in Abwehr und Angriff* (Leipzig: Brandstetter, 1941), 3, 26, 34, 68.

123. Ibid., 59–60, 83–84.

124. Ibid, 13.

125. According to Lindemann, these consisted of "ganz tiefgreifende Erschütterung im Islam und im Abendland (nach H. E. Corsepius)"; "gewaltiger Zivilisationsumbruch"; and furthermore, the "Übernahme westlicher Zivilisation ist nicht gleichbedeutend mit Einräumen abendländischer Sitten und Gebräuche," ibid., 10, 44, 54, 49.

126. Ibid., 8–10, 25 ("Rassekampf in Indien").

127. See also Bernard Lewis, *Faith and Power: Religion and Politics in the Middle East* (New York: Oxford University Press, 2010), 61–63.

128. Lindemann, *Der Islam im Aufbruch*, 9, 32, 54–55.

129. See also Schmitz-Kairo, *All-Islam*, 136–142.

130. Lindemann, *Der Islam im Aufbruch*, 69–71.

CHAPTER 5. AL-HUSAINI'S REVOLT

1. Amin al-Husaini, *Mudhakkirat al-Hajj Muhammad Amin al-Husaini* [The memoirs of al-Hajj Muhammad Amin al-Husaini], ed. Abd al-Karim al-Umar (Damascus: Al-Ahali, 1999), 16–17; Jennie Lebel, *The Mufti of Jerusalem: Hajj Amin al-Husaini and National Socialism* (Belgrade: Čigoja Stampa, 2007), 40.

2. Ibid., 151.

3. Ibid., 80–81.

4. Ibid., 57.

5. Brynjar Lia, *The Society of the Muslim Brothers in Egypt: The Rise of an Islamic Movement 1928–1942* (Reading: Ithaca Press, 1998), 154.

6. Al-Husaini, *Mudhakkirat*, 25–26.

7. Reinhard Schulze, *Islamischer Internationalismus im 20. Jahrhundert* (Leiden:

Brill, 1990), 94–100. Ibrahim Abu Shaqra, *Al-Hajj Amin al-Husaini mundhu wila-datihi hatta thaurat 1936* [Amin al-Husaini from his birth until the revolution of 1936] (Latakia: Al-Manara, 1998), 25.

8. Al-Husaini, *Mudhakkirat*, 17.

9. Abu Shaqra, *Al-Hajj Amin al-Husaini*, 189.

10. Lia, *The Society of the Muslim Brothers in Egypt*, 29, 47, 55.

11. Basheer M. Nafi, *Arabism, Islamism, and the Palestine Question, 1908–1914: A Political History* (Ithaca: Reading, 1998), 112.

12. This and other points made in this chapter are fully documented in the following chapters.

13. Nafi, *Arabism, Islamism, and the Palestine Question*, 115.

14. *Palestine and Transjordan, July 17, 1937; New York Times*, July 14, 1937; Yehoshua Porath, *The Emergence of the Palestinian Arab Nationalist Movement*, vol. 2 (London: Frank Cass, 1974), 225–230; USArchII, Department of State, RG59 890G.00/434, Knabenshue to Murray, November 27, 1937; 867N.01/1011, Murray to Hull, January 15, 1938; 867N.01/1021, Knabenshue to Hull, January 22, 1938; *al-Istiqlal*, June 9, 1938.

15. Zvi Elpeleg, "Why Was an 'Independent Palestine' Never Created in 1948?" *Jerusalem Quarterly* 50 (1989), 3–22; the agreement is reported by Hanna Asfur in *Bayan Nuwaihid al-Khut, al-Qiyadat wa al-Muassasat as-Siyasiyya fi Filastin, 1917–1948* [The leadership and political institutions in Palestine] (Acre: Silsilat ad-Dirasat, 1984), 403.

16. Nasir ad-Din an-Nashashibi interviewed on the grand mufti and Fakhr an-Nashashibi in an Arte TV program by Heinrich Billstein, *Turban and Swastika, The Grand Mufti and the Nazis*, aired September 12, 2009.

17. *Muatamar al-Umma al-Islamiyya* [Conference of the Islamic Nation], King David Hotel, Jerusalem, February 11, 1931.

18. Abu Shaqra, *Al-Hajj Amin al-Husaini*, 184–186.

19. BArchAAP, Deutsche Reichsbank, B25/01, No. 6790, "Die jüdische Industrie in Palestina; Jahresberichte der Haavara 1934–39"; "Erster Jahresbericht der Haavara, 01.01.35"; "Verwendung der durch die Haavara transferierten Gelder"; "Haavara Ltd. and Its Activities 1934–38."

20. David Ben Gurion at the Histadruth Convention in 1934, in Tom Segev, *Simon Wiesenthal: The Life and Legends* (New York: Doubleday, 2010), 469.

21. Lebel, *The Mufti of Jerusalem*, 41.

22. Edgar Flacker, "Fritz Grobba and Nazi Germany's Middle Eastern Policy, 1933–1942" (Ph.D. diss., London University, 1998), 121.

23. USArchII, FMS, P-207, "Die deutsche Ausnutzung der arabischen Eingeborenenbewegung im zweiten Weltkrieg," Supplement, Stuttgart, August 29, 1957. This document mentions payment to the grand mufti of £1,000 sterling via Fuad Hamza (Munich, September 1938); of £800 sterling via Musa al-Alami (Berlin, October 1938).

24. Flacker, "Fritz Grobba and Nazi Germany's Middle Eastern Policy," 122.

25. Amin al-Husaini, "Islam-Judentum: Aufruf des Großmuftis an die islamische Welt 1937," in Muhammad Sabri, *Islam-Judentum-Bolschewismus* (Berlin: Juncker & Dünnhaupt, 1938), 22–32.

26. Ibid.

27. Al-Husaini, *Mudhakkirat*, 174.

28. Tilman Nagel, *Mohammed* (Munich: Oldenbourg, 2008), 491.

29. Al-Husaini, "Islam-Judentum," 26–27.

30. UKArchK, CO733/326/75023/2, Cox to Moody, February 11, 1937; *Palestine*, March 10, 1937, 74–75; UKArchK, FO371 5551/19/31, August 18, 1936.

31. Luigi Goglia, "Il Mufti e Mussolini: Alcuni documenti italiani sui rapporti tra nazionalismo palestinese e fascismo negli anni trenta," *Storia Contemporanea* 17, no. 6 (1986): 1215.

32. USArchII, FMS, P-207, Fritz Grobba, "Supplement des Gesandten a.D. Dr. Fritz Grobba," in "German Exploitation of Arab National Movements in World War II" (see above, Chapter 4, note 61), 18; Fauzi Qawuqji, "Memoirs 1948," *Journal of Palestine Studies* 1, no. 4 (1972): 27–58: there were sixty-three al-Futtuwa members in 1939; Lebel, *The Mufti of Jerusalem*, 51; USArchII, RG 338, FMS, P-207, General der Flieger a.D. Hellmuth Felmy, "Die deutsche Ausnutzung der arabischen Eingeborenenbewegung im zweiten Weltkrieg," in "German Exploitation of Arab National Movements in World War II" (see above, Chapter 4, note 61), 19, 57.

33. Al-Husaini, *Mudhakkirat*, 40; Zvi Elpeleg, *Through the Eyes of the Mufti: The Essays of Haj Amin* (Portland: Mitchell Vallentine, 2009), 11.

34. Grobba, "Die deutsche Ausnutzung der arabischen Eingeborenenbewegung im zweiten Weltkrieg," Supplement, 19.

35. Helmut Mejcher, "Saudi-Arabiens Beziehungen zu Deutschland in der Regierungszeit von König Abd al-Aziz Ibn Saud," in *Der Nahe Osten in der Zwischenkriegszeit*, ed. Linda Schatkowski Schilcher and Claus Scharf (Stuttgart: Steiner, 1989), 109–127; Michael Wolffsohn, "The German-Saudi Arms Deal on 1936–1939 Reconsidered," in *The Great Powers in the Middle East, 1919–1939*, ed. Uriel Dann (New York: Holmes & Meier, 1988), 283–300, 288.

36. Grobba, "Supplement," 20, 23, 30, 33, 40; Flacker, "Fritz Grobba and Nazi Germany's Middle Eastern Policy," 123.

37. Grobba, "Supplement," 21–24; Wilhelm Kohlhaas, *Hitler-Abenteuer im Irak* (Freiburg: Herder, 1989), 9, 22.

38. Kohlhaas, *Hitler-Abenteuer im Irak*, 9, 22; Grobba, "Supplement," 18–19, 23.

39. USArchII, Office of U.S. Chief of Counsel For Prosecution of Axis Criminality, No. 792, PS, Original OKW Files Flensburg, Report for Admiral Canaris on Ibn Saud and the Grand Mufti, Staff Evidence, September 17, 1945.

40. Grobba, "Supplement," 18–19.

41. USArchII, Department of State, RG59 867N.00/588, Wadsworth to Hull, June 12, 1937.

42. *Falastin*, April 16, June 15, 1937; Benjamin Shwadran, *Jordan: A State of Tension* (New York: Council for Middle Eastern Affairs Press, 1959), 227; Elie Eliacher, "An Attempt at Settlement in Transjordan," *New Outlook* 18, no. 3 (1975): 71–75; USArchII, Department of State, RG59 867N.00/509, Wadsworth to Hull, June 8, 1937; 867N.00/522, June 26, 1937; Eliahu Elath, *Shivat Zion ve-'Arav* [The return to Zion and the Arabs] (Tel Aviv: Dvir, 1974), 137, 238–241.

43. Memo, July 29, 1937, *Documents on German Foreign Policy, 1918–1945* (Washington, D.C.: U.S. Government Printing Office, 1951), 758–762.

44. Ibid.

45. Robert Woolbert, "Pan-Arabism and the Palestine Problem," *Foreign Affairs* 16, no. 2 (January 1938): 316–317; Jacob C. Hurewitz, *Struggle for Palestine* (New York: Greenwood Press, 1968), 89–93; Porath, *The Emergence of the Palestinian Arab Nationalist Movement*, 2:89–93. UKArchK, FO371 551622/31, Mackereth to Foreign Office, September 15, 1937.

46. John Glubb, *A Soldier with the Arabs* (New York: Harper, 1957), 143; Hurewitz, *Struggle for Palestine*, 62.

47. USArchII, Department of State, RG59 867N.01/960, Allen to Hull, October 11, 1937; *Palestine* 12, no. 38 (September 22, 1937): 302, and no. 39 (September 29, 1937): 305; *New York Times*, September 19 and 22, 1937; Porath, *The Emergence of the Palestinian Arab Nationalist Movement*, 275; *Rose al-Yusuf*, February 4, 1938; USArchII, Department of State, RG59 867N.01/960, Allen to Hull, October 11, 1937.

48. Lukasz Hirszowicz, *The Third Reich and the Arab East* (London: Routledge & Kegan Paul, 1966), 34, citing Grobba, "Supplement"; Stephen Longrigg, *Iraq 1900–1950* (New York: International Book Center, 1953), 272.

49. UKArchK, FO371 E3906/22/31, Ormsby-Gore to Secretary of State, July 2, 1937.

50. Alec Kirkbride to League of Nations, *Permanent Mandates Commission Minutes*, 36th session, 94; Ann Dearden, *Jordan* (New York, 1958), 55; *New York Times*, November 7, 1937; Glubb, *A Soldier with the Arabs*, 155; *Palestine & Transjordan*, September 26, 1936.

51. On the details, see Barry Rubin, *The Arab States and the Palestine Conflict* (Syracuse: Syracuse University Press, 1982).

52. *New York Times*, October 6 and 7, November 10 and 25, and December 7, 1938; *Times* (London), October 6, 7, and 8, December 7, 1940; Christopher Sykes, *Crossroads to Israel* (Bloomington: Indiana University Press, 1978), 192–193.

53. *Documents on German Foreign Policy*, 746, 754, 779. See also David Yisraeli, "The Third Reich and Palestine," *Middle East Affairs* (October 1971): 347.

54. USArchII, Department of State, RG59 67N.01/1280 and /1346, Knabenshue to Hull, November 14 and 25, 1938; U.S. Department of State, RG9 867N.01/1384 and 1429, Knabenshue to Hull, December 30, 1938. Maurice Peterson, *Both Sides of the Curtain* (London: Constable, 1950), 143.

55. USArchII, Department of State, RG59 867N.01/1364, King Ibn Saud to President Roosevelt, December 15, 1938; see also RG59 867N.01/1365 and *New York Times*, January 15, 1939.

56. Ibid., November 12, 1938.

57. USArchII, Department of State, RG59 890G.911/15, Knabenshue to Hull, February 16, 1939.

58. *Great Britain and the East*, February 2, 1939.

59. UKArchK, FO371 E754/6/31, Lampson to Foreign Office, January 20, 1939; *Journal d'Egypte*, January 19, 1939; USArchII, Department of State, RG59 867N.01/1446, Fish to Hull, February 9, 1939.

60. USArchII, Department of State, RG59 867N.01/1441 and /1447, Johnson to Hull, February 7 and 11, 1939; UKArchK, FO371 E1660/6/31 and E1661/6/31; Hurewitz, *Struggle for Palestine*, 116; David Ben-Gurion, *My Talks with Arab*

Leaders (New York: Keter Books, 1973), 219, 230–231; *New York Times,* February 8, 10, and 16, 1939.

61. *New York Times,* February 8, 10, and 16, 1939.

62. UKArchK, FO371 E1668/6/31 and E1448/6/31, February 23 and 24, 1939; Michael Cohen, "The Palestine White Paper, May 1939: Appeasement in the Middle East," *Historical Journal* 16, no. 3 (1973): 584.

63. UKArchK, FO371 E1717/6/31, Peterson to Foreign Office, March 2, 1939; USArchII, Department of State, RG59 867N.01/1472, Bullitt to Hull, March 10, 1939, interview with Weizmann; 1485, Kennedy to Hull, March 20, 1939, interview with MacDonald.

64. UKArchK, FO371 E1253/6/31 and E1254/6/31, Bullard to Foreign Office, February 18, 1939; UKArchK, E1334/6/31, February 20, 1939, and 1459, Johnson to Hull, February 21, 1939.

65. UKArchK, FO371 E1875/6/31, March 7, 1939; Cohen, "The Palestine White Paper," 586–588; *New York Times,* February 27, 1939.

66. *New York Times,* February 27, 1939.

67. Ibid.

68. UKArchK, FO371 File 23231, Lampson to Foreign Office, March 23, 1939; E2541/6/31 and E2724/6/31; E2691/6/31, Lampson to Foreign Office, April 12, 1939; Cohen, "The Palestine White Paper," 590–591.

69. UKArchK, FO371 E2956/6/31, E3029/6/31, and E3158/6/31, Lampson to Foreign Office, April 23, 24, and 28, 1939; E3156/6/31, Houston-Boswell to Foreign Office, April 29, 1939.

70. UKArchK, FO371 E3160/6/31, E3029/6/31, and E3158/6/31, Lampson to Foreign Office, April 23, 24, and 28, 1939; E3156/6/31, Houstoun-Boswell to Foreign Office.

71. UKArchK, FO371 E3160/6/31 and E3161/6/31, Lampson to Foreign Office.

72. Ibid.

73. The meeting notes including all the quotations below are in UKArchK, FO371 E3945/6/31, Lampson to Foreign Office.

74. *Parliamentary Papers,* Cmd. 6019 (1939), 1–12.

75. Al-Husaini, *Mudhakkirat,* 276, 295.

76. *Documents on British Foreign Policy,* ser. 3, ed. Ernest L. Woodward, vol. 4 (London: H.M. Stationery Office, 1978), 209; Chaim Weizmann, *Trial and Error* (New York: Harper, 1966), 406.

77. UKArchK, FO371 E2362/10/31, Peterson to FO, April 11, 1938.

78. UKArchK, FO371 E3673/6/31 and E4904/6/31, Lampson to Foreign Office, May 18 and June 28, 1939; E4794/6/31, Newton-Butler to Foreign Office, June 28, 1939; USArchII, Department of State, RG59 867N.01/1557, Fish to Hull, May 20, 1939; *New York Times,* May 19, 1939; *Times* (London), May 18, 1939; Weizmann, *Trial and Error,* 408; Palestine and Transjordan, July 9, 1939; *Jarida Misr al-Fatah,* July 8, 1939.

79. USArchII, Department of State, RG59 867N.01/1603/1/2, 1613, 1622, 1632, Knabenshue to Hull, May 25 and 26, June 8 and 29, 1939; UKArchK, FO371 E3700/6/31, Houstoun-Boswell to Foreign Office, May 19, 1939; E4788/72/93 ad E4929/6/31, Newton to Foreign Office, June 28 and July 4, 1939; E5422/83 1, Bennett to Foreign Office, July 29, 1939.

80. UKArchK, E5422/831, Bennett to Foreign Office, July 29, 1939.

81. Flacker, "Fritz Grobba and Nazi Germany's Middle Eastern Policy," 124.

82. Glubb, *A Soldier with the Arabs*, p. 159; Hurewitz, *Struggle for Palestine*, 146–155; *Akher Sa'a* (Cairo), no. 1977 (September 13, 1972): 11–13.

83. *Akher Sa'a* (Cairo), no. 1977 (September 13, 1972): 11–13; Majid Khadduri, *Arab Contemporaries* (Baltimore: Johns Hopkins University Press, 1973), 239.

CHAPTER 6. THE NAZI–ARAB/ISLAMIST ALLIANCE PREPARES FOR BATTLE

1. Volker Koop, *Hitler's Fünfte Kolonne* (Berlin: Berlin-Brandenburg Verlag, 2009), 265–274.

2. Albrecht Fueß, *Die deutsche Gemeinde in Ägypten von 1919–1939* (Hamburg: Lit-Verlag, 1996), 94.

3. Koop, *Hitlers Fünfte Kolonne*, 271.

4. Seton Lloyd, *The Interval* (Oxford: Alden Press, 1986).

5. Rainer Michael Boehmer, *Uruk* (Mainz: Zabern, 1985).

6. Manfred Steffen to Wolfgang G. Schwanitz, August 2, 2010, on his father Willi Georg Steffen.

7. Adam Falkenstein, *Topographie von Uruk*, vol. 1 (Leipzig: Harassowitz, 1941); Wilhelm Kohlhaas, *Hitler-Abenteuer im Irak* (Freiburg: Herder, 1989), 26, 32, 62, 114; Ekkehard Ellinger, *Deutsche Orientalistik zur Zeit des Nationalsozialismus 1933–1945* (Berlin: Deux Mondes, 2006), 477, 502.

8. Friedrich Freiherr Kreß von Kressenstein, *Mit den Türken zum Sueskanal* (Berlin: Vorhut, 1938), 109; *Mitteilungen des Bundes der Asienkämpfer* 2, no. 1 (January 1, 1920): 3; (January 3, 1920): 4.

9. Paul Leverkuehn, *Der geheime Nachrichtendienst der Wehrmacht im Kriege* (Frankfurt: Athenäum, 1964), 162; for the Abwehr's structure, see Chantal Metzger, *L'empire colonial français dans la stratégie du Troisième Reich (1936–1945)*, vol. 2 (Brussels: Lang, 2002), 958–960.

10. RGVArkhM, 7-1-368, Haut-Commissariat de la République Francaise en Syrie et au Liban, "Liaison britannique Beyrouth, Mufti Hajj Amin al-Husaini, Hashim Jaishi, Abd al-Latif Salah, Très Secret," Beirut, August 3, 1939, 1; 7-1-969, 14, "Traduction d'un rapport sur les fraoti's arabes en Palestine, 1939," 1–2.

11. USArchII, T120, R901, F61169, "Return of Adil Azma, secret, Aleppo, 07/05/41, signed Rahn"; Adil Azma, "Functions, secret, Berlin, 07/08/41, signed Grobba"; F14696, B15765-769, "Organisation und Arbeitsplan der Abwehr im Orient, Abwehr II in Türkei, Apparat durch Verhaftungen zerschlagen, Geheime Reichssache, Berlin 18.04.41, gez. Grobba"; T77 R1432 F702, "An OKW/Amt Ausland Abwehr II, III, Mufti, Munir Rais, Fauzi al-Qawuqji, Nach Eintreffen Pässe, Nachrichtennetz schaffen, S-Tätigkeit einleiten, Übergangsorganisation Syrien, Türkei, Geheime Kommandosache, Sonderstab F, 05.12.41, gez. Stabschef Meyer-Ricks"; RGVArkhM, 7-1-660, 6713, "Activité de Hajj Amin et intrigues Anglo-Irakiennes, Fauzi Qawuqji, Adil Azma, Adil Arslan," October 18, 1940.

12. Hans-Jürgen Döscher, *Das Auswärtige Amt im Dritten Reich* (Berlin: Siedler, 1987), 175.

13. Wolfgang G. Schwanitz, ed., *Germany and the Middle East,* 1871–1945 (Princeton: Wiener, 2004), 184–85.

14. Barry Rubin, *Istanbul Intrigues* (New York: McGraw-Hill, 1989), 35.

15. Jeffrey Herf, *Nazi Propaganda for the Arab World* (New Haven: Yale University Press, 2009), 9, 39, 44.

16. Kurt Munzel, "Der Gebrauch des Genetivexponenten im arabischen Dialekt von Ägypten" (Diss., Erlangen University, 1948); Kurt Munzel, *Ägyptisch-Arabischer Sprachführer* (Wiesbaden: Harassowitz, 1958; 2d ed., 1983).

17. Friedrich C. Andreas, "Die Iranier," in *Unter fremden Völkern,* ed. Wilhelm Doegen (Berlin: Stolberg, 1925), 376.

18. Georg Graf von Kanitz, "Turkestan" (1911), in *Die Karawane des Gesandten,* ed. Martin Kröger (Göttingen: Vandenhoeck & Ruprecht, 2009), 92–102; Rudolf Nadolny, "Persien" (1913) (report to Reich Chancellor Theobald von Bethmann Hollweg, Sarajevo, June 17, 1913), in "Rudolf Nadolny," ibid., 115–125.

19. Ellinger, *Deutsche Orientalistik zur Zeit des Nationalsozialismus,* 348, 491: Walther Hinz, *Irans Aufstieg zum Nationalstaat im fünfzehnten Jahrhundert* (Berlin: De Gruyter, 1936), 124.

20. Stefan R. Hauser, "German Research on the Ancient Near East and Its Relation to Political and Economic Interests from Kaiserreich to World War II," in Schwanitz, *Germany and the Middle East,* 155–179.

21. Erich F. Schmidt, *Flights Over Ancient Cities Of Iran* (Chicago: University of Chicago Press, 1940).

22. Hauser, "German Research on the Ancient Near East."

23. PArchAA, Iran, Schacht Türkei/Iran, "Liste 15 deutsche Firmevertreter bei Schacht, Teheran, 24.11.36, Schmidt-Dumont"; "Aide mémoire Trade, Four Year Plan, Iran Raises Exports about 50 Mio. Mark, 1–3, Teheran, 24.11.36, Wohltat"; "Aide mémoire, plan Iran-Germany, Tehran, 12/21/36," 10, signed Melchers.

24. PArchAA, RAV Teheran 28, Besuch Schacht Bd. 1, Bd. 2, Türkei/Iran, "Liste 15 deutsche Firmevertreter bei Schacht, Teheran, 24.11.36, Schmidt-Dumont"; "Aide mémoire Trade, Four Year Plan, Iran Raises Exports about 50 Mio. Mark, 1–3, Teheran, 24.11.36, Wohltat"; "Aide mémoire, plan Iran-Germany, Tehran, 12/21/36," 10, signed Melchers.

25. PArchAA, RAV Teheran 28, Besuch Schacht Bd. 1, "Liste 1, Deutsche, Soirée des Gesandten, Teheran 23.11.36."

26. PArchAA, Iran, Schacht Türkei/Iran, "To State Secretary Dieckhoff, Near East Report, Tehran, 8/1/37," 24.

27. PArchAA, RAV Teheran 28, Besuch Schacht Bd. 1, Bd. 2, "Iran 20.–25.11.36"; "Großkreuz Humayun an Präsident Dr. Schacht"; "Reisebericht, I-III, Reichsbankpräsident Schacht, streng vertraulich, Teheran 30.11.36," 5; "Teheran, deutsche Presseschau, 03.12.36"; PArchAA, Iran, Schacht Türkei/Iran, "To State Secretary Dieckhoff, Near East Report, Tehran, 8/1/37, 11, signed Smend."

28. Arabic names of Golden Square: Al-Halaqa adh-Dhaabiyya or al-Murabba adh-Dhahabi; the four main leaders were Fahmi Said, Kamil Shabib, Salah ad-Din as-Sabbagh, Mahmud Salman.

29. Dennis Kumetat, "The Failure of German Business and Economic Policy toward Iraq in the 1930s: An Example of the German Arms and Steel Company

Otto Wolff of Cologne," *Al-Abhath: Journal of the American University of Beirut* 55–56 (1907–1908): 147–173.

30. Salah ad-Din as-Sabbagh, *Fursan al-Uruba fi al-Iraq* [Knights of Arabdom in Iraq] (Damascus, 1956), 109; Mustafa Dawud Kabha, "Tamarrud 1941 fi al-Iraq" [The 1941 uprising in Iraq], *al-Qalam* (Nazareth) 1, no. 2 (March 20, 1987): 26–31.

31. USArchII, FMS, P-207, USArchII, FMS, P-207, Fritz Grobba, "Supplement des Gesandten a.D. Dr. Fritz Grobba," in "German Exploitation of Arab National Movements in World War II" (see above, Chapter 4, note 61), 17, 33.

32. Edgar Flacker, "Fritz Grobba and Nazi Germany's Middle Eastern Policy, 1933–1942" (Ph.D. diss., University of London, 1998), 60.

33. Grobba, "Supplement," 26; Amin al-Husaini, *Mudhakkirat al-Hajj Muhammad Amin al-Husaini* [The memoirs of al-Hajj Muhammad Amin al-Husaini], ed. Abd al-Karim al-Umar (Damascus: Al-Ahali, 1999), 55; Fritz Grobba, *Männer und Mächte im Orient* (Göttingen: Musterschmidt, 1967), 130.

34. Peter Wien, *Iraqi Arab Nationalism* (New York: Routledge, 2006), 31; Grobba, "Supplement," 26; Flacker, "Fritz Grobba and Nazi Germany's Middle Eastern Policy," 58.

35. Grobba, "Supplement," 32.

36. Ibid., 77.

37. Grobba, "Supplement," 33; David M. Rosen, *Armies of the Young: Child Soldiers in War and Terrorism* (New Brunswick: Rutgers University Press, 2005), 206–207; Flacker, "Fritz Grobba and Nazi Germany's Middle Eastern Policy," 143.

38. Kohlhaas, *Hitler-Abenteuer im Irak*, 18; Flacker, "Fritz Grobba and Nazi Germany's Middle Eastern Policy," 120.

39. Grobba, "Supplement," 19–20.

40. Ibid., 21.

41. Grobba to Foreign Ministry, November 9, 1937, *Documents on German Foreign Policy*, 767–772.

42. Barry Rubin, "Anglo-American Relations in Saudi Arabia, 1941-1945," *Journal of Contemporary History* 14, no. 2 (April 1979): 253–267.

43. Grobba, "Supplement," 32.

44. BMArchLo, 371-23342, 371-2334, October 22, 1939, High Commissioner to London; documents of Wilhelm Stellbogen (press attaché, Deutsches Nachrichtenbüro), and Hasan al-Banna (Jihad in Palestine), including receipts and notes of October 18, 1939, October 16, 1939 dealing with Stellbogen's flat, Egyptian Military Secret Service, are found in Asam al-Aryan, "Al-Ikhwan wa al-Amirikiyun" [The Brothers and the Americans], *Ash-Asharq al-Ausat* (December 16, 2005); see also Lia, *The Society of the Muslim Brothers in Egypt*, 241.

45. Lia, *The Society of the Muslim Brothers in Egypt*, 241.

46. Ibid., 179; For Auni Abd al-Hadi see also Avi Shlaim, "The Balfour Declaration and Its Consequences," in *Yet More Adventures with Britannia: Personalities, Politics and Culture in Britain*, ed. Wm. Roger Louis (London: Tauris, 2005), 251–270.

47. Grobba, "Supplement," 12, 29.

48. Sylvia Keddourie, ed., *Arab Nationalism: An Anthology* (Berkeley: University of California Press, 1962), 44.

49. Majid Khadduri, *Arab Contemporaries: The Role of Personalities in Politics* (Baltimore: Johns Hopkins University Press, 1973), 240–243; Geoffrey Furlonge, *Palestine Is My Country: The Story of Musa Alami* (New York: Praeger, 1969), 127–128; Majid Khadduri, *Independent Iraq* (New York: Oxford University Press, 1951), 170–171; Lukasz Hirszowicz, *The Third Reich and the Arab East* (London: Routledge & Kegan Paul, 1966), 82; Jacob C. Hurewitz, *Struggle for Palestine* (New York: Greenwood Press, 1968), 147.

50. *Documents on German Foreign Policy,* series D, 11:241; Khadduri, *Independent Iraq,* 166–169, 281–285.

51. Trefor Evans, *The Killearn Diaries* (London: Sidgwick and Jackson, 1972), 125–127; George Kirk, "More Lessons of Palestine," *The 19th Century and After* (December 1948): 64; Khadduri, *Arab Contemporaries,* 238.

52. Muhammad Abd ar-Rahman Burj, *Aziz al-Misri wa al-Haraka al-Wataniyya al-Misriyya* [Aziz al-Misri and the Egyptian national movement] (Cairo: Markaz ad-Dirasat bil-Ahram, 1980), 71–77.

53. *Times* (London), May 30, 1941; Michael Cohen, "A Note on the Mansion House Speech," *Asian and African Studies* 11, no. 3 (1977): 375–386.

54. Anwar Sadat, *Revolt on the Nile* (New York: Day, 1957), 39.

CHAPTER 7. AL-HUSAINI IN SEARCH OF AN EMPIRE

1. USArchII, FMS, P-207, Fritz Grobba, "Supplement des Gesandten a.D. Dr. Fritz Grobba," in "German Exploitation of Arab National Movements in World War II" (see above, Chapter 4, note 61), 26; Fritz Grobba, *Männer und Mächte im Orient* (Göttingen: Musterschmidt, 1967), 130.

2. USArchII, T120, R63, S71, F50682 ff., Bureau of Secretary of State to Ribbentrop, B50692, report on meetings of von Papen and Shaukat in Ankara and Grobba and Haddad (August 26, 1940 in Berlin), secret, Berlin, August 27, 19, signed Grobba; To Mackensen, Meeting with Haddad (alias Taufiq Ali ash-Shakir) on Greater Arabia, Secret, Berlin, September 7, 1940.

3. USArchII, T120, R901, F61123, B23, "Notice on the Arab Question," Berlin, March 7, 1941.

4. PArchAA, Nachlaß von Hentig, vol. 84, von Oppenheim to Grothe on Shakib Arslan, Berlin, September 4, 1941, 1.

5. Karl-Heinz Roth, "Berlin-Ankara-Baghdad: Franz von Papen and the German Near East Policy During the Second World War," in *Germany and the Middle East, 1871–1945,* ed. Wolfgang G. Schwanitz (Princeton: Wiener, 2004), 190–191: Naji Shaukat in Ankara, later Haddad also went to Ankara for talks with Franz von Papen.

6. PArchAA, Botschaft Ankara, vol. 555, B488069–71, Grand Mufti to "Excellence Papen," Baghdad, June 21, 1940, 1–3, signed Grand Mufti de Palestine; B488097–98, July 22, 1940, signed Le Grand Moufti de Palestine; telegram, Uthman Kamal Haddad alias Taufiq Ali ash-Shakir in Ankara, Tarabya, secret, June 8, 1940, 1–2.

7. Urs Schwarz, *Schicksalstage in Berlin* (Lenzburg: Müller, 1986), 28.

8. USArchII, T120, R63, S71, F50682 ff., Bureau of Secretary of State Ribbentrop's order, "the Italian envoy gave indeed to premier al-Kailani this text on the Arab independence on behalf of his government 07/07/40 in Baghdad," secret, Berlin, September 24, 1940, signed Woermann.

9. Raoul Aglion, "Allah's Divided Children," *The Nation*, May 24, 1941, 607–609.

10. Durable Dranger, "Max von Oppenheim in the Middle East," *Time*, June 16, 1941.

11. USArchII, T120, R901, F61124, declaration in support of Arab independence drafted by Haddad in Berlin; B50712–13, document from Rome, September 14, 1940, signed Mackensen; order by von Ribbentrop concerning the declaration, and text of declaration, B50714–16, signed Woermann (seen by von Ribbentrop on September 28, 1940).

12. USArchII, T120, R63, S71, F50682 ff., To von Papen, information addressed to von Papen on von Weizsäcker–Haddad conversation on declaration in support of Arab independence, Berlin, October 18, 1940, signed Grobba; account of Weizsäcker–Haddad conversation for the Italians, Berlin, October 19, 1940; account of Weizsäcker–Haddad conversation, Berlin, October 21, 1940, signed Weizsäcker. PArchAA, Nachlaß von Hentig, vol. 84, B326021–22, To Habicht, [Union Jack] plan draft addressed to Habicht, Berlin, July 25, 1940, signed von Oppenheim; Wolfgang G. Schwanitz, "Max von Oppenheim und der Heilige Krieg: Zwei Denkschriften zur Revolutionierung islamischer Gebiete 1914 und 1940," *Sozial.Geschichte*, 19, no. 3 (2004): 28–59.

13. USArchII, T120, R63, S71, F50682 ff., B50723–24, von Weizsäcker–Haddad conversation on declaration in support of Arab independence, Berlin, October 18, 1940, signed von Weizsäcker.

14. USArchII, T120, R63, S71, F50682 ff., B255094, Bureau of Secretary of State to von Ribbentrop.

15. BArchPAA, 61123, B283, German radio declaration in support of Arab independence of December 5, 1940; for the German and the Arabic text see also *Berliner Lokal-Anzeiger*, December 5, 1940.

16. USArchII, T120, R63, S71, F50682 ff., B255092-01, Bureau of Secretary of State to von Ribbentrop; B50692, declaration of al-Lajna al-Qaumiyya fi Bairut [National Committee in Beirut], Beirut, January 14, 1941, text of declaration in support of Arab independence, via von Hentig, Berlin, January 4, 1941, signed Woermann.

17. Amin Al-Husaini, *Mudhakkirat al-Hajj Muhammad Amin al-Husaini* [The memoirs of al-Hajj Muhammad Amin al-Husaini], ed. Abd al-Karim al-Umar (Damascus: Al-Ahali, 1999), 73–74.

18. USArchII, T120, R63, S71, F50682 ff., B481559–65, Bureau of Secretary of State, to Mackensen, Meeting with Haddad (who had been in Berlin since August 26, 1940, waiting to go to Rome) on Greater Arabia, Secret, Berlin, September 7, 1940, signed von Weizsäcker.

19. See Hitler's speech before the Reichstag, January 30, 1939.

20. USArchII, T120, R901, 61123, B50688, von Papen und Naji Shaukat, "Italiener angeblich für unabhängiges Großarabien, Geheim, Aufzeichnung, 21.07.40,

Tarabya 31.07.40, gez. Kroll"; B50686–87, "06.07.40, von Papen-Shaukat, nordarabisches Reich unter irakischer Führung, weitere Treffen in Ankara für Wiederaufnahme der Beziehungen," gez. Woermann; B50689–90, "Heute Treff Großmuftis Sekretär (will weiter nach Rom und Berlin), Großarabien, einig mit Saudi-Arabien, Anschluss Jordaniens an Palästina, Entfernung Abdullahs, Geheim, Trabya 06.08.40, gez. Von Papen."

21. USArchII, T120, R901, 61123, B72–73, "Die Person des Großmufti, Berlin März 1941."

22. USArchII, X-411, Von Hentig report on Syria and Greater Arabia, secret, Berlin, February 26, 1941.

23. PArchAA, R901, 61123, Abetz to Woermann, "Syrische Frage," Paris, February 25, 1941.

24. PArchAA, R901, 61123, "Bedeutung des Irak-Öls für die Kriegführung," Berlin, May 3, 1941.

25. PArchAA, R901, 61123, "Waffenlieferungen nach dem Irak, geheime Reichssache, Berlin 6.3.41, gez. Ripken."

26. PArchAA, R901, 61123, "Aufzeichnung zur arabischen Frage, geheime Reichssache, Berlin, 7.3.41."

27. USArchII, R901, 61169, Von Hentig, "Groß-Arabien und die Lage in Syrien, Geheime Reichssache," Berlin, February 26, 1941, 14, 16ff; "Stellungnahme zum Bericht von Hentigs, Geheime Reichssache, Berlin 7.3.41"; Chantal Metzger, *L'empire colonial français dans la stratégie du Troisième Reich (1936–1945)*, 2 vols. (Brussels: Lang, 2002), 2:830–833, 841–842.

28. PArchAA, vol. 555, from Ankara Embassy, "A Son Excellence Monsieur l'Ambassadeur de la Grande Allemagne à Ankara" (Papen), 1–2, Baghdad, June 21, 1940, signed Grand Moufti de Palestine.

29. RGVArkhM, 7-1-998–46, "Renseignement, Von Hentig, Roser, Adil Arslan, Saadi al-Kailani, Umar Dawuq, Riad as-Sulh, Akram az-Zuwaitar, Mukhtar as-Sulh, Ihsan Jabiri, Amin al-Husaini," Paris, February 28, 1941.

30. USArchII, T120, R63, S71, F50682 ff., B255147, "Déclaration officielle de l'Allemagne et de l'Italie concernant les Pays Arabes," paragraph 7: "L'Allemagne et l'Italie reconaissent l'illegalité du 'Jewish National Home' en Palestine. Elles reconaissent à la Palestine et aux autres Pays Arabes le droit de résoudre la question des éléments juifs en Palestine et dans les autres Pays Arabes selon l'intérêt national arabe de la même manière qu'était résolue cette question dans les pays de l'Axe. Il s'en suit aussi qu'aucune immigration juive ne sera permise dans les Pays Arabes" (Berlin, March 1, 1941). USArchII, T120, R63, S71, F50682 ff., B255146–48, Bureau of Secretary of State to von Ribbentrop, and B50692, to Woermann: Uthman Kamal Haddad suggests a refined version of paragraph 3 ("Si la France accorde l'indépendance à la Syrie, l'Allemagne et l'Italie n'auront acune objection à cet égard."), and advances a new draft of the "Déclaration officielle de l'Allemagne et de l'Italie concernant les Pays Arabes," Berlin, March 1, 1941, signed Grobba.

31. USArchII, T120, R901, F61123, draft of letter to al-Husaini from Hitler, March 1941, signed Weizsäcker, 2; see also T120, R63571, F50682, B51223–25, "Materialien zur arabischen Frage, Geheime Reichssache," Berlin, October 14, 1942.

32. USArchII, T120, R901, F61123, B32–33, 36, note on the Arab question, Berlin, March 7, 1941.

33. PArchAA, R901, 61123, "A Son Excellence Le Führer de la Grande Allemagne, Geheime Reichssache, Baghdad, 20.01.41," signed Muhammad Amin al-Husaini, Grand Mufti de Palestine; to the Grand Mufti, secret, Berlin (March 4), 1941, signed Freiherr von Weizsäcker; al-Husaini, *Mudhakkirat*, 74–75.

34. Al-Husaini, *Mudhakkirat*, 35, 73; Grobba, "Supplement," 57: Some dozen Palestinians were in Baghdad with al-Husaini; PArchWGS, Nachlaß Günther Pawelke, vol. 6, Werner Junck to Pawelke, Duisburg, December 11, 1956.

35. USArchII, T77, R1432, F690, Cable 197 to Berlin and Special Command F: five hundred to a thousand al-Qawuqji men mobilized and need more weapons, discussion with Shammar leader in ar-Raqqa and Palestinian leader in Aleppo regarding anti-British uprising, will return today to Beirut, June 29, 1941, signed Meyer-Ricks, Rahn; F662, report by Meyer-Ricks on Syria, British steps and guerilla warfare by Arabs, and Vichy and Lebanon, June 22, 1941–July 4, 1941, Beirut, July 4, 1941, signed Meyer-Ricks; F691, Report on Special Command F and operations, southern Greece, July 14, 1941, signed Felmy (see also Rudolf Rahn, *Ruheloses Leben* [Düsseldorf: Diederichs, 1949], 260–262, 267, 317; PArchAA, Nachlaß von Hentig, vol. 84, Bl. 325927–28, to von Hentig, war news about Fritz Grobba, Fauzi al-Qawuqji, Shakib Arslan, Said al-Kailani, and Amin al-Husaini who luckily escaped, Berlin, October 31, 1941, signed von Oppenheim.

36. USArchII, T120, R901, F61169, B313977–79, cable to von Ribbentrop regarding talks under way since May 20, 1941, Warlimont visit to the French seeking support against the British in Syria and Iraq, supply of weapons from depots for Iraq, Paris, May 24, 1941, signed Abetz.

37. USArchII, T120, R901, F61169, cable to Ribbentrop, French Envoy in Ankara asks for transit permit to Syria, we ask von Papen to support him, Paris, June 21, 1941, signed Abetz.

38. Rahn, *Ruheloses Leben*, 229; see also Metzger, *L'Empire colonial français dans la stratégie du Troisième Reich*, passim.

39. USArchII, T120, R63571, F50682, to Woermann, regarding England and Iraq, Musa al-Husaini and Hamilton R. Gibb, signed Grobba, Berlin, October 16, 1940.

40. "Bila misyu, bila mistir, bi-s-sama Allah, wa ala-l-ard Hitlir." Gerhard Höpp, "'Nicht Ali zuliebe, sondern aus Hass gegen Mu'awiya': Zum Ringen um die Arabien-Erklärung der Achsenmächte 1940–1942," *Asien, Afrika, Lateinamerika* 27 (1999): 572.

41. Sami al-Jundi, *Al-Ba'th* (Beirut: An-Nahar, 1969), 27.

42. *Frankfurter Zeitung*, December 6, 1940.

43. Norman Stillman, *The Jews of Arab Lands in Modern Times* (Philadelphia: Jewish Publication Society of America, 1991), 106.

44. RGVArkhM, 7-1-998–46, "Renseignement, Von Hentig, Roser, Adil Arslan, Saadi al-Kailani, Umar Dawuq, Riad as-Sulh, Akram az-Zuwaitar. Mukhtar as-Sulh, Ihsan Jabiri, Amin al-Husain, Paris, 28.02.1941."

45. USArchII, RG338, FMS, P-207, Franz Halder, "Vorbemerkungen von Generaloberst a.D. Franz Halder," in "German Exploitation of Arab National Movements in World War II" (see Chapter 4, note 61), xii–xiii.

46. Anwar Sadat, *Revolt on the Nile* (New York: Day, 1957), 39.

47. Robert Lyman, *Iraq 1941* (Oxford: Osprey, 2005), 207; USArchII, RG 338, FMS, P-207, General der Flieger a.D. Hellmuth Felmy, "Die deutsche Ausnutzung der arabischen Eingeborenenbewegung im zweiten Weltkrieg," in "German Exploitation of Arab National Movements in World War II" (see above, Chapter 4, note 61), 37.

48. ArchPAA, 15916 FC, cable from grand mufti to German government, via Italy's embassy, Baghdad, May 3, 1941, signed al-Husaini, Mackensen; Felmy, "Die deutsche Ausnutzung der arabischen Eingeborenenbewegung," 34: OKW meeting on May 6, 1941; Ernst von Weizsäcker, *Erinnerungen* (Munich: List, 1950), 307.

49. In 1941 the code name Max Müller was used for the grand mufti but also for his secretary Kamal Uthman Haddad. The latter's other code name was Taufiq Ali ash-Shakir.

50. Grobba, "Supplement," 40: joint insurrection proposed by Rashid Ali to Ibn Saud in May 1940; Kohlhaas, *Hitler-Abenteuer im Irak*, 56, weapon deliveries to Iraq via Salonica and Athens, airplane deliveries to Werner Junck, May 15, 19, 1941.

51. Grobba, "Supplement," 44, 48–49, 51, 61; Felmy, "Die deutsche Ausnutzung der arabischen Eingeborenenbewegung," 34.

52. Felmy, "Die deutsche Ausnutzung der arabischen Eingeborenenbewegung," 55.

53. Ibid., 54.

54. PArchWGS, "Weisung Nr. 30, Mittlerer Orient, 23.05.41, gez. Jodl"; al-Husaini, *Mudhakkirat*, 76–78; Grobba, "Supplement," 53.

55. USArchII, RG 338, FMS, P-207, General der Artillerie a.D. Walter Warlimont, "Die deutsche Ausnutzung der arabischen Eingeborenenbewegung im zweiten Weltkrieg," in "German Exploitation of Arab National Movements in World War II" (see Chapter 4, note 61), 180; Kohlhaas, *Hitler-Abenteuer im Irak*, 57, 94; al-Husaini, *Mudhakkirat*, 72.

56. Kohlhaas, *Hitler-Abenteuer im Irak*, 90; Grobba, "Supplement," 57.

57. Grobba, "Supplement," 50–51: PArchWGS, Nachlaß Günther Pawelke, vol. 6, "Meine Erinnerungen an die Ereignisse des Tages unserer Ankunft in Baghdad, aus dem Gedächtnis aufgezeichnet am 20.11.56, gez. O. Krückmann"; Felmy, "Die deutsche Ausnutzung der arabischen Eingeborenenbewegung," 37.

58. Halder, "Vorbemerkungen von Generaloberst a.D. Franz Halder," xiii.

59. PArchWGS, Nachlaß Günther Pawelke, vol. 6, "Ursprung des Irakunternehmens, Wilhelm Melchers, Nürnberg, 11.08.47," 2.

60. PArchWGS, "An Oberst Junck, Kriegsgerichtliche Untersuchung eingestellt, alle Vorwürfe laut Grobbas Bericht 01.07.41, gegenstandslos, 20.09.41, gez. Kastner."

61. Al-Husaini, *Mudhakkirat*, 70–71.

62. Bernd Philipp Schrödder, *Iraq 1941* (Freiburg: Rombach, 1980), 41–58.

63. Felmy, "Die deutsche Ausnutzung der arabischen Eingeborenenbewegung"; Warlimont, "Die deutsche Ausnutzung der arabischen Eingeborenenbewegung."

64. PArchWGS, to Naji Shaukat, Arabic letter with codenames, Rome, September 28, 1942, signed Amin al-Husaini; on the Farhud see Ruth Bondy, *The Emis-*

sary: A Life of Enzo Sereni (Boston, Little, Brown, 1977), 193; Hayyim Cohen, "The Anti-Jewish Farhud in Baghdad," *Middle Eastern Studies* 3, no. 1 (October 1966): 2–17.

65. *Time,* July 21, 1941.

66. Warlimont, "Die deutsche Ausnutzung der arabischen Eingeborenenbewegung," 163–165.

67. Grobba, "Supplement," final remarks on Churchill, Falkenhayn, Verdun, Hitler, and his enemies about the missed chance in the Middle East, 79–82; Winston S. Churchill, *The World Crisis, 1911–1914* (London: Butterworth, 1931), 79–80; Göring made the same point to Hitler on the "enemies' weakest point in the South," as he claimed after World War II, adding a remark on the "endless, unbeatable Russia in the East," see USArchII, RG332, B104, State Department Special Interrogation Mission, Hermann Göring, by DeWitt C. Poole and Harold C. Vedeler, Wiesbaden, November 9, 1945.

68. USArchII, RG263, CIA, B58–60, Hajj Amin al-Husaini, Biographic Sketch No. 60, confidential, Washington, April 24, 1951, 2; al-Husaini, *Mudhakkirat,* 92.

69. USArchII, T120, R63571, F50682, to Ribbentrop, urgent Tehran cable, Berlin, June 6, 1941, signed Woermann.

70. PArchWGS, Diary, Abwehr Major Erwin Lahousen, Grand Mufti in Tehran's Japanese Embassy, Berlin 03.09.1941, signed Lahousen; al-Husaini, *Mudhakkirat,* 82–83, 179.

71. Al-Husaini, *Mudhakkirat,* 90–92.

72. Ibid., 89.

73. Ibid., 93–94.

74. Daniel Carpi, "The Mufti of Jerusalem, Amin al-Husaini, and His Diplomatic Activity during World War II (October 1941–July 1943)," *Studies in Zionism,* no. 7 (1983): 106–107.

75. Al-Husaini, *Mudhakkirat,* 96, 100.

76. BArchPAA, F8367P, B14828–837, propaganda against the British in the Middle East, secret, Berlin, August 7, 1941, signed Grobba; USArchII, T77, R1432, S71, F695, Amt Ausland/Abwehr, "An Krummacher, Abwehr II, Sonderstab F, Leitstelle Naher Orient, Ministerpräsident al-Kailani, 11,000 türkische Pfund (Hälfte Italiener, Hälfte Botschaft Ankara), Geheime Kommandosache," Berlin, November 5, 1941.

77. Jana Forsmann, *Testfall für die "Großen Drei"* (Cologne: Böhlau, 2009), 43.

78. Grobba, "Supplement," 78–79.

79. USArchII, T120, R28541, F28202, "Notiz für den Führer, gez. Fuschl, 7.09.42," 6.

80. Ata Taheri, *Deutsche Agenten bei iranischen Stämmen 1942–1944,* ed. Burkhard Ganzer (Berlin: Schwarz, 2008), 13, 91–97.

81. USArchII, FMS, P-207, Warlimont, "Die deutsche Ausnutzung der arabischen Eingeborenenbewegung," 163–166, 181.

82. "Unterredung zwischen dem Führer und Graf Ciano, Berlin, 29.11.1941," in Hans-Adolf Jacobsen, *Der Weg zur Teilung der Welt: Politik und Strategie von 1933 bis 1945* (Koblenz: Wehr & Wissen, 1977), 128, doc. 64.

83. PArchAA, F41797, E261172–74, "An Auswärtiges Amt Berlin, für Ettel

vom Großmufti, geheim, Rom 13.08.42, gez. Bismarck: Die Lage der Juden in den arabischen Ländern bis 18.07.42."

84. USArchII, T120, R901, 61125, B E261249–50, "Ministero degli Affari Esteri, Appunto, Segreto, Roma," September 13, 1942; see also Luigi Goglia, "Il Mufti e Mussolini," in *Storia Contemporanea* 16, no. 12 (1986): 1201–1253.

85. USArchII, Office of Naval Intelligence, C-9-E 25524, box 116, OSS 25681, Kirk to Hull, November 20–26, 1942, report of December 6, 1942, and OSS 26373, December 11, 1942, Kirk to Hull, December 3, 1942. See also Felmy, "Die deutsche Ausnutzung der arabischen Eingeborenenbewegung," and Warlimont, "Die deutsche Ausnutzung der arabischen Eingeborenenbewegung." Detailed accounts of Arab activities in Germany are contained in USArchII, RG226, OSS XL 14167, interrogation of Carl Rekowsky, August 14, 1945. See also Anthony R. De Luca, "'Der Grossmufti' in Berlin: The Politics of Collaboration," *International Journal of Middle East Studies* 10, no. 1 (February 1979): 125–138.

86. USArchII, T120, R28, B28202 ff.3, B28414–7, "Die Länder des arabischen Raumes im Nahen Osten, Geheim, 'Westfalen,'" May 31, 1942.

87. BArchPAA, F41796, E260591, cable to Hitler before leaving for Rome, Berlin, February 13, 1942, signed Amin al-Husaini.

88. Al-Husaini, *Mudhakkirat*, 116.

89. Taqi ad-Din al-Hilali, *Die Einleitung zu al-Birunis Steinbuch, mit Erläuterungen übersetzt* (Leipzig: Harassowitz, 1941).

90. PArchWGS, letter From al-Burqiba to al-Husaini, reporting receipt of his letter of January 22, 1943 on North African affairs, enclosing a memorandum to the Axis powers by Said Taufiq and Ramzi al-Ajaqi, and asking the grand mufti to intervene that he can come to Berlin for direct talks with the Germans, January 29, 1943.

91. Al-Husaini, *Mudhakkirat*, 117, 208.

92. Ibid., 116–117.

93. USArchII, RG218, B59, Joint Psychological Warfare Committee, "Abd al-Karim, Investigation Request to OSS, Joint Chiefs of Staff, Secret," Washington, D.C., August 4, 1942. BArchPAA, F41796, BE260924, "Arabische Mitarbeiter Rashid Ali al-Kailanis und des Grossmuftis, Rom 14.04.42, gez. Granow," report on Free Arab broadcast and al-Umma al-Arabiyya; BArchPPAA, 61123, B51074–75, report that al-Husaini is waiting for the Axis radio declaration and will choose co-workers for Radio Athens, Rome, March 28, 1942.

94. Memorandum on Arab Northwest Africa, Rome, November 18, 1942, Berlin, January 16, 1943, in al-Husaini, *Mudhakkirat*, 118–119. USArchII, R901, 61125, B302991–97, "Telegramm, Deutsch-italienische Besprechung über Tunis im Palazzo Chigi, Bey von Tunis, al-Husaini, al-Burqiba, Deutsch-Arabische Lehrabteilung, Rom 2.01.1943"; Metzger, *L'Empire colonial français dans la stratégie du Troisième Reich*, 2:963–969.

95. BArchPAA, F41796, BE260924, "Arabische Mitarbeiter Rashid Ali al-Kailanis und des Grossmuftis, Rom 14.04.42, gez. Granow": report on Free Arab broadcast, Al-Umma al-Arabiyya, and al-Husaini's and al-Kailani's visit to Rome, May 5–11, 1942; BArchPPAA, 61123, B51074–75, report that al-Husaini is waiting for the Axis radio declaration and will choose co-workers for Radio Athens, Rome, March 28, 1942.

96. PArchAA, R27327, B297998-01, "An Kapp, Memorandum, Propagandas-chriften der Araberfeinde, November 1942."

97. USArchII T120, R392, S930, F297916, German Foreign Ministry, special files of Envoy Ettel who was attached as the ministry's representative to the grand mufti of Jerusalem; B297924, "Arabien Komitee 38. Sitzung," Berlin, December 3, 1942: Following the earlier mentioned exchange of letters between al-Kailani and Groß of the Race-Political Office of the Nazi Party, October 17, 1942, about henceforth using anti-Judaism instead of anti-Semitism, twenty thousand leaflets were printed by OKW, the German Supreme Command, in a run to be distributed by airplanes over North Africa. See also B298067, Yunis Bahri of Bukarest, too OKW, Berlin, October 30, 1942.

98. German racist and Islamist leaflets for Arabs of November 17, 1941 in Metzger, *L'Empire colonial français dans la stratégie du Troisième Reich*, 2:909–915.

99. Von Ribbentrop letter of April 28, 1942 in Al-Husaini, *Mudhakkirat*, 115–116.; Wolfgang G. Schwanitz, *Islam in Europa, Revolten in Mittelost* (Berlin: Weist, 2013), 165.

100. PArchAA, Abwehr Afrika to Ritter, on German economic activities in French North Africa, Algeria, Morocco, on agents, and on allied landing in western Africa, Berlin, May 14, 1942, signed Canaris; see also Metzger, *L'Empire colonial français dans la stratégie du Troisième Reich*, Annex 44, 2:896–898.

101. Maurice M. Roumani, *The Jews of Libya* (Brighton: Sussex Academic Press, 2009), 34–37.

102. Robert Satloff, *Among The Righteous* (New York: Public Affairs, 2006), 42–44.

103. Daniel Carpi, *Between Mussolini and Hitler: The Jews and the Italian Authorities in France and Tunisia* (Hanover: Brandeis University Press, 1994), 205–227; Satloff, *Among The Righteous*, 31–33.

104. Shraga Elam and Dennis Whitehead, "Rauff vs. the Yishuv," *Haaretz*, July 4, 2007; Rauff's letter on Special Vans, Berlin, July 5, 1942, at http://www.holo caust-history.org/19420605-rauff-spezialwagen/rauff-1.gif.

105. USArchII, RG263, CIA B106, Name Index (2nd rel.) "Walter Rauff, Memorandum to Dr. Voss and his friends (original message 06/01/45, 2), Secret, Cairo 02/09/54," 1.

106. Klaus-Michael Mallmann and Martin Küppers, *Halbmond und Haken-kreuz: Das Dritte Reich, die Araber und Palästina* (Darmstadt: Wissenschaftliche Buchgesellschaft, 2006), 146, 203.

107. For documentation on Walther Rauff, see Wolfgang G. Schwanitz, "Amin al-Husaini and the Holocaust: What Did the Grand Mufti know?" *World Politics Review Exclusive,* May 5, 2008, 1.

108. Mallmann and Küppers, *Halbmond und Hakenkreuz*, 207.

109. Rahn, *Ruheloses Leben*, 295–302.

110. Gerhard Höpp, "In the Shadow of the Moon: Arab Inmates in Nazi Concentration Camps," in Schwanitz, *Germany and the Middle East*, 224. USArchII, RG263, EZZ-18, CIA Name Files (2nd release), B107, Walter Rauff, "German Intelligence Service in Tunis during the occupation, Colonel Rauff as Gestapo chief of Tunis, Secret, 11/15/43."

111. Satloff, *Among the Righteous*, 19–20.

112. USArchII, RG263, EZZ-18, CIA Name Files (2nd release), B107, Walter Rauff, "Head of SD in Milan, Secret, 07/02/44." USArchII, RG263, EZZ-18, CIA Name Files (2nd release), B107, "Walter Rauff, Personal-Bericht 1938, gez. Albert; Personalangaben 08.09.38, gez. Rauff; Bewährung als Führer SD Einsatzkommando Tunis, Winter 1942–43, Stellungnahme und Antrag Botschafter Rahns, Verleihung des Deutschen Kreuzes in Silber, gez. Wolff; Lebenslauf handschriftlich Rahn, Personalbericht, 23.04.38, gez. Rauff."

113. PArchAA, Botschaft Rom, Q, vol. 161, B304529–304531, "Niederschrift des Großmufti über seine beabsichtigte Tätigkeit in Nordafrika, übergeben General Amé, darin Briefinhalt, 26.07.42, an von Ribbentrop, Rom," August 29, 1942.

114. BArchPAA, R27766, Rahn to Foreign Ministry, predicting results of arming Arabs such as looting and pogroms against Jews, Tunis, December 5, 1942; see also Mallmann and Küppers, *Halbmond und Hakenkreuz*, 209.

115. USArchII, R901, 61169, B95–99, report to Woermann on Arabs, French, German-French relations, Europe, and ideological warfare, "Geheime Kommandosache," Paris, February 28, 1942, signed Rahn.

116. Al-Husaini, *Mudhakkirat*, 122.

117. USArchII, T120, R63, S71 F50682, B51137, report to Grobba, on Arab Legion and on plans made by al-Husaini in Rome, February 7–May 11, 1942, Berlin, May 22, 1942, signed Woermann.

118. USArchII, T120, R901, 61125, B33, agreement with the German Supreme Command (OKW) about the use of the Arab Freedom Corps, September 12, 1942 (replacing the agreement of January 1942 between Grobba, al-Kailani, General Felmy, and the grand mufti); see also BE261249–50, Ministero degli Affari Esteri, "Appunto, Segreto, Roma, 09/13/42." BArchAAL, 61124, B71–77, "Befehlshaber Sonderstab F, Bericht über die Tätigkeit des Sonderstabes F in der arabischen Frage, Großmufti rekrutierte eine Kompanie aus arabischen Gefangenen, Felmys Besprechungen Anfang Mai und Mitte Juli 1942 mit al-Husaini und al-Kailani, Name Freiheitscorps, Verträge, 15.08.42, gez. Felmy."

119. USArchII, T120, R901, 61125, B31–32, Supreme Command S.I.M., Center of the Grand Mufti in North Africa (translation from Italian), September 10, 1942.

120. Daniel Carpi, "The Mufti of Jerusalem, Amin al-Husaini, and His Diplomatic Activity During World War II (October 1941–July 1943)," *Studies in Zionism*, no. 7 (spring 1983): 119.

121. BArchAAP, F61124, "Betrifft Sonderverband 288," January 13, 1942.

122. USArchII, R901, 61125, B55–56; see also Mallmann and Küppers, *Halbmond und Hakenkreuz*, 216–217.

123. Sadat, *Revolt on the Nile*, 8–44; James Heyworth-Dunne, *Religious and Political Trends in Modern Egypt* (Washington, D.C.: privately published, 1950), 25–26; Geoffrey Warner, *Iraq and Syria, 1941* (London: Davis-Poynter, 1974), 24–27; Abd ar-Rahman Azzam, *Die Freiheitskämpfe der Tripolitaner* (Berlin: Der Neue Orient, 1918).

124. Sadat, *Revolt on the Nile*, 18–44.

125. Ibid.

126. Report to Foreign Office, "Security Summary Middle East," February 12, 1942, in Brynjar Lia, *The Society of the Muslim Brothers in Egypt: The Rise of an Islamic Movement 1928–1942* (Reading: Ithaca Press, 1998), 267–268.

127. Wajih Atiq, *Al-Malik Faruq wa Almaniya an-Naziyya* [King Faruq and Nazi Germany] (Cairo: Al-Fikr, 1992), 90, 187.

128. Sadat, *Revolt on the Nile*, 18–44; Heyworth-Dunne, *Religious and Political Trends in Modern Egypt*, 25–26; Warner, *Iraq and Syria*, 1941, 24–27.

129. *Stimme des Freien Arabertums*, June 25, 1942, quoted in Jeffrey Herf, "Hitlers Dschihad," *Vierteljahreshefte zur Zeitgeschichte*, no. 2 (2010): 270–72.

130. "Aufzeichnung des Gesandten Ettel, Unterredung mit Großmufti am 27.06.42, Augenblick bald gekommen, Ägypter zum offenen Aufruhr aufzurufen, Geheime Reichssache, Berlin 27.06.42, gez. Ettel," *Akten Zur Deutschen Auswärtigen Politik, 1918–1945*, Serie E, 1941–1945, vol. 3, June 16–September 9, 1942 (Göttingen: Vandenhoek & Ruprecht 1974), 1473/367993, 71–72; Atiq, *Al-Malik Faruq wa Almaniya an-Naziyya*, 178, 187.

131. "Ettel an Auswärtiges Amt, Amin Zaki Bey mit Faruqs Antwort für Hitler, Faruq grüßt Großmufti, Istanbul 24.07.42, gez. Ettel," *Akten Zur Deutschen Auswärtigen Politik, 1918–1945*, Serie E, 1941–1945, 3:222–223, Nr. 129; Atiq, *Al-Malik Faruq wa Almaniya an-Naziyya*, 115–134; al-Husaini, *Mudhakkirat*, 171.

132. Jehan Sadat, *Ich bin eine Frau aus Ägypten* (Munich: Heyne, 1987), 70; John W. Eppler, *Rommel ruft Kairo* (Gütersloh: Bertelsmann, 1959), 202–203, 295–298.

133. Anwar as-Sadat, "Rommel at al-Alamainin: An Egyptian View (1942)," in *A Middle East Mosaic*, ed. Bernard Lewis (New York: Random House, 2000), 314–316.

134. Wajih Atiq, *Al-Jaish al-Misri wa alman fi atha al-Harb alamiyya ath-Thaniyya* [The Egyptian Army and the Germans during World War Two] (Cairo: Cairo University Press, 1993), 63.

135. "Ettel an Auswärtiges Amt, Amin Zaki Bey mit Faruqs Antwort für Hitler, Istanbul 24.07.42, gez. Ettel," *Akten Zur Deutschen Auswärtigen Politik, 1918–1945*, Serie E, 1941–1945, 3:222–223, Nr. 129; see also Atiq, *Al-Jaish al-Misri*, 112.

136. Ettel/Tismer document, Berlin, July 28, 1942, and Tismer document, Berlin, July 31, 1942, Muhammad Radwan on a British plan to attack Marsa Matruh cutting off German-Italian troops at al-Alamain and the death of the other pilot, Ahmad Sayyid Husain, in Atiq, *Al-Jaish al-Misri*, 223–225, 227.

137. BArchPAA, F14073, 364869; "Ettel an Auswärtiges Amt, Amin Zaki Bey mit Faruqs Antwort für Hitler (Fussnote 2 zur Ankunft der beiden ägyptischen Flieger am 06.07.07.42, Telegramm 28.07.42) Istanbul 24.07.42, gez. Ettel," *Akten Zur Deutschen Auswärtigen Politik, 1918–1945*, Serie E, 1941–1945, 3:222–223, Nr. 129; see also Gerhard Höpp, "Der Koran als 'Geheime Reichssache': Bruchstücke deutscher Islampolitik zwischen 1938 und 1945," in *Gnosisforschung und Religionsgeschichte*, ed. Holger Preißler and Hubert Seiwert (Marburg: Diagonal, 1994), 435–446.

138. BArchPAA, FC4030, B363198, "An Tismer, Büro Ettel, Aufruf al-Husainis und al-Kailanis an die Ägypter, Broschüre Der Islam und die Demokratien, Ber-

lin 07.01.43, gez. Winkler"; B363199, "'Bayan Samahat al-Mufti al-Akbar ila ash-Shab al-Misri,' Rundfunkerklärung des Großmuftis an das ägyptische Volk, 3.07.42."

139. BArchPAA, F14009, B321578–80, "Radio-Erklärung des Großmufti, 3.07.42."

140. Reinhard Stumpf, "Einleitung," in *Marsch und Kampf des Deutschen Afrikakorps,* vol. 1: 1941, ed. Generalkommando des Deutschen Afrikakorps (1934; reprint, Berlin: Mittler 1994), 9–25.

141. "Tötet die Juden bevor sie Euch töten, Stimme des Freien Arabertums, 7.07.42," in Herf, "Hitlers Dschihad," 274; see also Jeffrey Herf, *Nazi Propaganda for the Arab World* (New Haven: Yale University Press, 2009), 112–113.

142. Abwehr II chart in Metzger, *L'Empire colonial français dans la stratégie du Troisième Reich,* 2:958.

143. PArchWGS, Diary of Erwin von Lahousen, head of Sabotage Department, Abwehr II, B208, July 13, 1942.

144. Oscar Reile, *Treff Lutetia Paris: Der Kampf der Geheimdienste im westlichen Operationsgebiet, in England und Nordafrika 1939–45. Im "Dienst" Gehlens 1949–61* (Munich: Welsermühl, 1973), 231–232.

145. BArchPAA, FC4030, B363196, "Notiz, Großmufti im Rundfunk, Martyrerrede 11.11.42, Amerikaner und Juden in Nordafrika, 25.11.42, Berlin 08.01.43."

146. BArchPAA, 61124, B205–206, "An Canaris, Geheimbrief an Bey von Tunis, al-Husaini will Reise mit Canaris nach Tunis, Berlin, 08.12.42"; USArchII, R901, 27332, B390957, report to Ettel on Nine Points of an Islamic Pact and Bloc of North Africa, February 1943.

147. Mallmann and Küppers, *Halbmond und Hakenkreuz,* 214.

148. "Telegraf, 6,000 Deutsche, Kairo gibt Spezialisten Verträge," *Sächsische Zeitung,* July 29, 1947; "Deutsche gegen Israel," ibid., January 15, 1949.

CHAPTER 8. GERMANY'S MUSLIM ARMY

1. Von Ribbentrop to von Papen, Berlin, September 26, 1941, in Franz von Papen, *Der Wahrheit eine Gasse,* 2 vols. (Munich: List, 1952), 2:547–548; Rudolf Rahn, *Ruheloses Leben* (Düsseldorf: Diederichs, 1949), 400.

2. PArchWGS, Higher Command to German Afrikakorps, explaining that after the hot season is over in fall 1941 as discussed with the Italian Higher Command, a German-Italian offensive will drive the British out of Egypt and the Suez Canal area, at the same time proceeding through Turkey, Syria, and Palestine, "geheime Kommandosache," June 28, 1941.

3. Edgar Flacker, "Fritz Grobba and Nazi Germany's Middle Eastern Policy, 1933–1942" (Ph.D. diss., University of London, 1998), 187.

4. Jan Lipinsky, *Das Geheime Zusatzprotokoll zum deutsch-sowjetischen Nichtangriffsvertrag vom 23. August 1939 und seine Entstehungs- und Rezeptionsgeschichte von 1939 bis 1999* (Frankfurt: Lang, 2004); Heinz Tillmann, *Deutschlands Araberpolitik im Zweiten Weltkrieg* (Berlin: Deutscher Verlag der Wissenschaften, 1965), 140.

5. BArchPAA, 61123, FS, Hitler's order to train Arabs for desert war, and to in-

clude Rashid Ali al-Kailani as leader of the training, "geheime Kommandosache," January 13, 1942.

6. USArchII, RG263, CIA Records, al-Husaini letters, April 19, 1943; PArchWGS, al-Husaini to von Ribbentrop on Muslims of Albania, asking for declaration of independence, Berlin, December 9, 1943.

7. BArchPAA, F4925, B390726–31, "Unaufrichtigkeit des Großmufti gegenüber deutschen militärischen Stellen," Berlin, October 26, 1942.

8. USArchII, T120, R901, 61124, B38–39, Arab leaders in Istanbul, Adil al-Azma, Nabil al-Azma, Akram Zuwaitar, asking Berlin through Ishaq Darwish for an official declaration on the Middle East, especially on Iraq, Syria, Lebanon, Transjordan, Palestine, Arab emirates, including recognition of the independence of the Arab kingdoms and their right of unification July 4, 1942; USArchII, T120, R901, 61125, "An Ettel, Großmuftis Nachricht an Kamil Muruwwa: Ich habe für Salim und Kameraden das Nötige gesandt (Randvermerk: 'freigelassene Araber [in Frankreich]'), Sofia, 12.02.43."

9. BArchPAA, F61124, B45–48, "Stellungnahme zum Schreiben des Auswärtigen Amts vom 05.08.42, DAL keine Arabische Legion, Soldatenzahlen Araber, Geheime Kommandosache, 14.08.42, gez. Felmy"; USArchII, T120, R28 S541, F28202, B28455–60, "Notiz für Gesandten von Rintelen, Unterredung Jodl-Felmy, Deutsch-Arabische Lehrabteilung ca. 4.000 Mann mit Sonderausbildung, darunter zwei Kompanien Araber, eine hat 170 Mann aus dem Vorderen Orient, die andere 100 Marokkaner, DAL wird zur Zeit von Griechenland in den Kauskasus verlegt, unser Vordringen in arabische Welt für Frühjahr 1943 erwartet, Geheim, Führerhauptquartier, 31.08.42."

10. USArchII, T120, R901, 61125, B29–30, report on meeting of Canaris, Felmy, von Lahousen, Meyer-Ricks, Amé, and Simen with al-Husaini, top secret, Rome, September 15, 1942, signed Canaris; R901, 61124, B70, cable on several hours of meeting between Canaris and al-Husaini, no command for al-Husaini over troops of Cape Sounion, he was depressed, signed Mackensen, top secret, Rome, September 17, 1942; B62890–91, report on the grand mufti's argument against using Arabs in the Caucasian theatre of war, and memorandum to Keitel on the movement of the Cape Sounion camp, Rome, September 29, 1942, signed Amin al-Husaini.

11. Otto Bräutigam, *So hat es sich zugetragen: Ein Leben als Soldat und Diplomat* (Würzburg: Holzner, 1968), 334–335, 405–409, 469.

12. Alexander Kirk to Foreign Office, "Basic Trends of Axis Broadcasts for Arabs," Cairo, April 18, 1942, in Herf, "Hitlers Dschihad," 270.

13. USArchII, T454, R16, Eastern Ministry and Occupied Soviet Areas, 1941–45, Too I 855/42; Bräutigam, *So hat es sich zugetragen*, 501, describes three principles of Rosenberg's ministry in ruling the occupied areas from the summer of 1942: liberation from Bolshevism, establishment of sovereign states, and winning of the hearts and minds of the population, including for the fight against partisans.

14. USArchII, T454, R16, Eastern Ministry and Occupied Soviet Areas, 1941–45, report by Oberkriegsverwaltungsrat on the visit to the Uraza Bairam festival in Kislovodsk, October 11, 1942, 4, 5.

15. USArchII, T454, R16, Eastern Ministry and Occupied Soviet Areas, 1941–

45, Ic/AO 3719/42, report by High Command of Army Group B to Army High Command (OKH) on the Kalmyks after the fall of Elista, August 26, 1942, with details of militias, volunteers, horsemen bands, agents, and insurgency, secret, January 18, 1942, signed Sordenstern.

16. Bräutigam, *So hat es sich zugetragen*, 627–628: Mende took over the Department of Alien Peoples in late August 1943.

17. Ibid., 295–297.

18. Ibid., 321.

19. Bernd Bronwetsch, "Die sowjetischen Kriegsgefangenen zwischen Stalin und Hitler," *Zeitschrift für Geschichtswissenschaft* 41, no. 2 (1993): 135–142; Camilla Dawletschin-Linder, "Die turko-tatarischen Kriegsgefangenen im Zweiten Weltkrieg im Dreiecksverhältnis zwischen deutscher Politik, turanistischen Aspiration und türkischer Außenpolitik," *Der Islam* 80 (2003): 1–29; Timothy Snyder, *Bloodlands: Europa zwischen Hitler und Stalin* (Munich: Beck, 2010), 220–229.

20. PArchAA, Nachlaß Von Hentig, V84, B325943–45, report to von Oppenheim on Tatars and other Muslims in the field, October 11, 1941, signed von Hentig.

21. Maria Keipert and Peter Grupp, eds., *Biographisches Handbuch des deutschen Auswärtigen Dienstes 1871–1945*, vol. 2, ed. Gerhard Keiper and Martin Kröger (Paderborn: Schöningh, 2005), 403–404; on the Brotherhood of Tatar Fighters, the Törek Tatarlarynyň Milli Körash, and the Tatarischer Kampfbund (Idel-Ural Turktataren), see Sebastian Cwiklinski, *Wolgatataren im Deutschland des Zweiten Weltkriegs: Deutsche Ostpolitik und tatarischer Nationalismus* (Berlin: Schwarz, 2002), 99–102, 121–126.

22. BArchPAA, 61174, B198, OKW to Foreign Office, January 31, 1941; see Dawletschin-Linder, "Die turko-tatarischen Kriegsgefangenen im Zweiten Weltkrieg," 18.

23. BArchPAA, von Papen to Foreign Office, Ankara, July 25, 1941, see Dawletschin-Linder, "Die turko-tatarischen Kriegsgefangenen im Zweiten Weltkrieg," 15.

24. Volker Koop, *Hitlers Muslime: Die Geschichte einer unheiligen Allianz* (Berlin: Bebra, 2012), 19.

25. Bernd Lemke, *Der Irak und Arabien aus der Sicht deutscher Kriegsteilnehmer und Orientreisender 1918 bis 1945* (Frankfurt: Lang, 2012), 324–349.

26. Bräutigam, *So hat es sich zugetragen*, 420–421.

27. Von Papen, *Der Wahrheit eine Gasse*, 2 vols. (Munich: List, 1952), 2:553–554; Sebastian Cwiklinski, *Wolgatataren im Deutschland des Zweiten Weltkriegs* (Berlin: Schwarz, 2002), 18–19.

28. Bräutigam, *So hat es sich zugetragen*, 496–497.

29. USArchII, T454, R16, Eastern Ministry and Occupied Soviet Areas, 1941–45, "Auswahl von Fragen, die aus den Reihen der Kaukasischen Legionäre gestellt wurden, geheim, 25.08.42."

30. Bräutigam, *So hat es sich zugetragen*, 435.

31. Joachim Hoffmann, *Die Ostlegionen 1941–1943: Turkotataren, Kaukasier und Wolgafinnen im deutschen Heer* (Freiburg: Rombach, 1976), 24–25.

32. USArchII, T454, R16, Eastern Ministry and Occupied Soviet Areas, 1941–45, letter of Cora von Mende to "Sir Thomas," October 1946, 4; Dawletschin-

Linder, "Die turko-tatarischen Kriegsgefangenen im Zweiten Weltkrieg," 16–17; Patrik von zur Mühlen, *Zwischen Hakenkreuz und Sowjetstern: Der Nationalismus der sowjetischen Ostvölker im Zweiten Weltkrieg* (Düsseldorf: Droste, 1971), 84.

33. Bräutigam, *So hat es sich zugetragen,* 467.

34. PArchWGS, Abwehr Diary of Erwin von Lahousen, Stalag IIIA, entry of November 29, 1941, 178, on Luckenwalde prisoners and Abwehr II.

35. USArchII, T120, R63, S71, F50682 ff., report to Weizsäcker that Hitler agreed to an Indian Legion to be organized under the leadership of State Secretary Keppler, but decided to postpone an Arab Legion as suggested on December 22, 1941, until discussions to be held with the military, results to be given to Hitler via von Ribbentrop, "Geheime Reichssache," Berlin, December 24, 1941, signed Woermann; Note from OKW regarding Indian Legion, Arab Legion, Grobba, and von Lahousen, Berlin, December 24, 1941, signed von Weizsäcker; Hoffmann, *Die Ostlegionen 1941–1943,* 26–27.

36. BArchPAA, 61124, B45–48, "Stellungnahme zum Schreiben des Auswärtigen Amts, 05.08.42, Namensgebung Deutsch-Arabische Lehrabteilung, Geheime Kommandosache, 18.04.42, gez. Felmy."

37. East Turk Armed Formation: Osttürkischer Waffenverband des SS-Hauptamtes in Dresden.

38. PArchWGS, letter to Major Morrison on the Eastern Ministry's function and structure, Detmold, October 31, 1945, signed von Mende, 2. See also Bräutigam, *So hat es sich zugetragen,* 394, 592.

39. Bräutigam, *So hat es sich zugetragen,* 301, 302–303, 318–321, 371.

40. Hitler's Order No. 41, April 5, 1942, for Operation Blue, and for later Operations Herron and Edelweiss up to the Caspian Sea.

41. Dietrich Eichholz, *Krieg um Öl: Ein Erdölimperium als deutsches Kriegsziel (1938–1943)* (Leipzig: Leipziger Universitätsverlag, 2006), 122–132.

42. USArchII, T454, R16, Eastern Ministry and Occupied Soviet Areas, 1941–45, report to Leibbrandt and Schickedanz on a trip to Turkey, August 14–29, 1942, secret, Berlin, September 1, 1942, 15.

43. See Chapter Seven. USArchII, T120, R901, 61123, B168–185, "Vordringen Deutschlands über den Kaukasus nach dem arabischen Raum, Geheime Reichssache, 05.02.42, gez. Grobba."

44. USArchII, T120, R901, 61124, B65–66, "Sonderstab F Oberkommando Wehrmacht, Amt Ausland/Abwehr unterstellt, Geheime Kommandosache, Berlin 15.08.42, gez. Canaris."

45. USArchII, T120, R901, 61124, B68–69, "Sonderstab F bzw. Deutsches Orientkorps, Mitteilung General Felmys, Arabisches Bataillon ehedem Deutsch-Arabische Lehrabteilung, Umwandlung in Korpsverband, Geheime Reichssache, Berlin 03.09.42, gezeichnet Grobba"; B149–150, "Die Vertetung des Auswärtigen Amts für die neuen Aufgaben südlich des Kaukasus, Iranisch-Arabischer-Türkischer Raum, u.a. Ausbildung fremder Verbände, H.Qu. OKH, 06.09.42"; PArchAA, Handakten Ritter, "Bericht arabisches Freiwilligen-Bataillon Tunis 14.12.42," 1–4; 61125, B16–19, "An Prüfer, Deutsch-Arabische Lehrabteilung, Araber, Einsatzziel Irak und Iran, die 30–40 Palästinenser des Großmuftis, Geheime Reichssache, Berlin 20.11.42, gez. Schuurre."

46. Amin al-Husaini, *Mudhakkirat al-Hajj Muhammad Amin al-Husaini* [The memoirs of al-Hajj Muhammad Amin al-Husaini], ed. Abd al-Karim al-Umar (Damascus: Al-Ahali, 1999), 120–121.

47. USArchII, R901, 61125, B105, "Irak und englische Judenpolitik in Palästina, Absehen von der Erwägung, schriftliche Zusicherung zu veröffentlichen, Geheime Reichssache, Berlin 10.02.43, gez. Prüfer."

48. BArchPAA, Großmufti Bosnien, 69287, B168–175, "Notizen über al-Husainis Gespräche, Berlin 28.04.43, gez. Winkler"; B181 reports that in Sarajevo the Grand Mufti wore four costumes—Croatian, German-Italian, Arabian, and Islamic.

49. In Rome in August 1942 al-Husaini gave an interview for the Sarajevo weekly *Osvit* claiming that the Axis victory would be a victory of the Islamic nations, and he met with the Bosnian student Mustafa Busulajetish on December 19; *Mudhakkirat*, 137.

50. PArchAAP, "An Weizsäcker, Muslime in Kroatien, Beilage, Angriffe auf Muslime, Berlin 09.06.42, gez. al-Husaini."

51. Al-Husaini, *Mudhakkirat*, 138–139.

52. BArchPAA, Großmufti Bosnien, 69287, B00144–75, "Politische Lage, der Besuch April 1943."

53. Bernwald in Guido Knopp, *Die SS: Eine Warnung an die Geschichte* (Bertelsmann: Munich, 2002), 298.

54. Al-Husaini, *Mudhakkirat*, 143.

55. PArchWGS, "Reichsleiter Baldur von Schirach, Vermerk, SS-Standartenführer Bock, Großmufti von Palästina, Besuch der Staatsoper, Wien 07.04.43, gez. Generalkulturreferent Walter Thomas."

56. Al-Husaini, *Mudhakkirat*, 140: Five points of Bosnian and Croatian recruitment into Waffen SS.

57. Jennie Lebel, *The Mufti of Jerusalem Haj-Amin el-Husseini and National-Socialism* (Belgrade: Čigoja Stampa, 2007), 193.

58. BArchBe, AA, NS19/2181, Reichsführer SS, "An Brandt, Treffen Großmufti-Goebbels, Goebbels-Hitler, geheime Kommandosache, Rolle der SS und Großmufti, Grunewald, 27.05.44," 2–3, remarks of Berger.

59. BArchPAA, Großmufti Bosnien, 69287, B00146, B00150, "An Professor Six, Politische Lage, der Besuch April 1943, Panislamische Kampftruppe, Konfliktfall Türkei, Teufelsdivision, Gefahrenmoment panislamischer Truppe, Berlin 04.05.43, gez. Konsul Winkler"; B168–175, "Notizen über al-Husainis Gespräche, SS-Division soll panislamische Kampftruppe werden, Türken und Bosniaken, Großmufti als Kalif, Berlin 28.04.43, gez. Winkler."

60. Al-Husaini, *Mudhakkirat*, 123, 129–145.

61. Ibid., 149; Lebel, *The Mufti of Jerusalem*, 191.

62. Al-Husaini, *Mudhakkirat*, 391, 436.

63. USArchII, T120, R63, S71, F50682; BArchPAA, R101202, "Reise des Großmuftis nach Holland, Amsterdam, Rotterdam, Volendam, 25.08.–29.08.43, Geheim, Berlin 07.09.43, 10.09.43, gez. Melchers"; al-Husaini, *Mudhakkirat*, 121.

64. BArchB, An Chef des SS Hauptamtes Berger, F2922, B699837–38, "An

Berger, Empfang türkischer Offiziere 14.12.43, die mit Aufstellung Islamischer Division beauftragt, Sympathie der deutschen Führung für Muslime und islamische Sache, vier Bitten der türkischen Offiziere, al-Husaini's Vorschlag, Krim-Tataren aus SS und Wehrmacht in die Islamische Division eingliedern, Berlin 15.12.43, gez. Amin al-Husaini."

65. Al-Husaini, *Mudhakkirat*, 432, 436.

66. "British Spy Records Show Nazi Plans for Palestinian Jews," Associated Press, July 5, 2001.

67. Police report from the Sir Martin Gilbert Archival Collection, the Churchill War Papers, London, in David G. Dalin and John F. Rothman, *Icon of Evil* (New York: Random House, 2008), 61, 184.

68. Al-Husaini, *Mudhakkirat*, 437.

69. Ibid., 146; Lebel, *The Mufti of Jerusalem*, 148–149.

70. Lebel, *The Mufti of Jerusalem*, 148–149; al-Husaini, *Mudhakkirat*, 122, 138, 141, 145.

71. USArchII, RG226, OSS Records, R&A Research Reports, XL5487, "Intelligence Report No. 1, Tall Afar Parachute Expedition, Secret, Basra 12/27/44," 1–15.

72. Cwiklinski, *Wolgatataren im Deutschland des Zweiten Weltkriegs*, 31–32.

73. BArchB, 2, 699597, Reichsministerium für die besetzten Ostgebiete, "Arbeitsgemeinschaft Turkestan und Richtlinien für die besetzten Ostgebiete, 1944"; 2, 699592, "Übersicht Kaukasische Leitstelle"; 2, 699386–88, "Abteilungsbefehl 2, Berlin Grunewald, 30.09.41, gez. Olzscha"; 2, 699382–83, "Übersicht Gesamtgliederungen der Verbände."

74. Lebel, *The Mufti of Jerusalem*, 235.

75. Al-Husaini, *Mudhakkirat*, 148–149, al-Husaini calls Djozo Hasan Sulaiman Juzu instead of Husain, likely his mistake; Lebel, *The Mufti of Jerusalem*, 230–236.

76. Al-Husaini, *Mudhakkirat*, 149.

77. USArchII, T83/2/3, Conversation of Hitler with Jodl, Warlimont, Fegelein, von Below, and others, top secret, at headquarters near Rastenburg (July 31, 1944), 9–12, 42–43; for *Volksdeutsche* see Detlef Brandes, Holm Sundhaussen, and Stefan Troebst, eds., *Lexikon der Vertreibungen* (Vienna: Böhlau, 2010), 708–11.

78. Al-Qur'an 43:61.

79. Ibid.

80. Harald Möller, "Wie sich die SS einmal mit dem Koran beschäftigte und dabei auf den Iran stieß," *Orient* 45, no. 2 (2004): 329–332.

81. BArchP, RF85, F3347 and Berlin Document Center, Research Department, Special Box 6, Das Arabische Büro, letter to Himmler, Berlin, July 16, 1943, signed Amin al-Husaini, 1; BArchPAA, R101202, "Reise des Großmuftis nach Holland, in seiner Wohnung ein gerahmtes Bild von Himmler und sich selbst, Geheim, Berlin 07.09.43, gez. Melchers."

82. Al-Husaini, *Mudhakkirat*, 164–165.

83. PArchAA, Personalakte Grobba, vol. 4827, "An Reichsminister des Auswärtigen, Gesandter Dr. Fritz Grobba in Bagdad ein Hochgrad-Freimaurer in Loge Zur Beständigkeit, seit 1934 gedeckt, Berlin, 26.03.1937, gez. M. Bormann."

84. BArchAAL, F56474, B351003–04, report dictated by Prof. Pierre Schrumpf: the grand mufti on the Turkish regime, Tevfik Rüstü Aras, and the Jews, Grobba on the Jews of Baghdad, Berlin, November 29, 1941.

85. Al-Husaini coined the expression after the 1967 Middle Eastern war, *Mudhakkirat,* 209.

86. Klaus Kreiser, *Atatürk: Eine Biographie* (Munich: Beck, 2008), 178.

87. We thank Klaus Kreiser of Berlin for additional information on Kemal Dogan Bek who served with Mustafa Kemal 1913 in Benghazi.

88. Al-Husaini, *Mudhakkirat,* 213.

89. Ibid., 214.

90. Hadassa Ben-Itto, *The Lie That Wouldn't Die: The Protocols of the Elders of Zion* (London, Mitchell 2005).

91. Al-Husaini, *Mudhakkirat,* 214, 219–220.

92. Ibid., 213–14.

93. PArchWGS, protocol of the Wannsee Conference, Berlin, January 20, 1942, 4–5.

94. Ibid.; see also http://www.ghwk.de/wannsee/dokumente-zur-wannsee-konferenz/?lang=de.

95. USArchII, T120, R63571, F50682, B50794–96, Anlage 8, "Entwurf [des Sekretärs] des Großmuftis für eine offizielle Erklärung Deutschlands und Italiens über arabische Länder, 8 Punkte, Gesandten Grobba Ende Februar 1941 übergeben, Geheime Reichssache, 1/3/41."

96. PArchWGS, order to Heydrich, to prepare an overall solution for the Jewish question in Europe and submit a draft for the desired Final Solution of the Jewish question, Berlin, July 31, 1941, signed Göring; see also http://www.ghwk.de/wannsee/dokumente-zur-wannsee-konferenz/?lang=de. For a short time Jews were deported also from Germany to the occupied Soviet areas after the Wannsee Conference. But the main part of the Holocaust happened in occupied Polish and Soviet areas; Bräutigam, *So hat es sich zugetragen,* 417; see also Snyder. For Hitler's order in May of 1941 to liquidate all Jews of Eastern Europe, see also Joachim Fest, "Hitlers Krieg," *Vierteljahreshefte für Zeitgeschichte* 38, no. 3 (1990): 371.

97. Meanwhile Himmler forbade the emigration of Jews with regard to the dangers of the war and the possibilities of the East, PArchWGS, Protocol of Wannsee Conference, Berlin, January 20, 1942, 5; http://www.ghwk.de/wannsee/dokumente-zur-wannsee-konferenz/?lang=de.

98. Al-Husaini, *Mudhakkirat,* 112.

99. BArchPAA, 61123, B135–141, December 12, 1941, signed Grobba.

100. BArchPAA, 61123, B135-141, "Empfang des Großmufti durch den Führer, 1.12.1941, gez. Grobba."

101. USArchII, T120, R63, S71, F50682, B50970, minutes of Rintelen's phone call about four decisions following the al-Husaini–Hitler conversation, taken by the Führer and von Ribbentrop; von Ribbentrop wants new minutes after talks with Rome, Berlin, November 18, 1941, signed Woermann.

102. "Unterredung zwischen dem Führer und Graf Ciano, Berlin, 29.11.1941," in Hans-Adolf Jacobsen, *Der Weg zur Teilung der Welt: Politik und Strategie 1939–1945* (Koblenz: Wehr & Wissen 1977), 128–129, doc. 64.

103. [New] invitation to Hofmann, for the Wannsee Conference, now to be held on January 20, 1942, Berlin, January 8, 1942, signed Heydrich; see also http://www.ghwk.de/wannsee/dokumente-zur-wannsee-konferenz/?lang=de. PArchAA, "Schreiben Sicherheitspolizeichef Reinhard Heydrich an Unterstaatssekretär Martin Luther, Berlin 08.01.1942," 1. See also the other documents there.

104. Bräutigam, *So hat es sich zugetragen*, 465.

105. So stated by Hitler to the Nazi leadership in Berlin on August 12, 1941, according to a note of that date in the diary of Joseph Goebbels, *Die Tagebücher von Joseph Goebbels: Sämtliche Fragmente*, ed. Elke Fröhlich, 23 vols. (Munich: Saur, 1987–2008), 1.5; see also Volker Ullrich, "Hitlers bösester Befehl," *Die Zeit*, August 1, 1998, 29.

106. International Military Tribunal, Nuremberg, Document UK-81, Affidavit C, Dieter Wisliceny, January 3, 1946; see also *Nazi Conspiracy and Aggression*, vol. 8 (Washington, D.C.: U.S. Government Printing Office, 1946), 606–619.

107. For more on Krumey, Kastner, Wisliceny, and Eichmann in Budapest see Shlomo Aronson, *Hitler, the Allies, and the Jews* (New York: Cambridge University Press, 2007), 228.

108. International Military Tribunal, Nuremberg, Document UK-81, Affidavit C, Dieter Wisliceny, January 3, 1946; see also *Nazi Conspiracy and Aggression*, 8:606–619.

109. Eichmann heard from Heydrich in late summer 1941: "Der Führer hat die physische Vernichtung der Juden befohlen." Voice recording of the Eichmann trial in Jerusalem, at http://www.ghwk.de/wannsee/dokumente-zur-wannsee-konferenz/?lang=de.

110. PArchWGS, AA, Referat D IIIg, B372040–42, "Wünsche und Ideen des Auswärtigen Amts zu der vorgesehen Gesamtlösung der Judenfrage in Europa, Anliegende Aufzeichnung wird als Vorbereitung für die morgige Sitzung bei SS-Obergruppenführer HEYDRICH Herrn Unterstaatssekretär Luther vorgelegt, Berlin, 08.12.1941," initialed "R" (Rademacher), 1–3. See also http://www.ghwk.de/wannsee/dokumente-zur-wannsee-konferenz/?lang=de.

111. The voice recordings of Eichmann's trial in Jerusalem give information on methods of killing as mentioned at the Wannsee Conference, the chain of command from the start of mass murder to Hitler's order, and Eichmann's function as expert for transports; at http://www.ghwk.de/wannsee/dokumente-zur-wannsee-konferenz/?lang=de.

112. See also Fritz Grobba, *Männer und Mächte im Orient* (Göttingen: Musterschmidt, 1967), 260–261.

113. For Hoffmann's photo of the meeting, captioned "Führer meets premier Rashid Ali al-Kailani," see *Völkischer Beobachter*, July 20, 1942.

114. See Chapter One.

115. Four-page handwritten affidavit from the Nuremberg trials, "Betr. Grossmufti von Jerusalem," July 26, 1946, signed Dieter Wisliceny, in Wolfgang G. Schwanitz, *Amin al-Husaini und das Dritte Reich* (Lawrenceville, 2008), 1–6.

116. Affidavit of Dr. Rudolf Kastner at the Nuremberg trial, in e.g. Dalin and Rothman, *Icon of Evil*, 169.

117. The grand mufti might have sent the Jordanian Abu Ghanima, the Pal-

estinian Rasim al-Khalidi, or the Egyptian Mustafa al-Wakil to visit the camp, though this is less likely.

118. PArchAA, R100702, F1784–85, "Wunsch Kailanis ein KZ zu besichtigen," Berlin, June 26, 1942, signed Grobba; Grobba, report and doc. 1-2, in *Germany and the Middle East 1871–1945*, ed. Wolfgang G. Schwanitz (Princeton: Wiener, 2004), 218–220.

119. PArchWGS, Four-page handwritten affidavit from the Nuremberg trials, "Betr. Grossmufti von Jerusalem," July 26, 1946, signed Dieter Wisliceny, in Schwanitz, *Amin al-Husaini und das Dritte Reich*, 1–6.

120. Kilian Bartikowski, "Benito Mussolini," in *Handbuch des Antisemitismus*, ed. Wolfgang Benz, vol. 2.2 (Berlin: De Gruyter Saur, 2009), 569–571.

121. PArchWGS, "An von Ribbentrop (Botschafter Prüfer durch al-Husaini übergeben), Balkan Juden 500 Erwachsene und 4000 Kinder, Berlin 15.05.43, gez. al-Husaini."

122. Al-Husaini, radio broadcast to the Islamic world, Islamic New Year 1364, December 17, 1944, *Barid ash-Sharq* 6, no. 52 (1944): 3–6.

123. BArchPAA, 13300, B51442–43, "Aufzeichnung, Großmufti bei Steengracht, 4,000 jüdische Minderjährige und 500 Erwachsene aus Bulgarien nach Palästina verhindern, Bulgarien unternahm bereits entsprechenden Schritt, al-Husaini regt arabisch-islamische Abteilung im Auswärtigen Amt an, Berlin 17.05.43, gez. Prüfer."

124. USArchII, RG263, CIA B106, Card Index, Jews, Bulgaria, conversation of al-Husaini with the Bulgarian Ambassador, an order was issued to prevent the Jews from leaving Bulgaria, al-Husaini announced that he will forward a memo on the bad situation of Bulgarian Muslims, Berlin, June 16, 1943, 1.

125. Aronson, *Hitler, the Allies, and the Jews*, 228.

126. For the affidavit of Dr. Rudolf Kastner at Nuremberg see, e.g., Dalin and Rothmann, *Icon of Evil*, 169.

127. Al-Husaini, *Mudhakkirat*, 189–196.

128. Ibid. For al-Husaini's letter to the government of Budapest of June 28, 1943 see, e.g., The Nation Associates, ed., *The Arab Higher Committee, Its Origins, Personnel and Purposes: The Documentary Record. Submitted to the United Nations* (New York, May 1947), unpaginated.

129. Al-Husaini, *Mudhakkirat*, 196.

130. The Nation Associates, *The Arab Higher Committee*.

131. Al-Husaini, *Mudhakkirat*, 196–197.

132. PArchWGS, testimony of Hermann Krumey, Court of Justice, Frankfurt am Main, May 27, 1961, 1–2: "It has been pointed out to me that the 20 June 1942 teletype to Eichmann does not mention the term 'special treatment,' but that in my teletype to Ehlich, dated 22 June 1942, I dictated the following sentence: 'I have notified IVB4 of the transfer of these children, on the assumption that they are destined for special treatment.' I would like to state regarding that: I do not remember exactly what was in my mind when I drafted the teletype. It is my opinion that I did not then take the words 'special treatment' to mean extermination. I am sure that at that time I was not aware of and familiar with the term 'special treatment' in the sense of extermination. The children were a special matter within our camp operation and required a special treatment relative to our conditions. In using the

phrase, 'on the assumption that they are destined for special treatment,' I consider that I indicated that the children required to be given a special treatment, as they could not simply be included in our normal evacuation procedures, but would have, for example, to be accommodated in homes. I would explain the fact that I contacted Eichmann on this assumption by saying that his section, IVB4, was the office which, as far as I was concerned, was responsible here because of the aspect of transport. IVB4 always decided where our transports were to be sent. That is why I also inquired of them in this instance, since, after all, the children had to be evacuated from our camp, and I wanted to know where they were to go."

133. At the trial of Adolf Eichmann, Morning Session 50, Document 281, 1961, Prosecutor Steiner stated that Wisliceny had described conversations with Eichmann, Later Wisliceny made one correction: "I have read these descriptions and find them correct, except for this, that Eichmann was born in Palestine, and that the Mufti was a permanent partner of Himmler's; this is not what I said." The Nizkor Project, Session 50, http://www.nizkor.org/hweb/people/e/eichmann-adolf/transcripts/Sessions/Session-050-07.html.

134. According to Dieter Wisliceny: "The Mufti is one of the originators of the systematic destruction of European Jewry by the Germans, and he has become a permanent colleague, partner and adviser to Eichmann and Himmler in the implementation of this programme." Here Wisliceny adds: "I have read these descriptions and find them correct, except for this, that Eichmann was born in Palestine, and that the Mufti was a permanent partner of Himmler's; this is not what I said." The Nizkor Project, Session 50, http://www.nizkor.org/hweb/people/e/eichmann-adolf/transcripts/Sessions/Session-050-07.html.

135. PArchWGS, al-Husaini diary, 1944, entries for November 7, 9, and 10, 1944: "Eichmann."

136. ISArchJ, Mufti War Time Papers, B 186–89, report to von Ribbentrop regarding the Division of Arab and Muslim Volunteers, German press reports of November 2, 1944, and al-Husaini's presence in Berlin between November 2 and 9, 1944, where he met, among others, the head of the Middle Eastern desk Dr. Melchers, Oybin spa, December 11, 1944, signed al-Husaini.

137. Affidavit of Dr. Rudolf Kastner at Nuremberg trial in, e.g., Dalin and Rothman, *Icon of Evil*, 169.

138. Goebbels mentions a conversation between Hitler and himself on unrest in India, see Fröhlich, *Die Tagebücher von Joseph Goebbels* 1.4:621, entry for May 1, 1941.

139. Chris Hale, *Himmler's Crusade* (New York: Bantam, 2004), 284–300; Johannes Glasneck and Inge Kircheisen, *Türkei und Afghanistan: Brennpunkte der Orientpolitik im zweiten Weltkrieg* (Berlin: Deutscher Verlag der Wissenschaften, 1968), 206–208, 214–215.

140. Hale, *Himmler's Crusade*, 207–234.

141. USArchII, FMS, P-207, Fritz Grobba, "Supplement des Gesandten a.D. Dr. Fritz Grobba," in "German Exploitation of Arab National Movements in World War II" (see above, Chapter 4, note 61), 76: report on meeting of von Ribbentrop with Schäfer, von Hentig, and Grobba; ibid., addendum, 2: at the end of December 1939 von Ribbentrop had revived the Tibet project with the Soviets.

142. A Goebbels diary entry for April 20, 1941 mentions a report by the semiofficial German news agency Transocean of Moscow. Fröhlich, *Die Tagebücher von Joseph Goebbels* 1.4:597:.

143. Wilhelm Kohlhaas claims that Alfred Rosenberg likely opposed the joint Nazi-Soviet Amanullah project for ideological reasons, giving anti-Bolshevism priority, *Hitler-Abenteuer im Irak* (Freiburg: Herder, 1989), 12, 18, 23, 37. But there was a revival of that plan by the Abwehr and the SD in April of 1940; Glasneck and Kircheisen, *Türkei und Afghanistan*, 268.

144. Glasneck and Kircheisen, *Türkei und Afghanistan*, 213.

145. Grobba, "Supplement," 76; Flacker, "Fritz Grobba and Nazi Germany's Middle Eastern Policy, 1933–1942," 204; Kohlhaas, *Hitler-Abenteuer im Irak,* 12; Glasneck and Kircheisen, *Türkei und Afghanistan*, 213, 234–235.

146. USArchII, RG 338, FMS, P-207, General der Artillerie a.D. Walter Warlimont, "Die deutsche Ausnutzung der arabischen Eingeborenenbewegung im zweiten Weltkrieg," in "German Exploitation of Arab National Movements in World War II" (see Chapter 4, note 61), 152, 159.

147. USArchII, R901/61124, meeting of May 14, 1942, between von Ribbentrop, Grobba, and Felmy on political preparations for the German advance into Arab lands and the Indian Legion, "Geheime Kommandosache," Berlin, May 30, 1942, signed Grobba.

148. PArchAA, R27326, B367937–44, "Angriffe Radio Londons auf al-Husainis Appell an die Inder und indischen Muslime, Entgegnung al-Husainis, 13.09.42"; see Hans Lindemann, *Der Islam im Aufbruch, in Abwehr und Angriff* (Leipzig: Brandstetter, 1941), 74–75, on Hindus and Muslims in northwestern India.

149. USArchII, T120, R36, 28202, Grand Mufti's secret organization, principles, distribution, former officers and youth, 72 branches alone in India, 28.11.41, signed Grobba.

150. *Oriente Moderno* 22 (1942): 368–370; see also "Amin al-Husaini: Rundfunkrede an die Inder, Berlin, 22.08.1942," in *Mufti-Papiere*, ed. Gerhard Höpp (Schwarz: Berlin, 2001), 63–65.

151. USArchII T120, R392, S930, F297916, B367923–27, German Foreign Ministry, special files of Envoy Ettel, attached in the service of the grand mufti of Jerusalem, the Faqir of Ipi (also Faqir Ibi, al-Husaini, *Mudhakkirat,* 84–85), al-Husaini's Arabic letter, top secret, Berlin, January 18, 1943.

152. For Ashmawi, see Israel Gershoni and James Jankowski, *Egypt: Dictatorship versus Democracy in the 1930s* (Stanford: Stanford University Press, 2009), 220–223.

153. USArchII, RG263, CIA Records, Ent ZZ-18, B58–60 (2nd rel.), Cairo Station Files, report on Salih Mustafa Ashmawi's recent visit, his statement on April 19, Al-Ikhwan al-Muslimun, and messages of the grand mufti, secret, Cairo, April 27, 1943.

154. Al-Husaini, *Mudhakkirat,* 231.

155. Grobba, "Supplement," 35.

156. Jan Kuhlmann, *Subhash Chandra Bose und die Indienpolitik der Achsenmächte* (Berlin: Schiler, 2003), 318–322.

157. USArchII, T77, R1432, F698–699, Special Command F, letter to Meyer-Ricks on talks with Bose, Fauzi al-Qawuqji, and Kapp on a joint Arab-Indian Committee for a general uprising of Indian troops, based in Basra, Berlin, November 9, 1941, signed Krummacher.

158. Paul Leverkuehn, *Der geheime Nachrichtendienst der Wehrmacht im Kriege* (Frankfurt: Athenäum, 1964), 178–179.

159. Al-Husaini, *Mudhakkirat*, 104, 206–208; Kuhlmann, *Subhash Chandra Bose und die Indienpolitik der Achsenmächte*, 191, 232, 284, 317; Claudia Preckel, "Philosophers, Freedom Fighters, Pantomimes: South Asian Muslims in Germany," in *Islam and Muslims in Germany*, ed. Ala al-Hamarneh and Jörn Thielmann (Leiden: Brill, 2008), 308–309.

160. Al-Husaini, *Mudhakkirat*, 84–85.

161. Grobba, "Supplement," 76–78: Lebel, *The Mufti of Jerusalem*, 166: Faqir, Arabic for "poor," was a Dervish and Sufi honorific title, not a code name as Lebel suggested.

162. Lindemann, *Der Islam im Aufbruch*, 75.

163. Aga Khan, *Die Memoiren des Aga Khan: Welten und Zeiten* (Munich: Desch, 1954), 344.

164. Paul Schmidt, *Statist auf diplomatischer Bühne 1923–1945* (1949; reprint, Wiesbaden: Aula, 1984), 375.

165. H. R. Trevor-Roper, *Hitler's Table Talk 1941–1944*, rev. ed. (New York: Enigma, 2007), August 28, 1942, midday, 504.

166. PArchAA, R27649, B371052–53, "An Prinz Max Hohenlohe, Der Führer, Aga Khan, Fühlungnahmen und andere inoffizielle Kanäle nach England, Berlin, 24.07.1940, gez. Hewel."

167. PArchAA, R27649, B371041–42, "An Prinz Max Hohenlohe, Ihr Gespräch mit Aga Khan verwendet, interessiert uns, der Khan trägt doch zu sehr auf 2 Schultern, Berlin, 23.01.1941, gez. Hewel."

168. Aga Khan, *Die Memoiren des Aga Khan*, 432, 355, 357, 403.

169. PArchAA, R27649, B371054, "Hewels Notiz, Erkundungen seines Sekretärs über Aga Khan in der Schweiz und Gespräche mit ihm, September 1939, Skeptiker des britischen Kriegerfolgs, offener Polemiker, Rückwirkung auf Islam, grosse Stellung und Bedeutung die London Aga Khan beimisst, machtvolle Person, die Islam im Orient repräsentiert, seine Äußerungen verfolgen auch gewisse Zwecke, Berlin 24.07.1940."

170. PArchAA, R27649, B371052–53, "An Prinz Max Hohenlohe, Der Führer, Aga Khan, Fühlungnahmen und andere inoffizielle Kanäle nach England, Berlin, 24.07.1940, gez. Hewel."

171. PArchAA, R27649, B371044–46, "An Hewel, Prinz Max Hohenlohe über Treffen mit Aga Khan zu England, Indien und Mittelmeer, Zürich, 09.08.1940."

172. PArchAA, R27649, B371063–66, "An Hewel, Gespräch mit Aga Khan und Botschaft an den Führer, Khedive und König von Ägypten, Ägypten erobern, Kampf gegen England ist Kampf gegen die Juden, Istanbul an Russland, Schloss Rothenhaus bei Görkau, 25.07.1940, gez. Max Hohenlohe."

173. PArchAA, R27649, B371048–49, "An Hewel, Max Hohenlohes Memorandum über Aufenthalt in der Schweiz 04.–10.08.1940 zu England Coventri-

sieren und Blockade, USA Kriegeintritt, Aga Khan, Geldschwierigkeiten, Pariser Rennpferde, iranischer Staatsbürger."

174. Lindemann, *Der Islam im Aufbruch*, 24.

175. Al-Husaini, *Mudhakkirat*, 179–186; Grobba, "Supplement," 89.

176. Lindemann, *Der Islam im Aufbruch*, 16; Paul Schmitz-Kairo, *All-Islam: Weltmacht von morgen?* (Leipzig: Goldmann, 1937; 2d ed., 1942), 243–244.

177. See also IArchStJ, B919, Arabic letter to Japan's foreign minister, signed "Amin al-Husaini, Rais al-Muatamar al-Islami al-Alami [President of the Islamic World Conference]."

178. ISArchJ, Mufti War Time Papers, B917–18, note to Foreign Minister of Japan regarding the Islamic Liberation Army and a pact between the Islamic leadership and Japan, Berlin, June 22, 1944, signed Amin al-Husaini; Arabic letter of al-Husaini to the Muslims of Japan, with an appeal and condolences on the occasion of the passing of the mufti Abd ar-Rashid Ibrahim, in The Nation Associates, ed., *Le Haut Comité Arabe: Ses origines, ses membres, ses buts. Documents d' archives soumis aux Nations Unies en mai 1947* (New York: Nation Associates, 1947), 57.

179. Al-Husaini, *Mudhakkirat*, 180–84.

180. Al-Husani's Arabic radio broadcast on the occasion of the Muhammad's birth, March 1944, in *Barid ash-Sharq* 6, no. 53 (1944): 7–9.

181. BArchB, Reichsführer SS, F3347, B2576076–77, "al-Husaini's Aufruf und Flugblätter an Araber in alliierten Heeren, Berlin, Oybin 23.01.45"; USArchBDC, Special File 6, Grand Mufti, 1–2; NS 19/2637, B39–40.

182. BArchBe, AA, NS19/2181, Reichsführer SS, "An Brandt, Treffen Großmufti-Goebbels, Goebbels-Hitler, geheime Kommandosache, Grunewald, 27.05.44," 2–3.

183. Grobba, "Supplement," 69.

184. Ibid.

185. USArchII, CIC Reports, Grand Mufti's Hidden Documents, Confidential, December 1, 1944, 1–2; CIB Files, Grand Mufti, Bad Gastein Report, March 11, 1945, 1; USArchII, CIC Reports, al-Husaini, al-Kailani, and Abwehr II, May 22, 1945, 1.

186. PArchWGS, al-Husaini's timeline and program of visits in the Muslim Indian Shababiyya military camps for the Arab Legion, January 20, 1945, 1.

187. Al-Husaini, *Mudhakkirat*, 153–154.

188. PArchWGS, letter to Nahum Goldmann regarding Eichmann, al-Husaini, Argentina, and Linz, March 30, 1954, signed Simon Wiesenthal, 1–4.

189. Foreign Ministry agreement with Amin al-Husaini, April 5, 1945, in Schwanitz, *Gold, Bankiers und Diplomaten: Zur Geschichte der Deutschen Orientbank 1906–1946* (Berlin: Trafo, 2002), 294.

CHAPTER 9. A BID FOR PARTNERSHIP IN THE AXIS

1. See, e.g., the grand mufti's and his aides' articles on India in *Barid ash-Sharq*, especially "Wathia'q an mauqif muslimi al-Hind" [The truth about Muslims of India], ibid., 47 (1943): 18.

2. BArchB, F4925, B390798–04, Al-Husaini to Ettel complaining of Minister Grobba's indiscretions, October 1942.

3. USArchII, T120, R901, 61125, B30, Canaris on spy centralization by al-Husaini in North Africa, Rome, September 15, 1942.

4. Donald M. McKale, *Curt Prüfer: German Diplomat from the Kaiser to Hitler* (Kent, Ohio: Kent State University Press, 1987), 197, 33.

5. Amin Al-Husaini, *Mudhakkirat al-Hajj Muhammad Amin al-Husaini* [The memoirs of al-Hajj Muhammad Amin al-Husaini], ed. Abd al-Karim al-Umar (Damascus: Al-Ahali, 1999), 119.

6. In late October 1942 Schellenberg's title was head of the security police and the security service, SD.

7. PArchAA, R27325, B390752–53, "Handakte des Gesandten Ettel, Ag. Ausland Nr. 1903/42, geh. Kds. Ausl. II, A2, Amt Ausland Abwehr, Notiz, Betrifft: Mufti als Mitarbeiter, Bericht des VO/Mufti Rom Nr. 10/42g, 11/20/42, Notiz, Vier Gründe Mufti auf der Seite der Achse, Geheime Kommandosache 2/12/42, 5/11/42."

8. BArchPAA, F15557, B368056–60, October 20, 1942, report on details of al-Husaini's Greater Arab Empire as told to the Italians and Germans on September 15, 1942.

9. Al-Husaini, *Mudhakkirat*, 121.

10. PArchWGS, Office Of Chief Of Council For War Crimes, Doc. No. NG-5462–5570, "Eidesstattliche Erklärung" (on financial affairs of Germany's Arab guests] of Carl Rekowski, October 5, 1947, 8, 10.

11. USArchII, FMS, P-207, Fritz Grobba, "Supplement des Gesandten a.D. Dr. Fritz Grobba," in "German Exploitation of Arab National Movements in World War II" (see above, Chapter 4, note 61), 75.

12. See also The Nation Associates, ed., *The Arab Higher Committee, Its Origins, Personnel and Purposes: The Documentary Record. Submitted to the United Nations* (New York, May 1947), unpaginated.

13. PArchAA, Personalakte Grobba, I-IV, 4828, IV (1939–45), "Besoldung-Bezüge, Berlin 05.01.40, gez. Diederich."

14. Ibid.

15. USArchII, T120, R28541, 28202, UStS/Pol. Nr. 959, November 6, 1941.

16. Jennie Lebel, *The Mufti of Jerusalem: Haj-Amin el-Husseini and National-Socialism* (Belgrade: Čigoja Stampa, 2007), 153.

17. USArchII, T120, R901, 61125, B42–43, Ribbentrop, Al-Kailiani, Felmy, (2.) "Militärabommen mit dem Oberkommando der Wehrmacht über die Verwendung des arabischen Freiheitscorps, unterzeichnet am 12.09.42 in Rom, Großmufti erhielt Kopie, Geheime Reichssache, Berlin 13.01.43, gez. Prüfer."

18. USArchII, T77, R1432, F565–689, Special Command F, Adil Azma to Fauzi al-Qawuqji on conversations regarding a draft of a pact with Germany in Baghdad, Istanbul, September 15, 1941 (completed after September 20, 1941), 12: conversations in Istanbul between September 6 and 20, 1941 in a group to which Rashid Ali al-Kailani belonged; USArchII, T120, R63, S71, F50682, B50971–75, report to Woermann on Arab drafts of pacts of friendship and alliance between the Axis powers and Iraq, Syria, Lebanon, and Transjordan, including seven para-

graphs of a draft of a pact between Germany, Italy, and Iraq, signed by Rashid Ali al-Kailani, Naji Shaukat, Muhammad Hasan Salman, Berlin, December 12, 1941, signed Grobba.

19. The grand mufti used in German the term "Präsident des islamischen Welt-kongresses" (president of the Islamic World Congress, Rais al-Muatamar al-Islami al-Aam, or later, al-Alami), although the original name was the General Islamic Congress; also in PArchWGS, letter to von Ribbentrop, Oybin, December 11, 1944, signed Al-Husaini, 3.

20. Lebel, *The Mufti of Jerusalem*, 227.

21. BArchPAA, F41796, E260921–24, April 14, 1942.

22. USArchII, OSS 61, Master Cards, al-Kailani in Hitler's Near East Council, advisory body, August 20, September 30, 1942.

23. BArchPAA, F16096, "Al-Qanun al-Asasi li-Hizb al-Umma al-Arabiyya [Statute of the Arab Nation Party]," point 3: "Tard al-Yahud min al-Buldan al-Arabiyya wa muharabat al-Yahudiyya al-Alamiyya [Driving Jews out of Arab lands and fighting against world Jewry]." See also Al-Husaini's handwritten Arabic letter to Naji Shaukat about the founding of a secret organization in Baghdad in February 1942, including codenames, Rome, September 28, 1942, signed Amin Al Husaini.

24. USArchII, T120, R63, S71, F50682, B51112, mentions the grand mufti's Pan-Arab flag as a black, white, and green triangle with a red triangle at the staff, Berlin, April 22, 1942.

25. USArchII, T120, R901, 61125, B28, September 15, 1942.

26. BArchAAP, F61124, B49–50, August 14, 1942.

27. PArchAA, Inland IIg 410, F2842, B393064–66, December 16, 1943.

28. PArchAA, R27326, B367937–44, September 13, 1942; Hans Lindemann, *Der Islam im Aufbruch, in Abwehr und Angriff* (Leipzig: Brandstetter, 1941), 74–75.

29. BArchAAL, F4170, "An U.St.S. Henke, Aufzeichnung über Besuch der Sachbearbeiter Dr. Boehm und Hofheinz für islamische Fragen im SS-Hauptamt, Großmufti, AA Referat für islamische Fragen und Erwin Ettel, Berlin 03.03.44."

30. Elke Fröhlich, ed., *Die Tagebücher von Joseph Goebbels: Sämtliche Fragmente*, 23 vols. (Munich: Saur, 1987–2008), 1.3:589–591.

31. BArchBe, AA, NS19/2181, Reichsführer SS, "An Brandt, Treffen Großmufti-Goebbels, Goebbels-Hitler, geheime Kommandosache, Grunewald, 5/27/44," 2–3, gez. Berger."

32. Fröhlich, *Die Tagebücher von Joseph Goebbels*, 2.12:188–89.

33. BArchAAL, F13300, An Steengracht, Aufzeichnung Prüfer [Grand Mufti honorary president of the Islamic Central Institute of Berlin], Berlin 17.05.43, gez. Prüfer; PArchWGS, Talk, al-Husaini, Gerhard von Mende, Mullah Institutes Armed Forces and SS, secret, Oybin, 27.07.44, 3, signed von Mende.

34. The Rome institute was established by the Societá Amici dell'India, Istituto Italiano per il Medio ed Estremo Oriente, on April 29, 1942, Jan Kuhlmann, *Subhash Chandra Bose und die Indienpolitik der Achsenmächte* (Berlin: Schiler, 2003), 232; see also Ranjan Borra, "Subhash Chandra Bose, The Indian National Army, and the War of India's Liberation," *Journal of Historical Review* 3 (1982): 407–439.

35. Gerhard Höpp, *Muslime in der Mark: Als Kriegsgefangene und Internierte*

in Wünsdorf und Zossen, 1914–1924 (Berlin: Arabisches Buch, 1997); Lebel, *The Mufti of Jerusalem,* 224–225, 240.

36. "Der Großmufti über den Befreiungskampf des Islams," *Deutsche Allgemeine Zeitung,* December 19, 1942, 1.

37. Hitler, *Mein Kampf* (Boston: Mariner, 1999), 357, 455, and 552.

38. "Der Großmuftii über den Befreiungskampf des Islams," *Deutsche Allgemeine Zeitung,* December 19, 1942.

39. "Dieser Krieg kann dem Islam die Freiheit bringen: Großmufti von Jerusalem and die Muslime der Welt," *Völkischer Beobachter,* December 20, 1942, 4; "Der Großmufti über den Befreiungskampf des Islams," *Deutsche Allgemeine Zeitung,* December 19, 1942, 1.

40. PArchWGS, Aktennotiz Dr. Koeppen, "Aufgabengebiet 'Überstaatliche Mächte,' Großmufti, Reichsleiter Rosenberg, Araber und Bezeichnung Antisemitismus, Berlin, 5/17/43, gez. Dienstleiter Hans Hagemeyer."

41. Al-Husaini, *Mudhakkirat,* 161; *Weltkampf* was published by the Hoheneichen Verlag in Munich for the Hohe Schule, Außenstelle Frankfurt am Main.

42. PArchWGS, Office Of Chief Of Council For War Crimes, Doc. No. NG-5462–5570, "Eidesstattliche Erklärung" of Carl Rekowski, October 5, 1947, 6.

43. PArchWGS, "An Rosenberg, Rosenbergs Artikel im *Völkischen Beobachter* 'Schmarotzerschutz: Heilige Pflicht der Demokratien.'" Berlin, August 2, 1944.

44. Lebel, *The Mufti of Jerusalem,* 240, suggested, perhaps following Kamal ad-Din Jalal, that the grand mufti got his "Points of Contact between Islam and National Socialism" from Rosenberg. This is unlikely. The stump speech about those points contains chosen verses of al-Qur'an and hadith that Rosenberg could not have known. The language of al-Husaini's speeches was inspired, even in wording, however, by Hitler's writings and speeches. Al-Husaini was often invited to Hitler's public speeches, and received translations of others in writing.

45. Zvonimir Bernwald's testimony is in the TV show by Stefan Meining, "The Pact between Radical Muslims and Hitler." German ARD, Report Munich, July 17, 2006, 5.41 min; Lebel, *The Mufti of Jerusalem,* 231.

46. PArchWGS, al-Husaini's stump speech, "Islam and National Socialism," 1943, 5, and "Rede vor den Imamen der bosnischen SS-Division, 04.10.44," 5; see also Gerhard Höpp, ed., *Mufti-Papiere* (Berlin: Schwarz, 2001), 218–222.

47. "Gemeinnutz geht vor Eigennutz" was part of the NSDAP program of 1920. The mint of Berlin produced one-reichsmark coins with this legend from 1934 on.

48. BArchP, AA, R27327, 298019–23; HA Ettel 6, 207; TL 15451.

49. PArchWGS, "Aktennotiz Dr. Koeppen, Aufgabengebiet 'Überstaatliche Mächte,'"Großmufti, Reichsleiter Rosenberg, Araber und Bezeichnung Antisemitismus, Berlin, 17.05.43, gez. Dienstleiter Hans Hagemeyer."

50. Grobba, "Supplement," 27; *Weltkampf: Die Judenfrage in Geschichte und Gegenwart,* no. 3 (1944): 168 (inquiry by Rashid Ali al-Kailani and response by Prof. Dr. Walter Groß of the NSDAP Office of Racial Policy, October 17, 1942; Groß explains that term "anti-Semite" is incorrect and that "anti-Jewish" ("Judengegner") is preferable and adds that the expression "anti-Semitism" is also incorrect, since it would apply to Arabs and other speakers of Semitic languages); see also Lebel, *The Mufti of Jerusalem,* 239.

51. Grobba, "Supplement," 27.

52. "Araber und Muslime befinden sich im Krieg mit dem Judentum," Radio Berlin, January 28, 1944, in Jeffrey Herf, "Hitlers Dschihad," *Vierteljahreshefte für Zeitgeschichte*, no. 2 (2010): 259–86.

53. Muhammad Sabri, *Islam-Judentum-Bolschewismus* (Berlin: Juncker & Dünnhaupt, 1938), 5–21, including Amin Al-Husaini, "Islam-Judentum: Aufruf des Großmuftis an die islamische Welt 1937," 22–32; for Sabri see also Gerhard Höpp, *Texte aus der Fremde* (Berlin: Arabisches Buch, 2000), 75–77.

54. For instance, for Bosniaks in SS units, see Veliki Muftija Jeruzalemski, *Islam i židovstvo* [Islam and Jewry] (Zagreb: Croat Printing, 1943); see also Lebel, *The Mufti of Jerusalem*, 312.

55. Sabri, *Islam-Judentum-Bolschewismus*, 19–20: He quoted the French Communist Jean Barthel: "If Muhammad were alive today, he would be a Communist."

56. Ibid.

57. "Tötet die Juden bevor sie euch töten, Stimme des Freien Arabertums," 7.07.42, in Jeffrey Herf, "Hitler's Dschihad," in *Vierteljahreshefte für Zeitgeschichte*, (2010) 2, 274.

58. Al-Husaini, *Mudhakkirat*, 160–161.

59. PArchWGS, Deutsches Historisches Institut Moskau, "Dienstkalender Heinrich Himmler 1943–1944, Auszüge, Termine des Reichsführer-SS am 4. Juli 1943 (Hochwald)," 329; rechts unten abgezeichnet 'Gro[othmann]'; Programm für den Besuch Seiner Eminenz des Groß-Mufti am 4. Juli 1943 in der Feld-Kommandostelle des Reichsführer-SS, 10.45–17.50 Uhr, 530–531, links unten gez. voll 'Grothmann', darin dessen handschriftliche Ergänzung einer Uhrzeit, 15.30 Uhr: Abholung des Gastes durch den Reichsführer-SS in seiner Wohnung. Darin sind erwähnt al-Husainis diverse Termine mit SS-Sturmbannführer Grothmann, SS-Obergruppenführer Berger, SS-Gruppenführer Best, SS-Obergruppenführer von dem Bach, SS-Brigadeführer von Herff, SS-Brigadeführer von Scholz, SS-Obersturmbannführer Tiefenbacher, SS-Obersturmbannführer Brandt, SS-Standartenführer Rode und Major Wiederhold." We are thankful to Rainer Karlsch, Wladimir J. Sacharow, and Matthias Uhl for locating these documents.

60. Al-Husaini, *Mudhakkirat*, 124; Paul Schmidt, *Statist auf diplomatischer Bühne 1923–1945* (1949; reprint, Wiesbaden: Aula, 1984), 543–544.

61. Simon Wiesenthal, *Großmufti, Großagent der Achse* (Salzburg, Ried 1947), 45: Wiesenthal relies on a statement by Dieter Wisliceny of January 26, 1946.

62. BArchAAP, F4191, B408995, Sonder, Telegramm Nr. 2864, "Winkelmann teilt Ankunft al-Husaini am 07.10.1944 in Budapest mit, insgesamt sechs Personen, bittet mich, für Betreuung zu sorgen, unbekannt, was er machen soll, ob Besuch politischer Charakter und Sprachregelung zu erwarten [handschriftliche Randnotiz: RAM hat fernmündlich Westfalen, A[lois] Brunner (Sonderzug Westfalen, Büro von Ribbentrops Dienstzug—WGS) gebeten, dieses Telegramm nicht oder wenigstens gleichzeitig mit Vortragsnotizen dem RAM vorzulegen, 06.10.], Budapest, 05.10.44, gez. [Edmund] Veesenmayer."

63. Peter Z. Malkin and Harry Stein, *Eichmann in My Hands* (New York: Warner, 1990), 38.

64. Al-Husaini, *Mudhakkirat*, 159.

65. David G. Dalin and John F. Rothman, *Icon of Evil* (New York: Random

House, 2008), 57–59; Raul Hillberg, *The Destruction of the European Jews,* rev. ed. (New York: Holmes & Meier, 1985), 504–505.

66. Jean-Claude Pressac and Serge Klarsfeld, eds., *The Struthof Album Study of the Gassing at Natzweiler-Struthof of 86 Jews Whose Bodies Were to Constitute a Collection of Skeletons: A Photographic Document* (New York: The Beate Klarsfeld Foundation, 1985).

67. According to Hitler's instruction of December 12, 1941. See also Heinrich Himmler's activities schedule, Berlin, December 18, 1941; Volker Ullrich, "Hitlers bösester Befehl," *Die Zeit,* August 1, 1998, 29; Otto Bräutigam, *So hat es sich zugetragen: Ein Leben als Soldat und Diplomat* (Würzburg: Holzner, 1968), 599.

68. Ernst Jäckh, "Deutsch-türkische Interessengemeinschaft," in *Der Schwabenspiegel,* September 22, 1909; Jäckh, "Der Schwabe Friedrich List als Orient-Prophet," ibid., December 2, 1910; Jäckh, "Friedrich Lists deutsch-englische Orientprophetie," ibid., April 14, 1910.

69. Al-Husaini, *Mudhakkirat,* 126–127.

70. Ibid., 171.

71. PArchWGS, Deutsches Historisches Institut Moskau, Dienstkalender Heinrich Himmler 1943–1944, Auszüge, "Termine des Reichsführer-SS am 8. Mai 1944, 14.00–23.00 Uhr, 385; rechts unten gez. kurz 'Gro[thmann],' darin aufgeführt al-Husainis diverse Termine mit SS-Obergruppenführer Berger, SS-Standartenführer Wagner, SS-Sturmbannführer Weibrecht, SS-Gruppenführer Johst, SS-Sturmbannführer Grothmann, SS-Brigadeführer Fegelein, General Reinecke und Oberst Westhoff; handschriftlich Uhrzeit des Treffens al-Husainis mit Berger '23.00 Uhr' nachgetragen [durch Grothmann]."

72. Al-Husaini, *Mudhakkirat,* 124–125.

73. Ibid., 124.

74. Astrid Ley and Günther Morsch, *Medizin und Verbrechen: Das Krankenrevier des KZ Sachsenhausen 1936–1945* (Berlin: Metropol, 2007), 392.

75. PArchWGS, diary of Amin al-Husaini 1944, entries for November 7, 9, and 10, 1944: "Eichmann."

76. For a detailed discussion of these themes in PLO propaganda, see Barry Rubin, *The PLO Between Anti-Zionism and Antisemitism* (Jerusalem: Hebrew University Sassoon Center, 1993).

77. This account is taken from the postwar interrogation of Erich Mansfeld, USArchII, RG338, and 238, M1270, July 30, 1945.

CHAPTER 10. THE WAR AFTER THE WAR

1. Barry Rubin, *The Arab States and the Palestine Conflict* (Syracuse: Syracuse University Press, 1982), 133–147.

2. USArchII, RG226, OSS L42785, May 4, 1944; L32219, August 15, 1944; ad L44470, August 17, 1944. See also OSS 89863, August 9, 1944. Detailed minutes of the meeting are in OSS 101239, October 12, 1944; OSS 95754, Henderson to Stettinius, September 1, 1944; and OSS 11401, January 18, 1945.

3. An excellent analysis of wartime Palestinian politics is in OSS 54614, January 6, 1944.

4. For the text of the Palestine resolution, see Jacob C. Hurewitz, *Struggle for*

Palestine (New York: Greenwood Press, 1968), 192; OSS L52078, December 29, 1944.

5. King Abdallah of Transjordan, *Memoirs* (New York: Cape, 1950), 253.

6. USArchII, RG263, CIA, NF, EnZZ-18, B58–60, security summaries to the effect that the mufti hopes soon to publish files refuting false accusations on his alleged pro-Axis activities as spread by the Jews, June 9, 1947.

7. *Life,* October 27, 1952.

8. Joseph B. Schechtman, *The Mufti and the Fuehrer* (New York: Yoseloff, 1965), 163.

9. PArchWGS, "Schnellbrief, An Staatspolizei(leit)stellen, Inspekteure der Sicherheitspolizei und des SD im Altreich und Wien, Evakuierung von Juden, Geheim," Berlin, January 31, 1942, signed Eichmann, 1: "The most recently started measures and the evacuation of Jews to different areas in the East are to be regarded as the start of the final solution of the Jewish question. . . ."

10. Amin Al-Husaini, *Mudhakkirat al-Hajj Muhammad Amin al-Husaini* [The memoirs of al-Hajj Muhammad Amin al-Husaini], ed. Abd al-Karim al-Umar (Damascus: Al-Ahali, 1999), 128.

11. USArchII, CIA, NF, RG263, EnZZ-18, B14, "Interrogation of PW Dieter Wisliceny on the German SD and the persecution of Jews 1933–44, Confidential," August 27, 1945, signed Kurt Sichel.

12. Adolf Eichmann, "I Transported Them To The Butcher: Eichmann's Own Story," pt. 1, *Life,* November 28, 1960. The former SS officer Willem M. Sassen recorded interviews with Eichmann on sixty-seven tapes in 1955, and two excerpts appeared in *Life* magazine in 1960. Based on it, the filmmaker Raymond Ley produced a ninety-minute documentary drama, *Eichmanns Ende: Liebe, Verrat, Tod,* for ARD TV which aired in Germany on July 25, 2010.

13. Al-Husaini, *Mudhakkirat,* 163.

14. USArchII, RG263, CIA, NF, EnZZ-18, B58–60, CIC Reports, instruction to 12th Army Group that eleven al-Husaini–related persons are to be apprehended, giving place of residence so far as known, profession, place and date of birth: Safwat al-Husaini (farmer, Jerusalem, October 20, 1900), Salim al-Husaini (journalist, Jerusalem, November 16, 1913), Sad ad-Din Abd al-Latif (*waqf* director, Jerusalem, April 9, 1999), Dr. Farhan Jandali (eye doctor, Khums, April 3, 1918, with wife and child), Dr. Zafir Hifni (lawyer, Aleppo, October 10, 1908), Dr. Maruf ad-Dawalibi (jurist, Aleppo, December 15, 1904, with wife and child), Ramzi al-Ajati (engineer, Aleppo, October 1, 1906), Fauzi Mudarris (farmer, Aleppo, May 10, 1913) Yusuf Rushdi (journalist, Tunis, July 15, 1907), Baha Tabba (merchant, Beirut, May 21, 1904), hardly legible entry (likely bodyguard Habib Hasan, chauffeur, Beirut, March 15, 1912), secret, June 5, 1945; add to this Hasan Abu as-Saud, secret, June 17, 1945.

15. Al-Husaini, *Mudhakkirat,* 128–129; David G. Dalin, *Hitler's Pope* (Washington, D.C.: Regnery, 2001), 137; an unpublished manuscript by Yigal Carmon tells the story of the American officer who took over al-Husaini's archive in Berlin.

16. The Nation Associates, ed., *The Arab Higher Committee, Its Origins, Personnel and Purposes: The Documentary Record. Submitted to the United Nations* (New York, May 1947), 2; Al-Husaini, *Mudhakkirat,* 128.

17. Tom Segev, *Simon Wiesenthal: The Life and Legends* (New York: Doubleday, 2010), 394–96; Simon Wiesenthal, *Ich jagte Eichmann* (Gütersloh: Mohn, 1961), 19.

18. Wiesenthal, *Ich jagte Eichmann*, 26, 44–45.

19. Simon Wiesenthal, *Großmufti, Großagent der Achse* (Salzburg: Ried, 1947).

20. ArhJugBG, Inv. Br. 553, 574–173, memorandum to the State Department to take the initiative to indict al-Husaini as a war criminal and issue instructions to the War Crimes Commission, for he was a major supporter of the Axis and was directly involved in the murder of millions of Jews in Europe, New York, mid-1945, 1–6.

21. Jennie Lebel, *The Mufti of Jerusalem: Hajj Amin al-Husaini and National Socialism* (Belgrade: Čigoja Stampa, 2007), 232–233; Alexandr Danilov, "Postsoviet Transformation: From Chaos of Revolutions to Democracy with Human Face," in *States and Nations between Local and Global,* ed. International Sociological Association (Moscow: Russian State University for Humanities, 2009), 31: Hussein Djozo, "Đihad," *Glasnik vrhovnog islamskog starješinstva u SFRJ* [Journal of the Islamic community elders in the Federal Republic of Yugoslavia] (1973): 7–8; Ibrahim Dzafic, *Der Korankommentar von Husein Djozo (1912–1982)* (Marburg: Tectum, 2008).

22. Lebel, *The Mufti of Jerusalem*, 260–264; Schechtman, *The Mufti and the Fuehrer*, 175.

23. USArchII, RG263, CIA, NF, EnZZ-18, B58–60, security summaries, report that Sad ad-Din Arif of the Arab Higher Committee, a leading arms smuggler, met al-Husaini to draw money for supplies and weapons, that Ahmad Hilmi approved and checks were signed by Ishaq Darwish, September 4, 1945.

24. USArchII, RG263, CIA Name Files, EnZZ-18, B58–60, security summaries, report of grand mufti's arrest (AP), London, May 21, 1945.

25. USArchII, RG263, CIA Name Files, IN 36881.

26. USArchII, RG263, CIA Name Files, ISLD telegram, report of a new French policy in the Levant involving a mutually convenient agreement between Paris and al-Husaini, Beirut, August 28, 1945.

27. USArchII, RG263, CIA Name Files, Jane Burell, Washington, D.C., March 7, 1946; al-Husaini, *Mudhakkirat*, 38, 48, 233.

28. For details see Schechtman, *The Mufti and the Fuehrer*, 169–174.

29. USArchII, RG263, CIA NF, EnZZ-18, B58–60, security summaries, report on the grand mufti, Jane Burell, Washington, D.C., March 7, 1946.

30. Justice Robert H. Jackson, *New York Post*, June 18, 1946; see also Schechtman, *The Mufti and the Fuehrer*, 181; al-Husaini, *Mudhakkirat*, 253–254.

31. The United Zionist Revisionists of America, Statement, al-Husaini and the U.S. Administration, mid-1946, reprinted in Schechtman, *The Mufti and the Fuehrer*, 180; see also al-Husaini, *Mudhakkirat*, 252–253; the World Jewish Congress proposed that Eichmann be tried at Nuremberg in part regarding his close contacts with al-Husaini; see Segev, *Simon Wiesenthal*, 113.

32. USArchII, RG263, CIA, NF, EnZZ-18, B58–60, security summaries, report on censorship of the *New Yorker Morgen Journal*'s accusations against al-Husaini concerning the extermination of Jews and demanding his trial as a war criminal, Cairo, June 25, 1945.

33. Andrew Roth, "The Mufti's New Army," *The Nation,* November 16, 1946, 551–52.

34. *New York Post,* April 20, 1946.

35. The quote by al-Banna is at the end of page 28 and the beginning of page 29 (see footnote 86). Footnote 54 reads: "Hassan al-Banna and the Mufti of Palestine" in "Contents of Secret Bulletin of Al-Ikhwan al-Muslimin dated 11 June 1946," Cairo (23 July 1946). NARA RG 226 (Office of Strategic Services) Washington Registry SI Intelligence, Field Files, Entry 108A, 190/16/28/3–7, Box 15, Folder 2.

36. Al-Husaini, *Mudhakkirat,* 392, 427.

37. Ibid., 73, 259, 334, 390–393.

38. Ibid., 334–335; Benny Morris, 1948: *A History of the First Arab-Israeli War* (New Haven: Yale University Press, 2008), 101.

39. ArchBStU, XAXXII, 18852, "Profile terroristischer Gruppen, Berlin, 1/3/89," 54–55.

40. Al-Husaini, *Mudhakkirat,* 73, 259, 334, 390–393.

41. Ibid., 427, 438. 493.

42. Morris, 1948, 121, 152–53. According to Morris, Salama, for example, had a German adviser who was killed in battle on April 5, 1948.

43. For a detailed discussion of these issues in the 1930s and 1940s, along with documentation for these assertions, see Rubin, *The Arab States and the Palestine Conflict.*

44. Barry Rubin and Judith Colp Rubin, *Yasir Arafat: A Political Biography* (New York: Oxford University Press, 2003), 14–17.

45. Gamal Abd El Nasser, *Die Philosophie der Revolution* (Cairo: Mondiale, 1953), 62.

46. USArchII, RG263, CIA, B58–60, Biographic report on al-Husaini mentioning his twenty Palestinian bodyguards, secret, Washington, D.C., November 19, 1951, 3.

47. USArchII, RG263, CIA, B58–60, Biographic report on al-Husaini, Habib Hasan, al-Husaini's declining power, and his four close advisers, secret, Beirut, January 30, 1950; on al-Husaini's habits and his mysterious [Soviet] visitors between midnight and three in Cairo, secret, Beirut, May 19, 1950.

48. Al-Husaini, *Mudhakkirat,* 185–187.

49. USArchII, RG263, CIA, B58–60, Ex-Mufti and his supporters, Middle East and Pakistan, confidential, Washington only, Cairo, November 26, 1951, 1–2.

50. USArchII, RG263, CIA, B58–60, report on al-Husaini, Sukkar, Ramadan, al-Kashani, and terrorist circles, secret, Beirut, September 27, 1951. USArchII, RG263, CIA Records, Ent ZZ-18, B58–60 (2nd rel.), report on accomplices in King Abdallah's assassination fleeing to the Gaza strip, July 31, 1951, 1; report on activities of the former grand mufti and the Arab Higher Executive, and on the leader of the mufti's terrorist organizations in various countries, Abdullah at-Tal, secret, Beirut, September 27, 1951, 1–2; report that Egypt's officials consider the mufti deeply involved in the assassination of King Abdullah, secret, Cairo, October 12, 1951, 1. The assassination of as-Sulh has been historically attributed to the

Syrians based only on newspaper speculation, but the CIA concluded that it had been done by al-Husaini's men, also Syrians.

51. See Chapter Eleven.

52. Al-Husaini, *Mudhakkirat*, 84–86.

53. USArchII, RG263, CIA, B58–60, report on al-Husaini's use of funds from Pakistan, Alluba, and Khaliq az-Zaman, July 23, 1950; Alluba, funds transfer, Permanent Islamic Congress, August 24, 1950.

54. USArchII, RG263, CIA, B58–60, Biographic report on al-Husaini, al-Kashani, and the Soviets, secret, Washington, D.C., November 19, 1951, 5.

55. USArchII, RG263, CIA, B58–60, report on al-Husaini, the Jamiyyat Fidaiy-yun al-Filastin, and al-Kashani's role on its board, secret, Karachi, April 25 and May 13, 1952.

56. USArchII, RG263, CIA, B58–60, report on al-Husaini, the Arab League delegation to Bonn, and counterintelligence, Washington, D.C., September 11, 1952, 1–3.

57. Ibid.

58. USArchII, RG263, CIA, B58–60, report on al-Husaini, the Arab Higher Committee, the Muslim Brothers, al-Kashani, security information, and the Levant States, July–August 1951, 1–2; Biographic Report, Al-Husaini, relations with al-Kashani, secret, Washington, D.C., January 5, 1952, 2, 4–5; report on Islamic World Congress in Jerusalem, March 12–December 9, 1953; report on al-Husaini and al-Kashani in Lebanon, confidential, Beirut, December 1, 1953, signed Raymond A. Hare.

59. USArchII, RG263, CIA, B58–60, report on al-Husaini's new intelligence service with Egyptian officials, secret, Beirut, January 8, 1951.

60. USArchII, RG263, CIA, B58–60, report on al-Husaini's assassins against collaborators in all Arab lands, May 26, 1949; on al-Husaini's remarks that if U.S. and Britain stay out, the Arabs will liquidate Israel and on World War III, June 23, 1951, 2.

61. USArchII, RG263, CIA, B58–60, al-Hajj Amin al-Husaini, Biographic Sketch No. 60, April 24, 1951, 6.

62. Aidar Khairutdinov, *Musa Dzharullakh Bigiev* (Kazan': Fan, 2005), 81–83; see also Batyr Baishev, documentary film *And the Moon was Glowing* on the Tatar philosopher Musa Jarullah Bigi (1875–1941). There is some debate, however, over the identity of Wiesenthal's main informant. See Segev, *Simon Wiesenthal*, 88–89; Wiesenthal, *Ich jagte Eichmann*, 137.

63. Wiesenthal, *Ich jagte Eichmann*, 135.

64. Ibid., 140, 148–149.

65. Amtsgericht Hamburg, Vereinsregister, 69 VR AR 112154, Gründungsprotokoll Deutsche-Muslim-Liga, Hamburg, January 30, 1954, 1–3.

66. USArchII, RG263, CIA NF, EnZZ-18, B30–31, Eichmann, letter to Nahum Goldmann on Eichmann, al-Husaini, Argentina, and Dr. Ibn Ajma Bey Bigi, Linz, March 30, 1954, signed Simon Wiesenthal, 3.

67. Wiesenthal, *Ich jagte Eichmann*, 149.

68. Ibid., 138, 155.

CHAPTER 11. THE ARAB STATES' USEFUL NAZIS

1. USArchII, RG263, CIA, NF, EnZZ-16, B80, report on von Leers, statement of Cesar Ugarte Jr., April 29, 1965, 1–2.

2. USArchII, RG263, CIA, NF., EnZZ-18, B58–60, Regional Security Officer, memorandum on Cesar Ugarte, Odessa, Nazis, Lists, Cairo, April 29, 1965, 1–8; Amin al-Husaini, *Mudhakkirat al-Hajj Muhammad Amin al-Husaini* [The memoirs of al-Hajj Muhammad Amin al-Husaini], ed. Abd al-Karim al-Umar (Damascus: Al-Ahali, 1999), 177.

3. Uki Goñi, *Odessa: Die wahre Geschichte* (Berlin: Assoziation A, 2006), 9–10.

4. Tom Segev, *Simon Wiesenthal: The Life and Legends* (New York: Doubleday, 2010), 215–216.

5. USArchII, RG263, CIA, NF, EnZZ-16, B80, Leers, Intel Sum 1954–59, FBI report, Walter Maria Kotschnig reported to have been responsible for attendance of Roehm, Himmler, and Leers at meetings, 1925–33, January 11, 1952, September 1, 1956.

6. Ibid., 4.

7. USArchII, RG263, B17/18, Gehlen, Russian Experts of German Intelligence Service, Secret Control, January 8, 46; CIA Biographic Sketch of General Reinhard Gehlen 1961.

8. Statement of Udo Grobba to Wolfgang G. Schwanitz, August 22, 2002.

9. Wolfgang G. Schwanitz, "The Jinnee and the Magic Bottle: Fritz Grobba and the German Middle Eastern Policy 1900–1945," *Germany and the Middle East 1871–1945,* ed. Schwanitz (Princeton: Wiener, 2004), 87–117.

10. USArchII, RG319, B5, Revision note Number 4 on the German intelligence services, February 17, 1945.

11. USArchII, RG263, CIA, NF, EnZZ-18, B38–41, report on "Utility" (Reinhard Gehlen's CIA cover name), the odium he inspired, and the GIS, French, and British positions, May 1950, 1–8.

12. USArchII, RG263, CIA, B58–60, report on al-Husaini and a German in Cairo, Grobba and Clodius in Soviet captivity, the ex-mufti in Kabul contacting Germans and Soviets, and the oil crisis in Persia, secret, Bonn, September 22, 1951; al-Hajj Amin al-Husaini, Biographic Sketch, April 24, 1951, 6; Biographical Information on al-Husaini, Einhorn, secret, Washington, D.C., November 19, 1951, 3.

13. PArchWGS, Nachlaß Günther Pawelke, vol. 6, letter of Werner Junck to Pawelke, Duisburg, October 29, 1956.

14. PArchAA, Geheimarchiv Akte Dr. Voigt, Bd. 66, Nr. 6446, April 3, 1958.

15. Wolfgang G. Schwanitz, *Berlin-Kairo: Damals und heute* (Berlin: DAG, 1991), 85–110.

16. Andrea Röpke, "Stille Hilfe," *Antifaschistisches Infoblatt* 70 (2006): 1, 10–13, 12.

17. USArchII, RG263, CIA, NF, EnZZ-18, B58–60, Amin al-Husaini, Regional Security Officer, memorandum on Cesar Ugarte, Odessa, Nazis, Lists, Cairo, April 29, 1965, 1–8; Al-Husaini, *Mudhakkirat*, 177.

18. Segev, *Simon Wiesenthal*, 163–165.

19. Nationalrat der Nationalen Front der Deutschen Demokratischen Republik,

Dokumentationszentrum der staatlichen Archivverwaltung der DDR, ed., *Braunbuch: Kriegs- und Naziverbrecher in der Bundesrepublik: Staat, Wirtschaft, Verwaltung, Armee, Justiz, Wissenschaft* ([Ost-]Berlin: Staatsverlag, 1965).

20. Nationalrat der Nationalen Front der DDR, ed., *Braunbuch: Kriegs- und Nazi-Verbrecher in der BRD und in Westberlin,* 3d ed. ([East] Berlin: Staatsverlag, 1968).

21. Segev, *Simon Wiesenthal,* 156.

22. USArchII, RG263, CIA, NF, EnZZ-16, B80, Johann von Leers; see also Counter Intelligence Corps, Alleged Member of ODESSA Group, April 19, 1948, in Heinz Schneppen, *ODESSA und das Vierte Reich* (Berlin: Metropol, 2007), 19.

23. USArchII, RG263, CIA, NF, EnZZ-16, B80, report on Johann von Leers, his Middle Eastern connections, his past in the RSHA and Abwehr, and his connection with Eichmann, March 19, 1958, 2.

24. Wiesenthal, *Ich jagte Eichmann* (Gütersloh: Mohn, 1961), 180–185, 197–198.

25. Heike B. Görtemaker, *Eva Braun: Leben mit Hitler* (Munich: Beck, 2010), 254, 280.

26. Sefton Delmer, *Black Boomerang* (London: Viking, 1962).

27. "Oberländer, Der Stöpsel," *Der Spiegel,* January 27, 1960, 5.

28. Amtsgericht Hamburg, München, Vereinsregister, AR 112154, To Regierungsdirektor Nentwig, Bayerisches Staatsministerium für Arbeit und soziale Fürsorge, Munich, Notification of the establishment of a self-contained Islamic community, Bonn, April 17, 1957, Namanjani's letter of November 5, 1958 on behalf of the Islamic Community in Munich with the name Ecclesiastical Administration of Muslim Refugees in the German Federal Republic.

29. Ian Johnson, *A Mosque in Munich: Nazis, the CIA, and the Rise of the Muslim Brotherhood in Europe* (New York: Houghton Mifflin Harcourt, 2010).

30. Wolfgang G. Schwanitz, "Stalin in Mecca," *Common Knowledge* 15, no. 3 (Fall 2009): 512–13.

31. Erik Lommatzsch, "Hans Globke und der Nationalsozialismus: Eine Skizze," *Historisch-Politische Mitteilungen* 10 (2003): 95–128.

32. USArchII, RG263, CIA, NF, EnZZ-18, B80, Johann von Leers, Regional Security Officer, memorandum on Cesar Ugarte, ODESSA, Nazis, Lists, April 29, 1965, 1–8; for a different version of the CIA information linked to Federico Schwend, see Guido Knopp, *Die SS: Eine Warnung an die Geschichte* (Munich: Bertelsmann, 2002), 343.

33. Regierungsdirektor Nentwig, Bayerisches Staatsministerium für Arbeit und soziale Fürsorge, München 22, Prinzregentenstrasse 5, April 17, 1957.

34. "Alte Kameraden," *Der Spiegel,* January 20, 1965. Kai Hermann, "Die Karriere eines SS-Offiziers: Zech-Nentwig: Britischer Agent, Legationsrat, Industrieller, Zuchthäusler," *Die Zeit,* January 5, 1964, 18.

35. Wiesenthal, *Ich Jagte Eichmann,* 221–222.

36. USArchII, RG263, CIA, NF, EnZZ-16, B80, von Leers, Intel Sum 1954–59, 100 Fascist Personalities, January 9, 1956, 2.

37. Wolfram Meyer zu Uptrup, *Kampf gegen die "jüdische Weltverschwörung"* (Berlin: Metropol, 2003).

38. USArchII, RG263, CIA, NF, EnZZ-16, B80, von Leers, Intel Sum 1954–59, Reichsverräter, January 15, 1956, 1–6, 1.

39. Ibid.; Dr. Hans A. Euler, "What Eva Perón Meant to Argentina," *Der Arbeitgeber* (1952): 15–16; Karl Neubert, "Weltpolitk," *Der Weg,* September 4, 1952; Felix Schwarzenborn, ibid., August 7, 1953, August 29, 1956.

40. USArchII, RG263, CIA, NF, EnZZ-16, B80, von Leers, Intel Sum 1954–59, Hasan Fahmi Ismail, October 31, 1956, 1.

41. USArchII, RG263, CIA, NF, EnZZ-16, B80, von Leers, Statement of Cesar Ugarte Jr., April 29, 1965, 1–2.

42. USArchII, RG263, CIA, NF, EnZZ-16, B80, von Leers, Intel Sum 1954–59, Bandung Conference, June 15, 1956, 5.

43. USArchII, RG263, CIA NF, Entry ZZ-16, B12, report on Johann von Leers's conversion to Islam by ex-grand mufti, on Gesine von Leers, Otto Skorzeny and Ernst von Kayser, on al-Husaini's outreach to Algeria, Morocco, Yemen, Pakistan, and on less frequent consultations of al-Husaini by Abd an-Nasir, October 15, 1957, 1–3.

44. Ibid.

45. USArchII, RG263, CIA, NF, EnZZ-16, B80, Leers, Intel Sum 1954–59, Dr. Hans A. Euler, "What Eva Perón Meant to Argentina," *Der Arbeitgeber* (1952): 15–16; Karl Neubert, "Weltpolitk," *Der Weg,* September 4, 1952; Felix Schwarzenborn, *Der Weg,* August 7, 1953, August 29, 1956.

46. USArchII, RG263, CIA, NF, EnZZ-16, B80, von Leers, Intel Sum 1954–59, reports on von Leers visit by Priester, September 30, October 25, 1957; on Leers and Priester article for states of Bandung Conference, National Aid, and Nikolaus von Rychkowsky, January 30, 1958; on Priester, Kirkut, and Husayni, December 4, 1958, 1.

47. USArchII, RG263, CIA, NF, EnZZ-16, B80, von Leers, Intel Sum, von Leers and seven top ODESSA members in Cairo, April 29, 1965, 1–8, 8.

48. USArchII, RG263, CIA, NF, EnZZ-16, B80, von Leers, Intel Sum 1954–59, von Leers registered by Amt VI (RSHA), September 5, 8, 1956, 1.

49. USArchII, RG263, CIA, NF, EnZZ-16, B80, Leers, Intel Sum 1954–59, Leers chief adviser to Abd an-Nasir, February 2, 1959, 1.

50. "Nasser und die 'Weisen von Zion,'" *Der Tagesspiegel,* October 31, 1958.

51. Shauqi Abd an-Nasir, *Thaurat Abd an-Nasir* [Abd an-Nasir's Revolt] (Nicosia: Al-Arabi, 1981), see also his works on back cover.

52. USArchII, RG263, CIA, NF, EnZZ-16, B80, von Leers, Intel Sum 1954–59, report on "Spider's Web" organization and Kernmayr, February 2, 1959, 2.

53. Ibid.

54. Ibid., von Leers Activities, October 24, 1957, 1–2.

55. USArchII, RG263, CIA, NF, EnZZ-16, B80, von Leers, Intel Sum 1954–59, von Leers, Eisele, May 4, 1958, 1.

56. Zvi Elpeleg, ed., *Through the Eyes of the Mufti: The Essays of Haj Amin,* translated and annotated by Rachel Kessel (London: Vallentine Mitchell, 2009); see the review by Wolfgang G. Schwanitz in *Jewish Political Studies Review,* December 24, 2012, 136–141.

57. William Stevenson, "Nazis in Egypt, The Expose That Nasser Could Not Take," *New York Post,* August 25, 1956.

58. Anne Sharpley, "He Threw Me Out," *Washington Daily News,* May 15, 1956.

59. USArchII, RG263, CIA, NF, EnZZ-16, B80, von Leers, Intel Sum 1954–59, *Al-Jihad* of Jerusalem article, September 12, 15, 1956.

60. USArchII, RG263, CIA, NF, EnZZ-16, B80, von Leers, Intel Sum 1954–59, Exploit Nazis, August 31, 1956, 1.

61. Röpke, "Stille Hilfe," 10–11.

62. Rudolf Augstein, "Ludwig Zind," *Der Spiegel,* December 17, 1958.

63. USArchII, RG263, CIA, NF, EnZZ-16, B80, von Leers, Intel Sum 1954–59, von Leers; mentioned in connection with escape to Egypt of camp physician Dr. Eisele and anti-Semite Ludwig Zind, *Frankfurter Rundschau,* January 12, 1959, January 12, 1958.

64. USArchII, RG263, CIA, NF, EnZZ-16, B80, von Leers, Intel Sum 1954–59, French Foreign Legion, July 31, 1956, 1.

65. In the 1950s René Vautier joined the FLN in Algeria and established a film unit called Groupe Farid with Ahmad Rashidi and Jamel Shandarli. They produced *L'Algérie en flammes,* in 1958.

66. Boualem Sansal, *Das Dorf des Deutschen oder das Tagebuch der Brüder Schiller,* trans. Ulrich Zieger (Gifkendorf: Merlin, 2009), 100, 200, 133–134, 241–262.

67. Ibid.

68. "Ex-Nazi Officials In Cairo Named, Anti-Semitic Campaign," *Daily Telegraph,* January 20, 1960.

69. For doubts on the identity of Louis (Ludwig) Heiden, see Samir Ata Allah, "Louis al-Hajj," *Al-Majalla,* May 29, 2008.

70. The list was launched by the Simon Wiesenthal Center in 2002. As of April 1, 2010, Alois Brunner and Aribert Heim were both on the list. See also http://www.operationlastchance.org/; http://de.wikipedia.org/wiki/Operation_Last_Chance.

71. "6,000 Deutsche, Kairo gibt Spezialisten Verträge," *Telegraf,* July 29, 1947; "Deutsche gegen Israel," *Sächsische Zeitung,* January 15, 1949.

72. Wiesenthal, *Ich jagte Eichmann,* 137, 139, 179, 194.

73. See "List of experts in both units, 4/30/53," in Wolfgang G. Schwanitz, *Deutsche in Nahost 1946–1965,* 2 vols. (Munich: Haensel-Hohenhausen, 1998), 1:208.

74. USArchII, RG263, CIA, NF, EnZZ-18, B107, Ernst Otto Remer, Dietrich von Mirbach on Remer and al-Husaini, Cairo, April 27, 1953, 1; report on Remer's monthly allowance, his contact with the Supreme Guide of Ikhwan, and Sophia Tauwil, Cairo, September 18, 1954, 1.

75. USArchII, RG263, CIA, NF, EnZZ-16, B80, von Leers, Intel Sum, report on von Leers and "Spider's Web" organization, names in media, March 5, 1965, 1.

76. USArchII, RG263, CIA, NF, EnZZ-18, B107, Ernst Otto Remer, Frederyk Kulikowski, Cairo, July 27, 1955, 1; Remer suspected of working with the East, December 20, 1955, 1–2; Remer of Varel near Oldenburg possible Bloc agent, his illegal arms trade with Oriental Trade Company, October 17, 1961, 1–2.

77. On Nazis and spies, see Joel Beinin, *The Dispersion of Egyptian Jewry: Culture, Politics, and the Formation of a Modern Diaspora* (Berkeley: University of California Press, 1998).

78. See reviews by Wolfgang G. Schwanitz of Shabtai Teveth, *Ben-Gurion's Spy: The Story of the Political Scandal That Shaped Modern Israel,* Orient 38, no. 3 (1997): 567–570, and Khalid Muhi ad-Din, "Wa al-An Atakallamu" [And now I am talking], *Der Islam* 73, no. 2 (1996): 360–363.

79. USArchII, RG263, CIA, NF, EnZZ-16, B80, von Leers, on his Middle Eastern connections, the RSHA, Abwehr, "Utility" (Gehlen), Mohn, Leverkuehn, Rademacher, and Eichmann, von Leers, Secret, Munich, March 19, 1958, 1–3.

80. Ibid.

81. PArchAA, B372020–21, Aufzeichnung, "Sitzung RSHA, 06.03.42, weitere Behandlung Judenfragen, Sterilisierung der rund 70.000 Mischlinge, Mischehen, Geheime Reichssache, Berlin 7.03.42"; B372009–11 "An Luther, Gaus, Woermann, Weizsäcker, Ergebnisse Mischlinge, Geheime Reichssache," Berlin, November 6, 1942, Rademacher, see also http://de.wikipedia.org/wiki/Franz_Rademacher#cite_note-4. See also Eckart Conze, Norbert Frei, Peter Hayes, and Moshe Zimmermann, *Das Amt und die Vergangenheit: Deutsche Diplomaten im Dritten Reich und in der Bundesrepublik* (Munich: 2010), 186.

82. Ernst Klee, *Das Personenlexikon zum Dritten Reich* (Frankfurt: Fischer, 2005), 476.

83. USArchII, RG263, CIA, NF, EnZZ-16, B80, von Leers, Two agents on Middle Eastern connections, RSHA, Abwehr, "Utility" (Gehlen).

84. USArchII, RG263, CIA, NF, EnZZ-18, (2nd rel.), B106, Walter Rauff, Recruiting Germans for Arab Legion, post in general staff of Arab army, Secret, March 4, 1949; Von Strachwitz about forty-seven Germans employed in Syria, Rauff is said to reorganize the Second Bureau along Gestapo lines, Secret, November 5, 1949.

85. USArchII, RG263, CIA, NF, EnZZ-18, B106, Walter Rauff, Advisor for Syrian Army Second Bureau, June 10, 1949; Aid to Midani, Syrian Chief of Intelligence, Secret, July 29, 1949.

86. See also Lutz Hachmeister, "Presseforschung und Vernichtungskrieg: Zum Verhältnis von SS, Propaganda-Apparat und Publizistik," in *Die Spirale des Schweigens: Zum Umgang mit der nationalsozialistischen Zeitungswissenschaft,* ed. Wolfgang Duchkowitsch et al. (Münster: Lit, 2004), 78.

87. Bodo Hechelhammer, *Walther Rauff und der Bundesnachrichtendienst* (Berlin: Bundesnachrichtendienst, 2011); Jost Dülffer, "Im Einsatz für den BND," *Frankfurter Allgemeine Zeitung,* September 27, 2011, 8.

88. For Rauff see also Gerald Steinacher, *Nazis auf der Flucht: Wie Kriegsverbrecher über Italien nach Übersee entkamen* (Innsbruck: Studienverlag, 2008), 204–255; Shraga Elam and Dennis Whitehead, "Rauff vs. the Yishuv," *Haaretz,* July 4, 2007.

89. Wiesenthal, *Recht,* 288, 290.

90. BArchAAP, "Telegramm, Winkelmann teilt Ankunft al-Husaini . . . , 5/10/44."

91. Simon Wiesenthal, *Recht, nicht Rache: Erinnerungen* (Frankfurt: Ullstein, 1988), 300.

92. USArchII, RG263, CIA NF, EnZZ-18, B30–31, Eichmann, letter to Dr. S. J. Roth, *Arbeit-Zeitung* article, December 6, 1962, 1–3.

93. *Arbeiter-Zeitung,* 1962, in Wiesenthal, *Recht, nicht Rache,* 292.

94. Ibid.; *Bunte* interview with Brunner, October 10, 1985.

95. *Times of Israel,* January 10, 2013, http://www.timesofisrael.com/mossad-tried-to-kill-saddam-in-the-1970s-new-documentary-reveals/.

96. "Nazi Butcher in Syria Haven," *Chicago Sun-Times,* November 1, 1987.

97. USArchII, RG263, CIA, NF, EnZZ-16, B19, Alois Brunner, Nazi war criminal in Damascus, November 5, 1987, signed Shultz, 1–3.

98. Andreas Förster, "Gerichtsstand Ostberlin," http://www.profil.at/articles/1130/560/303091/stasi-gerichtsstand-ostberlin.

99. USArchII, RG263, CIA, NF, EnZZ-16, B19, Alois Brunner, Kennedy's cable to Ambassador Djerejian, confidential, Washington, D.C., July 3, 1991, 1.

100. USArchII, RG263, CIA, NF, EnZZ-16, B19, Alois Brunner, European Parliament on Brunner, September 12, 1991, 1–2.

101. USArchII, RG263, CIA, NF, EnZZ-16, B19, Alois Brunner, Alois Brunner, dead or alive? January 6, 1993, 1–2.

102. "Leader of the Azerbaijan Legion, Portrait of Dudansky," *Unser Herr,* July 20, 1943.

103. USArchII, RG263, CIA B106, Name Index, al-Husaini and Head of Azerbaijan National Committee Abd ar-Rahman Fatalibeyli-Dudanginsky . . . , July 15, 1949, 1–2.

104. USArchII, RG65, FBI, NF, 136AB, B175, F105–285524-Sec.1, François Genoud.

105. PArchAA, Aktenbestand (AB) V5/Band (Bd)88/Bd1447, Einzelfälle, AB4/Bd840, AB11/Bd382, AB11/Bd1392, AB36/Bd112, AB36/Bd300.

106. Al-Husaini, *Mudhakkirat,* 227.

107. PArchAA, V5, B14, 4J, Landgericht Berlin, Zivilkammer 171 (Kammer für Wertpapierbereinigung).

108. PArchAA, V5, B14, 47, "An Deutsche Botschaft Ankara, Entschädigungsansprüche des al-Hajj Amin al-Husaini, Bonn, 13.05.74, gez. Däumer."

109. PArchAA, V5, B14, 4J, Landgericht Berlin, Zivilkammer 171, "Beschluss im Verfahren 1,100,000 AEG Aktien (53.380), unbekannte Verwahrart, unbekannte Stücknummern, Geschäftsnummer 171 KWpE 16/71, Antragsteller François Genoud vertreten durch Dr. Hans Flächsner, Westberlin, 03.04.74, 2–8, gez. Muhs."

110. PArchAA, V5, B14, 47, "Devisenfonds des Goßmufti Amin al-Husaini und zur Person (contra), geheim, Bonn, 15.08.67, gez. Söhnke," 1–3.

111. PArchAA, V5, B14, 47, "Devisenfonds des Großmufti Amin al-Husaini (bester Freund), geheim, Bonn, 17.08.67, gez. Linsser"; also suggested in section IB4 (VLR Schirmer) and IB5.

112. USArchII, RG65, FBI, NF, 136AB, B175, F105–285524-Sec.1, Genoud, FBI/CIA on subject, secret, Berne, June 6, 1975.

113. USArchII, RG65, FBI, NF, 136AB, B175, F105–285524-Sec.1, Genoud, possible ineligibility, secret, Washington, D.C., June 7, 1975, signed Kissinger. See also USArchII, RG65, FBI, NF, 136AB, B175, F105–285524-Sec.1, Genoud, FBI Director, memorandum that Genoud was found to be ineligible under Sec. 212 (A) (28) F of the Immigration and Nationalities Act, secret, August 14, 1975.

114. USArchII, RG65, FBI, NF, 136AB, B175, F105–285524-Sec.1, report of

Genoud's contacts with extreme right-wing, anti-Zionist circles, and dinner in Hotel de la Paix, secret, Lausanne, July 21, 1986.

115. USArchII, RG65, FBI, NF, 136AB, B175, F105–285524-Sec.1, report on Genoud, Libya, and France, secret, Paris, August 12, 1986.

116. Himmat was listed by the UN Security Council as a person associated with al-Qaida on November 9, 2001, and Nada on September 3, 2002, See the UNSC summaries of April 6, 2009, http://www.un.org/sc/committees/1267/NSQI05301E .shtml.

117. Wolfgang G. Schwanitz, "'Doppelte': deutsche Gesandte in Kairo 1953–1963," in *Misr wa Almaniya fi al-Qirnain at-Tasi'a Ashara wa al-'Ishrin fi dhau al-Watha'iq* [Egypt and Germany in the nineteenth and twentieth centuries as reflected in archives], ed. Wajih Atek and Wolfgang G. Schwanitz (Cairo: Dar ath-Thaqafa, 1998), pt. 2, 212: "NSDAP Member List of 10/20/52."

118. Wilhelm Kohlhaas, *Hitler-Abenteuer im Irak* (Freiburg: Herder, 1989), 15.

119. Helmut Glenk, Horst Blaich, and Manfred Haering, *From Desert Sands To Golden Oranges: The History of the German Templer Settlement of Sarona in Palestine 1871–1947* (Victoria, B.C.: Trafford, 2005).

120. Eckart Conze, Norbert Frei, Peter Hayes, and Moshe Zimmermann, *Das Amt und die Vergangenheit: Deutsche Diplomaten im Dritten Reich und in der Bundesrepublik* (Munich: Blessing, 2010), 664.

121. Ibid., 654.

122. Ibid., 387.

123. PArchWGS, Nachlaß Günther Pawelke, vol. 1, "Frontflugspange, 20 Feindflüge, Gefechtsstand, 18.04.1941, 07.06.41, gez. Junck."

124. USArchII, HICOG Bonn, report on Israeli attack against Pawelke, *Journal de Jérusalem, Jerusalem Post, Frankfurter Allgemeine Zeitung*, November 18, 1952.

125. See the good study of Ekkehard Ellinger, *Deutsche Orientalistik zur Zeit des Nationalsozialismus 1933–1945* (Berlin: Deux Mondes, 2006).

126. "Muff im Talar," *Der Spiegel*, November 20, 1967; "Prof. Spuler suspendiert," *Hamburger Abendblatt*, November 17, 1967; "9.11.67—Studentenprotest an der Hamburger Uni," *Die Welt*, November 29, 1999.

CHAPTER 12. HOW THE AXIS LEGACY SHAPES TODAY'S MIDDLE EAST

1. Tariq Ramadan, "Whither the Muslim Brotherhood?" *New York Times*, February 9, 2011, http://www.nytimes.com/2011/02/09/opinion/09iht-edramadan09 .html?_r=2&ref=global.

2. See Chapters Six and Nine.

3. Daniel Schwammenthal, "The Mufti of Berlin: Arab-Nazi Collaboration Is a Taboo Topic in the West," *Wall Street Journal*, September 24, 2009.

4. Gilbert Achcar, *The Arabs and the Holocaust* (New York: Picador, 2010), 130; Meir Litvak and Esther Webman, *From Empathy to Denial: Arab Responses to the Holocaust* (New York: Columbia University Press, 2009). For the apologetic approach, see Muhammad Kabha, "The Palestinian National Movement and Its

Attitude toward the Fascist and Nazi Movements 1925–1945," *Geschichte und Gesellschaft* 37 (2011): 437–450.

5. See, for example, Albert Hourani, *Arabic Thought in the Liberal Age 1798–1939* (New York: Oxford University Press, 1962).

6. On the moderates' weaknesses, impediments to their success, and reasons for their defeats, see Barry Rubin, *The Long War for Freedom: The Arab Struggle for Democracy in the Middle East* (New York: John Wiley, 2005).

7. USArchII, RG263, CIA, NF, EnZZ-16, B58–60, report on al-Husaini, Arafat, the West Bank as a base for a Palestinian state, secret, Beirut, December 29, 1968, 1–2. All material on the al-Husaini–Arafat discussions is taken from this document.

8. M. P. Waters [pseudonym of Maurice or Moshe Pearlman], *Mufti Over The Middle East* (London: Barber/Narod Press, 1942), 18–26.

9. ArhJugBG, Inv. Br. 553, 574–173, memorandum to the State Department, New York, mid-1945, to take the initiative to indict al-Husaini as a war criminal and issue instructions to the War Crimes Commission as a major supporter of the Axis, directly involved in the murder of millions of Jews in Europe. A following list comprises the names of some of the Arab political and spiritual leaders murdered by the Grand Mufti's gangsters up to 1939 as set out in an Arabic document, published in Cairo, January 2, 1939. The document charges him with direct responsibility for these murders: Shaikh Ali al-Khatib, imam of the Sakhra Mosque; Shaikh Said al-Khatib, preacher of the al-Aqsa Mosque; Shaikh Abd ar-Rahman al-Khatib, instructor in Arabic and religion at the Rashidiyya School; Shaikh Mahmud Ansari, supervisor of the *haram* area of the al-Aqsa Mosque; Shaikh Abd al-Hafiz Humuri, a Hebron religious authority; Farid Hamad Allah, a Tulkarm leader; Abd as-Salam Barqawi, a Jenin dignitary; al-Hajj Ali Harzun, deputy mayor of Lydda; Shaikh Said Hunaidi, an elder killed during prayers at the mosque of Lydda; Shaikh Ali Abu Salim, head of the village of Batilli, who together with four members of his family—Abd, Hasha, Jamal, and Rushdi—was murdered on the night of a religious festival; Mustafa Yusuf al-Khatib of Dair Nazzam; Ali al-Hajj Muhammad, chief of the village of Allar; Muhammad Irshad and Ahmad Irshad, two brothers from Jenin; Hasan Sidqi Dajjani, Jerusalem leader and noted lawyer; Khalil Taha, a well-known Haifa leader; Taufiq Hiyas, a relative of Khalil Taha; Ibrahim Bey Khalil, a Hebron leader and treasurer of the fund for orphans; Nasir ad-Din, mayor of Hebron; Shaikh Ibrahim Abd ar-Razzaq, head of the village of Bait Rima; Ahmad Abd ar-Razzaq, the brother of the above; Ahmad Abd ar-Rahman, head of the village of Imatin; Nimr Sab, mayor of Qilqiliyya; Ibrahim Badr, chieftain of Dair ash-Shaikh, assassinated with his wife, three children, and valet; Muhammad Marqa, dignitary of Hebron. Attached is a letter to the editor of the *New York Times*, January 2, 1944, and an article, "Mufti Held Disturber," by A. S. Yehuda, New School for Social Research, New York, December 30, 1943.

10. PArchAA, R27327, B297993–7, "Memorandum an Karl Kapp, Propaganda der Araberfeinde, Berlin, 02.11.1942."

11. USArchII, RG263, CIA, NF, EnZZ-16, B58–60, report on al-Husaini, Arafat, and the West Bank as a base for a Palestinian state, secret, Beirut, December 29, 1968, 1–2.

12. USArchII, RG263, CIA, NF, EnZZ-16, B58–60, report on al-Husaini, Arafat, and the West Bank as a base for a Palestinian state, secret, Beirut, December 29, 1968, 1–2.

13. USArchII, RG263, CIA, NF, EnZZ-16, B58–60, report on and urgent meeting between al-Husaini and Arafat, on February 20, 1969 in Beirut while Arafat was en route from Moscow to Amman via Beirut, on the dispute between them, and al-Husaini's letter to the king, March 4, 1969, 1–2.

14. Ibid.

15. BArchBe, SAPMO, NL182/1333, "An Ulbricht, Stoph, Honecker, Axen [Umlaufnote, SED Politbüro] Neuorientierung für den Palästinensischen Widerstand auf der Botschafter Konferenz in Moskau am 19.08.1969: Einladen, Ausrüsten, Nutzen und Bewaffnen der Führer palästinensischer Organisationen für gemeinsame Aktion, Radikale zügeln, Ostberlin 1.10.69, gez. Otto Winzer."

16. USArchII, RG263, CIA, NF, EnZZ-16, B58–60, report on clash of Arafat's Fatah with al-Husaini's Islamic Conquest Fidaiyin, a new right-wing Fidaiyin splinter group under Brigadier Rashid Araikat, in which five Islamic Conquest supporters were killed and fifty-five joined the Fatah, in a refugee camp close to Amman in mid-June 1969, June 30, 1969, 1–2.

17. Filastin al-Thawra, January 1970; Walid Khadduri, ed., International Documents on Palestine 1969 (Beirut: The Institute for Palestine Studies and The University of Kuwait, 1972), 300.

18. For a detailed discussion of this issue, see Barry Rubin and Judith Colp Rubin, Yasir Arafat: A Political Biography (New York: Oxford University Press, 2003).

19. Fatah, "The Seven Points" (January 1969, passed by the Central Committee of Fatah), in The Israel-Arab Reader: A Documentary History of the Middle East Conflict, ed. Walter Laqueur and Barry Rubin (New York: Penguin, 2008), 130–131.

20. Rubin and Rubin, Yasir Arafat, 69–70.

21. For a detailed discussion of these events see ibid., 185–216.

22. Mahmud Abbas, "Sviazi mezhdu sionizmom i natsizmom (1933–1945) (diss., Moscow University, 1982); see also his Al-Wajh al-Akhar: Al-Alaqat as-Sirriyya baina an-Naziyya wa as-Sahyuniyya [The other point of view: The secret ties between the Nazis and the Zionist movement] (Amman: Dar Ibn Rushd, 1984), 253; and Through Secret Channels (Reading: Garnet, 1995).

23. Bernard Lewis, Semites and Anti-Semites: An Inquiry into Conflict and Prejudice (New York: Norton, 1987), 161.

24. On the Brotherhood's history, see Barry Rubin, Islamic Fundamentalists in Egyptian Politics, 2d rev. ed. (New York: Palgrave-Macmillan, 2008).

25. Two rare exceptions are Ali Bader's 2008 novel, The Tobacco Keeper, and the remarks of Rashid Al-Khayoun, interviewed on al-Arabiyya Television, December 4, 2009, translated in MEMRI Special Dispatch No. 2750, January 13, 2010, http://www.memritv.org/clip/en/0/0/0/0/0/0/2312.htm.

26. USArchII, RG263, CIA, B58–60, RLB-1788, report on meeting between Fedor Pisarenko of the Soviet legation and Halina Abd al-Karim al-Jauni, secret, Beirut, December 27, 1949; Ad-Dawalibi publicly for Soviet alliance according to al-Husaini's instruction, April 15, 1950.

27. USArchII, FMS, P-207, Fritz Grobba, "Supplement des Gesandten a.D. Dr. Fritz Grobba," in "German Exploitation of Arab National Movements in World War II" (see above, Chapter 4, note 61), 75.

28. Barry Rubin, *The Truth About Syria* (New York: Palgrave-Macmillan, 2007).

29. Michel Aflaq, *Fi Sabil al-Ba'ath* [For the Ba'th] (Beirut: Dar at-Tali'a, 1959), 40–41, quoted in Franck Salameh, "Does Anyone Speak Arabic?" *Middle East Quarterly* (Fall 2011), http://www.meforum.org/3066/does-anyone-speak-arabic.

30. See Chapter Six.

31. On the struggle between Iran and the Saudi regime, see, for example, Barry Rubin, *Cauldron of Turmoil* (New York: Harcourt Brace Jovanovich, 1992).

32. David Barnett and Efraim Karsh, "Azzam's Genocidal Threat," *Middle East Quarterly* (Fall 2011): 85–88. This article for the first time tells the full story of the Azzam quote and its documentation.

33. See, for example, Barry Rubin and Judith Colp Rubin, *Anti-American Terrorism and the Middle East* (New York: Oxford University Press, 2002).

34. Götz Nordbruch, *Nazism in Syria and Lebanon: The Ambivalence of the German Option, 1933–1945* (New York: Routledge, 2009), 20–21, 33–34.

35. Grobba, "Supplement," 72–73, Arab News Bureau Sofia; PArchWGS, NG-5462–5570, report from Rekowski: twenty-five hundred marks monthly for Kamil Muruwwa, seven hundred U.S. dollars monthly for Mr. Glock of Lisbon (8, 10).

36. Eyal Ziser, *Lebanon: The Challenge of Independence* (London: I. B. Tauris, 2000), 174.

37. USArchII, RG263, CIA, B58–60, al-Husaini's interview with al-Hayat, copies sold ten times their price, secret, Jerusalem, December 15, 1953, 1.

38. Kamil Muruwwa, "Nam, al-Mufti al-Akbar qabil Hitler" [Yes, the Grand Mufti met Hitler], *Al-Hayat,* no. 37 (March 19, 1946); "Haqiqat Dahrina" [A truth of our lifetime], ibid., no. 650 (June 22, 1948); Kamil Muruwwa, *Qul Kalimatuka wa Imshi* [Say your word and beat it], vol. 1, nos. 1–1426 (Beirut: Al-Hayat, 1970), 37, 113, 650–651.

39. *New York Times,* April 19, 1988, http://www.nytimes.com/1988/04/19/us/anti-semitism-charges-lead-to-delay-on-religion-prize.html?sec=&spon=&pagewanted=all.

40. Barry Rubin, *The PLO Between Anti-Zionism and Antisemitism* (Jerusalem: Hebrew University Sassoon Center, 1993) provides many examples.

41. Anti-Defamation League of B'nai B'rith, "Open Letter To King Fahd of Saudi-Arabia," press release, New York, February 7, 1985, 1.

42. USArchII, RG263, CIA, B58–60, "Ex-Grand Mufti and support for Said Ramadan, exiled Egyptian Ikhwan leader in Damascus, Islamic congresses in Jerusalem 1956, Mecca, finance," December 16, 1954, 1.

43. USArchII, RG263, CIA, B58–60, report on activities of the Ikhwan al-Muslimin leader Muhammad Said Ramadan and the ex-grand mufti in Karachi, February 21, 1963, 1.

44. USArchII, RG263, CIA, B58–60, "Al-Husaini, Ramadan, 9/54 arrests, Syrian Muslim Brothers," December 11, 1954.

45. USArchII, RG263, CIA, B58–60, report on the ex-grand mufti's money for Ramadan's newspaper *Al-Muslimun*.

46. USArchII, RG263, CIA, B58–60, report on Ramadan's newspaper *Al-Muslimun*; see also Ralph Ghadban, *Tariq Ramadan und die Islamisierung Europas* (Berlin: Schiler, 2006), 60; Brynjar Lia, *The Society of the Muslim Brothers in Egypt: The Rise of an Islamic Movement 1928–1942* (Reading: Ithaca Press, 1998), 155.

47. USArchII, RG263, CIA, B58–60, report on the al-Husaini Clan, Said Ramadan, Saudi Arabia, the Saud–an-Nasir dispute, and Jamal al-Husaini's spy system in Lebanon and Syria, secret, May 8, 1962, 1–2.

48. PArchAA, Nachlaß von Hentig, vol. 84, 326011–12, von Oppenheim to LR Otto von Grote on Shakib Arslan, Sanusi, and Ismail Hakki Bey, Berlin, April 9, 1941.

49. Grobba, "Supplement," 69, 73, on monthly allowance for Amir Shakib Arslan, editor of *Islam* and *La Nation Arabe* in Lausanne, from the Foreign Ministry's Press Department; PArchWGS, Office Of Chief Of Counsel for War Crimes, Doc. No. NG-5462–5570, Rekowski, 9; PArchAA, Nachlaß von Hentig, vol. 84, 326010, von Oppenheim to Melchers, money request for Shakib Arslan, Berlin, April 10, 1941; ibid., 32608–09, von Oppenheim to Woermann, money request for Shakib Arslan, Berlin, April 10, 1941.

50. Said Ramadan, *Islamic Law: Its Scope and Equity* (London: P. R. Macmillan, 1961); Said Ramadan, *Das islamische Recht: Theorie und Praxis* (Wiesbaden: Otto Harrassowitz, 1980); Ghadban, *Tariq Ramadan und die Islamisierung Europas*, 60.

51. Ghadban, *Tariq Ramadan und die Islamisierung Europas*, 56–57; Lia, *The Society of the Muslim Brothers in Egypt*, 155; Reinhard Schulze, *Islamischer Internationalismus im 20. Jahrhundert* (Leiden: Brill, 1990), 203; Amin al-Husaini, *Mudhakkirat al-Hajj Muhammad Amin al-Husaini* [The memoirs of al-Hajj Muhammad Amin al-Husaini], ed. Abd al-Karim al-Umar (Damascus: Al-Ahali, 1999), 88. For an Egyptian government evaluation, see Archiv des Bundesbeauftragten für die Unterlagen des MfS, Berlin, MfS, X/111, minutes of conversation between Erich Mielke and Sharawi Juma, top secret, East Berlin, July 3, 1969, 1–8.

52. Barry Rubin, *The Muslim Brotherhood: A Global Islamist Movement* (New York: Palgrave-Macmillan, 2010); Barry Rubin, *Survey of Islamism*, 2 vols. (New York: M. E. Sharpe, 2009).

53. Vereinsarchiv, Islamische Gemeinschaft Deutschland, Hamburg, VerArch AGH, Deutsche Muslim-Liga e.V., VR112154, "Protokoll, gez. Anna Bohnsack, Hamburg, 24.06.61," 84–86.

54. VerArchAGM, Islamische Gemeinschaft in Deutschland, VR6256, "An Ramadan, Genf, Forderung Generalversammlung Moscheebaukommission, verfehlte Neuwahl Vorstand, Abstimmungsresultat Generalversammlung 26.11.61, Ablehnung Kandidatur Said Ramadans und Ali Kantemirs, München 22.12.61."

55. Bayerisches Staatsministerium des Inneren, ed., *Verfassungsschutzbericht 2008* (Munich: Bayerisches Staatsministerium des Innern, 2009), 62; see also Bundesministerium des Inneren, ed., *Vorabfassung Verfassungsschutzbericht 2005* (Berlin: Druckerei Alt-Moabit, 2006), 221.

56. Himmat was listed by the UN Security Council as a person associated with al-Qaida on November 9, 2001, and Nada on September 3, 2002, See the UNSC summaries of April 6, 2009, http://www.un.org/sc/committees/1267/NSQI05301E.shtml.

57. *The 9/11 Commission Report: Final Report of the National Commission on Terrorist Attacks on the United States* (New York, 2006), 366.

58. Video of Clapper testimony, http://www.youtube.com/watch?v=r66wLuAn5Mo.

59. Ramadan, "Whither the Muslim Brotherhood?"

60. Ayman al-Zawahiri, *Knights under the Prophet's Banner.* The book was published in *al-Sharq al-Awsat,* December 2–12, 2001, and translated by the U.S. Department of Commerce, Foreign Broadcast Information Service (FBIS), December 2, 2001 (FBIS-NES-2001–1202–12).

61. PArchAA, R27327, B297998–01, An Kapp, Memorandum, Propagandaschriften der Araberfeinde, November 1942.

62. See Chapter Eight.

63. Sayid Qutb, "Our Struggle with the Jews," quoted in Ronald L. Nettler, *Past Trials and Present Tribulations: A Muslim Fundamentalist's View of the Jews* (Oxford: Pergamon Press, 1987), 86–87.

64. Hamas Covenant, August 18, 1988, Article 15, http://avalon.law.yale.edu/20th_century/hamas.asp.

65. Al-Aqsa TV on February 28, 2010, http://www.memritv.org/clip/en/o/o/o/o/o/o/2415.htm, http://www.memri.org/report/en/o/o/o/o/o/o/4035.htm.

66. Rubin and Rubin, *Anti-American Terrorism and the Middle East,* 137–142.

67. Al-Jazeera, January 28–30 2005, http://www.memritv.org/clip_transcript/en/2005.htm.

68. "Muslim Brotherhood Supreme Guide, 'The U.S. Is Now Experiencing the Beginning of Its End'; Improvement and Change in the Muslim World 'Can Only Be Attained Through Jihad and Sacrifice,'" MEMRI, Special Dispatch No. 3274, October 6, 2010, http://www.memri.org/report/en/o/o/o/o/o/o/4650.htm.

69. For a discussion of this issue, see Barry Rubin, *Modern Dictators: Third World Coupmakers, Strongmen, and Populist Tyrants* (New York: McGraw-Hill, 1987).

Index

Page numbers in *italics* indicate illustrations